The Politics of Neocorporatism in France

The Politics
of Neocorporatism
in France

Farmers, the State, and
Agricultural Policy- making
in the Fifth Republic

John T. S. Keeler

New York   Oxford
OXFORD UNIVERSITY PRESS
1987

Oxford University Press

Oxford   New York   Toronto
Delhi   Bombay   Calcutta   Madras   Karachi
Petaling Jaya   Singapore   Hong Kong   Tokyo
Nairobi   Dar es Salaam   Cape Town
Melbourne   Auckland

and associated companies in
Beirut   Berlin   Ibadan   Nicosia

Published by Oxford University Press, Inc.,
200 Madison Avenue, New York, New York 10016

Oxford is a registered trademark of Oxford University Press

Library of Congress Cataloging-in-Publication Data
Keeler, John T. S.
    The politics of neocorporatism in France.
    Bibliography: p.
    Includes index.
    1. Fédération nationale des syndicats d'exploitants agricoles—History.
    2. Trade-unions—Agricultural laborers—France—History.
    3. Agriculture and state—France—History.
    I. Title.
HD6688.A3F435   1987   331.88'13'0944   86-5172
ISBN 0-19-504078-3

Printing (last digit): 9 8 7 6 5 4 3 2 1
Printed in United States of America
on acid-free paper

For my parents,
Priscilla Anne Keeler
and
William Everett Keeler

Acknowledgments

This book could not have been completed without the assistance of many institutions and individuals on both sides of the Atlantic. It is a pleasure to acknowledge the debts that I owe to all of them. Vital financial support was provided at various stages of the project by the Council for European Studies, the Center for European Studies of Harvard University, and the Graduate School Research Fund of the University of Washington. A Pre-Dissertation Fellowship from the Council enabled me to spend the summer of 1974 in Paris undertaking preliminary research on the dissertation from which much of this book was derived. A grant from the Harvard CES in the fall of 1975 allowed for a second research trip to France, devoted for the most part to the case studies of Aisne and Corrèze. Return visits to these two departments and the case study of Landes were made possible in the summer of 1976 by a Krupp Foundation Fellowship in European Studies awarded by the Harvard Center. Funding from Washington's GSRF enabled me to complete some final work in Paris during the summers of 1980 and 1983.

A great deal of the information on which this book is based could not have been obtained without the cooperation of scores of members and employees of the major organizations of French agriculture. Not all of them can be listed here (the names of all of those interviewed may be found in Appendix A), but some must be given special thanks. Much to my surprise a number of gracious Parisians managed to make my research not a chore but rather an enjoyable experience— even during the infamous *mois d'août*: Monique Genay, Charles Keryhuel, and Georges Muller at the APCA library; Christian Bonnetier, Philippe Bourgeois, and Christian Labbé of the FNSEA staff; Paul Kerdraon and Jean-Claude Pichon, editors of the CNJA's *Jeunes Agriculteurs*; and Madeleine Trébous, editor of *Paysans*. In the three case-study departments, numerous people went to heroic lengths to respond to what must have seemed like an endless barrage of requests for assistance. There is no way to thank adequately those who took hours away from their own work to discuss organizational affairs, arrange interviews, drive me to meetings, compile statistics, and dig through dusty newspapers and documents in search of some crucial piece of the puzzle. The following individuals provided such invaluable help and somehow remained affable throughout the weeks during which my project consumed much of their time: Marie Boulanger, Jean-Pierre Prévot, and Jean-Philippe Tronche of Aisne; Collette Crumeyrole, Pierre Faurie, and Nicole Vernat of Corrèze; Francis Barets, Jean Bourlon, Jean-Paul Lemaroc, and Jacques Ramon of Landes. Many of these people invited me to their homes at the first opportunity, treated me to their finest cuisine and cognac, and did everything possible to make me feel like a special guest; some even loaned me their automobiles for weekend trips or offered to do my laundry!

Of all the men and women throughout the French countryside who have helped and befriended me over the years, two deserve my warmest thanks: Mme. Dominique Arnould, the librarian of the Chambre d'Agriculture in Laon, and her husband, M. Dominique Arnould, the mayor of Pouilly-sur-Serre. These remarkable people have not only taught me a great deal about the human dimension of French agriculture, but have also made me feel that I have a home-away-from-home in rural France. Their kindness, energy, and infectious optimism have often made me believe "le ciel est bleu" even during the bleaker periods of research and writing.

The following scholars merit thanks for discussing my research project, reading various drafts of chapters, and providing useful criticisms along the way: John Ambler, Michel Crozier, Henry Ehrmann, Peter Gourevitch, Rolf Heinze, Miles Kahler, Peter Katzenstein, Ira Katznelson, Peter Lange, Gerhard Lehmbruch, Margaret Levi, Michael McCann, Donald McCrone, David Pinkney, Hans-Jurgen Puhle, George Ross, William Safran, Martin Schain, William Schneider, Ezra Suleiman, Sidney Tarrow, Yves Tavernier, Jean-Claude Thoenig, James Townsend, Sidney Verba, Frank Wilson, James Q. Wilson, Gordon Wright, Laurence Wylie, and John Zysman. Joel Krieger and Joel Migdal facilitated completion of the book with the sort of stimulation and encouragement that only special friends can provide. Suzanne Berger offered invaluable suggestions at the initial stage of my research and read several drafts of the entire manuscript. I thank her not only for this, but also for the inspiration which her own work provided. It was her *Peasants Against Politics* that introduced me to the French peasants and assured me it would be possible to undertake a study entailing interviewing and observation in the French countryside.

My debt to Stanley Hoffmann would be impossible to exaggerate. It was he who first aroused my interest in the study of French politics and introduced me to the stimulating environment of 5 Bryant Street. He has guided my research on French agricultural politics ever since it began as a seminar paper for his Social Science 117 course. Whatever merit this book might have must be credited above all to the criticism and encouragement that he provided and the standards of scholarship that he set. Needless to say, any failings of this work are my own responsibility.

Susan Rabiner, Henry Krawitz, and Judy Mintz of Oxford University Press deserve my thanks for their encouragement as well as for their skill and patience in guiding this book through the production process.

Kevin Lake, Shanny Peer, and Bart Salisbury served as able research assistants at various points. Karen Davidson, Cynthia Ketcham, Sharon Clarke, Berkeley Parks, and Patricia Scanlon typed several drafts of the manuscript; they should be thanked not only for performing their job in a professional manner, but also for remaining patient when my requests seemed unreasonable.

As our friends from Seattle to Paris can attest, the full extent of my debt to Patricia could be acknowledged fully only in another volume of several hundred pages. No one could hope to have a better wife and best friend. The good times involved in the preparation of this book were enhanced immeasurably by her enthusiasm for picnicking in the parks of Mont-de-Marsan, dancing at the Naves fête, climbing the château d'eau in Pouilly, and sharing the innumerable delights of Paris. The bad times were made bearable by her understanding and her uncanny ability to comfort. In a very real sense, this is her book as well as mine.

This book is dedicated to my parents, Priscilla Anne Keeler and William Everett Keeler. Growing up in their home necessarily entailed developing a fascination with politics and an appreciation of spirited debate. Without that experience, I would probably not have ever considered pursuing a career in political science. Without their love and support, I would definitely not have managed to complete this project.

Seattle, Wash.   *J. T. S. K.*
June 1985

Contents

Acronyms

AAA	Agricultural Adjustment Administration
ADASEA	Association Départementale pour l'Aménagement des Structures des Exploitations Agricoles
AFBF	American Farm Bureau Federation
ANDA	Association Nationale pour le Développement Agricole
APCA	Assemblée Permanente des Chambres d'Agriculture
CAC	County Agricultural Committee
CAP	Common Agricultural Policy
CDJA	Centre (Cercle) Départemental des Jeunes Agriculteurs
CETA	Centre d'Etudes Techniques Agricoles
CFDT	Confédération Française Démocratique du Travail
CGA	Confédération Générale de l'Agriculture
CGC	Confédération Générale des Cadres
CGPME	Confédération Générale des Petites et Moyennes Entreprises
CGT	Confédération Générale du Travail
CNASEA	Centre National pour l'Aménagement des Structures des Exploitations Agricoles
CNJA	Centre (Cercle) National des Jeunes Agriculteurs
CNMCCA	Confédération Nationale de la Mutualité, de la Coopération et du Crédit Agricole
CNPF	Conseil National du Patronat Français
CNSTP	Confédération Nationale Syndicale des Travailleurs-Paysans
CRJA	Centre Régional des Jeunes Agriculteurs
CSO	Conseil Supérieur d'Orientation de l'Economie Agricole et Alimentaire
CUMA	Coopérative d'Utilisation du Matériel Agricole
DBV	Deutschen Bauernverband
DJA	Dotation Jeune Agriculteur
DSA	Directeur des Services Agricoles
EEC	European Economic Community
FASASA	Fonds d'Action Sociale pour l'Aménagement des Structures Agricoles
FCSEA	Fédération Corrézienne des Syndicats d'Exploitants Agricoles

FDSEA	Fédération Départementale des Syndicats d'Exploitants Agricoles
FEN	Fédération d'Education Nationale
FFA	Fédération Française de l'Agriculture
FLSEA	Fédération Landaise des Syndicats d'Exploitants Agricoles
FNSEA	Fédération Nationale des Syndicats d'Exploitants Agricoles
FNSP	Fédération Nationale des Syndicats Paysans
FO	Force Ouvrière
FORMA	Fonds d'Orientation et de Régulation des Marchés Agricoles
FRSEA	Fédération Régionale des Syndicats d'Exploitants Agricoles
GAEC	Groupement Agricole d'Exploitation en Commun
IVD	Indemnité Viagère de Départ
JAC	Jeunesse Agricole Catholique
MADARAC	Mouvement d'Action et de Défense pour l'Amélioration du Revenu des Agriculteurs Corréziens
MODEF	Mouvement de Défense des Exploitants Familiaux
MONATAR	Mouvement National des Travailleurs Agricoles et Ruraux
MRG	Mouvement des Radicaux de Gauche
MRP	Mouvement Républicain Populaire
NFU	National Farmers' Union (Britain/United States)
PCF	Parti Communiste Français
PS	Parti Socialiste
PSU	Parti Socialiste Unifié
RPF	Rassemblement du Peuple Français
RPR	Rassemblement du Peuple pour la République
SAFER	Société d'Aménagement Foncier et d'Etablissement Rural
SEGL	Syndicat des Exploitations de la Grande Lande
SFIO	Section Française d'Internationale Ouvrière
SICA	Société d'Intérêt Collectif Agricole
SLIR	Syndicat Landais d'Initiatives Rurales
SMI	Surface Minimum d'Installation
SMIC	Salaire Minimum Industriel de Croissance
SNPMI	Syndicat Nationale de la Petite et Moyenne Industrie
SOFRES	Société Française d'Enquêtes par Sondages
SUAD	Service d'Utilité Agricole et de Développement
TVA	Taxe sur Valeur Ajoutée
UDF	Union pour la Démocratie Française
UDR	Union Démocratique pour le République
USAA	Union des Syndicats Agricoles de l'Aisne
UTH	Unité de Travailleur-Homme

The Politics of Neocorporatism in France

Introduction

Neocorporatist Theory
and the Case of France

"L'Hiver sera chaud!" was the warning shouted out by a mob of 3,000 angry farmers who engaged in a bloody confrontation with riot police outside the regional prefecture of Strasbourg in December of 1981. As a wave of demonstrations rocked the French countryside from Alsace to Brittany and from the Ardennes to the Spanish border, the winter did indeed prove to be hot for those in charge of agricultural policy within François Mitterrand's new Socialist government. Not since 1961 had such an extensive and violent outpouring of anger been witnessed in the agricultural sector.[1] Thousands of farmers waving placards and chanting antigovernment slogans paraded through virtually all of the provincial capitals. Everything from rocks to manure was hurled at the prefectures, windows were broken, official cars were overturned, railroad tracks were destroyed, and countless highways were blocked by tractors. Although no deaths were reported, scores of protesters and police were injured in violent encounters all across the country.[2]

Two unprecedented events in the early months of 1982 symbolized for the public what the press was beginning to term "la révolte des paysans." In early February, on a farm in Normandy, Minister of Agriculture Edith Cresson found herself surrounded by 1,200 protesters who pelted her with eggs and insults. As the mob became ever more frenzied and made it impossible for her to leave by limousine, she was forced to escape by running across a meadow with her outnumbered guards and leaping into a helicopter summoned by the anxious *gendarmes mobiles*. Since television cameras were present, dramatic scenes of the disheveled and mud-splattered minister fleeing from "her" farmers were broadcast into millions of homes, providing what to many seemed a vivid illustration of the Socialists' fading popularity and faltering capacity to govern.[3] No one could remember when a minister of agriculture had been treated more rudely. The next month, on 23 March, Parisians witnessed the largest

3

demonstration of farmers in the history of the capital. A crowd of nearly 100,000 protesters brought traffic to a halt as they marched behind thirty tractors along a 3-mile-long route from the Place de la Nation to the Porte de Pantin. This manifestation of agricultural discontent was spectacular enough not only to make front-page news all across France, but even to receive extensive coverage in the New York *Times* and a mention in the evening news programs on American television.[4]

Attempts to explain the onset of the "hot winter" of 1981–82 focused on a wide variety of factors ranging from the farmers' disillusionment with an eighth consecutive year of declining agricultural income to their allegedly sexist disdain for Cresson, the first woman in French history to hold the post of minister of agriculture. Almost all informed observers agreed, however, that the key problem underlying this explosion of rural unrest was the recent "divorce" between the government and the most powerful of agricultural organizations, the FNSEA (Fédération Nationale des Syndicats d'Exploitants Agricoles). It was FNSEA activists who organized most of the antigovernment demonstrations throughout the countryside from late 1981 to early 1982, and it was the national elite of the FNSEA who orchestrated the drive to bring the peasants to Paris in March of 1982. In fact, the FNSEA's role was so prominent that much of the popular press depicted the winter of rural discontent as a personal test of wills between Cresson and the president of the FNSEA, François Guillaume. Socialist spokesmen predictably blamed the divorce on the FNSEA and explained it in purely partisan terms. The leader of the Socialist contingent in the National Assembly, for example, branded Guillaume as "a political agitator of the Right," while the Socialists' newspaper reported fears within Cresson's cabinet that the conservative leaders of the FNSEA hoped to destabilize the Socialist government through demonstrations, as the truckers' union had done in Allende's Chile.[5] More detached analysts acknowledged that the partisan leanings of the FNSEA elite were no doubt a factor, but they stressed that one of the government's initial moves upon assuming power in 1981 had constituted a virtual application for divorce: the decision to impose from above a vital change in the structure of relations between the state and interest groups within the agricultural sector.

The leaders of the FNSEA decided to launch their nationwide protest movement only after the Socialist government declared its intention to dismantle the corporatist system of group-state relations which, since its establishment by the Gaullists in the early 1960s, had accorded the FNSEA a monopoly of representation among unions within the agricultural sector and even allowed it to comanage (*cogérer*) sectoral affairs in Paris and throughout the countryside. This system of corporatist *cogestion* had been a major factor enabling the process of agricultural modernization—the transformation from subsistence polyculture to specialized production for a market economy, the mechanization of work, the consolidation of small farms, and the concomitant exodus from the land of thousands of farmers—to unfold without creating the sort of widespread "climate of disintegration" which many observers expected and feared more than two decades ago.[6] Furthermore, as President Valéry Giscard d'Estaing noted in a celebrated speech of 1977, the state's special relationship with the FNSEA had facilitated the development of an agricultural economy strong and competitive enough to serve as "the oil of France," producing an annual export surplus on the order of 20 billion francs.[7] However, critics on the Left and even some on the Right had long complained that the corporatist system involved a sacrifice in state authority, an acceptance of questionable and even illegal uses of public funds for the advancement of private organizational interests, and a systematic stifling of union pluralism—in short, as one union rival of the FNSEA put it, a veritable reconstruction of the infamous Vichy regime's Corporation Paysanne.[8]

Given the illegitimacy of the corporatist system in the eyes of many on the Left, along with the fact that the FNSEA elite possessed strong if informal ties to the parties of the Center-Right, Edith Cresson's Ministry of Agriculture decided to place a high priority on revamping the traditional structure of group-state relations. In her first major speech as minister, Cresson issued what might be termed an anticorporatist manifesto. "It is necessary," she proclaimed, "to end the confusion between the role of professional organizations and that of the state. The former must negotiate and contest if they feel it necessary; the state must make the decisions." Not only was the FNSEA to be deprived of its "right" to comanage the sector, it was also to be stripped of its status as the only officially recognized union representative for agriculture—a status that had reinforced FNSEA hegemony by providing "le syndicalisme officiel" with tangible benefits (e.g., state subsidies and exclusive seats on commissions) as well as an aura of authority. Announcing that she was merely acknowledging "the union pluralism which exists in reality," Cresson broke the FNSEA's monopoly by according official recognition to three additional unions: the Communist-dominated MODEF (Mouvement de Défense des Exploitants Familiaux), the predominantly Socialist CNSTP (Confédération Nationale Syndicale des Travailleurs-Paysans), and the extremely conservative FFA (Fédération Française de l'Agriculture).[9]

Understandably, the government's intention to impose this new pluralist order was viewed as a grave threat by the leaders of the FNSEA, who protested vehemently against what they considered to be "systematic efforts to destabilize" their organization.[10] In the words of L'Express, the FNSEA's representative monopoly and its extraordinary power to control the "utilization of a large share of public funds" for the sector were advantages that "François Guillaume [was] not ready to abandon without a struggle."[11] As Guillaume and others made clear throughout the winter of 1981–82, "la révolte des paysans" was in large part an antipluralist revolt orchestrated by an organization fearful of being reduced from the status of a quasi-official policy-maker to that of a mere pressure group.

Even as an effort was being made to institute "pluralism" in the agricultural sector, therefore, it ironically became more evident than ever that analysts of

French politics and policy must understand the role that the politics of corporatism has played in France since the advent of the Fifth Republic. By the same token, interest group theorists were provided with a graphic demonstration of the need to incorporate the French case into their comparative discussions of the "neocorporatist" phenomenon.

THE NEOCORPORATIST THEORETICAL PERSPECTIVE

France has so far received scant attention in the burgeoning literature on (neo)corporatism, a literature so vast that it has made corporatist studies appear to be "a growth industry" and almost "a major 'field of study' itself."[12] The neglect of France by interest group theorists and comparativists can be explained in part by the fact that French politics specialists have produced relatively few useful studies of the dynamics of group-state relations. "Most of the available studies," as Ezra Suleiman lamented some years ago, "have centered on rather sensational cases . . . single issues of major policy where energies are galvanized." This concentration on "explosive issues" and "interest group battles . . . ultimately solved in parliament" has provided "little insight into the role of pressure groups in the French political system, for there is no attempt to comprehend the complex mechanisms and relationships that generally play a role in the group's attempts to influence decisions." "There is need," Suleiman concluded, "for less concentration on the sensational cases that come and go . . . and above all there is a need for specific case studies."[13] One could add that there has long been a need for studies that deal not solely with group-state interactions in Paris, but also with the multifarious related interactions in the provinces, for it is on the subnational level—where policies are implemented with group support or against group resistance, where state officials strive to defuse or stifle unrest before it can become a problem for the national government, where the rank and file question organizational policy and decide whether or not to reject the orientations taken by distant national leaders—that interest groups and the state face perhaps their most demanding tasks and give substance to the formal working relationships agreed upon in Paris.

While the data gap described by Suleiman has doubtless contributed to the neglect of France in the corporatist literature, a more fundamental reason for this inattention has probably been the way in which Philippe Schmitter's "Still the Century of Corporatism" has served to structure debates over and research on the phenomenon of corporatism in liberal democratic polities. In this seminal article, Schmitter was concerned with offering "to the political analyst an explicit alternative to the paradigm of interest politics which has heretofore completely dominated the discipline of North American political science: pluralism."[14] Pluralism, according to Schmitter, could be defined as

> a system of interest representation in which the constituent units are organized into an unspecified number of multiple, voluntary, competitive, nonhierarchically ordered and self-determined (as to type or scope of interest) categories which are not specifically licensed, recognized, subsidized, created or otherwise controlled in leadership selection or interest articulation by the state and which do not exercise a monopoly of representational activity within their respective categories.[15]

Noting that the pluralist paradigm had often been observed to be "of little utility in describing the likely structure and behavior of interest-group systems in contemporary developing polities," Schmitter proceeded to present "corporatism" as a rival paradigm or "heuristic concept" allegedly better suited as a conceptual guide to analyzing and understanding the dynamics of interest group behavior and group-state relations in a host of empirical cases:

> Corporatism can be defined as a system of interest representation in which the constituent units are organized into a limited number of singular, compulsory, noncompetitive, hierarchically ordered and functionally differentiated categories, recognized or licensed (if not created) by the state and granted a deliberate representational monopoly within their respective categories in exchange for observing certain controls on their selection of leaders and articulation of demands and supports.[16]

While the corporatist paradigm provides a new perspective on many aspects of interest group behavior, its central theoretical departure from the traditional pluralist approach can be summed up quite simply. In the words of Collier and Collier, "it takes as a starting point the role of the state in shaping interest representation."[17] The pluralist paradigm leads one to expect that the state will play at most a *passive* role in determining the mode of interest group activity; for example, groups may pattern their institutions after those of the state in order to facilitate access, and particular groups may be powerful within their respective sectors in part because their resources enable them to succeed in gaining access. In contrast, the corporatist paradigm leads one to expect that the state will act as an "architect of political order," bolstering certain groups at the expense of others and thereby profoundly affecting group dynamics.[18] In Schmitter's terms, the state is not "an arena for which interests contend or another interest group with which they must compete," but rather "a constitutive element engaged in defining, distorting, encouraging, regulating, licensing and/or repressing the activities of associations."[19]

Stimulating though it was, Schmitter's initial conceptualization of corporatism was also somewhat problematic and limited in its utility. By defining corporatism as a "Macro-Gestalt" or an ideal-typical system, Schmitter directed attention almost exclusively toward the politywide approximations of such a system said to be present in, for example, Switzerland, Austria, the Netherlands, and Scandinavia.[20] As critics soon noted, however, "corporatism as a structural configuration is rarely an adequate description of total societies."[21] Accordingly, analysts such as Pempel and Tsunekawa have encouraged "greater disaggregation in all thinking about corporatism as a concept" and have stressed the need for the consideration of variance across sectors within polities.[22] Schmitter himself, in a follow-up article, has acknowledged that "different interest sectors . . . may be organized and relate to the state in quite different ways" and that "in point of fact, all the interest intermediation systems of Western Europe are 'mixed.' They may be predominantly of one type, but different sectors . . . are likely to be operating according to different principles or procedures."[23]

This trend toward a more disaggregated, sectoral approach to the study of corporatism has led to extensive analyses of some polities (e.g., Britain and West Germany) previously neglected. Still, however, the applicability of the corporatist paradigm to some sectors of the French case has received relatively little attention.[24] The data gap has no doubt been a factor here once again, but a more important reason has been the resistance to corporatist development in the one sector—labor—which has been the principal focus of discussion in the corporatism literature over the past few years.[25] Within this literature France has been mentioned only in a negative sense, that is, as a "deviant" noncorporatist case. For example, recent studies of the labor sector by Schain and by Cox and Hayward concluded that "among the advanced capitalist societies in Western Europe," the "corporatist model" is "probably least applicable to France."[26] Given the paucity of articles devoted to other sectors, the current corporatism literature strongly implies that the French interest group system as a whole can and should be viewed as functioning in essentially pluralist terms. Indeed, one analyst has gone so far as to argue explicitly that "France seems to be an exception to the purported trend toward corporatism," and that French interest group politics can be described as "a near classic case of interest group pluralism."[27]

A central purpose of this book will be to demonstrate that, contrary to such implicit or explicit judgments, a neocorporatist theoretical perspective *is* useful and to some extent even indispensable in explaining the dynamics of interest groups and group-state relations in contemporary France. It will be argued that since the advent of the Fifth Republic, group-state relations within all of the major socioeconomic sectors (including, to some degree, labor) have been affected by a corporatization process encouraged by the state. Interest group dynamics have been less fully and evenly corporatized in France than in many other West European polities, but the corporatization trend has entailed important consequences for intragroup and intergroup relations as well as the nature of group-state interaction in the policy-making process. Before moving to a discussion of the French case, it will be necessary to develop the theoretical framework within which this case is to be analyzed and to explain why the phenomenon of "corporatization" is politically significant.

Critics of the ideal-typical, "Macro-Gestalt" conceptualization of corporatism have stressed the need for an alternative approach that is not only disaggregated but also *dynamic*, that is, "more sensitive to changes over time."[28] As Collier and Collier have argued, corporatism should "not be conceived narrowly as either present or absent, but rather as a variable that may assume different values, as a phenomenon that may be present to varying degrees," as a "set of dimensions . . . along which cases may be arrayed."[29] In the same vein, Claus Offe has urged that corporatism be treated as a "concept that does not describe a situation, but rather an 'axis' of development. In other words, political systems can be more or less corporatist, more or less advanced in the process of corporatization, depending on the degree to which public status is attributed to organized interest groups," that is, the degree to which groups are assigned "certain semipublic or public functions" as well as "resources" that affect not only group-state relations but also "internal relations between rank-and-file members and executive members."[30]

If one accepts the need for such a dynamic approach, then one must define "corporatism" not in ideal-typical terms à la Schmitter, but rather in generic terms applicable to a variety of more or less fully developed types. For the purposes of this book, therefore, corporatism will be defined as a system of interest intermediation in which a limited number of groups within a sector are formally incorporated into the public policy-making process (i.e., granted seats on public committees, commissions, or councils) and provided by the state with certain benefits in exchange for their cooperation and their restraint in the articulation of demands. This definition acknowledges that it is at least theoretically possible for more than one group within a sector to receive official status from and behave as clients of the state; given the political difficulties involved in developing or sustaining an intensely cooperative relationship between the state and a number of rival groups, it is assumed that the more fully developed types of corporatism will feature a single client. "Corporatization" will be defined as a change in the system of interest intermediation involving an increase in the extent to which the official group(s) is incorporated into the policy-making process, receives benefits, provides cooperation, and shows restraint.

Corporatization thus defined is a multifaceted phenomenon entailing politically important changes not simply in the mode of group-state interaction, but also in the dynamics of intragroup and intergroup relations. The more a sector is "corporatized," the more the dynamics of interest group politics within the sector will resemble the ideal type elaborated by Schmitter. Seldom, however, will empirical cases manifest fully all of the characteristics associated with the ideal type. For example, unless rival groups are outlawed (and few if any will be in democratic polities) one should not expect to find sectoral interests represented in a "singular-monopolistic" group functioning in a "noncompetitive" situation due to the "compulsory" nature of membership. Instead, in what could be termed a case of "strong corporatism," one should expect to find interests represented in a hegemonic (or nearly monopolistic) official group functioning in a competitive situation strongly skewed in its favor by various state-sponsored measures which provide individuals with potent incentives to join the official group rather than its nonofficial rivals.

As Schmitter has acknowledged in a recent essay, " the real world is almost always located somewhere in between" his ideal types of pluralism and corporatism.[31] What analysts need, therefore, is a theoretical framework that specifies points along the pluralism–corporatism continuum and stipulates what sort of group dynamics should be observable at each point. No such analytical structure has yet been provided in the literature on the corporatist perspective, although at least two authors have made tentative steps in this direction.[32] In this book, therefore, I will employ a theoretical framework that is original yet quite consciously informed by many of the earlier, less elaborate efforts. Moreover, I will demonstrate how the framework can be used to track the development of corporatization within a single sector of one polity, to compare the degrees of corporatization obtained by various sectors of one polity, and/or to compare the degrees of corporatization obtained within a single sector of various polities.

As Figure I.1 indicates, the framework posits five points along the pluralism–corporatism continuum. Near the ends of the continuum one finds the "strong pluralism" and "strong corporatism" types, the characteristics of which are described schematically in Table 1.1. In terms of Figure 1.1, "corporatization" signifies movement from left to right along the continuum. As a sector becomes more "corporatized," change occurs in each of the dimensions listed on the left margin of Table 1.1: the role of the state in shaping interest intermediation increases, as state officials enhance the status of the official group or groups to the detriment of nonofficial groups; the official group(s) enjoys increasingly biased influence through formal incorporation into the public policy-making process; membership within the official group(s) becomes increasingly attractive (or all but compulsory) in light of the resources provided by the state; the official group(s) thus enjoys increasing "partial immunity" from members' criticisms, and the official group(s) serves increasingly as a "transmission belt" between members and the state rather than as a "defender" of its members; and competition between the official group(s) and its rivals becomes increasingly skewed in favor of the state's client(s), as its competitive advantage is enhanced through the receipt of more tangible and intangible benefits.

For example, the transformation from "strong pluralism" to "structured pluralism" involves the initiation of an effort by the state to designate certain groups as official sectoral representatives and to incorporate them to a very limited degree into the policy-making process. In this type of group-state system, the official groups are accorded only modest benefits (in terms of biased influence and competitive advantage) and can thus be expected to provide in exchange only a modest degree of cooperation and restraint. The nature of group-state interaction, intragroup relations, and intergroup relations in such a system diverges somewhat from the patterns associated with ideal-typical or strong pluralism, and this fact may at times be of some political importance, but the system generally functions according to pluralist dynamics.

Figure I.1 Points on the pluralism-corporatism continuum

Strong Pluralism	Structured Pluralism	Weak Corporatism	Moderate Corporatism	Strong Corporatism
—— X ——	—— X ——	—— X ——	—— X ——	—— X ——

Table 1.1 The dynamics of "strong pluralism" and "strong corporatism" systems

	Strong Pluralism	Strong Corporatism
Role of the state in shaping the pattern of interest intermediation	The state plays no active role, serving simply as a *broker* vis-à-vis competing interest groups.	The state plays a very important role as *architect* of political order, acting so as to bolster an official client group.
Nature of group-state interaction in the public policy-making process	Groups attempt to influence policy by pressuring or lobbying state decision-makers. No groups are *formally* incorporated into the public policy-making process. If any public committees/commissions exist, they provide groups with no genuine influence; thus groups may even refuse to participate in them.	The *official client* benefits greatly from biased influence, i.e., structured access to state decision-makers and/or devolved power for the administration of public policy. *Nonofficial groups* must resort to lobbying and other traditional pressure tactics.
Nature of intragroup (elite-member) relations	The behavior of group elites is essentially responsive to the demands of members; demand responsiveness may well be imperfect, but this is due to oligarchic tendencies rather than intervention by the state. Groups essentially act as "defenders" of their members vis-à-vis the state.	The behavior of official client elite is often not very responsive to member demands; group leaders enjoy a good deal of "immunity" from members' criticism through benefits received from the state in exchange for their cooperation and restraint. The official client group acts as a "transmission belt" between members and the state, often striving to mobilize members in support of policy and to discipline dissidents.
Nature of intergroup relations	Groups compete for members and influence without state interference. Members join and remain within a group due to attractiveness of incentives derived from endogenous sources or nonstate exogenous sources.	The *official client group* enjoys an enormous competitive advantage, as the state provides it with resources or even makes membership compulsory. *Nonofficial groups* receive no such resources and may even be repressed by state.

When corporatization advances to the point of "weak corporatism," which one can expect to happen only rarely without the presence of a group capable of serving as the sole client for the sector, pluralist theory is no longer useful as a means of explaining interest-group dynamics. The official group of such a system is incorporated more fully into the policy-making process and provided with more significant benefits in exchange for a corresponding degree of cooperation and restraint. Pluralist theory is inapplicable to such a system because a group which is accorded a significant degree of public status ceases, in Offe's words, "to be exclusively determined in its actions and accomplishments by the interests, ideologies, need perceptions, and so forth of its members."[33]

As this study will illustrate, the degree to which the corporatization process proceeds in a particular sector of a democratic polity depends on the calculations made both by those "above" (the state actors emphasized by Offe) and those "below" (the group actors emphasized by Schmitter).[34] Whereas authoritarian (or state) corporatism à la Vichy may simply be imposed from above in a roughly uniform fashion, the corporatization of a regime such as the Fifth French Republic develops in an uneven, ad hoc manner through recognition by the state (that is, the officials of the government and the bureaucracy) and the would-be clients that a corporatist relationship would be *mutually* beneficial. A highly corporatist group-state relationship can thus be expected to emerge and remain stable only if state actors (weighing the potential utility of the would-be client in making intervention in the sector's economy workable and socially acceptable as well as its potential utility as a source of electoral support) and interest-group actors (weighing the utility of client status in reinforcing their organization and in producing desired policy/political outcomes) both view such a relationship as preferable to a more pluralist alternative. From the perspective of the state actors, corporatization is a means not only of facilitating intervention in a sector where the services of a client are needed, but also of altering what Nordlinger terms the "resource-weighted societal parallelogram of preferences" through reinforcing the resources of those groups whose policy/political preferences converge with those of the state.[35] From the perspective of the interest group actors, corporatization is a means of obtaining not only increased influence within the policy-making process, but also various benefits that can enhance the group's organizational status.

One of the goals of this book is to clarify theoretically and illustrate empirically the dynamics of such a mutually beneficial relationship, that is, "the delicate combination of ruling imperatives, organizational goals, and member interests that lies at the heart of the corporatist effort."[36] The case to be examined in depth, that of the French agricultural sector, suggests the following model of group-state relations in a stable system of "strong corporatism." The agreement by an interest group to perform the role of an official client involves the exchange of some *gains* for some *losses*. What a client loses, above all, is a certain measure of its freedom to articulate the demands of its members. It becomes less able to appear as their ardent defender during times of sectoral unrest, because the maintenance of its client status is contingent upon acceptance of the obligation to "behave responsibly and predictively, and to refrain from any non-negotiable demands or non-acceptable tactics."[37] Indeed, the client is sometimes obliged to act as an agent "of mobilization and social control for the state vis-à-vis [its] members."[38] The gains an official client group receives in exchange for fulfilling its obligations to the state are essentially of two types. The more obvious and more often discussed type is *biased influence*: structured access to the decision-making centers of the state and/or devolved power for the administration of public policy. But the second type of gain, related to but analytically distinct from the first, is of more fundamental importance for the client: *competitive advantage*. If a corporatist client is to continue to respect its obligations to the state, which will at times mean disregarding the sentiments of many of its members, then it must receive organizational supports or benefits from the state sufficient to provide it with at least "partial immunity from its members," that is, to assure that its unpopular behavior will not imperil its sectoral hegemony by generating a massive departure of hostile members for nonofficial rivals.[39]

In explaining the ability of official clients to derive competitive advantage from their relationship with the state, neocorporatist theory assumes that group members (or prospective members) behave according to the sort of logic developed in the works of "incentive" theorists. Since this book will deal to a great extent with the intragroup and intergroup dimensions of the politics of corporatism, it is important that this assumption be acknowledged and justified. In his seminal book, *The Logic of Collective Action*, Mancur Olson makes the now familiar argument that "large and powerful economic lobbies" manage to recruit and retain members not because they effectively articulate members' interests, as traditional pluralist theory assumed, but "because they perform some function in addition to lobbying for collective goods." Rational, self-interested individuals cannot be expected to join an organization simply because they agree with its policy goals and wish to further its efforts to produce certain public policy benefits. Such benefits are public or collective goods, by nature available to all individuals in the relevant population regardless of whether or not they are group members. Large organizations such as socioeconomic interest groups must thus support themselves by "providing some sanction, or some attraction, distinct from the public good itself, that will lead individuals to help bear the burdens of maintaining the organization." Organizations successful in enrolling members, Olson argues, can be expected to possess either "the authority and the capacity to be coercive" or a supply of "selective incentives," "positive inducements," that the group can offer to members and effectively withhold from those who refuse to become members.[40]

Virtually all students of interest groups now accept the notion that "selective incentives" or sanctions are crucial in determining the ability of groups to obtain members. However, critics of Olson have demonstrated empirically that, in Moe's words, "political goals simply appear to have much greater inducement value for members than his theory leads us to expect."[41] James Q. Wilson has provided a less parsimonious model which stresses the importance of selective incentives, but which allows one to account for the significance of groups' political goals as well as other forms of inducement. Beginning with the assumption that "people join associations for a variety of reasons"—including organizational goals or "stated purposes"—and that they are "more or less rational about action taken on behalf of these reasons," Wilson presents a typology of incentives that organizations may employ to attract members. The four principal types of incentive, according to Wilson, are the following: (1) *material incentives*—"tangible rewards," that is, "money, or things and services readily priced in monetary terms"; (2) *specific solidary incentives*—"intangible rewards arising out of the act of associating that can be given to, or withheld from, specific individuals," for example, "offices, honors and deference"; (3) *collective solidary incentives*—"intangible rewards created by the act of associating that must be enjoyed by a group if they are to be enjoyed by anyone," for example, "such collective status or esteem as the group as a whole may enjoy"; and (4) *purposive incentives*—"intangible rewards that derive from the sense of satisfaction of having contributed to the attainment of a worthwhile cause"; these rewards "depend crucially on the stated objectives" or political goals of the organization. As Wilson notes, these incentive types "vary in the extent to which they implicate the stated purposes . . . of the organization."[42] Both solidary and purposive incentives are limited in appeal to those who are attracted to the political goals and/or elites and/or other members of an organization. In contrast, material incentives, especially crucial services, may well appeal to those who are indifferent or even hostile to the ideas or personalities associated with an organization.

To understand the relationship between incentive theory and neocorporatist theory, one need merely note the importance of the *source* of the benefits organizations have at their disposal for distribution to members in the form of selective incentives. These benefits may derive entirely from within the group, for example, from membership dues or from group-sponsored activities; in this case the benefits can be said to have an *endogenous* source. Alternatively, benefits may be derived from sources outside the group, for example, from another interest group, a political party, a foundation, or the state; these benefits may be said to have an *exogenous* source.[43] Pluralist theory leads one to expect that interest groups will function either entirely with endogenous resources, or with these in combination with nonstate exogenous resources. Neocorporatist theory, in contrast, assumes that some interest groups—the official clients of the state—will benefit from a substantial supply of exogenous resources provided by the state. It is these resources that provide official clients with a competitive advantage and are most crucial in sustaining a client at a time when its "purposive incentives" are of diminishing appeal.

The state can bolster a client organization by enhancing its ability to attract members with all three of the nonpurposive types of incentive. An organization's capacity to deliver specific solidary incentives can be increased through the allocation of seats on prestigious public committees, councils, and commissions; these are offices or honors that many of the more ambitious members (or potential members) of an organization prize. The collective solidary incentives offered by an organization can also be enhanced by the state; simple "recognition" of the group, along with any powers devolved to it by the state, can lend the group an aura of authority and thus increase its "collective status or esteem." By far the most visible and the most demonstrably important manner in which the state can reinforce a client, however, is to provide it with money and other resources translatable into material incentives. When a client organization receives a direct cash subsidy, or when it is indirectly provided with resources through grants of money, personnel, or infrastructure to a semipublic agency that the organization controls, then it will be able to offer members a variety of services and other material incentives with which non-official rival organizations will be hard-pressed to compete. In addition, it should be noted that client organizations which wield power through their control of public bodies at the local level may employ what might be termed "negative" material incentives; that is, they may be in a position to deny valued goods to nonmembers.

Advantageous though the "gains" of client status may be, under certain circumstances interest group elites may find that they are insufficient to offset the "losses" which that status entails. In other words, client group elites may decide, if faced with widespread dissent by their members and/or the possibility of a damaging organizational scission, that they must terminate their cooperation with the state and articulate members' interests without restraint. Such a case could be categorized as one of corporatist *instability* generated *from below*. It is also quite possible, of course, for corporatist instability to be generated *from above*, that is, by the state. "Instead of just facilitating the management of the state," corporatist arrangements could "eventually threaten the status and resources of public authorities and party politicians and introduce additional rigidities and irrationalities into public policy making. State bureaucrats might find that devolution of authority to corporatist intermediaries deprives them of their unique status and of important instruments for resolving broader public issues and intersectoral conflicts."[44] One would expect such an occurrence to be especially likely in a case where a new government obtains power and inherits a network of corporatist clients which, because of their policy/political ties to the old regime, seem likely to frustrate rather than facilitate the government's efforts to make policy and maintain social peace. In such a case, an example of which will be provided in this book (see Chapter 8), the state is apt to decrease (if not cease) its cooperation with the client, reduce (if not eliminate) the benefits traditionally provided to the client, and compel the client to decrease (if not abandon) its cooperation and restraint. If this alteration of the traditional mode of behavior by actors either above or below persists for long, of course, it will engender what can be termed *decorporatization*, that is, the establishment of a stable system of group-state relations at some point closer to the pluralist end of the continuum described in Figure I.1

THE UNEVEN CORPORATIZATION TREND IN FRANCE

As numerous analysts have observed, the single most important factor in stimulating corporatization within democratic polities has been "a shift in the nature and extent of public policy," specifically an acceleration of the "coercive intervention of the modern bureaucratic state."[45] Samuel Beer, one of the first to perceive the trend toward neocorporatist group-state relations, has referred to this phenomenon as "Herring's law": "The greater the degree of detailed and technical control the government seeks to exert over [private] interests, the greater must be their degree of consent and active participation."[46] Another classic formulation of this "law" has been provided by Andrew Shonfield: "The increased range and subtlety of the relationship between the public and the private sectors have made it less feasible to govern effectively by decree. The system will not function unless private organizations give their willing collaboration to the pursuit of public purposes. What is therefore required is the opposite of a bully state—rather a wheeling and dealing type of public authority constantly seeking out allies, probing and maneuvering for the active consensus."[47]

The operation of the Herring-Shonfield law has been visible to some degree in France ever since the 1940s. During the Fourth Republic, successive governments "relied heavily on state intervention and planning" to manage the economy and, inspired by the ideal of an *économie concertée*, "developed a corporatist network to intensify the participation of private interests in the making of public policy."[48] Near the end of the Fourth Republic, Georges Lavau noted that public-private collaboration had been institutionalized in "countless" councils, committees, and commissions and that these constituted "a very important but little known factor of the political effectiveness of pressure groups."[49] Important though this development was, it amounted to no more than a relatively modest alteration in the system of group-state relations, that is, the creation in most sectors of what we have termed structured pluralism. Throughout the Fourth Republic period, the corporatization process was limited by the nature of both the principal interest groups and the state. Compared to those of many other polities, the peak interest groups in most French sectors were relatively weak in terms of resources and capacity to mobilize and discipline their members (and thus facilitate intervention); even where they were willing, therefore, they were not able to serve as very effective clients for the state. Even more important, however, was the fact that the state was relatively restricted in its capacity to wheel, deal, maneuver, and probe in the manner discussed by Shonfield. On the one hand, governments that generally endured for less than a year were incapable of cultivating clients with assurances of biased influence and organizational benefits. On the other hand, as long as parliament and the political parties dominated the political system, traditional lobbying or pressure tactics retained their central importance for all interest groups and enabled nonofficial groups excluded from the system of structured representation to exert considerable if sporadic influence within the policy-making process.

With the advent of the Fifth Republic in 1958, three major factors combined to further the corporatization trend and to give it a distinctive French flavor. First, state intervention increased dramatically as the new regime sought, in Stanley Hoffmann's words, to "pursue economic modernization and handle the resulting social costs with maximum efficiency and minimum friction." Achieving these goals would necessitate not only a "formidable extension of state functions and operations," but also a "complicated symbiosis" between the state and organized interests which would allow "the state, as the dispenser of subsidies, favors and power, to orient these groups and to carry out policies which cannot be enforced by bureaucrats alone."[50] Second, the constitutional changes introduced by the Gaullists entailed "a massive transfer of power" from parliament to the executive and the bureaucracy.[51] While the government thus felt increasingly compelled to attempt to enlist group assistance in pushing through the disruptive and complex program of modernization, interest groups in turn were forced to rechannel their efforts from lobbying in parliament to interacting with the new or strengthened decision-making centers of the state. Selected groups were provided by the state with a variety of benefits (subsidies, privileged access, and even devolved power) which served not only as incentives for their cooperation, but also as a means of strengthening their organizations and rendering them more useful clients. Third, the weak and shifting governments of the Fourth Republic were replaced by a stable majority of the Center-Right which would remain intact for twenty-three years. What this meant was that the government's rhetorical commitment to *concertation* with "social partners" translated into genuinely intimate group-state relationships mainly in those sectors whose leaders were relatively comfortable with the politics and policies of the Center-Right and whose constituents were a major focus of electoral concern for the government.

The transition to the Fifth Republic thus produced a pronounced but uneven and somewhat unusual corporatization process. Schmitter, Lehmbruch, and others have noted that corporatization has tended to develop primarily in polities where the "strength of reformist social-democratic parties" has been "greatest and most protracted."[52] However, the French case shows that—as in Japan—a strongly interventionist Center-Right government can produce an anomalous form of "corporatism without labor." In the Japanese case, as Pempel and Tsunekawa have demonstrated, this "curious anomaly" can be explained largely by the fact that the Left has been excluded from governing coalitions since the time of the occupation. Organized labor, "consistently allied with political parties on the 'outs,'" has been as hostile to the regime as the regime has been to it and thus has "neither succeeded in acquiring, nor faced the need to resist, any significant pressure for national level corporatist connections." In contrast, however, the organizational representatives of big business and agriculture—the "key sectoral components" of the ruling Liberal Democratic Party—have developed strong corporatist ties with the government and the bureaucracy.[53]

In the French case, one finds that a similar government coalition acting in concert with its chief sectoral allies to guide the process of economic modernization led in the two decades after 1958 to the development of a roughly comparable "unbalanced corporatist structure." The unbalanced or uneven nature of the French corporatization process can be explained as the result of variance, from sector to sector, in the degree to which the state and the respective interest groups perceived as beneficial the development of corporatist ties. As schematically depicted in Table 1.2, group-state relations were corporatized to some extent even in the labor sector, where a "strong pluralism" system was transformed to a "structured pluralism" system; corporatization developed more fully in the business sector, with a "structured pluralism" system evolving into a "moderate corporatism" system, and even further in the agricultural case, where a "strong corporatism" system emerged. The remainder of this section will be devoted to a brief account of developments within the labor and business sectors and will thus establish a cross-sectoral comparative perspective for the subsequent, much more detailed analysis of the agricultural case.

Labor

While the major trade unions were officially recognized by the state and offered some possibilities for formal participation in the policy-making process during the Fourth Republic, the unions were too weak (all of them together could claim to represent little more than 20% of the workers) to serve as effective clients and were ideologically resistant to doing so. "With their relatively anemic membership, intense rivalries, and anti-capitalist ideologies," notes Kuisel, the unions "participated diffidently and on the periphery of [the] corporatist network. Thus the CGT withdrew from the planning apparatus in 1947, and those trade union federations that chose to remain assumed a more critical stance. Similarly, unions lost control of the governing boards of the nationalized firms in the 1950s and even drifted away from their *ministère de tutelle*, the labor department."[54] Those trade unionists who did agree to participate in the planning process during the 1950s felt "like interlopers in some club meeting or family circle," and their meager input was ignored and even ridiculed. In the words of Stephen Cohen, the *économie concertée* was a "partnership of big business, the state, and, in theory though not in practice, the trade unions."[55] One might say that the unions were merely "formally" formally incorporated into the policy-making process during

Table 1.2   The uneven corporatization trend in France, 1958–81

	Labor Sector	Business Sector	Agricultural Sector
Degree of state need for client in facilitating intervention and achieving policy goals	Low–Moderate Union cooperation potentially useful but not necessary	Moderate CNPF cooperation quite useful, but direct state-firm relations a viable alternative in some cases	Very High FNSEA cooperation crucial for achievement of modernization and maintenance of social peace
Degree of group-state consensus on political and policy goals	Very low in case of CGT/CFDT; Moderate in FO case	Rather low until late 1960s; moderate to high thereafter	Very high from 1959 onward in regard to CNJA; high from 1964 onward with reformed FNSEA
Capacity of group(s) to mobilize and discipline members	Low	Low until late 1960s; moderate thereafter	Low–moderate, but improving as state subsidies and devolved power allow for expansion of staff and improved communications between Paris and the provinces.
Nature of transformation of group-state system from 1958–81	Strong pluralism to structured pluralism (FO is exception)	Structured pluralism to moderate corporatism	Structured pluralism to strong corporatism

this period. At the dawn of the Fifth Republic, labor thus stood as the only one of the major socioeconomic sectors whose dynamics could still be best described as an example of "strong pluralism."

The factors that precluded the corporatization of the labor sector during the 1950s continued, for the most part, to block progress throughout the first two decades of the Fifth Republic. The contradictory partisan orientations of the unions and the government remained the principal obstacle. As cross-national studies have shown, strong corporatist relationships involving industrial trade unions have tended to emerge only in countries "where confessional and social democratic unions have dominated the labor movement"[56] while the Socialists have been "the leading party in government" or at least part of the governing coalition.[57] In the French case, the predominant union—the Confédération Générale du Travail (CGT)—was very closely tied to the Communist Party and, of course, the Left was excluded from power at the national level. Charles de Gaulle may well have been thinking of his efforts to deal with the unions when he wrote in his memoirs that economic policy is "a sphere in which all is asperity."[58]

During the years in which the Center-Right parties controlled the government, the leaders of the largest unions viewed participation in the planning process and other forms of formal interaction with the state as "a very real trap," that is, as no more than a chance to win small concessions at the risk of losing ideological purity, diluting the class consciousness of the workers and, ultimately, reinforcing the capitalist system to which they were fundamentally opposed.[59]

While the lack of a political/policy consensus between unions and the state was the most fundamental factor limiting corporatization, the persistent organizational weakness of the unions was very important as well. From the perspective of the government, an attempt to develop significant corporatist ties with the unions appeared to be not merely politically impractical, but also (except in times of crisis, as will be discussed later) not so potentially useful as to be worthy of much effort. "Because of their inability to mobilize a mass base effectively," the unions' "advice and acquiesence generally [was] not considered necessary by the state for the successful development and implementation of policy." Neither the state nor the employers could expect many "benefits of social order" from collaboration with union organizations with "so little authority over strike action."[60]

Despite what in retrospect seem to have been insuperable obstacles to corporatization, there were at least two periods when the development of at least "weak corporatism" was somewhat of a possibility. In the early days of the Fifth Republic, a majority of the leaders of France's second largest union (the Confédération Française des Travailleurs Chrétiens, CFTC, renamed in 1964 the Confédération Française Democratique du Travail, CFDT)[61] did express a willingness to collaborate with the government in exchange for an expansion of union rights, an increase in the role of labor within the planning process, and other benefits. Had the "Gaullists played their cards correctly," it has been suggested, "the nation's second largest and fastest growing union organization . . . appeared available . . . as an ally in an enlightened conservative moderniz- ation scheme." However, only a few "Left Gaullists" manifested interest in cultivating such an ally. As the government assumed an increasingly conservative orientation, the CFTC became disgruntled, pursued a course of "contestative participation," and then—as the CFDT—was radicalized by the events of May 1968, through which it "discovered" the class struggle and became committed to a socialist alternative.[62]

It was the shock of the May 1968 student-worker revolt which gave rise to the second period of tentative movement toward corporatization. In its efforts to resolve the crisis, the government was compelled to call together the major unions and the Conseil National du Patronat Français (CNPF) for a series of tripartite negotiations unparalleled in the postwar era.[63] Inspired by the successful outcome of these "Grenelle talks," the first government of the post–de Gaulle era in 1969 sought to assure social stability through an enduring improvement in industrial relations, the linchpin of what Prime Minister Jacques Chaban-Delmas termed a "New Society."[64] This initiative of Chaban-Delmas and his social advisor, Jacques Delors (who would later become minister of finance in the government of Mitterrand), "was precisely the sort of combination of concrete economic benefits and increases in union rights in return for industrial peace and union participation in parts of the policy processes which might very well have been accepted eight or nine years earlier" by the CFTC/CFDT, but it simply "came much too late" to stand a chance of the sort of sweeping success for which its sponsors hoped.[65] The CFDT, the CGT, and the minority unions did participate in summit negotiations with organized business and the state from 1969 through the early 1970s and signed a host of agreements concerning matters such as employment security, technical education, and the monthly payment of wages.[66] With a few exceptions, however, the CGT and (somewhat later) the CFDT refused to cooperate with Delors's ambitious *politique contractuelle*, a scheme designed to offer "real concessions" on the wage front "in exchange for certain limitations on their traditional freedom of action."[67] As the CGT and CFDT dismissed the *politique contractuelle* as "class collaboration" or "an enterprise of seduction," the corporatist experiment produced little lasting change in group-state relations within the labor sector.[68] An opinion poll administered in 1971 showed that it was by no means only the union elites who were reluctant to play this game; fully 42% of wage and salary earners agreed that "unions who sign such contracts are over-committing themselves and cannot defend the real interests of the employed" (32% disagreed and 26% gave no reply). At the same time, it became clear that support for this "progressive" policy was fragile within the government as well as the business community. Chaban-Delmas was heavily criticized by conservatives of his own party for attempting this "opening to the Left" and, largely for this reason, was ousted as Prime Minister in 1972.[69]

With the departure of Chaban-Delmas and the onset of the economic crisis produced by the oil shock of 1974, the first "serious attempt to build a process of corporate consultation" gave way to a more traditional mode of relations between unions and the state.[70] The announcement of the Barre Plan of economic austerity in 1976, which had been "prepared without any consultation with the union organizations," marked the complete breakdown of union-state corporatist contacts. Efforts by Raymond Barre's government to revivify the corporatist bargaining process in 1979, accompanied by President Giscard d'Estaing's pledge to seek "a 'social consensus' through collective consultations," proved fruitless once again. By this time it was clear that the Center-Right government was not genuinely convinced that corporatist consultation with the ideologically hostile and organizationally weak trade unions could provide a sound "basis of long-term social stability."[71] As for the CGT and CFDT, their political opposition to the conservative government increasingly precluded serious consideration of the sort of self-imposed constraints that even a weak corporatist relationship would entail. In the short run, this would require them to be satisfied with what Georges Séguy of the CGT once termed "liberty in a cage," and in the long run it might impair the chances of an electoral victory for the united Left.[72]

The failure of the more dramatic possibilities for corporatization of the labor sector during the Center-Right era should not be allowed to obscure the fact that the "strong pluralism" system of the 1950s did evolve, at least, into what could be categorized as a system of "structured pluralism." As Ashford has argued, there were "more efforts to open new links between business and labor over the past twenty years than ever before," and initiatives of the state led to a significant increase in the degree to which trade unions were incorporated into the policy-making process. The two major unions participated not only in tripartite bargaining sessions at the summit, but also in a vastly expanded network of official bodies with some role in the administration of policy regarding, for example, unemployment compensation and health insurance. In fact, the degree of accommodation practiced by the CGT and CFDT was sufficient to engender condemnation by extreme Leftists affiliated with nonrecognized unions. The major unions were subjected to sardonic criticism for their agreement to negotiate at the summit in the "New Society" era, and their participation in advisory bodies led to the charge that they had "accept[ed] the idea of cooperation at all levels with the state . . . and an even more or less complete fusion between the highest levels of trade union bureaucracy and certain state organs. . . . This collaboration is detrimental to the interests of the workers."[73]

Another element of the limited but significant increase in the corporatization of the labor sector during the Center-Right era was an effort by the state to affect the dynamics of interest representation through subsidization. Under the Fourth Republic, the state had provided trade unions with only meager and "indirect" subsidies derived from union membership in the Economic Council. Soon after the Fifth Republic was launched, however, the Gaullist government established an important direct subsidy program, that for *promotion sociale collective*. An examination of the rationale behind this program and of the manner in which the Ministry of Labor allocated the program's funds during the years of conservative government will demonstrate that these subsidies seem to have been conceived and used as a means of altering the pattern of labor representation, that is, of bolstering the smaller, more moderate unions at the expense of their larger and more radical rivals.

In the text of the *promotion collective* bill that the Gaullists presented to parliament in 1959, the program was described as a means of enabling recognized trade unions to provide their elites with the "economic and social education" necessary for effective participation in the tripartite consultative bodies that the government sought to promote.[74] The wording of the text revealed no broader, partisan intent. However, the spokesmen for the government in the parliamentary debates clearly implied that the program was unlikely to be implemented in a nonpartisan manner. It was argued, for example, that the subsidy effort would help to produce a "competent workers' elite" through encouraging "the union organizations to put aside the myth of the class struggle and the influence of Marxist *dirigisme*" and thus make it possible "to establish collaboration . . . between management groups and labor unions."[75] More generally, the legislation was portrayed as part of the government's effort to "restore the social unity of the country."[76] A Communist deputy expressed considerable skepticism about the program, noting that a member of the government had depicted it as a means of altering the lamentable situation in which one of five French voted Communist, while another of its backers had claimed—in words "which remind us of a certain regime . . . at Vichy"—it would accelerate recognition of the fact that "the notion of class struggle is becoming more anachronistic every day."[77] One indication that the program might indeed be intended to alter the current balance of union power was the fact that the commission report on the *loi project* mentioned only the CFTC, Force Ouvrière (FO), and the Confédération Générale des Cadres (CGC) as unions already undertaking efforts to educate workers; no reference at all was made to the efforts of the CGT.[78] Given that the CGT was openly committed to striving for the delegitimation of the Gaullist regime, simple political logic could have led one to expect that funds would not flow readily into CGT coffers.[79]

During the first decade of the program's operation, the CGT was accorded from one eighth to one fourth as much funding as its rivals received.[80] The CGT repeatedly protested against what it viewed as a discriminatory policy and demanded that the funds be distributed not by the Ministry of Labor, but rather by a commission composed solely of trade union representatives.[81] In the face of such charges, the government justified its allocation of funds by explaining that the unions were paid in proportion not to their size, but to their "efforts at genuine union education"; clearly if indirectly, the CGT was thus informed that many of its "educational sessions" were ineligible for subsidization because they dealt with "politics" and involved partisan indoctrination.[82]

A fascinating footnote to the May 1968 revolt is the fact that the Grenelle talks apparently led to a modification of this "discriminatory" policy. CGT leader Georges Séguy has stated that Prime Minister Georges Pompidou raised the possibility of increased state funding for the CGT in return for "a softer CGT stand," but that he (Séguy) rebuffed the overture by saying that "there could be no question" of such a bargain.[83] This may indeed have been Séguy's position; obviously CGT behavior during the crisis was determined by political calculations concerning a wide variety of matters, some of which were much more important than the prospect of obtaining an increase in state funding. Nevertheless, it is notable that the CGT did air its grievance regarding the subsidy issue during the Grenelle negotiations, that the CGT did take a relatively "soft" stand during the crisis, and that the government altered the traditional subsidization policy soon thereafter. "The ultimate irony of the May–June 1968 crisis," notes Ross, "was that General de Gaulle was able to terminate the 'Events' by relying in part on the predictability of the CGT's behavior." The CGT controlled the strikes, maintained a "strong apolitical stance" and sabotaged the activities of Leftists who saw "the May crisis as an opportunity for politicizing unionists."[84] And in 1969 the CGT began to receive *promotion collective* subsidies equal to those given the other recognized unions.[85]

Yet the CGT continued to receive far less than would seem truly equitable, given its membership (2.4 million in 1978, compared to 1.15 million for the CFDT, 900,000 for FO, and 225,000 for the CFTC-Maintenue) and its popularity (44.9% of the vote in 1978 elections for the *comités d'entreprise*, compared to 21.1% for the CFDT and 9.6% for FO). Understandably, then, throughout the years of Center-Right government the CGT and, to a lesser extent, the CFDT both believed "that their more moderate rivals obtain[ed] a higher proportional share than [was] justified." By the mid-1970s, even the CGT was receiving 3 million francs per year—just under 20% of its total budget—from

Table I.3   Trade Union Subsidization Versus Electoral Support

	1975		1976		1977		1978		1979	
	State Subs.[a]	Vote % in C d'E[b]	State Subs.	Vote % in C d'E	State Subs.	Vote % in C d'E	State Subs.	Vote % in C d'E	State Subs.	Vote % in C d'E
CGT	2,615	44.6%	3,000	47.9%	3,000	43.5%	3,000	44.9%	3,480	40.3%
	29.2%[c]		29.1%		29.1%		29.1%		29.1%	
CFDT	2,615	20.2%	3,000	19.8%	3,000	21.0%	3,000	21.1%	3,480	21.3%
	29.2%		29.1%		29.1%		29.1%		29.1%	
FO	2,615	8.6%	3,000	9.0%	3,000	9.0%	3,000	9.6%	3,480	9.8%
	29.2%		29.1%		29.1%		29.1%		29.1%	
CFTC	1,100	2.4%	1.295	2.6%	1,295	2.9%	1,295	2.6%	1,500	2.8%
	12.3%		12.6%		12.6%		12.6%		12.6%	

Sources: Data on state subsidies (for "formation économique et sociale des travailleurs appelés à exercer des responsabilité syndicales") are taken from "Syndicats II: Organisations syndicales," a supplement to *Liaisons sociales*, avril 1980, 126. Th "electoral support" (percentage of "suffrage exprimés" in elections for the *comités d' entreprise*, first college) data are from Gérard Adam, *Le Pouvoir syndical* (Paris: Dunod, 1983), p. 161.

[a] Subsidies are in thousands of francs.

[b] C d'E—*comités d'entreprise*.

[c] This is the percentage of subsidies accorded to the four major trade unions; the CGC and the Fédération de l'Éducatic Nationale (FEN) also received subsidies.

the state. For FO and some of the other "moderate" unions, the degree of budgetary dependence on the state was apparently even higher.[86]

It is intriguing to note that FO, the principal beneficiary of the state's subsidy allocation formula (see Tables I.3 and I.4), played an increasingly useful role from the government's perspective from the late 1960s through 1981. While the CFDT disappointed Delors by turning uncooperative during the peak years of the *politique contractuelle*, FO along with the CFTC "were there to play the game of reformism." Indeed, "FO was incontestably the pillar of the *politique contractuelle*," as it agreed to sign many significant accords to which the CGT and CFDT were staunchly opposed.[87] Over the next decade, as the two largest unions generally rebuffed overtures of the state and employers, it was FO that did the most to prevent a stalemate in the collective bargaining process. Small though it was, FO was able to have such an impact because of the French law stipulating that "agreements signed by one union are binding on all employees within that bargaining unit irrespective of their union affiliation."[88] From 1974 to 1980, FO signed *all* contracts offered in the public sector every year except 1977, while the CGT and CFDT refused to sign *any*. In the private sector, FO signed in 70–80% of the cases, whereas the CGT signed 40–55%, and the CFDT slightly more. Meanwhile, despite its principled opposition to *cogestion*, FO also assumed an increasingly important and privileged role in the policy-making process.[89] The FO leadership eagerly sought official positions within the union–state–employer councils, worked closely with the FNSEA (an organization shunned for political reasons by the CGT and CFDT) to coordinate policy positions on issues of concern to both workers and farmers, and, in general, served as "the Giscard regime's trade union interlocutor while vaunting the virtues of *concertation*."[90] At least in part because of the funding and status derived from its special relationship with the state, FO increased both its membership and its share of votes in

Table I.4 Subsidization per Percent Vote Received by Unions in Comités d'Entreprise Elections (in thousands of francs)

	1975	1976	1977	1978	1979
CGT	58.6	62.6	70.0	66.8	86.4
CFDT	129.5	151.5	142.9	142.2	163.4
FO	304.1	333.3	333.3	312.5	355.1
CFTC	458.3	498.1	446.6	498.1	535.7

Sources: Data on state subsidies (for "formation économique et sociale des travailleurs appelés à exercer des responsabilités syndicales") are taken from "Syndicats II: Organisations syndicales," a supplement to *Liaisons sociales*, avril 1980, 126. The "electoral support" (percentage of "suffrage exprimés" in elections for the *comités d'entreprise*, first college) data are taken from Gérard Adam, *Le Pouvoir syndical* (Paris: Dunod, 1983), p. 161.

professional elections throughout the 1970s while the CFDT made smaller proportional gains and support for the CGT decreased.[91] Within the "structured pluralist" system of the labor sector, therefore, FO benefited from functioning as what could be termed a "weak corporatist" exception.

Business

In comparison to the labor sector, the business sector may seem by some measures to have been highly corporatized during the years of the Fourth Republic. A single peak interest group, the CNPF, was able to claim the affiliation of all but "a few . . . generally insignificant employers' associations. . . . unity in sheer organizational terms [had] been achieved more fully than ever before."[92] The CNPF participated in a host of public advisory bodies and its representatives on the planning commissions outnumbered those of all trade unions combined by a ratio of two to one.[93] The Council and its affiliated trade associations enjoyed "generally excellent relations with the administration," and in collecting industrial statistics, administering regulations, and performing a number of other functions for the state, they continued to shoulder some of the responsibilities that had been introduced by the Organization Committees of the state-corporatist Vichy regime.[94] Moreover, some of the services the CNPF provided to the business community were subsidized by the state.[95] These facts having been acknowledged, it must be stressed that the relationship between organized business and the state during the Fourth Republic was not truly of a corporatist nature. In terms of the framework we have introduced it should be categorized merely as an example of "structured pluralism."

How and why was the corporatization of the business sector limited from the late 1940s through the 1950s? On the one hand, state officials had little need to promote the development of an authoritative national interlocutor for the business community. Given the resistance of the major unions (as well as the employers), the sort of tripartite negotiations which would become common after the late 1960s were as yet seldom on the government agenda.[96] Furthermore, state officials felt that many of their most important interactions with the business sector could be best conducted not through a peak interest group, but rather through direct dealings with the directors of selected firms. As Zysman has noted, the planning officials "worked with individual private businessmen to devise and implement their industrial strategies. Official business organizations were intentionally avoided, because the Planners feared they might be constrained by traditional business attitudes and policy commitments."[97] That brings us to the other side of the equation: throughout this period, the CNPF was neither able nor willing to perform as an effective client. Impressive though its membership figures seemed, the CNPF represented "an organic unity . . . more seeming than real."[98] The CNPF had been termed a "council" rather than a "confederation" at its founding in 1946 precisely because its affiliates wished to underscore the limitations placed on the authority of the organization's national elite. CNPF leaders were barred by statute from making policy commitments not *previously* approved by the membership, and they had virtually no capacity to enforce organizational discipline.[99] Constrained by the "veto" power of its affiliates, and pressured by the small businessmen forcefully represented within the Council by the semiautonomous CGPME (Confédération Générale des Petites et Moyennes Entreprises), the CNPF leaders generally pushed for traditional protectionist policies during the 1950s and thus often found themselves at odds with governments committed to a modernization process entailing the elimination of many inefficient firms. To cite only a few specific examples, the CNPF condemned the Monnet Plan, refused to endorse the second modernization plan, opposed the European Coal and Steel Community, and expressed serious reservations (but insufficient hostility, in the view of some firms) concerning France's entry into the European Economic Community.[100]

On the surface, at least, relations between the CNPF and the state changed very little during the initial years of the Fifth Republic. While the government of the new regime at times displayed an increased sense of need for a national *interlocuteur patronal*, the CNPF remained a weak organization and continued to appear as "an incarnation of the stolider aspects of French management."[101] Indeed, to the reported consternation of the Gaullist government, the CNPF issued in 1965 a "Liberal Charter" which expressed a deep hostility toward the drift of state policy and seemed to foreclose the possibility of expanded group-state cooperation or tripartite negotiations. The key sections of the charter called for a renunciation of "illusions of systematic *dirigisme*," a reduction in the encroachments of the interventionist state, and resistance to any reform of the traditional mode of industrial relations which might enhance union rights at the expense of employers.[102]

As determined as this statement seemed to be, in retrospect it would appear as an ephemeral triumph for the forces of tradition within the CNPF. Two factors were already operating to create the conditions necessary for a change in the structure and orientation of the organization. First, as the number of small businesses was steadily declining, the political weight of larger firms (now rapidly growing in size through mergers) within the CNPF was increasing. The managers of these firms, most of whom were former civil servants, shared the government's commitment to state-guided growth efforts (which seemed ever more imperative in the context of the heightened competition created by European integration) and welcomed the prospect of increased cooperation between the public and private sectors. Within a few years, as Suleiman's study has documented, roughly 70% of the French industrial elite would feel that it was easy to communicate effectively with the public sector and that a rigid separation between the two sectors was not desirable.[103] Second, a new generation of employers (organized as the Centre des Jeunes Patrons) was arguing for a reinforcement of CNPF authority, an expansion of the national elite's role, and a more "modernist" policy orientation vis-à-vis unions as well as the state. A renewal of the CNPF's leadership from 1963 to 1967 brought to power some figures who were part of that movement and others who were at least sympathetic to its ideas.[104] The significance of these factors would become evident in the wake of May 1968.

During the second week of the general strike of 1968, Prime Minister Pompidou attempted to resolve the crisis by convening the leaders of the CNPF and the trade unions for a series of summit negotiations now known as the Grenelle talks. More than ever before, the state needed an *interlocuteur valable* for the business sector and, in effect, the anxious officials of the government compelled the CNPF elite to assume that role more fully than organizational statutes allowed. Faced with governmental pressure to act, and cognizant of the obvious need to contribute to a restoration of order, the CNPF representatives committed the entire business community to accept a host of concessions to the unions. "In one blow, the Grenelle Accords increased the minimum wage (SMIC) by 30 percent, provided a general wage increase of about 10 percent, and made plans for a 1968 law creating union committees (*sections syndicales*) in firms with over fifty employees."[105] While many employers viewed the concessions as prudent and necessary, others responded with outrage. Some of the CGPME members assessed the wage agreements as ruinous, whereas larger firms were particularly concerned about the expansion of union rights. Tire magnate François Michelin charged the CNPF with irresponsibility and convinced the entire trade association for rubber to terminate its affiliation with the Council. For the future of the CNPF, reactions to the mode of the national elite's behavior were perhaps even more important than those regarding the content of the accords. Whereas Michelin and others felt that the Council could not be forgiven for having arrogated powers that properly belonged to the affiliates, a large segment of the membership drew a very different conclusion. They believed that the leaders' limited authority had compelled them to act in an excessively unassertive manner and thus interpreted the May events as evidence of a need to expand the powers of the CNPF's governing body. As debates on these issues grew increasingly intense following the May crisis, it became clear that the CNPF was experiencing a crisis of its own and that only a reform of the organization could resolve it.[106]

After more than a year of intraorganizational negotiations, "a new CNPF" was created with reforms of the Council's statutes at an extraordinary general assembly in late 1969. A majority within the organization believed that, faced with an increasingly powerful state and union movement as well as a challenging economic situation, the CNPF must be given the means to transcend its traditional minimalist, defensive posture. The CNPF was thus officially declared to be a "confederation," although the word "council" was retained in its title, and the authority of the national elite to sign accords binding the affiliates was significantly increased. Given resistance by some trade associations to what was termed "hari-kari . . . for the benefit of a monolithic and centralized organiz-ation," the power to negotiate wage deals was reserved for the various professional branches, but in other areas the sort of negotiations that the CNPF had undertaken in 1968 were accorded legitimacy. The CNPF was thus not quite transformed into a veritable "superprofession," but it was rendered much more than the "simple liaison organism" it had been in the past. If some employers viewed the strengthened CNPF as "an artificial construction imposed by the state and the unions," most agreed that it was now a necessity. The principal losers in this revamping of the CNPF were the small, inefficient employers. Organizational reform, along with changes in the elite over the next few years (most notably the increasing influence of François Ceyrac, a proponent of a strong and "modernist" *patronat* who was elected president of the CNPF in 1972) served to reduce the influence of the PME and reorient CNPF policy toward goals more compatible with those of the government.[107]

For the governments of the Center-Right, collaboration with the "new CNPF" was of unprecedented importance during the 1970s for reasons related to both policy and politics. In terms of policy, the goal of achieving social peace and stable modernization through the *politique contractuelle* could be reached only with a CNPF willing and able to negotiate in good faith at the summit.[108] During the early 1970s, under Ceyrac's leadership, the CNPF fulfilled this role to an extent which greatly pleased the government while alienating a sizeable fraction of the employers (especially, as usual, the PME). The more disgruntled *patrons* went so far as to attribute the elite's continued willingness to engage in national-level talks with the unions to the fact that "the CNPF, which is close to the government, represents the desire of the latter for national negotiations."[109] Even in the Giscard-Barre era, when a variety of factors combined to diminish the significance of contractual negotiations, the CNPF continued to be an indispensable partner for the government. Ceyrac worked closely with Prime Minister Barre to develop a program for the training and employment of young persons in 1977 and encouraged employers to support Barre's National Employment Pact in 1978.[110] The concerted drive for growth and an expansion of exports also increased state reliance on the expertise and mobilizational capacity of the CNPF staff, which by the late 1970s had grown (with 220 full-time employees) to twice its size in the 1950s and was supported by an annual budget of 70 million francs.[111]

In terms of politics, it was the steady bipolarization of French politics and the growing threat of a victory by the united Left that compelled the government to cultivate closer contacts with the *patronat*. Government officials encouraged the CNPF to expand its public relations efforts as a counter to the CGT and other unions, to dampen employer protests (which they believed could lead at least disgruntled *petits* to vote for the Left) over austerity policies, and to contribute financially to the electoral campaigns of conservatives. Fearful of what implementation of the Common Program would entail, the CNPF was willing to comply even when, as was especially the case during the era of the Barre Plan, it disagreed with significant elements of the Center-Right government's policy. From 1973 onward, the CNPF abandoned its traditional practice of "apolitisme" and called upon employers to vote against the enemies of free enterprise while also (more discreetly) soliciting their financial support. It is estimated that the CNPF and its affiliates contributed approximately 20 million francs to more than one hundred deputies during the 1978 electoral campaign alone.[112]

For the CNPF, the client status developed during the 1970s entailed both the gains and the losses typically associated with corporatism. The intimacy of the CNPF's relationship with the state led observers to refer to the *patronat* as a "third component of the majority," while Ceyrac's visibility in the policy-making process was sufficient to earn him a ranking—according to an opinion poll of the mid-1970s—as one of the nine most influential Frenchmen.[113] At the same time, however, the relationship between the CNPF and the state generated increasing opposition from some employers, especially the CGPME. The CGPME became increasingly alienated from the CNPF, and in the late 1970s a rival employer's organization—for which the CGPME was compromised through its formal ties to the CNPF—known as the SNPMI (Syndicat Nationale de la Petite et Moyenne Industrie) emerged to voice vociferous opposition to the government's austerity program and condemn the CNPF as an accomplice. The SNPMI charged the CNPF with being "tied to the government by the game of subsidies" and announced that it would provide the "*contre-pouvoir* expected by public opinion."[114] Such opposition impaired the CNPF's efforts to portray itself as the sole spokesman of a united business community, but it failed to pose a major competitive threat. On the one hand, the Center-Right government refused to grant official recognition to the CNPF's rival; the SNPMI was forced to wait until the Socialist majority achieved power in 1981 to acquire that status. On the other hand, the CNPF employed its impressive array of services as a means of staving off the departure of dissident members. Those contemplating support for the CGPME or SNPMI were contacted by CNPF staffers who threatened to "cut the bridges" if the *patronat* were openly opposed.[115]

By the end of the Center-Right era, therefore, the business sector had evolved from a system of "structured pluralism" to what could most appropriately be termed a system of "moderate corporatism." As the state's need for a business client increased, the CNPF's capacity to mobilize and discipline members improved and the political/policy goals of the CNPF converged with those of the state, the degree of sectoral corporatization increased along all four of the dimensions cited earlier. However, as will be demonstrated in the following chapters, the business sector remained less fully corporatized than the agricultural sector. In regard to the central dimension of group-state relations, some interview data collected by Frank L. Wilson in 1979 illustrate rather neatly the situation of the business sector between agriculture and labor on the scale of corporatization. In Wilson's interviews, representatives of the agricultural sector were found to be the ones who most commonly "often" participated in government committees (72.3%), engaged in formal meetings with government officials (78.6%), and benefited from private contacts with government officials

(92.9%); representatives of the business sector recorded the second highest percentages in each of these categories (63.6%, 69.7%, and 72.7%, respectively), while those of the labor sector recorded the lowest figures by far (41.7%, 41.7%, and 8.7%, respectively).[116]

THE POLITICS OF NEOCORPORATISM IN THE FRENCH AGRICULTURAL SECTOR

At the dawn of the Fifth Republic, one could feel relatively safe in making at least two key assumptions about the future of French agriculture. First, one could expect the continuation, in one form or another, of the agricultural modernization process that had been accelerating since the end of World War II. Second, one could expect that proposals for increased state intervention to guide this process and hasten the rural exodus would continue to be resisted by the farmers' chief organizational spokesman, the FNSEA. Virtually all of the farmers were united in viewing the rural exodus as a "scandal" and the interventionist state as the "permanent enemy" of the agricultural sector.[117] True, some members of what would become known as the "new generation" of French farmers were beginning to question the prudence of such a purely defensive posture, but they were as yet a small and powerless minority. At this point it was nearly as difficult as it had been during the Liberation period to imagine that, in the words of Michel Crozier, "the French peasant milieu could respond to this natural pressure other than by a passive resistance and sporadic agitations."[118]

More than two decades after the founding of the Fifth Republic, it is clear that the first assumption was valid—but the second was not. The modernization process has indeed continued, but since the early 1960s it has been actively encouraged by the FNSEA. Abandoning its unconditional opposition to the rural exodus, the FNSEA began just over twenty years ago to support reform policies that would increase agricultural efficiency and productivity at the expense of a tremendous decrease in the number of farms and farmers. Moreover, through developing a corporatist relationship with the state unmatched in either intimacy or originality by interest groups of other French sectors, the FNSEA acquired the right to "comanage" agricultural policy in Paris and throughout the countryside. How can one explain this unanticipated development of "strong corporatism" in the French agricultural sector? To what extent has the development of corporatism affected not only the policy-making process, but also the dynamics of intragroup and intergroup relations within the sector? These are the major empirical questions on which this book will focus.

As Leo Panitch noted not long ago, one result of the "Macro-Gestalt" conceptualization of corporatism is that research has been "oriented away from the questions of why corporatism has developed in particular sectors and amongst

particular groups, . . . the role that it plays and the contradictions it intro-
duces."[119] A central purpose of this study is to contribute to the closing of this gap
in the corporatist literature; this is apparently the first book-length study to
explore the development, structure, and dynamics of "neocorporatism" in a
single sector of a major democratic polity. It is also apparently the first to provide,
through departmental case studies, an illustration of the degree to which the
development of what we have termed a "strong corporatism" system can vary in
its impact—its "role," its "contradictions," and its political implications—from
region to region.

The fieldwork on which this study is primarily based was carried out during
a series of trips to Paris and the French countryside between 1974 and 1983. Visits
in 1974, 1980, and 1983 were devoted mainly to research in Paris, whereas visits in
1975 and 1976 focused on departmental case studies. The data were derived from
(1) more than one hundred interviews, generally two to four hours in length, with
officials of the major French agricultural organizations and the state (the names
and positions of the individuals interviewed are listed in Appendix A);
(2) attendance at farmers' union meetings, conferences, and demonstrations;
(3) observation of interactions between union members and officials *en permanence* at the local level; (4) observation of interactions between union elites and
state officials during both formal and informal meetings; and (5) research in both
private and public archives (a list of those consulted is included in the
Bibliography). The information collected through these means provides the
empirical basis for Part II and, in conjunction with a wide variety of published
sources, for Parts I and III as well.

Part I will present a nationwide perspective on the development, structure,
and dynamics of the "strong corporatism" system in French agriculture. Chapter
1 will discuss the relationship between the farmers and the state in the
precorporatist or "structured pluralism" period, the years of the Fourth
Republic, when FNSEA hegemony was predicated—rather like that of the
CNPF during the same era—on a popular rejection of modernization and staunch
opposition to the *dirigisme* of the state. Chapter 2 will examine the origins of
neocorporatism during the initial years of the Fifth Republic. Here it will be
shown that, as the Gaullists came to power intent on accelerating the
modernization process, the state's need for a corporatist client in the agricultural
sector drastically increased. Whereas the state could deal "firm by firm" or
"branch by branch" within the business sector, and thus had only a limited need
for a peak client such as the CNPF, it could hardly deal farm by farm with
agriculture. The sector consisted of millions of extremely small (even the largest
farm produced a smaller fraction of total sector output than the smallest firm) and
inaccessible production units. Control over or even communication with the
sector sufficient to engineer coherent reform thus required assistance from the
FNSEA's private bureaucracy; reliance on the product associations was not a
satisfactory alternative, as these were essentially Paris-based lobbying organizations with meager mobilizational ability in the countryside. As the state's need

for a client increased, government officials encouraged the emergence of a "new generation" elite willing to set the FNSEA on a course compatible with the policy and political goals of the state. This new elite, bolstered by state resources and pressure, recast the FNSEA as a peak interest group not only willing but also able to serve as an effective client. Chapter 3 will deal with the evolution of FNSEA-state relations, intragroup politics, and intergroup competition during the era of strong corporatism, focusing on the efforts of the FNSEA elite to cope with the "losses" entailed in the organization's assumption of the client role. It will be demonstrated that the obligation to "behave responsibly" during this troubled period of corporatist modernization led to unprecedented tension within the FNSEA and the emergence of some formidable "nonofficial" rival unions. In the face of these challenges, as Chapter 4 will show, the FNSEA maintained its sectoral hegemony largely through its corporatist "gains," that is, the biased influence and competitive advantage that it was accorded by the state. The FNSEA elites enjoyed "partial immunity" from internal and external pressure, as the union's incentive system was enriched by a variety of exogenous resources flowing from the state.

To what degree did FNSEA hegemony throughout the countryside grow to depend on the "partial immunity" derived from the state during the era of strong corporatism? And to what degree did the privileged relationship which the FNSEA enjoyed with the state at the national level vary at the department level because of contextual particularities? At the outset of my research, it was hypothesized that the FNSEA's national-level client status would lead the state to accord a privileged policy-making role, entailing the sort of corporatist gains and losses discussed earlier, to all of the FNSEA's departmental branches (Fédérations Départementales des Syndicats d'Exploitants Agricoles, FDSEAs) regardless of variations in their socioeconomic, organizational, and political context. Three departments—Aisne, Corrèze, and Landes—which differ greatly in regard to these contextual variables were selected for intensive case studies which, in terms of Harry Eckstein's typology of case studies, could be termed "plausibility probes."[120] One of these departments (Landes) was selected in part because it could also serve as what Eckstein terms a "crucial-case study" (of the "most likely" form) for testing an alternative hypothesis suggested by recent literature on the limits to the power of the French state: despite the FNSEA's national-level client status, state officials would be forced by the political pressure of local notables aligned with rival unions to deny a privileged policy-making role to the FNSEA's affiliate in departments where the FNSEA was organizationally weak and unpopular.[121]

As Part II will show, my case studies of corporatism and syndical politics at the grass roots essentially support the initial hypothesis while also manifesting a significant degree of cross-departmental variance in FNSEA dynamics and some variance in the mode of group-state relations. Chapter 5 will demonstrate that the development of national-level corporatism during the Center-Right era had a relatively limited impact on syndical politics in Aisne. Here the FNSEA's departmental affiliate enjoyed what could be termed an *independent* hegemony which was simply materially bolstered, at the cost of some intragroup tension, by the advent of the national corporatist system. In contrast, as Chapter 6 will discuss, the development of corporatism made a vital contribution to the maintenance of FNSEA hegemony in Corrèze. FNSEA policy generated internal divisions and increased the competitive threat posed by "nonofficial" rival unions; as a result, the status of the FNSEA affiliate became *dependent* on the influence, power, and subsidies that flowed from the corporatist system. As Chapter 7 will illustrate, the impact of corporatism was enormous in Landes— greater, perhaps, than in any other department. Although state officials in Landes were at times compelled to diverge from the general pattern of relations with the FNSEA so as to accommodate an extremely popular "nonofficial" union, they did accord the FNSEA affiliate a privileged status and employed a variety of means to bolster it at the expense of its rival, thus providing the official union with a sort of *artificial* hegemony. In Landes and in Corrèze as well, opposition to the FNSEA—expressed in the Chamber of Agriculture, in the Conseil Général, and in the streets—was sufficient to give rise to questions concerning the legitimacy of the corporatist system, but not to force any appreciable change in its operation.

As noted earlier, the legitimacy of the corporatist system became a major issue at the national level once the Socialists won control of the presidency and the National Assembly in 1981. Indeed, Mitterrand's first minister of agriculture assumed office determined to dismantle the system in favor of a new pluralist order. Part III (Chapter 8) will examine the impact of this reform effort and attempt to derive from it some generalizations pertaining to the politics of decorporatization. It will be shown that even when a decorporatization strategy seems necessary for the achievement of a government's policy and political goals, it may prove to be so costly and disruptive as to be counterproductive. One of the major reasons for this is that, as the French agricultural case illustrates, an established client is likely to be a potent obstacle in the path of reform sought by a new government, a sort of obstructionist legacy of the old regime.

Should the development of agricultural corporatism in France be viewed as a curious anomaly explicable solely in terms of the particularities of the French case? Might it not be true, as various findings of this study suggest, that certain distinctive socioeconomic and political characteristics of agriculture generally render this sector unusually prone to a relatively high degree of corporatization? The concluding chapter will strive to answer these questions by elaborating a "corporatist imperative" hypothesis and testing that hypothesis through comparative analysis of group-state relations in the agricultural sectors of Great Britain, Italy, West Germany, and the United States. It will be shown that while agricultural corporatism has been widely perceived in France and elsewhere to be a national exception, it may be more properly viewed, within limits, as a cross-national rule.

I

The Development of Neocorporatism in French Agriculture

1

Establishing Syndical Unity
Against the State: 1944-58

On 12 October 1944, the Corporation Paysanne was formally dissolved by an ordinance of Charles de Gaulle's provisional government. The French experiment in authoritarian corporatism begun four years earlier thus came to a close, denounced by the new minister of agriculture as "a criminal enterprise in the service of Germany, modeled on the Hitlerite and especially the Italian corporative systems."[1] Discredited though it was by its transformation into an arm of the state which performed (albeit with reluctance and even resistance in some quarters) vital functions for the German occupiers, the Vichy Corporation did achieve something which would come to be viewed widely within the agricultural sphere as a constructive legacy: it showed that "peasant unity," a popular ideal previously precluded by intrasectoral political conflicts, could indeed become an institutional reality. Even agricultural leaders opposed on principle to "*l'unité imposée*" have acknowledged that the Corporation's propaganda and organizational efforts enhanced the visceral commitment to peasant unity in many rural areas and thus paved the way for those who sought to develop syndical unity in the postwar era.[2]

But given the socioeconomic and political diversity of the countryside, how could the unity of the peasantry imposed by the state during the Vichy regime be maintained once democracy had been restored? And how was the organizational embodiment of this ideal to relate to the state? These were the central questions to be dealt with during the decade following the dissolution of the Corporation. As this chapter will illustrate, two very different efforts were made to resolve these questions. During the immediate postwar period, a Socialist minister of agriculture attempted to use the power of the state to impose from above an organizationally unified peasantry dominated by the Left; in terms of the framework elaborated in the Introduction, this may be seen as an early effort by the Left to create a "strong corporatism" system of the sort that would emerge, years later, under the auspices of the Center-Right. Before long, however, this initial neocorporatist experiment was derailed by conservative forces within the agricultural sphere. During the years of the Fourth Republic, they succeeded in institutionalizing a form of peasant unity predicated on hostility to the state within the context of a "structured pluralism" system. Ironically, as subsequent chapters will show, it was the organization they created—the FNSEA—which would later embrace the state and serve as the linchpin of a new corporatist system in the Fifth Republic.

THE LEFT'S ABORTIVE ATTEMPT TO IMPOSE PEASANT UNITY FROM ABOVE

Soon after de Gaulle's triumphant return to Paris in August 1944, the agricultural committee of the National Resistance Council was asked to nominate a minister of agriculture for the provisional government. The committee's choice, quickly confirmed by a de Gaulle disinterested in agricultural affairs, was Pierre Tanguy-Prigent, a young Breton Socialist. Tanguy had achieved local prominence before the war by organizing an agricultural cooperative in the face of stiff resistance from a well-entrenched farmers' union led by staunch conservatives, and had then been elected as the youngest member of France's Chamber of Deputies in the 1936 election which brought the Popular Front to power. Since 1943, he had been the principal leader of an anti-Corporation resistance organization known as the CGA (Confédération Générale d'Agriculture). Once appointed as agricultural minister in September 1944, Tanguy found himself in the extraordinary position of controlling levers of power which, he felt, could enable him to transform the formerly clandestine and weak CGA into a peasant organization of unmatched strength and use that organization as a means of implementing sweeping reforms in the countryside.[3]

On 12 October, the same day that the Corporation Paysanne was dissolved, the provisional government issued an ordinance which in effect instituted the CGA as the organizational embodiment of peasant unity. On the one hand, the establishment of new farmers' organizations not approved by the state was forbidden. On the other, Tanguy was authorized "to appoint a National Committee for Agricultural Action, together with a series of local committees for each department, to supervise the establishment of the CGA." Once the National Committee had been appointed, it became clear that the "peasant unity" envisioned by Tanguy was to have a highly partisan flavor distasteful to many segments of the peasantry. Not only did the committee contain a vastly disproportionate number of Socialists and Communists, many of whom had worked with Tanguy during the Resistance, but its key figure was a bureaucratic official from a nonagricultural cooperative movement.[4] In the words of a conservative critic, "the mold and the corset were in place."[5] Even a group of authors politically sympathetic to Tanguy has acknowledged: "it seemed . . . that the Left, which had vehemently denounced the Corporation Paysanne, was imposing in just as authoritarian a manner a professional organization of a comparable nature."[6]

Similar though they may have seemed in 1944, there was a significant difference between the organizational venture of Tanguy and that of the Vichy era; while the former was launched in an authoritarian style, it was not to be sustained in that manner. At the CGA's founding "Congress of Peasant Unity" in March of 1945, Tanguy promised dissidents that CGA leaders would be elected according to more democratic procedures in the future and that the ban on the organization of rival organizations would be lifted once it seemed apparent that "selfish political rivalries" no longer threatened to destroy the chances of unifying the peasantry (the ban was rescinded in 1946).[7]

By most accounts, Tanguy and his associates believed that the Left could retain control of the dominant peasant organization even after the "corset" had been loosened. They were encouraged by the results of the 1945 legislative election, for this contest revealed that the Socialists had retained their prewar influence in the countryside while the Communists, benefiting from recognition of their contribution to the Resistance, made remarkable gains. In addition, the Socialists were confident that their control of the Ministry of Agriculture, their influence in the administration, and the attractiveness of their reform program would combine to generate a good deal of support from small farmers formerly under the sway of conservative notables.[8] As Chapter 8 will demonstrate, these optimistic calculations of Tanguy were remarkably similar to those which would be made three decades later by the next Socialist minister of agriculture, Edith Cresson.

For the achievement of Tanguy's reform goals, it was vital that these calculations prove accurate and that the CGA remain on good terms with the ministry. What the ambitious minister sought was to develop a modernized, efficient agriculture integrated into a planned economy in such a way as to increase productivity while also enhancing "social justice," especially through assuring the survival of the small farmers.[9] Among the specific programs he proposed were the following: expansion of cooperatives; establishment of a network of state marketing agencies modeled after the Office du Blé created by the Popular Front government; institution of a Statut du Fermage et du Métayage designed to protect sharecroppers and tenant farmers from exploitation by landlords (the impact of this reform, passed in 1945–46, is discussed in detail in Chapter 7); creation of an Office National Foncier which would buy land and sell or rent it to small farmers on favorable terms; and encouragement of *cooperatives de culture* entailing joint operation of voluntarily merged family farms.[10] While the realization of this reform program would involve a vast expansion of state intervention into the agricultural economy, Tanguy recognized that state agents would be incapable of making much progress alone, especially if faced with grass-roots resistance. "To achieve these reforms," as Gervais, Jollivet, and Tavernier have written, "the government would need the support of a professional organization which would play the game of collaboration and which was sufficiently capable of rallying the peasants so that they would agree to embark on the path that had been traced for them."[11] In other words, Tanguy would need a corporatist client on which his government could rely, and he envisioned the CGA as "the agency through which basic changes could be accomplished."[12]

Though Tanguy was sanguine about the Left's chances of increasing its following among the peasantry, he was realistic enough to recognize that—at least in the short run—most of the peasants would be difficult to win away from the forces of the traditional Right associated with prewar *syndicalisme* and, more recently, the Corporation. In constructing the CGA, therefore, he made a variety of moves intended to weaken the peasant-based syndical movement vis-à-vis the service organizations (such as cooperatives), whose technicians and bureaucrats were more sympathetic to the cause of reform as well as the parties of the Left. Within the CGA, the syndical federation—the FNSEA—was thus established as merely one of the broader confederation's seven branches, along with the federations of cooperatives, mutual aid societies, agricultural credit organizations, agricultural technicians, CFTC-affiliated farm workers, and CGT-affiliated farm workers. The FNSEA would be the largest of these branches, but Tanguy calculated that its conservative elements would be unable to outvote the combined forces of the Left in the CGA's central governing board. Hedging this bet, Tanguy acted not only to encircle the FNSEA within the confederation, but also to weaken its ability to recruit members. The minister's experience *sur le terrain* had made clear that the conservative union movement traditionally attracted peasants not only (or even primarily) through compelling ideas, but rather with a wide range of services. With a firm grasp of the sort of organizational logic articulated decades later by Mancur Olson, he thus issued an ordinance in October 1945 that made it illegal for agricultural *syndicats* to engage in economic service activities, all of which were to be reserved for other branches of the CGA. The conservative *syndicalistes* protested vehemently against what they astutely viewed as an attempt to "emasculate" their organization, but the ordinance remained in effect. As will be discussed later in this chapter, Tanguy's legal initiative of 1945 has had a long-term impact on the FNSEA, even though many departmental unions have developed imaginative tactics designed to mitigate its effect.[13]

Only after the CGA's six other branches had been established, its founding congress held, its initial executive boards selected, and the precautionary ordinance forbidding syndical engagement in economic operations issued did Tanguy give the green light for the formation of the FNSEA. As preparations for the first FNSEA elections were being made, some CGA leaders argued that only those farmers who had already formally joined the confederation should be allowed to vote; by some estimates, nearly two thirds of the total had refused to do so, at least in part for political reasons. Optimism, a concern for legitimation, or a combination of the two finally led the CGA leaders to decide that all farmers who wished would be allowed to vote. The result was a disaster for the Left. When the FNSEA election was held in January 1946, approximately 80% of those elected were individuals who had previously played no part in the CGA, and a significant number of them were former officials of the Corporation. With the exception of a few Leftist strongholds in central and southern France, "conservatives or Christian Democrats were swept into office" all across the country. As Gordon Wright has argued, the 1946 FNSEA election seemed to represent both "the peasants' conscious reaction against the organizers of the CGA, whose interests struck them as urban and political rather than rural and professional" and "the natural tendency of village communities to choose tried and trusted local spokesmen."[14]

If the January elections put Tanguy's plans for the CGA in jeopardy, then the decisions of the founding FNSEA congress in March 1946 signaled that they were almost certain to prove impracticable. Virtually all of the national syndical bureau's top posts were filled by conservatives or Christian Democrats, and a former member of the National Corporative Council—René Blondelle, the operator of a large farm from Aisne—was selected for the powerful position of secretary-general. Almost immediately, Blondelle and the Rightist faction began to develop a strategy for strengthening the FNSEA, increasing its autonomy from the CGA, and undermining the status of the confederation. By the time of the FNSEA's second national congress in 1947, the conservatives were prepared to launch a major offensive. Blondelle proclaimed that the peasant movement had been hampered by "the confusion of authority between the CGA and the FNSEA" and suggested, as the solution to this problem, that the CGA be reduced to the role of a coordinating body with most of its infrastructure and staff shifted to the more "apolitical" FNSEA. The vast majority of the congress accepted Blondelle's plan, thus dealing the CGA a blow from which it would never recover, although it managed to avoid complete liquidation until the mid-1950s. Only the combined forces of the technical or service branches—merged in the early 1950s as the Confédération Nationale de la Mutualité, de la Cooperation, et du Crédit Agricole (CNMCCA)—might have prevented the FNSEA's rise to prominence at the expense of a Left-dominated CGA, but it gradually became clear that the "Socialist" sympathies of most CNMCCA leaders had been exaggerated by Tanguy in the heady days of the Liberation; these men were of no mind to challenge the FNSEA, and many of them actually preferred Blondelle to the "political" leaders of the CGA.[15]

In retrospect it is clear that the CGA's fate was sealed in 1947, not only by the maneuvering of the Blondelle équipe, but also by a major shift in the political orientation of the Ministry of Agriculture. Tanguy continued to support the CGA, even as its authority eroded, but in October 1947 he was replaced by a moderate who gave way a month later to an influential Christian Democrat, Pierre Pflimlin. During the next three years Pflimlin, who was politically sympathetic to the FNSEA leaders, contributed to the consolidation of Blondelle's "coup" by effectively withdrawing state recognition from the CGA and treating the FNSEA as the principal representative of the agricultural sector.[16]

In sum, Tanguy-Prigent's attempt to impose from above a form of "peasant unity" dominated by the Left, a sympathetic client willing and able to collaborate in the implementation of an ambitious reform program, ended as a fiasco. Had Tanguy or another Socialist held the ministry beyond 1947, it is conceivable that the power and resources of the state might have been employed to reinforce the prospective client; even then, however, the CGA would most likely have proven to be ineffective. What this abortive neocorporatist venture illustrated was that the establishment of a viable "strong corporatism" system would require not only a willing (and perhaps more able) state, but also a client with more extensive support in the countryside. That combination would not appear, as the next chapter will show, until the dawn of the Fifth Republic. Meanwhile, during the interlude of the Fourth Republic, a very different sort of interest intermediation system would emerge with the newly established FNSEA as the central actor.

THE DEVELOPMENT OF SYNDICAL UNITY AGAINST THE STATE

As late as the early 1960s, in one of the first texts on the Fifth Republic, Maurice Duverger could assert: "At the present time, the only general agricultural group is the FNSEA. In contrast to industry and commerce, the farmers are not very divided by the struggle between the *petits* and the *gros*."[17] Given the intrasectoral divisions of the early postwar era, how was it possible for the FNSEA to develop and maintain a semblance of syndical unity throughout the 1950s? The remainder of this chapter will attempt to show that the FNSEA maintained its nationwide hegemony from 1946 until the end of the 1950s through the articulation of limited but almost universally popular policy objectives, ones which stressed the strategic necessity for peasant unity against a hostile state; and the establishment of an organizational structure that enabled even the poorest of the FNSEA's departmental branches, unlike their would-be syndical rivals, to provide members with at least minimal services. While the Federation's stated objectives or "purposive incentives," to borrow James Q. Wilson's term, were not the kind that could generate the fervid support of many farmers, they were the sort that would incite the active opposition of relatively few. Moreover, in the regions where opposition did arise, rival union movements were hard-pressed to compete with an FDSEA able to offer members a variety of services or "material incentives" subsidized by the FNSEA's central office.

Purposive Incentives: The FNSEA Program

"What is there in common," asked a *Le Monde* journalist some years ago, "between a small livestock raiser from the Creuse . . . and the grain and sugar beet farmer who drives tractors and harvestors on 200 hectares of rich land in the Somme? Nothing, if not the same tie to work on the land and the same submission to the caprice of the sun, rain, wind and snow." It thus seems clear, he concluded, that "syndical unity does not correspond to sociological or political reality."[18] As mentioned earlier, however, there was at least a minimal basis in "sociological reality" for the syndical unity that the FNSEA sought to develop from the late 1940s into the 1950s. Once the FNSEA had supplanted the CGA as the principal vehicle for the representation of peasant interests, it was able to benefit from the widespread desire for peasant unity which flowed from that "same tie to work on the land" and the seemingly endangered status of all farmers in an increasingly urbanized society. But it is apparent that what critics denounced as "the myth of peasant unity" was not a sufficient basis for the development and retention of syndical unity; the example of the CGA, which failed despite its ability to invoke this supportive ideal, stands as evidence for this contention.

The absence of serious syndical opposition to the FNSEA during the period under consideration can be explained largely by the Federation's effort to provide a *rational basis* for "the myth of peasant unity" through the avoidance of issues that would tend to divide its disparate membership. A coalition of farmers widely divergent in their socioeconomic and political interests, the FNSEA behaved in the manner of the coalition parties analyzed by Butler and Stokes in their study of British politics. Such parties, they note, normally try to avoid "position issues"—those on which there exist "rival bodies of opinion"—and orient their programs around "valence issues": those "on which there is essentially one body of opinion on values and goals," such as "peace and economic prosperity and national prestige." The organizational utility of valence issues, note Butler and Stokes, "is not that they mobilize the largest number of committed supporters but that they are likely to draw 'moderate' support from all segments of the electorate."[19]

Throughout the 1950s, the FNSEA was able to draw at least moderate support from virtually all segments of the peasantry by articulating a program that revolved around the central valence issue in French agriculture. The policy component of this program focused on the fight for "equitable"—that is, relatively high—prices for agricultural produce. The strategy proposed in this program for the realization of high prices was *contestation* (ranging from the application of pressure through lobbying in parliament, on one end of the continuum, to mass demonstrations on the other) against an allegedly malevolent state determined to maintain prices at the lowest possible level.

In a "restatement of the old corporative theme of the peasant world outside and against the industrial nation," the FNSEA argued that the essential interests of all farmers could be satisfied only through their united struggle for the obtainment of a level of prices that would provide the agricultural sector with an income at "parity" with that of the industrial sector. In the platforms of the FNSEA throughout the first postwar decade this policy demand was repeatedly expressed in variations of the slogan "the price of produce is the wage of the peasant family."[20] "Only by state action to raise farm prices," the FNSEA contended, "could the farmers be expected to go on tooling up for higher productivity; and only by state action to restore the proper balance between agricultural and industrial prices could the peasantry be assured of social justice."[21]

The FNSEA's "prices first" policy provided the union with purposive incentives of nearly universal appeal.[22] A fight for higher prices could promise tangible benefits to all farmers, from the very largest to the very smallest. Moreover, as Gordon Wright has explained, it could do so in the most appealing manner:

> A policy of raising prices was easy to grasp; its effect promised to be immediate; and its probable inflationary consequences could be ignored or argued away. No one seemed to care that most of the gains from higher prices would go to a small group of modernized farmers. For a peasant living near the subsistence level, a few hundred or a few thousand additional francs (even of the badly inflated kind) could loom as large as millions for the big one-crop producer.[23]

Concentration on the valence issue of (high) prices rendered possible the maintenance of syndical unity, for it linked the principal demands of small family farmers in France's polycultural regions to those of the large-scale farmers in the regions of modernized and specialized production. Although the partners in this coalition may have benefited unequally from the "prices first" policy, the policy nevertheless embodied a certain sort of equality; all farmers *of similar stature* benefited equally, a result that could not fail to appeal to the members of a society in which, as Laurence Wylie has remarked, "the necessity is felt to give equal treatment to *parallel elements* within [a] social organization."[24] In addition, the inequality of the coalition partners was of some mutual political advantage: the small farmers gained on the price front from the lobbying muscle of the well-endowed specialized producers, whereas the latter were able to make their case for higher prices by stressing the needs of the marginal *petits* and thus profit "from prices fixed on the survival costs of the least efficient producers."[25]

Along with the battle for higher prices, the FNSEA pressed for a number of complementary economic and social policies such as "rebates on the purchase of farm machinery, a reduced price for gasoline used in farm work, increased governmental credits for rural services and 'collective equipment' (water supply lines, electrification, and so on), improved social security for farmers, and state assistance in finding new export markets."[26] With very few exceptions, these policy demands were also formulated in such a manner as to render them valence issues. Policies that would acknowledge the disparity in the needs of agricultural groups and selectively aid certain segments of agriculture at the expense of others were assiduously avoided. The FNSEA repeatedly insisted that such measures were unnecessary, as state price supports could and should be sufficient to allow for the modernization and prosperity of even the smallest farmers. In the words of one FNSEA president of the 1950s, if prices "were normal, there would be no marginal farms." Moreover, the FNSEA argued, pushing for selective subsidy schemes would merely prove to be counterproductive, as it would divide the farmers (and the FNSEA) and weaken their political force. Syndical unity in the 1950s thus rested on an assumed harmony of agricultural interests and a conviction that distinguishing between the needs of different sectoral categories would be, in the expression of a Breton activist, "harmful, even criminal, at present. All of French agriculture will be saved or none of it."[27]

While the policy component of the FNSEA program in this era was predicated on valence issues, the strategy component was also designed to be nondivisive and thus serve to reinforce the cohesion of the Federation. Through a wide range of pressure activities encompassed by the term *contestation,* the Federation sought not merely to achieve its policy objectives but also to establish its image as the vigilant defender of the peasants against their "permanent enemy," the state.[28] A logical conclusion derived from the FNSEA's theory of "normal prices" was that the agricultural profession itself, and its union representative, bore no responsibility for the problems of the sector. These could be attributed wholly to an adversary state that failed to assure the "just" or "proper" functioning of the agricultural economy and forced the farmers to submit to the officious harrassment of "statist technocrats" in the Ministry of Agriculture.[29]

Despite its extreme antistatist rhetoric, the FNSEA did accept at least a minimal formal role in the formulation and administration of governmental policy during the 1950s; the interest intermediation system of this era was not one of "strong pluralism" but rather "structured pluralism." Like the CNPF in the business sphere, the FNSEA participated in scores of official committees, commissions, and councils. From 1953 onward, for example, FNSEA delegates played a significant role on advisory committees attached to state agencies charged with organizing markets for produce such as meat (SIBEV) and milk (Interlait).[30] Throughout the fifties, however, the power exercised by such bodies was quite limited. Though it was open to "limited *dirigisme,*" the FNSEA staunchly resisted the kind of extensive state intervention that might have increased its formal participation in the policy-making process, but also increased its apparent responsibility for or complicity in the administration of sectoral affairs. As Gervais and others have noted, the experiences of the Corporation Paysanne had made many FNSEA leaders cautious about assuming a collaborative role involving the integration of the Federation into the institutions of the state.[31] In this regard, the relatively liberal principles of the FNSEA leadership dovetailed with the sort of organizational strategy best suited for the maintenance of syndical unity.

The image of adversary union-state relations carefully cultivated by the FNSEA appealed to the "immense majority" of peasants who, in the 1950s, viewed the state as something "alien to them, habitually playing in their lives a constraining and harmful role."[32] Moreover, this image served to enhance the seeming necessity of the syndical unity embodied in the FNSEA. If one assumed that the state was the common enemy of all segments of agriculture, then the formation of rival unions stemming from political and/or socioeconomic cleavages would be seen as sheer folly. By continuing to evoke this image while engaging in *contestation* against successive governments, the FNSEA of the 1950s was thus able to discourage dissident movements and reinforce its legitimacy as the representative of the entire profession.

Even during this era, however, the FNSEA could not hope to appeal equally to all segments of the peasantry. Syndical unity was at best tenuous, given the persistence of political divisions within the agricultural sector and the way they were managed by the Federation's elites. For only three years after its founding in 1946 did the FNSEA's national bureau include representatives of all major partisan groups. From 1946 to 1949 the FNSEA was headed by a Christian Democratic president, Eugène Forget, who "worked unceasingly to mediate between factions" of the Right and Left while insisting that all currents of opinion be accommodated within an organization committed to political neutrality (*apolitisme*). Forget resigned under pressure in 1950, however, giving way to a new president—René Blondelle—and a secretary-general who were both conservative former *syndics* of the Corporation.[33] Moving quickly to consolidate the power of the Right-wing forces, the Blondelle *équipe* pushed "the last remaining Communists, and most of the Socialists as well . . . out of the FNSEA's Bureau." At the same time, some of the departmental federations controlled by Communists and/or Socialists were excluded from the FNSEA for alleged violations of organizational statutes (e.g., the failure to pay dues) and ideologically acceptable groups were bestowed with official FDSEA status.[34] From the time of the Blondelle purge until the dawn of the 1960s the FNSEA's national executive continued to be dominated by conservative *gros* (large farmers), concentrated in the prosperous North and Parisian Basin, acting in alliance with "moderate" Catholic small farmers from the less developed regions.[35]

The skewed balance of power within the Federation was manifested clearly, if informally, in the organization's relationship with the parliament of the Fourth Republic. The FNSEA exercised its influence primarily through a multiparty farm bloc organized as a parliamentary "intergroup," the Amicale Parlementaire Agricole (APA).[36] Initiated in 1951, and especially powerful between 1951 and 1956, the APA originally consisted of deputies elected under the auspices of an FNSEA program known as "civic action." Theoretically, the civic action program maintained the FNSEA's adherence to strict political neutrality. Candidates of all parties were offered the support of the FNSEA on the condition that they respond in the affirmative to a long list of questions designed to test their willingness to defend agricultural interests.[37] In practice, however, civic action "opened the way to a tacit FNSEA alliance with the parties of the liberal-conservative right, whose outlook coincided" with that of FNSEA president Blondelle and his associates. Most of the civic action deputies were affiliated with the Peasant party or the Republican-Independents. Eighty of those elected in 1951 were officials of agricultural organizations, and of these no more than one fourth belonged to the "big three" parties of the Liberation. Because the political result of civic action patently compromised the FNSEA's putative *apolitisme*, it generated considerable controversy within the Federation, especially in regions of Leftist and Christian Democratic strength; hence the program was discontinued in 1956. Yet the APA remained an organized force into the early years of the Fifth Republic and continued to draw almost exclusively from the Center and the Right; the "communists refused to participate . . . and the Socialists refrained until 1958."[38]

As one would expect, given the uneven nature of its links to the parties, the FNSEA's relationship with the governments of the Fourth Republic varied considerably even while the rhetoric of *contestation* remained relatively constant. The Federation enjoyed its most cordial relationship with the governments of the 1951–56 period, when the Independent-Peasant bloc was not only part of the governing coalition but also provided all of the ministers of agriculture.[39] It was with the conservatives excluded from the cabinets of Socialist Guy Mollet and Radical Maurice Bourgès-Maunoury in 1956–57 that the FNSEA assumed its most aggressive stance and urged APA deputies to harass the government most vigorously.[40] A comparison of the dynamics of the two major waves of mass peasant demonstrations during the Fourth Republic illustrates the political logic that guided *contestation*. In 1953, when an economic crisis provoked the small wine producers and cattle raisers of South and Central France to demand action against a moderate-conservative government, the FNSEA provided the agitators with moral support but attempted to dissuade them from continuing or expanding their demonstrations. A "safe-and-sane" demonstration was organized in Paris by the national bureau while the more violent protests of the rank and file were, if not contained, then at least discouraged.[41] The behavior of the FNSEA leaders was very different when, during the economically and politically troubled 1956–57 period, Socialist and Radical premiers headed governments which not only lacked Independent-Peasant members but also functioned without a minister of agriculture, assigning the tasks of that post to a mere *secrétaire d'état* attached to the Ministry of Finance. In response to the Mollet government's proposal of a new agricultural basic law calling for wide-ranging reform, denounced by FNSEA officials as a policy "that rests on the omnipresence and the omnipotence of the state," the Federation's *centrale* mobilized more than a million peasants for a nationwide demonstration on 19 May 1956. In the aftermath of that "historic day" the FNSEA continued to promote localized demonstrations until the Mollet government fell in May of 1957, never having submitted its reform bill to parliament. FNSEA-sponsored protest and parliamentary pressure became even more intense under the government of Bourgès-Maunoury which succeeded that of Mollet. During the summer of 1957, as the cabinet attempted to keep a lid on farm prices in the face of worsening inflation, the FNSEA announced that it was "breaking off relations" with the government and proceeded to launch "the most widespread and violent" nationwide demonstrations of the Fourth Republic era. Politically inspired though the FNSEA's *contestation* may have been, at least in part, it delivered impressive results which benefited virtually all farmers and seemed to provide a vivid illustration of the efficacy of syndical unity. The Federation's pressure compelled the government to call for a special session of parliament in September 1957, and Minister of Finance Felix Gaillard moved to defuse the agricultural unrest, issuing a decree that protected most farmers from inflation by indexing the prices of seven major farm products to the general price level.[42]

Victories such as the Gaillard decree certainly bolstered the image of the FNSEA, but they were insufficient to prevent disaffection on the part of many small/Leftist farmers cognizant of the political slant of the national bureau. After Blondelle replaced Forget and consolidated the conservatives' position in 1949, FNSEA membership declined markedly throughout the less developed small farming regions of the Center and the South. Many Leftists dropped out of the Federation in protest over its conquest by former officials of the Corporation, and a good number of small farmers did so suspecting "that their interests would be poorly served by syndical leaders who came from the large modernized wheat- and beet-growing regions of the North."[43] From the mid-1950s onward, moreover, a number of the FNSEA's departmental branches in the predominately poor and Leftist regions assumed a stance of "passive dissidence" vis-à-vis the Federation's national leadership.[44]

What is remarkable from the perspective of the 1980s, however, is the fact that, despite these manifestations of dissatisfaction with the FNSEA, efforts to organize rival union organizations were limited in scope and essentially unsuccessful during the 1950s. In some departments, as case studies of Part II will illustrate, activists of the Left formed local unions to rival the FDSEA, but in general they did so only after being expelled from the FNSEA. In most departments with strong Leftist traditions a good many Socialists and even Communists remained within the FNSEA; according to one source, approximately 40% of the farmers holding Communist Party cards retained their FNSEA affiliation as of 1955. On the national level, no sustained rival union movement emerged. The one movement with the declared intention of becoming a nationwide challenger to the FNSEA, the Comité Générale d'Action Paysanne, faded within a year after it had been spawned by the unrest of 1953.[45]

One factor that served to forestall the formation of rival unions during this era was the flexibility of the FNSEA's federal structure. The "passive dissidence" mentioned earlier was hardly applauded by the national elite, but it was at least grudgingly tolerated. Departmental affiliates of the Federation were accorded sufficient independence to organize regional actions which went further than the national bureau would have liked and which on occasion openly contested the policies set in Paris. The most celebrated example of such quasi-autonomous regional action was that pursued in 1953 and intermittently thereafter by the Comité de Gueret, an informal group composed of delegates from the FDSEAs of eighteen departments of the Massif Central and the Vendée-Poitou.[46] As chapter three will discuss, the decreasing tolerance of such dissident movements would serve to precipitate rival union initiatives in the Fifth Republic.

Another factor which facilitated the maintenance of syndical unity during the 1950s was that, as a result of the FNSEA's orientation toward a program predicated on valence issues, rural activists of the Left were inclined to view as unnecessary or imprudent the launching of separate unions. As Yves Tavernier has noted, "the agricultural Left. . . did not speak a different language" during this era.[47] The Communists as well as the conservatives predominant within the FNSEA supported the preservation of all family farms, argued that most of the farmers' problems stemmed from prices kept excessively low by an adversary state, and favored a syndical strategy of persistent *contestation*.[48] Given this programmatic convergence and the freedom of maneuver afforded by the FNSEA's flexible structure, the Communists shared the Federation's assumption that syndical unity was the best means of defending the peasantry. Echoing the FNSEA bureau, Waldeck Rochet contended that the "division of the peasantry would inevitably bring a weakening of peasant action" and that "oppositionist activity should be conducted from within the FNSEA and not from outside it."[49] Though spokesmen of the Left at times criticized the "myth of peasant unity," most of them understood that the sentiment in favor of unity was kept alive by the FNSEA's concentration on the battle for high prices through *contestation*. Rather than sponsor a syndical scission which "a large number of its rural electors would not understand," the PCF—and other parties of the Left—thus opted for struggle within the unitary FNSEA.[50] It was only after the FNSEA had undermined the rational bases of the "myth of peasant unity" by deciding, in the 1960s, to engage in *concertation* with a Center-Right government seeking a drastic reduction in the farm population that the Communists and their allies on the Left would reconsider this strategy.

Material Incentives: The FNSEA's Service System

In explaining how the FNSEA maintained its nationwide implantation and syndical unity in the pre–Fifth Republic era, it is crucial to stress the role played not only by purposive incentives, but also by material incentives. As Terry Moe's study of American farmers' unions has shown, purposive incentives appear to account for a significant percentage of decisions to join particular organizations—more, at least, than extreme formulations of Olson's logic of collective action would imply. However, Moe's data also illustrate vividly the importance of tangible selective incentives, for instance, services ranging from the provision of information to cut-rate insurance. Fully 56% of the Farm Bureau members he queried stated that they would "drop out if their economic services were taken away," while the figure for the more ideological and narrowly based Farmers Union was 42%.[51] No such survey data exist for the French case, but sufficient evidence exists to demonstrate the importance of material incentives for agricultural organizations and the extent to which they contributed to the FNSEA's hegemony in the 1950s.

The typical French peasant, notes Henri Mendras, could scarcely understand "why one would ask him to support a union which would give him no immediate material advantage in return."[52] Responding to this desire for tangible benefits was relatively simple for the farmers' unions of the Third Republic. Virtually all of them maintained their membership through cooperative services, offering fertilizer, seeds, and other necessities at discount rates. So prevalent was the practice, in fact, that the unions were often functionally indistinguishable from cooperatives and were commonly dubbed *syndicats-boutiques*. As noted earlier, however, Tanguy-Prigent enacted a law designed to end this traditional practice in 1945. When the CGA was organized, all economic service activities were thus reserved for the cooperatives, the *mutualités*, and the Crédit Agricole, while the FNSEA was formally limited to the representation and defense of "the interests of the agricultural profession in the moral, technical, social, economic and legislative domains."[53]

This restriction of the FNSEA's capacity to provide material incentives was of little consequence during the first years of the organization's existence. Empowered by the state to control the rationing of scarce materials necessary for agricultural work, most departmental unions were able to organize with relative ease. Nearly all farmers were unionized as long as union membership was the only means of assuring access to such crucial goods as gasoline, fertilizer, and even rubber boots. However, after the departmental FNSEA branches were deprived of their rationing power in 1947, membership plummeted in most departments. With the end of rationing and the intensification of political conflicts within the Federation, membership in the FNSEA declined from almost 1.2 million in 1946 to 742,200 in 1950.[54]

Departmental unions reacted to this recruitment crisis in varied fashions, as the case studies of Part II will illustrate, but all of them sought to develop a system of material incentives. In some extreme cases, FDSEAs resorted to de facto (and illegal) mergers with cooperative organizations, thus reinstituting the prewar *syndicats-boutiques*.[55] Most local unions worked in concert with officials of the FNSEA's national office to create a variety of services which, without encroaching on the domain of the cooperatives and other "service" organizations, would respond to the vital needs of the farmers and thus induce membership. In a memorandum distributed to departmental elites by the FNSEA in the mid-1950s, the national vice-president in charge of *action syndical* proclaimed: "It is necessary for the union to be lively at the local level. A lively union . . . is one which provides services. A farmer with a need should always be able to satisfy it [directly] through the union or [indirectly] through the intermediation of the union."[56] In attempting to respond to the needs of members and prospective members, departmental unions generally instituted as many services as they could afford. These services varied by locality, but they commonly included the provision of such benefits as (1) a newspaper, usually free for members, offering information on subjects such as current prices and new farming techniques as well as union policy statements; farmers generally rate the provision of such news as a highly valued service, as Moe's data show; (2) advice on taxes and other legal matters; (3) assistance in filling out forms necessary for the receipt of subsidies, building permits, and so on; (4) mediation between members and the state bureaucracy; (5) cut-rate farm services, for example, disinfection of stables in livestock-raising areas.[57]

Useful though these services were, they were insufficient to enable the FNSEA to obtain a nationwide level of membership density (the number of members divided by the total number of farmers eligible for membership) as high as that achieved in nations where farmers' unions were allowed to offer a gamut of material inducements ranging from insurance to cooperative activities. As of the mid-1950s, for example, the FNSEA's nationwide membership density was no more than approximately 35%, a figure remarkably low when compared to the 80–90% levels reached by its counterparts in countries such as Britain and West Germany.[58] Quite clearly, then, the limitation on FNSEA activities imposed by Tanguy's Liberation ordinance had an important effect.

An examination of FNSEA membership density from department to department shows, however, that the impact of the Tanguy ordinance was highly uneven. As Figures 1.1 and 3.5 indicate, a geographic pattern of FNSEA membership density emerged in the 1950s and has remained relatively constant ever since. In the wealthy agricultural departments of the North and Parisian Basin, where large FDSEA budgets (e.g., 527,000 francs for Aisne in 1957) allowed for the hiring of many salaried staff personnel and the provision of an extensive array of services/incentives, almost all eligible farmers joined the union. In the relatively poor departments such as those of the Massif Central, meager budgets (e.g., 37,000 francs for Corrèze in 1957) severely restricted the development of services and, as a result, a much smaller percentage of eligible farmers enrolled in the union. To a degree, of course, the lower membership density of an FDSEA such as that of Corrèze reflected limits to the appeal of its policy positions or purposive incentives. However, a comparison of votes obtained in Chamber of Agriculture elections with membership density figures seems to confirm the importance of material incentives. In Aisne, the FDSEA received

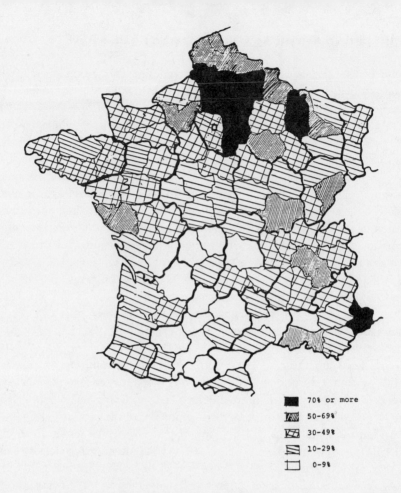

█	70% or more
▨	50-69%
▨	30-49%
▧	10-29%
▢	0-9%

Figure 1.1 FNSEA membership density (dues–paying members/active farmers) by department, 1958. (From Prugnaud, *Les Etapes*, p. 177.)

almost 100% of the chamber votes and achieved a membership density of roughly 90%; in Corrèze, the FDSEA received more than 50% of chamber votes throughout the 1950s, yet achieved a membership density of less than 30%.[59] In poor departments such as Corrèze, therefore, scant material incentives rendered impossible the recruitment of even all farmers in the FDSEA's "membership market," that is, those attracted to its purposive incentives.

This interpretation of the case study data can be supported by some ecological data for France as a whole. Table 1.1 utilizes data from the early 1970s to illustrate the extent to which, all across France, the ability of the FNSEA's departmental branches to attract votes/members correlated with measures of departmental wealth. On the one hand, the ability of the FNSEA to *win votes* was not markedly greater in the more prosperous departments; indeed, such indices of departmental prosperity as the amount of money per capita distributed as loans by the Crèdit Agricole and the number of kilograms of fertilizer used per hectare

Table 1.1.   The Correlation Between Indices of Departmental Wealth and Ability of
FNSEA to Attract Votes/Members

	Agricultural Income per Capita	CA Loans per Capita	Kg Fertilizer per ha	"Economic dues" Paid by FDSEA
%FNSEA Vote in the 1974 chamber election	.200	.177[a]	.190[a]	.212
FNSEA membership density in 1975	.434	.429[b]	.317	.517[b]

Sources: The agriculture income per capita data were derived from *résultat brut d' exploitation* per department (1968) contained in "Le Budget des Chambres d' Agriculture," a 1973 mimeo obtained in Landes, and data on the male agricultural population per department (1962) found in *Paysans* (août-novembre 1968), 31–32. Data on Credit Agricole loans per capita were derived from data on "*prêts individuels du Crédit agricole en cours au 1–1–67, en millions de F*" in the same issue of *Paysans*, 69–70, and the data on male agricultural population per department. Data on fertilizer use per hectare (1966–67) in each department were found in the same issue of *Paysans*, 69–70. Data on "economic dues" paid by each FDSEA (1975) were taken from "Cotisations 1975," 7 juillet 1975—a mimeo distributed by the FNSEA. The 1974 Chamber of Agriculture election results were taken from a mimeo entitled "Elections aux Chambres d'Agriculture: College des chefs d'exploitation—circonscriptions renouvelables en février 1974" obtained at the Ministry of Agriculture. Two sources were employed for the calculation of FNSEA membership density by department: "Cotisations 1975" and *Statistique agricole* (Paris: Ministère de l'Agriculture, mars 1969), tableau VII. The number of farms larger than 5 hectares was used as the best estimate of total farmers eligible for membership in calculating membership density.
Note: N = 85; the Paris region and Corsica were excluded. CA = Chamber of Agriculture.
[a] Not significant at the .05 level.
[b] Significant at the .001 level.

registered statistically insignificant correlations with the percentage of votes received by the Federation. On the other hand, the FNSEA's ability to *recruit dues-paying members* was far greater in the wealthier departments such as Aisne; all of the indices of departmental prosperity/development correlated significantly, and some rather strongly, with FNSEA membership density.

To fully understand the FNSEA's ability to retain its nationwide implantation and syndical hegemony in the 1950s, it must be recognized that the Federation made some effort to offset the effect of this variance in departmental capacity to finance services. Although the majority of FDSEAs functioned with budgets far lower than that of Aisne, and some of them (as in Landes, discussed in Chapter 7) could offer little more than a "syndicalisme de sentiment," virtually all of them were enabled to attract members with a stable if meager supply of material incentives. In this way they differed profoundly from most local rival unions; for example, the Communist-led FCSEA in Corrèze existed almost entirely on paper and thus achieved a membership density of less than 10% in the 1950s despite the fact that it regularly obtained more than 40% of the votes in chamber elections.[60] What sustained and stabilized the operation of many poor FDSEAs was the receipt of subsidies from the Federation's wealthier branches, distributed by the FNSEA's *centrale* in Paris. The subsidization process functioned in two ways, one constant and one intermittent. What might be termed a constant subsidy for the poorer FDSEAs flowed from the FNSEA's budget system. Each FDSEA contributed to the support of the national organization according to a formula that took into account not only the number of members it claimed, but also the relative prosperity of its department. Payments were made on the bases of both a flat rate for each member (the *cotisation syndicale*) and a variable rate geared to the agricultural wealth of the department (the *cotisation économique*) . As a percentage of total dues paid, the *cotisation syndicale* varied from more than 60% in the case of an extremely poor department to little more than 10% in the case of a very rich department.[61] In 1957, for example, the FDSEA of Aisne paid just under 40,000 francs to the FNSEA—a figure greater than the entire budget of the Corrèze FDSEA, which paid a mere 5,000 francs in national dues.[62]

In return for its modest payment, an FDSEA like that of Corrèze gained access to resources of the FNSEA's *centrale* without which its departmental service system would have functioned less smoothly, if at all. Through receipt of the national office's magazines, newsletters, and technical brochures, and through utilization of the *centrale*'s financing of things ranging from travel to telephone calls, each FDSEA was able to provide members with information and professional assistance which few unions unaffiliated with the FNSEA could hope to match.

In addition to this regular assistance, each FDSEA could call on the *centrale* for special organizational help if and when it was required. Upon request, national staff and elected officials would organize information and training sessions for local *cadres*, assist in the establishment of local services, and even—in cases of dire need—provide cash subsidies to assure the survival of a departmental union.[63] Would-be rival union movements were hard-pressed to compete with the FNSEA's subsidy system; those that did form and survive tended to rely on exogenous support as well, receiving money or staff support from local political party organizations. As Gordon Wright has explained, it was primarily the lack of financial resources necessary to sustain unions in the poor regions of France that led to the collapse of the Comité Générale d'Action Paysanne.[64]

An additional, exogenous source of subsidies which helped to sustain many FDSEAs of the 1950s was the publicly financed Chamber of Agriculture. Control of the departmental chamber provided many destitute FDSEAs with meager but essential infrastructural and financial support, facilitating the maintenance of a departmental headquarters (often housed in the chamber's building) and the employment of staff (sometimes paid partially or entirely by the chamber).[65] This sort of indirect state subsidy to the FNSEA was but a foreshadowing of the aid it would receive through the Fifth Republic's corporatist system, the origins of which will be discussed in the next chapter.

2

The Origins of the
Neocorporatist System: 1959–64

As noted in the Introduction, it is possible to isolate several variables that can be expected to play a large part in determining whether the system of interest intermediation within a particular sector will undergo a process of corporatization: the *degree of state need for a client* in facilitating intervention and achieving policy goals; the *degree of group-state consensus* on policy and political goals; and the *capacity of would-be clients* to mobilize and discipline members. Another factor must be added to this list of variables when analyzing sectors within polities whose governmental systems are experiencing significant change: *the capacity of the state* to cultivate and maintain ties with prospective clients, that is, to "wheel and deal" in the fashion described by Shonfield, to create new institutions within which clients can play an important role and to deliver benefits intended to bolster a client or sustain its cooperation. The central purpose of this chapter is to illustrate how changes in each of these variables during the early years of the Fifth Republic, summarized schematically in Table 2.1, generated a fundamental transformation of group-state relations in the French agricultural sector. In comparative perspective, as the concluding chapter will show, this transformation of a "structured pluralism" system into a highly corporatized system appears to have been remarkable in both its rapidity and its extent.

The single most important factor enabling such an unusually dramatic systemic change to occur was the extraordinary event of 1958, the fall of the Fourth Republic and its replacement by Charles de Gaulle's regime. In this new republic, state officials were *more eager* than their predecessors had been to cultivate corporatist ties with an agricultural client, for the Gaullist government sought to implement an ambitious reform program unattainable without sectoral collaboration. Given the shift in power from parliament to the executive, combined with a durable proexecutive majority in the parliament, state officials were also *more capable* of launching such initiatives than their counterparts of the Fourth Republic had been. Nevertheless, their corporatist modernization venture

Table 2.1 Political change and the corporatization of the agricultural sector, 1959–64

	Fourth Republic Era	Early Fifth Republic (1959–64)
Degree of state need for client in facilitating intervention and achieving policy goals	*Low–moderate*; predominately conservative governments keep intervention within traditional bounds and seek to increase productivity without pushing for structural reform. *Moderate–high* for Mollet's Socialist government, but reforms are opposed by FNSEA and rejected by parliament.	*Very high*; Gaullist government seeks rapid and extensive structural reform yielding modernization without a disruption of social peace. Such goals appear to be attainable only if an agricultural client will support intervention, comanage policy, and encourage members to take advantage of opportunities offered by reform agencies.
Capacity of state to cultivate ties with prospective clients	*Low*; weak, short-lived governments incapable of implementing ambitious institutional reforms or of assuring flow of benefits to clients.	*Very high*; with new governmental structure and solid majority, state officials now capable of instituting reform agencies and assuring flow of benefits to prospective clients.
Degree of group-state consensus on political and policy goals	*Moderate*, with conservatives in power, but consensus favors limited intervention, traditional policy and "structured pluralism." *Very low*, with left in power.	*Very high* from 1959 onward in regard to CNJA and only slightly less high from 1964 onward with reformed FNSEA. Both state officials and group leaders favor achievement of modernization through corporatization of group-state relations and continued comanagement.
Capacity of group to mobilize and discipline members	*Low–moderate*; FNSEA functions with limited means and fairly weak organizational network. Ability to discipline members limited, as maintenance of syndical unity requires tolerance of most forms of dissidence.	*Low–moderate, but increasing*; state subsidies and devolved power allow for expansion of salaried staff and improved communication between Paris and the provinces. Ability to discipline members remains low in some regions, but generally improves after 1964 as FNSEA power and centralization increases.

may well have proven unsuccessful if the onset of the new republic had not coincided fortuitously with another development unrelated to the shift in regimes: the maturation of a "new generation" of farmers who shared the Gaullists' vision for agricultural reform, were eager to collaborate in bringing such reform to fruition, and proved capable of transforming the hitherto hidebound FNSEA into an effective corporatist client.

THE NEW GENERATION AND THE CNJA

While conservative, tradition-minded men dominated the FNSEA throughout most of the decade of the 1950s, a new generation of farmers trained in critical thought and social activism was reaching maturity. What distinguished most of these young men from their elders was the education they had received from an influential youth organization, the JAC (Jeunesse Agricole Chrétienne). Even during the war years, while its ideology rested on traditional values, the JAC provided a radical organizational experience; it broke down the barriers that had previously perpetuated social isolation, brought young men together and required them to examine critically the status quo. After 1945 a change in national leadership made the JAC more of a radicalizing force, as its ideology incorporated some of the ideas of militant Leftist Catholicism. Under René Colson and a progressive group of clerical advisors, JAC doctrine "shifted away from the defense of traditional values of stability, oriented to an idealized peasant community of the past, and moved toward social and civic values more positively oriented toward change." Central to the new Jaciste creed was an ethic of participation and an emphasis on group activity. No longer was the peasant to be the savagely independent creature of Balzac's novels or the Marxian potato secure in his own little sack. "In order to develop himself," a JAC document proclaimed, the peasant needs to experience "group life," to "be related to others." Collective activity combined with critical thought, the Jacistes were taught, could bring about constructive reforms of rural and economic structures.[1]

By the mid-fifties the young farmers mobilized by the JAC's "silent revolution" were reaching the age (twenty-five to twenty-eight) when they would normally drop out of the movement, establish a family, and accept the responsibility of operating a farm. However, many of the former JAC activists wished to continue their organized reform activities. After considering a few other alternatives, the new generation of activists decided to channel their energies into reviving the moribund syndical youth movement, the Jeunes de la CGA. Through an agreement reached in 1956 between former Jacistes and the leaders of the FNSEA, the CGA youth section was transformed into a new organization, the CNJA (Cercle—later Centre—National des Jeunes Agriculteurs), endowed with "a more rigorous structure and more precise and important powers."[2] Instead of a mere social center or training group for the young, the CNJA was to be "a genuine organization of young professionals." Open to all farmers from twenty-one to thirty-five years of age, the CNJA was to function with some measure of autonomy. It was guaranteed "legal, administrative and financial" independence; however, its status was—and remains—ambiguous.[3] By statute it was declared to be a "component part" of the FNSEA; its chief officers were to have seats on the administrative council and the bureau of the FNSEA; and while it was to operate with "freedom of action and expression," it was intended to act "in close collaboration" with the FNSEA's administrative council so as not to contradict the senior organization's "general policy."[4]

For the first year or two of the CNJA's existence, the ambiguity of the organization's status seemed to have been resolved through acceptance of dependence on, or at least harmony with, the FNSEA. "Moderate" elements, "rooted mainly in certain conservative small-farming districts but led by sons of large modernized farmers from the northeast," manifested a "respectful attitude toward their seniors" and expressed "only mild aspirations toward agrarian reform."[5] After 1959, however, the status of the CNJA abruptly underwent an extraordinary transformation. A change in the CNJA elite, a response to this change by the state, and the outbreak of unprecedented unrest in the countryside combined to catapault the new and previously insignificant CNJA into the national spotlight. For a few years, from 1959 until roughly 1964, the CNJA appeared not only to be carving out an independent niche for itself among agricultural organizations but even to be "on the verge of . . . becoming predominant over its parent organization, the FNSEA." Indeed, as Roy Pierce has noted, the "pressure from the CNJA was great enough for some people to suggest that the old Third Republic conflict between 'left' and 'right' in French agriculture had been replaced with a conflict between generations."[6]

With the benefit of hindsight, the period of 1959 until 1964 must be interpreted quite differently. The change engendered by the new generation through the institutional vehicle of the CNJA was both more and less dramatic than it appeared in the early 1960s. In one sense, this period is but a parenthesis in the history of the FNSEA and the balance of power among French agricultural organizations. For after 1961, to a degree, and certainly after 1964 the "systematic opposition" of the CNJA to the FNSEA ended.[7] The FNSEA rapidly reassumed and maintained its position of dominance over the CNJA—a dominance it had never really relinquished in terms of relative organizational strength but only of political influence; and as the "generational conflict" of the time lessened, the traditional Left-Right conflict reappeared as the most important.

In another sense, however, the 1959–64 period initiated a permanent transformation of the status of the FNSEA. When the FNSEA recaptured its dominant position after 1964, it did so by coopting the major reformist leaders who had founded the CNJA and by adopting their program. The FNSEA thus abandoned its strict emphasis of "valence issues" and began to articulate policies predicated on more divisive "position issues" such as structural reform. Moreover, the FNSEA abandoned its emphasis on *contestation* and initiated a strategy of *concertation* with the state; in the process, the FNSEA began the transformation from a relatively autonomous "pressure group" to a corporatist official union.

THE REFORMERS' PROGRAMS VERSUS FNSEA TRADITION

In 1959 the former JAC reformers from the underdeveloped Center and South of France "secured a precarious one-vote majority in the CNJA's Conseil d'Administration and put their spokesmen—Hubert Buchou and Michel Debatisse—into the key posts of President and Secretary General." The CNJA's magazine began immediately to trumpet the cause of reform and the CNJA's 1959 congress became a forum for the expression of ideas anathematic to the FNSEA elders.[8] In February, before an FNSEA congress dominated by discussion of the Federation's traditional price policy, the young CNJA elite brashly unveiled its comprehensive program for reform.[9] With a reasoned attack on the core of the FNSEA's program, the young reformers initiated what was to become popularly known as the conflict of generations.

To Debatisse and the rest of the CNJA reformers, the FNSEA's portrayal of a "prices first" policy as the solution to the problems of all French farmers was deceitful and demogogic. By no means did the new generation deny the fundamental importance of prices; their contention was merely that "the question of agricultural prices must no longer constitute the sole pivot of union action."[10] A cursory examination of agricultural economics revealed that a high price, though universally popular, was not an umbrella that protected all farmers equally. To the contrary, high prices allowed the few farmers with large, specialized operations to prosper while leaving the mass of small, polycultural farmers in relative poverty. For example, a hike of one franc/*quintal* in the price of wheat would translate into a significant augmentation of income for the 2,000 farmers producing 3,000 *quintaux* per year, but would scarcely ameliorate the condition of the 350,000 *petits*, each of whom produced a mere 25 *quintaux* annually. To argue that a "prices first" policy could lead to "parity" between agricultural and nonagricultural incomes was thus misleading; as one observer noted, the traditional concentration on prices could only lead to "parity with the directors of a factory for the largest among us and with the janitors (*balayeurs*) of the same factory for the others."[11]

To allow the battle for high prices to be fought in the guise of protecting small, marginal farmers was thus, in the words of a prominent reformer, "one of the scandals of our century."[12] A rise in prices of as much as 20–30% would do little to alleviate the plight of the many small, inefficient producers. The continuation of traditional agricultural policy would merely engender their demise. Already such a trend was evident: 50,000 to 100,000 family farmers were compelled to abandon their properties each year, "chassés par la misère."[13] If this trend were allowed to continue, the reformers argued, a new agricultural equilibrium would eventually obtain: land and responsibility would be concentrated in the hands of a few rural capitalists, while formerly independent *chefs d'exploitation* would be reduced to the status of proletarian wage earners either on commercial farms or in factories.[14]

To obviate such a fate and truly defend the interests of the small- and medium-sized farmers, argued the young reformers, economic realities had to be recognized so that policies tailored to accommodate them could be developed. The corporative myth that all farmers share the same need—high prices—had to be abandoned. For the small farmer to be guaranteed a decent income, not only fair prices but also increased productivity would be necessary. This increase in productivity would entail professional education, the adoption of modern techniques and modern equipment and, most crucially, structural reforms to facilitate the enlargement of inefficiently small agricultural "enterprises."[15]

The push for structural reforms challenged one of the FNSEA's most fundamental principles, the notion that all family farms could be saved. But as the young militants pointed out, the persistent rural exodus and the excessively small size of many farms made this contention altogether implausible. The first step toward the formulation of a rational policy, they argued, was to admit that economic concentration and a concomitant diminution in the number of farms were ineluctable. The real choice facing French agriculture was not whether or not to save all family farms. Instead, it was whether to (1) let the process of concentration and rural exodus continue to be ignored by the FNSEA and the state, in which case it would proceed in its liberal and "anarchic" fashion; or (2) recognize the inevitability of the process and to attempt to control or guide it so as to save the largest possible number of family farms and minimize the attendant human sacrifices.

In defending the latter option, the reformers presented a comprehensive program of structural reform. They proposed, first of all, that the rural exodus be encouraged—but encouraged in a "humanized," "regulated," and "organized" manner. Aged farmers should be granted special pensions to allow them a secure and early retirement, while young farmers should be offered educational "reconversion" subsidies to facilitate their movement into nonagricultural occupations. This subsidy package would, on the one hand, increase the supply of land available for the enlargement of marginally viable farms and, on the other, reduce competition among young farmers for the purchase of much-needed land.[16]

Second, the reformers proposed that the land market be controlled so that parcels liberated by the exodus could be obtained by those farmers most in need rather than by those who already possessed viable farms and were relatively prosperous. An agency for land intervention should be instituted, they argued, to assure preferential treatment for small- or middle-sized farmers wishing to expand their modest enterprises. Moreover, a "selective credit policy" should be instituted to assist small farmers in buying necessary land and in making the requisite investments in land improvement, equipment, and so forth.[17]

Third, to assure the viability of family farms of modest dimension the young reformers urged the promotion of "group agriculture." Their model of group agriculture incorporated cooperative activity on several levels. On the level of production, the militants envisioned the consolidation of overly small farms into larger group enterprises. For example, four or five farmers whose holdings were not in themselves economically viable (*rentable*) would merge to create an enterprise of 100 or 150 hectares, thus permitting the more efficient utilization of their material resources (equipment, capital, etc.); such an arrangement, it was argued, would also allow for a division of labor, a decrease in hours of work, and even occasional vacations.[18] Entailed in such a venture was a new attitude toward the land. Each farmer would be forced to view his property not as a patrimony to be jealously defended against outside interference, but rather as a productive tool to be utilized in the most efficient manner possible. On the level of distribution, the reformers proposed the encouragement of producer groups (*groupements de producteurs*). Producers of various products were to form regional organizations in which the members would submit to production norms and marketing schedules determined by the group. Such discipline would afford the farmer bargaining power vis-à-vis giant corporations and allow him to become "master of his product." The more ambitious reformers proposed all-encompassing group activity which would allow the farmers to bypass the corporations altogether and to control completely their products: the "cooperative integration" of the totality of a sector of production (or of a vertical segment of a sector). Under such a scheme the farmers would engage not only in production and marketing, but in the processing of their products as well.[19]

As could be expected, the new generation's frontal attack on the dogma of the FNSEA was met—at least initially—with considerable verbal and organizational resistance by the traditional leaders of the Federation. For example, in a vituperative article entitled "No, Mr. Debatisse" published in September of 1959, an adjunct secretary-general of the FNSEA defended the traditional price policy and dismissed all aspects of the reformers' program. Gérard Boudy accused Debatisse and his colleagues of proposing the creation of totalitarian "kolkhoz" (collective farms)—of which, he suggested, they perhaps wanted to become the directors. Moreover, he questioned the very right of the reformers to express such ideas within the CNJA: "No. You have not received a mandate from the majority of farmers, young or older, to support such ideas."[20] Many other traditional leaders joined in the counterattack, accusing the CNJA of "causing an uproar . . . of supporting theses which will lead us infallibly to absolute *dirigisme* and even to the kolkhoz."[21] It was not surprising, therefore, when in February 1960 the young militants were defeated in their first attempt to exert some influence within the FNSEA; the traditional leaders resisted any attempt to incorporate the ideas of the reformers into the FNSEA program and easily blocked the efforts to elect former CNJA president Buchou to the FNSEA's national administrative council.[22]

After this initial failure, the reformers stepped up their efforts in two directions. Within the FNSEA, first of all, a concerted effort was made to increase their influence in local and departmental branches; CDJA (Centre Départmental des Jeunes Agriculteurs) officials exploited the positions reserved for them by statute in the FDSEAs' councils, while former CDJA officials ran for office in the FDSEA themselves. Secondly, the national CNJA leaders exploited to the full their opportunities to win acceptance for their ideas from the representatives of the state and thus gain an independent base of influence and prestige. As it turned out, this approach proved to be enormously successful.[23]

THE CNJA AND THE STATE

For the young reformers, the advent of the Fifth Republic was a godsend.[24] Establishing influence within the Fourth Republic, where parliament was supreme and the political contacts of the traditional FNSEA leaders were substantial, would have continued to be difficult into the 1960s. In the new regime, however, the rules of the game were completely different. Old-style lobbying "could produce little more than noisy reverberations," and it was "now better to know two well-placed civil servants than twenty deputies."[25] Moreover, it soon became apparent that not a few well-placed civil servants were eager to get to know the young proponents of agricultural reform. Many of the "young technocrats" of the new regime—in the Planning Commission and the offices of the president and the prime minister—hoped to initiate an innovative, coherent agricultural policy and were impressed by the fresh ideas and the dynamism of the new generation. "In the early months of the Fifth Republic, these officials made contact with the CNJA leaders, and consultations between the two groups became increasingly frequent."[26] In 1959, only a few years after its origin, the CNJA was granted two seats on the Economic and Social Council and its leaders were "elevated to the dignity of privileged interlocutors of the regime."[27] From 1959 onward the CNJA was regularly included, as an "officially recognized" organization, in all official interactions between the agricultural profession and the state. Accorded seats on all advisory councils and *commissions paritaires*, the CNJA thus achieved the status of one of the "great organizations" of agriculture along with the FNSEA, APCA (Assemblée Permanente des Chambres d'Agriculture), and CNMCCA.[28]

   Such special treatment of a new, unestablished organization generated hostile reactions on the part of many traditional agricultural leaders and even nonagricultural labor union officials. While the bureaucrats in the Ministry of Agriculture explained their recognition of the CNJA as a logical reaction to the importance the CNJA had acquired within the agricultural milieu, disgruntled opponents of the reformers questioned the CNJA's credentials and charged that the action of the state was nothing more than politically inspired "collusion."[29] In fact, there were good reasons to level such a charge. Three of the five criteria for "recognition" listed in the *Code du Travail* are "experience," "length of service" [*ancienneté*], and "independence."[30] Cleary the CNJA was lacking in regard to the first two of these characteristics and, while its policies manifested some "independence" from the FNSEA at this time, it was, as previously noted, a statutory component of the FNSEA. In none of the other West European countries was the youth organization affiliated with the major farmers' union granted independent "officially recognized" status.[31] In regard to the other two criteria, the number of members and the amount collected in dues, the credentials of the CNJA were only marginally better; in the few years of its existence it had hardly had time to demonstrate a stable membership and financial base. A decade later other syndical organizations such as MODEF would be denied "recognition" despite the fact that they more completely satisfied most of these criteria.

As Michel Bazex has noted, the accordance of "recognition" by the state is by no means purely "mechanical" and often stems at least partially from "political" motivations.[32] In the case of the CNJA's recognition, governmental sources admitted as much. Yves Tavernier has reported that a close collaborator of Prime Minister Michel Debré confided that the "promotion" of the CNJA represented a "political choice":

> The government intends to make the maximum effort to enable agriculture to modernize and become competitive internationally. These results can only be obtained by the implementation of profound reforms which necessitate the active cooperation (*concours*) of the farmers. The lack of education of the majority among them, their hostility to an evolution which condemns a certain number of them to leave, obliges us to solicit the support of the professional organizations. But if the state (*pouvoirs publics*) cannot find the desired cooperation in the traditional leaders, it has sensed in the young a greater receptivity.[33]

Here one finds the central motivation on the part of the government not only for CNJA recognition, but also for the encouragement of corporatization in the agricultural sector. The leaders of the Fifth Republic planned to increase drastically the degree of state intervention in the agricultural economy and to push ahead with structural reforms that "could not fail to pose problems and to create victims." What they needed was some "formula" for intervention that would render the drive for "economic efficiency compatible with *la paix sociale*."[34] As one top official from the Ministry of Agriculture confided some years ago, the new agricultural policy was expected to create "an explosive machine . . . when one builds up such an arsenal in a world which is not prepared . . . one knows quite well that at some moment there is going to be a reaction." The government knew that it was "playing with fire" and it thus recognized the need to cooperate with professional representatives who would not only increase the efficiency of state intervention but also "share the risks" by serving as "shock absorbers" in case of conflict.[35] As long as the FNSEA refused to provide its assistance and to perform the role of a corporatist client/shock absorber, the CNJA would be employed as a surrogate. Thus Michel Debré announced in March 1960 that the government had decided to rely upon "that generation of farmers which has perhaps more ambition than the preceding generations, which has a sort of modern ambition, as capable of progress as industry."[36]

On the part of the young reformers, there existed a complementary motivation for neocorporatist collaboration. The elaboration of a rational, comprehensive reform program for agriculture would necessitate the utilization of what Debatisse termed "the *rôle moteur* of the state"; only through extensive state intervention could the way be prepared for the farmers to "take charge of their economic destiny."[37] The structural reforms envisioned by the young militants could not be obtained through the old strategy of *contestation*, of an adversary relationship with the state manifested in pressure on parliament and periodic mass demonstrations. They would have to be achieved not through a "spirit of *revendication*" or a "passive conception of *droit à* . . .", but rather through a "spirit of initiative" and "active solidarity" with the state.[38]

As the reformers attempted to point out, their proposed change in union strategy was not in truth a total departure from past practice of the FNSEA. Despite its professed antistatism and its reliance on *contestation*, the FNSEA had long supported state intervention to regulate produce markets.[39] Moreover, the FNSEA had formally participated for years, at least to a modest degree, in the formulation and implementation of agricultural policy. The limited interventionist policy of the Fourth Republic had entailed FNSEA participation in the Planning Commision, scores of official national and departmental committees, as well as the chambers of agriculture.[40]

While there was indeed some continuity between past FNSEA practice and the strategy suggested by the reformers, the sort of cooperation with the state which they envisioned was nevertheless properly perceived as a qualitatively different variety. What they proposed was that the profession engage in what would later come to be popularly known as *concertation* or *cogestion* (comanagement), working intimately with the government to formulate all aspects of agricultural policy, collaborating with state officials to implement that policy, and even utilizing power devolved from the state to administer policy directly at the local level. Doing so would involve an assumption of responsibility for state policy on the part of the union much greater than in the past. Moreover, the reformers proposed that the profession cooperate with the state in the elaboration of a program predicated not solely on "valence issues" but also on more divisive "position issues." Their intention was to sanction the efforts of a relatively strong and "authoritarian" state to "break resistance" and to impose reforms leading to a fundamental change in agricultural structures.[41]

The changes in FNSEA policy and strategy proposed by the reformers were thus profound and controversial. In 1959 it was by no means clear that the reformers' ideas would ever be incorporated into the FNSEA program. From 1959 to 1962, however, the CNJA militants' collaboration with the government produced policy results which made serious consideration of their ideas unavoidable, thus paving the way for their conquest of the FNSEA. After lengthy consultation with the leaders of the CNJA and the other major agricultural organizations, the Debré cabinet introduced in April 1960 an agricultural "charter" intended to provide "the orientation of French agriculture for a generation and even longer."[42] The charter, or orientation law, espoused a central goal to which the FNSEA traditionalists as well as the CNJA reformers subscribed: the achievement of "parity" for agricultural income. However, it proposed to obtain this goal not through the guaranteed prices and *indexation* principle favored by the traditional FNSEA leaders, but rather through the long-range structural reforms advocated by the reformers. Parity was to be achieved through the state-encouraged development of dynamic middle-sized family farms—farms that would support two UTH (*unité de travailleurs hommes*) and thus allow for the utilization of modern technical methods of production and the efficient employment of labor and capital.[43] Although the measures proposed to achieve this reform were extremely vague, the law patently represented the government's acceptance in principle of a new direction in agricultural policy. "For the first time," as Gordon Wright has stated, "the word *structures* itself appeared in French farm legislation." While the traditionalists rejected the proposed charter as an evasion of price policy, the young reformers termed it "a first step in the right direction" and expressed regret only as to its "timidity."[44]

The reformers had thus made their first impact on agricultural policy; a much more profound impact was to follow. During the ten months following the promulgation of the orientation law, only two of its thirty proposed implementing decrees were issued. In May 1961, this governmental inaction generated the beginning of "the most extensive and violent jacquerie that modern France has known." As a number of observers have noted, this wave of demonstrations was distinguished from its many predecessors by virtue of the fact that it was the first to be led by reformers of the new generation, the first to focus its demands not on prices but on the necessity of sweeping structural reform.[45] With this demonstration of the popularity of the reformers and the gravity of their demands, the government moved to incorporate structural reforms even more fully into the agricultural charter.

In the wake of the unrest of the summer of 1961, one of the first governmental steps was the replacement of a conservative minister of agriculture with a reform-minded, dynamic former prefect: Edgard Pisani. If it is true, as one journalist has written, that Michel Debré "made" the CNJA by granting it official recognition and providing its reform ideas with some celebrity,[46] then it was Pisani who assured the lasting impact of the young reformers' ideas and laid the institutional foundation for the development of the neocorporatist system. Pisani was determined to break with the tradition of the agricultural ministry, which he categorized as "few ideas and some nice subsidies distributed with discernment," and to provide France with its first coherent agricultural policy. Believing that the greatest obstacle to reform was "the conservatism of the profession itself," Pisani continued and intensified the special relationship that Debré had established between the state and the new generation reformers.[47] Collaborating intimately with the "young turks," Pisani presented in early 1962 a "complementary law"—popularly known as the "Pisani Law"—designed to "reinforce the basic law of 1960 and go well beyond it."[48]

In its final form, the Pisani Law incorporated virtually all of the major provisions of the CNJA's reform program. First, it strengthened the most novel institution created by the original orientation law: a series of regional agencies known as SAFERs (Sociétés d'Aménagement Foncier et d'Etablissement Rural) "which would be authorized to buy land as it came on the market, to carry out necessary improvements (including the consolidation of microfundia into viable farms), and to sell or lease this land to qualified family farmers."[49] In the Pisani Law, the powers of the SAFERs were increased by according them a *droit de préemption*, a priority for the purchase of land placed on the market; although this priority right was later weakened through amendment, it did give the SAFERs the ability to obtain some valuable land that would have been bought by wealthy farmers or nonagricultural speculators.[50] Second, the new law established a Fonds d'Action Sociale pour l'Aménagement des Structures Agricoles (FASASA). The multifaceted FASASA responded to the reformers' desire to accelerate the rural exodus, but to do so in a controlled and "humanized" manner. The most important activity of the FASASA was to be the granting of a special subsidy—an IVD (Indemnité Viagère de Départ)—to those aged peasants who would agree to an early retirement and render their land available for redistribution. Also included within the FASASA program were two other activities. The FASASA was to offer (1) occupational training subsidies to young men wishing to abandon farming for another métier, and (2) special subsidies to farmers who would consent to move from overpopulated regions (the West and the North) to areas where the land was undercultivated (primarily the Southwest and the South).[51]

Two other major components of the Pisani Law responded to the reformers' desire for the development of "group agriculture." The law offered legal and financial encouragement for the organization of regional producer groups which would be empowered to negotiate collective marketing agreements for certain products. To compel merchants to deal with them and to influence prices significantly, such groups would need to embrace a majority of producers and collect a large portion of the total crop. Accordingly, the bill included a provision that would make a group's marketing agreements compulsory for all regional producers of a particular product upon the approval of two thirds of the producers.[52] The Pisani Law also outlined a legal foundation for the practice of group agriculture at the level of production, that is, the merger and communal operation of a number of contiguous family farms. Tax advantages, special loan rates, and subsidies for land improvement were offered to groups of two to ten farmers who would merge their operations into a single legal unit, a GAEC (Groupement Agricole d'Exploitation en Commun).[53]

While the content of the Pisani Law represented a triumph of the CNJA's reform program, the manner in which its provisions were to be implemented signaled another victory of equal importance for the reformers: acceptance by the government of the *cogestion* principle. A passage of the law noted simply that the new reforms were to be put in place and administered with "the collaboration of the professional agricultural organizations."[54] Over the next few years it would become clear that this phrase actually signified a fundamental transformation of the traditional system of agricultural policy-making and the role played not only by the CNJA, but also by the FNSEA. As will be discussed fully in Chapter 4, from the early 1960s onward the FNSEA-CNJA would serve as the linchpin of a corporatist policy-making network, comanaging funds for agricultural development, coadministering the SAFERs and other structural reform agencies, and sending legions of state-funded syndical employees into the countryside to promote programs such as the IVD. Indeed, in some policy areas the FNSEA-CNJA would benefit from nothing less than a "spectacular transfer" of state authority, the virtual "substitution" of *syndicalisme* for the administration.[55] Such a thorough process of corporatization would not have been possible, however, without a shake-up of the FNSEA's national elite and a commitment by the Federation to pursue modernization through *concertation*.

THE REFORMERS' CONQUEST OF THE FNSEA

The immediate effect of the government's adoption of CNJA-sponsored reforms was to increase greatly the influence and apparent independence of the FNSEA's youth branch. Its more important, long-term effect was to be the reconciliation of the CNJA and the FNSEA—or, more precisely, what a reporter for *Le Monde* termed the "absorption" of the CNJA by the FNSEA.[56] The CNJA, ironically, declined in influence because of its success: its first-generation leaders moved into positions of power within the FNSEA and forced the incorporation of reform ideas into the FNSEA program.[57]

As Yves Tavernier has noted, this process was accomplished through a combination of the strength of the reform movement and the flexibility of the FNSEA's traditional leaders. After defeating the reformers' effort to gain an important post within the FNSEA at its 1960 congress, the traditional leaders began to recognize the strength of their opposition; prominent young militants were acquiring FDSEA posts in an increasing number of departments and the widespread popularity of the reformers' programs in underdeveloped regions was becoming difficult to ignore. In 1961, therefore, the traditional leaders agreed to accept one of the chief reformers—Marcel Bruel—as secretary-general (second in command) of the FNSEA. Soon thereafter, in 1962, the central tenets of the reform program were incorporated into the FNSEA's official platform. While the

Federation's congress in February 1962 included spokesmen for the traditional price policy, it also served as a forum for the presentation of reports by both Bruel and Michel Debatisse (then CNJA secretary-general) on the importance of structural reform and differential policies for the disparate segments of agriculture.[58]

By accommodating the demands of the reform movement and coopting some of its principal leaders, the FNSEA had momentarily avoided the danger of a scission led by former CNJA elites. However, its adoption of a contradictory and controversial program contained the seeds of future conflicts. The rapid transformation of agriculture, the increasing activism of disadvantaged farmers, and the adoption of reform policy by the state made the retention of the traditional program all but impossible. Nevertheless, the future was to prove prescient the skepticism with which traditional FNSEA leaders greeted the optimistic proclamation of Michel Debatisse in his 1962 congress report: "It is best to look important truths in the face. They don't endanger our syndical unity nearly so much as a silence filled with equivocation. The oneness of agriculture is a myth, but its unity is real."[59] Maintaining a syndical unity predicated on divisive position issues was to prove to be an arduous, if not impossible, task.

A striking illustration of this fact ensued at the FNSEA congress of 1964, the culmination of the reformers' drive to aquire control of the Federation. Elections to the national administrative council engendered an unprecedented, open conflict. The result was a victory for the young reformers, as they won a slim majority (13) of the 25 council seats. The subsequent election of members to the national bureau manifested the sort of tensions that would continue to plague the FNSEA and the sort of compromises that the maintenance of "syndical unity" would entail. In announcing the composition of the new bureau the FNSEA was forced to issue a rather embarrassing communiqué which, as a *Le Monde* reporter remarked, represented the first time that the Federation had frankly admitted the existence of factions (*tendances*) in its midst. To "assure the equitable representation of all factions," the communiqué stated, two new bureau posts had had to be created. The most important of these, that of adjunct secretary-general, went to the reformers' most celebrated spokesman, Michel Debatisse. With the retention of Bruel as secretary-general, the reformers thus controlled two of the three most important positions in the national FNSEA bureau. The third and the most important post, that of the presidency, was retained by a young but relatively conservative representative of Blondelle's department (Aisne), Gérard de Caffarelli. Many of the more militant reformers were eager to replace Caffarelli with a representative of their own *tendance*, but such a step was halted by others who feared that this would be fatal to syndical unity. Any attempt to use the FNSEA purely as an instrument of reform would risk generating a reaction on the part of the conservative and wealthy farmers of the North and Parisian Basin. Short of provoking an outright scission, these *gros* could threaten to withhold their massive, crucial contributions to the FNSEA's budget and/or to pursue a vigorously independent policy through the specialized associations (such as that for wheat) which they controlled.[60]

Given the balance of financial power in agriculture and the structure of the FNSEA, the victory of the reformers could by no means be complete; the FNSEA could not be remade in the image of the CNJA during its most radical period. This would continue to be true even in later years when Michel Debatisse assumed first the secretary-generalship (1968) and then the presidency (1971) of the FNSEA. As an editorial in the CNJA's official magazine proclaimed on the latter occasion:

> The FNSEA is not and will never be the CNJA. Not only because of the age of its members but also because of its composition. . . . It must reckon with categories of farmers much more diverse than one finds within the CNJA, with the powerful specialized associations which carry great weight. Its role is often to arbitrate between the opposing interests within it. Its policy, as Michel Debatisse himself has emphasized, is to "find various solutions suited to all of the farmers, whoever they may be."[61]

Finding solutions "suited to all of the farmers" would not be an easy task, needless to say. By the mid-1960s, however, both the CNJA and the FNSEA were at least more materially capable than ever before of attempting to convince farmers throughout the countryside that the solutions they proposed were sound and supportable. Not only did the leaders of the FNSEA-CNJA enjoy unprecedented power and visibility through participation in the new network of comanagement agencies, but they were also able to undertake a vastly increased agenda of activities as a result of the subsidies which began to flow from the government. As early as 1964, the CNJA received 750,000 francs from the *promotion collective* program and another 900,000 francs from the Fonds National de la Vulgarisation du Progrès Agricole, a total of 1.65 million—more than *four times* the amount (402,000 francs) it collected in dues from members.[62] That same year the FNSEA also received a substantial if smaller sum, more than a half million francs (for *promotion collective*), and it would begin to receive much more after its client credentials were more firmly established. With these subsidies from the state, as Chapter 4 will document, the leaders of the FNSEA and its youth branch were rendered capable of vastly increasing their salaried staff personnel, improving elite contacts through stepped-up travel between Paris and the provinces, and organizing a wide variety of new educational and training sessions for members. Over the next two decades the FNSEA-CNJA elites would find their improved material capacity to be indispensable, for an increasing number of farmers would come to view the policy "solutions" proposed by the Federation as nothing less than a threat to their very existence.

3

Corporatist Modernization and Syndical Disunity: 1964–81

During the two decades that followed the rise to power of the "new generation" and the passage of the Pisani Law, the *anciens jeunes* transformed the image of the FNSEA in a manner which won considerable acclaim from observers outside the world of French agriculture. Many sociologists and journalists concerned with the modernization of France viewed the behavior of Michel Debatisse and his colleagues as a courageous, constructive response to the dramatic socioeconomic challenges facing the agricultural community. To Michel Crozier, for example, the French farmers served as evidence that "creative effervesence has not disappeared in France." Having "awakened themselves and taken their affairs in hand," he argued, they "effected a remarkable mutation at a social and economic cost much lower than that [paid by] many other countries."[1]

Contrary to the sanguine expectations of the young reformers, however, the reorientation of the FNSEA from a pressure group battling for high prices through *contestation* to an official union seeking modernization through *concertation* with the state proved to be extremely controversial within the agricultural sector. From the early 1960s until 1981, when the election of a Socialist government altered the terms of group-state relations, the fragile syndical unity maintained throughout the 1950s was subjected to enormous stress as a result of the "discriminatory" nature of the reforms that the FNSEA advocated and the compromising quality of the *concertation* strategy to which the Federation's elite clung even during periods of intense sectoral unrest. In many ways, the FNSEA of the Center-Right era stands as a classic example of a corporatist client struggling to maintain its status in the face of contradictory pressures exerted by the government above and its members below. As this chapter will show, the FNSEA's "responsible" and restrained behavior vis-à-vis the state furthered a process of corporatist modernization which was defensible on many grounds, but which also compelled the union to cope with a severe loss of support from below. On the other side of the equation, as the next chapter will illustrate, these losses were offset by benefits that flowed from above throughout the "strong corporatism" era.

THE FNSEA's REFORM POLICY

From the early 1960s onward, the reform policy of the FNSEA was guided by a vision of an ideal agricultural structure composed of farms which would be neither the tiny, inefficient units predominant in the past nor the giant, agribusiness concerns common to the United States, but rather a compromise between these two extremes: medium-sized, modernized family farms which would be economically efficient yet also "socially and humanly viable."[2] To "prepare the future"[3] in this manner while also attempting to assure equitable agricultural incomes in the short run, the FNSEA developed a complex package of policy demands based on the premise that the agricultural sector was composed of various categories of farmers with disparate needs. A report delivered at the 1967 CNJA congress expounded a typology of farmers and their needs which had previously been implicit in FNSEA-CNJA proposals and which soon became a leitmotif of the FNSEA's program.[4] The following "three agricultures" were delineated.

1. A *competitive agriculture* possessing sufficient land "to assure the full employment of labor and material" and utilizing the most advanced new techniques. The farmers in this category, capable of producing at a low cost below the level of fixed prices, could be assured of prosperity merely through the continuance of governmental market supports (price policy).

2. An *intermediate agriculture* which "is not yet perfectly competitive, but which has already largely commenced its evolution and which can win or lose the game depending on the agricultural policy followed." The farmers in this category were assumed to be relatively young, predominantly engaged in livestock production (most efficient for a medium-sized farm) and "animated by a desire for growth." Lacking the land, capital, and technical education necessary for such growth, these farmers needed state aid to improve and expand their enterprises sufficiently to move from category 2 to category 1.

3. An *agriculture victimized by change*, composed of the aged farmers living on excessively small farms and of the young farmers unable—because of their lack of land, capital, and/or education—to advance into category 1. The departure of these farmers was accepted as inevitable and viewed as a precondition for ameliorating the structures and increasing the incomes

of those who would stay on the land. What these farmers needed was "personalized subsidies" such as the IVD or occupational training grants.[5]

To serve the disparate needs of these three categories of farmers, the FNSEA advocated what it viewed as a diversified but coherent agricultural policy. On the one hand, it sought prices sufficient for the prosperity of categories 1 and 2. On the other hand, it sought additional aid for categories 2 and 3, aid in the form of subsidies differentiated both by region and by type of farm.[6]

This program would seem to have been well suited to the needs of the agricultural sector during a period of rapid socioeconomic and technological change. From 1962 onward, however, it gradually became evident that such a program—however reasonable—was poorly suited to the organizational needs of the FNSEA. "New generation" reformers argued in the early 1960s that the diversified reform program would serve to reinforce the unity of the FNSEA by responding better to the particular needs of each category of farmers than the valence-issue program ever could.[7] But this optimistic prediction was predicated on two rather unrealistic assumptions: that all farmers would comfortably fit into the abstract "categories" to which they were assigned and that the state would support FNSEA-sponsored reforms sufficiently to ensure the popularity of the FNSEA program. Unfortunately, these assumptions proved to be invalid.

In the abstract, the logic underlying the structural reform program was seductive. A "humanized exodus" from the land, it was argued, would allow the "maximum" possible number of farmers to remain on the land working viable farms. As long as structural reform policy remained in the theoretical stage, each relatively young farmer could imagine that *he/she* would be the one to stay in agriculture and benefit from structural improvements. Once the reform policy began to be implemented, however, it was inevitable that many farmers would be disappointed. As a *Paysans* editorial stated in 1970, some had simply expected too much:

> Unfortunately, the necessary means—and especially the financial means—have continued to be insufficient. But this is not the essential reason that some farmers, especially the young, have been led to say that the structural reform policy has failed. Indeed, many of them would not be satisfied even if the SAFER and the FASASA doubled or tripled their activity all at once. In general, they hoped for much more than could possibly be given. Reasoning in an unrealistic manner, some believed that it would be possible for every young farmer who so desired to install himself on a well-structured farm. However, the reality is something else.[8]

Even if the FNSEA-sponsored reform program had been fully financed, it would have entailed a cruel realization on the part of many young farmers, especially those in heavily populated regions: some farmers who wished to be included in category 2 would be forced into category 3. For example, since the SAFER could acquire only a limited amount of land under the best conditions, it could aid one farmer only by denying another. Tension between neighbors, members of the same union, was the inevitable outcome of such a program. As one critic has noted, the popularity of structural reform was bound to produce friction when it became clear that "many are called, but few are chosen."[9]

The reform program was certain to meet opposition not only from those "not chosen," but also from members of category 1. In the "three agricultures" scheme, these relatively prosperous farmers were assumed to be content with the present state of their large, modernized farms. In reality, however, many of them were eager to enlarge and improve their farms further. These "liberals" resented even the modest activities of SAFER, for example, and fought for the maintenance of a free market in land. Conflicts between pro-SAFER and anti-SAFER forces generated considerable tension within regions such as Nord-Picardie, where the implementation of the regional SAFER was blocked until the mid-1970s and where some of the more "savage liberals" defected from the FNSEA to join a conservative rival union, the FFA.[10]

While it was inevitable that the "discriminatory" reform program would give rise to some opposition, sectoral conflict could have been limited by a determined governmental effort to fulfill the promises of the early 1960s. However, successive governments of the Center-Right era exacerbated tensions and undermined the position of the FNSEA by failing to deliver on these promises. As the analysis of the global impact of modernization included later in this chapter will show, state policy was far more liberal than the new generation expected and the fruits of modernization were thus bitter for many farmers. The following examination of two key reform programs—the SAFER and the Dotation Jeune Agriculteur (DJA)—will provide a preliminary illustration of the way in which agricultural modernization policy produced relatively few "winners" and a great many alienated "losers."

When the SAFERs received their initial funding in the early 1960s, one journal lamented that a sum twenty-five times greater would be required to restructure one fourth of France's farm acreage within the next ten years.[11] No such funding proved to be forthcoming. From 1963 to 1978, all of the SAFERs combined were thus able to purchase only 1,098,000 hectares and sell 950,000 hectares; in a typical year, the SAFERs managed to acquire no more than 14–17% of the land placed on the market. As a result of the inadequacy of their funding and the restriction of their powers, the SAFERs directly benefited only about 5,000 to 7,000 farmers per year. Furthermore, the SAFERs did not succeed as hoped in controlling speculation and containing the rising cost of land. From 1965 to 1978, the price of farm land increased by 219% (32% in constant francs).[12] Some agricultural economists argued that the SAFERs may have exacerbated rather than attenuated the increase in the cost of land.[13] It is little wonder, then, that relatively few farmers have enthusiastically agreed with the FNSEA's assessment of the SAFERs' activities as "very positive."[14]

Another representative example of an FNSEA-sponsored reform that benefited some farmers but alienated many others is the DJA, a subsidy adopted in 1973 intended to assist the modernization efforts of young farmers recently installed as *chefs d'exploitation*. Proclaimed as a significant victory for the FNSEA-CNJA, the DJA program in its first three years enabled approximately 7,000 young farmers to receive installation subsidies of between 25,000 and 45,000 francs.[15] However, many farmers were denied the DJA because of their inability to meet all of the conditions necessary for its receipt, for example, the possession of a farm at least as large as the state-established *surface minimum d'installation* (SMI) for the department and the completion of 200 hours of technical education. An editorial in the CNJA's magazine in 1976 noted that "the conditions for the attribution of the *dotation* are so restrictive that . . . scarcely 30% of the requests could be satisfied in certain regions, notably the West." In the department of Manche, for example, only 25% of the farmers under thirty-five years of age who acquired farms in 1976 possessed sufficient acreage to surpass the SMI (set at 15.4 hectares in this case). Moreover, not even all of those young farmers who could have fulfilled the requirements for the DJA felt that it would be worth submitting to the multitude of "administrative annoyances" necessary for its obtainment. As one organizational leader commented, "Very often . . . when the youth sees the dossier, all the red tape, the 200-hour long course of study . . . the program of expenditures, etc . . . he prefers to abandon the farm."[16] A natural reaction on the part of many farmers was to blame the FNSEA-CNJA for the excessive complexities or inadequacies of programs such as the DJA. The tendency to do so was created not only by the FNSEA's sponsorship of such programs and positive reaction to their adoption, but also by the fact that it was usually union leaders and staff personnel who were charged with administering them.[17]

THE FNSEA's CONCERTATION STRATEGY

The reformers who assumed control of the FNSEA in the early 1960s argued, as discussed in Chapter 2, that the reshaping of France's antiquated agricultural system could not be accomplished through the traditional union strategy of "simple *contestation*," but would instead entail "active solidarity" with the state. Initially, then, the new strategy of *concertation* was defended on instrumental grounds as the only means of producing a form of modernization in line with the interests of most farmers. However, when *concertation* began to produce disappointing results and became a major source of organizational tension, the leaders of the FNSEA began to defend it in a very different manner. Over the years, the FNSEA elites developed a comprehensive rationale for the maintenance of *concertation* which portrayed this strategy as a virtual necessity.

The FNSEA leaders argued that their reliance on *concertation*, and their consequent refusal to engage in *contestation*, simply represented a realistic adaptation to changes in the political and economic environment of the Federation. "Between the success of political action undertaken through the parliamentary channel in 1957 and the failures of 1960 and 1964," a 1972 report declared, "an event occurred in 1958 which it would be foolish not to take into account." The application of pressure through parliament had become outmoded, as the Fifth Republic's institution of a powerful presidency and the presence of a stable governmental majority posed "in new terms the possibilities of action vis-à-vis the state." Moreover, the report continued, a second important event had further modified the dynamics of agricultural policy formation: the transfer of a significant portion of agricultural policy-making power from Paris to Brussels. The emergence of the European Community and the Common Agricultural Policy had further weakened the power of the national legislature and had necessitated a reevaluation of the traditional relationship between the FNSEA and the representatives of the state.[18] With "agricultural decisions being made at Brussels," Michel Debatisse stated, "it is important to make an ally of the minister who represents us."[19]

Concertation was held to be necessary not only because of changes in political structure, but also because of the dramatic increase of state intervention into the agricultural economy since the advent of the Fifth Republic. In the 1972 report cited previously, it was noted that observers outside of the agricultural sector were often "astonished" at the frequency and intimacy of contacts between the FNSEA and the state and were led to contrast the attitude of the farmers' unions with that of the workers' unions. But to criticize the FNSEA for its engagement in *concertation*, it was argued, was to ignore the uniqueness of the agricultural context. "In effect, the intervention of the state is permanent in the elaboration and application of agricultural policy."

> This interventionism is so great that the authors of the VI Plan have placed agriculture in the category of *secteurs administrés*. . . . in all the countries of the world, recognizing especially the consequences of economic evolution and the disequilibrium of international markets, the state has been compelled to play an extensive role in the agricultural domain. . . . Vis-à-vis the other [economic sectors], the role played by the state is much less extensive and it is this which explains, without any doubt, the greater frequency of relations between the agricultural union and the government.[20]

Given the extent of the state's involvement in the agricultural sector, the report contended, the FNSEA was compelled to negotiate or engage in dialogue with any government, whatever its composition might be. "Every day" the FNSEA found it necessary to contact the government or the administration regarding some matter pertaining to the defense of agricultural interests. Since "this defense" would be "no longer possible" if relations between the FNSEA and the state were severed, a rupture of relations could be considered only in the most "grave cases."[21]

This official rationale for the strategy of *concertation* was by no means without substance. State intervention in agriculture did indeed increase enormously after the advent of the Fifth Republic (in large part, as the FNSEA neglected to acknowledge, because such a development was encouraged by the Federation). The budget of the Ministry of Agriculture increased from 3.8 to 34 billion francs between 1960 and 1976, while over the same period state spending on agriculture swelled from 5.4% to 13.5% of total public expenditures.[22] The maintenance of dialogue with the state was doubtless useful for the guidance of this intervention and the "daily defense" of agricultural interests. Especially with the complications arising from the shift of decision-making power (especially in the area of price setting) to Brussels, it was reasonable for the FNSEA elite to be concerned with maintaining the French agricultural minister as an "ally" and with employing "forms of action" that were, in the words of the 1972 report, "seriously deliberated and then applied with determination under the control of those who have responsibility for them."[23]

However compelling this rationale for permanent *concertation* may have seemed to the FNSEA leaders, it proved to be less than cogent for many farmers at the *base*. An opinion poll of 1973 demonstrated this fact vividly. When asked to name "the most effective type of action" for a farmers' union to pursue, only 46% of the farmers responded "permanent *concertation* with the government and state administration." The other 47% of the farmers who responded favored action ranging from "negotiations after an *action de revendication*" (29%) or "union action reinforced by political action" (13%) to "systematic opposition" (5%). Responses to another question showed, moreover, that even some farmers who favored *concertation* questioned the tenacity with which the FNSEA defended their interests. Fully 55% of all farmers queried felt that the FNSEA and CNJA "allow themselves to be influenced by the government," while only 38% felt that the officially recognized interlocutors of the state were "really independent." Finally, only 47% of the farmers queried manifested sufficient confidence in the FNSEA to state that it should be allowed to retain its privileged position as the sole farmers' union recognized by the state as an official interlocutor. Maintenance of the FNSEA's present status was favored by 66% of the farmers with 50 or more hectares of land, 65% of those specializing in wheat or other grains, and 66% of those politically aligned with the Center-Right majority; in contrast, the FNSEA's privileged position was supported by only 45–47% of the farmers with less than 50 hectares of land, 41–47% of the livestock raisers, and 22% of those politically aligned with parties of the Left.[24]

It was the retention of the *concertation* strategy even in the face of widespread dissatisfaction with the government's agricultural policy that eroded the FNSEA's 1950s image as the "independent" defender of the agricultural sector. The espoused principle of the FNSEA was to maintain a *concertation* course except "in the grave cases when all dialogue has truly become impossible."[25] In the eyes of the FNSEA leaders, cases sufficiently grave to justify engagement in *contestation* emerged only during one period—1964–65—between the early 1960s and the election of May 1981. Not once after 1965, even during times of acute agricultural crisis when *concertation* seemed to many farmers to have lost its instrumental function, did the FNSEA sever relations with the government and mobilize its troops in a systematic manner to apply extreme pressure for changes in agricultural policy. Those calling for boycotts of group-state negotiating sessions were advised to remember the proverb "those absent are always wrong,"[26] and the demonstrations that were organized were designed to be "moderate" and restrained. An examination of the FNSEA's behavior during selected agricultural crises of the 1960s and 1970s will demonstrate why, to many farmers, *concertation* began to "convey the impression of the complicity of the Federation in the orientations taken" by the government.[27]

1964–65: Forced Contestation

In 1964, three months of negotiation with the government—including an audience with President de Gaulle—failed to bring about any compromise measures that would alleviate the effects of the government's austerity program on the agricultural sector. The majority of the FNSEA elite refused to accept minority demands for an appeal to parliament for a censure motion, or for national mass demonstrations; instead, it agreed to launch a nationwide strike of milk deliveries for home consumption. Though the strike proved to be a technical success, it evoked no response from the government. The government placed the proponents of *concertation* in a difficult position by refusing to engage in a dialogue with the striking farmers or to convoke a "commission of sages" as suggested by some FNSEA leaders. Only after the government had rendered the continuance of the *concertation* strategy impossible did the FNSEA adopt *contestation* measures. In October of 1964, the FNSEA broke off relations with the government and issued an appeal to parliament for a motion of censure; the motion was proposed, and, though not adopted, did receive 209 votes.[28]

Still resentful over its treatment during this 1964 affair, the FNSEA was moved to engage in *contestation* again in 1965. At a time when government reports were indicating that agricultural income had declined in 1964, the Gaullist government announced (on 30 June) that it was halting negotiations in Brussels, at least ostensibly over the issue of the financial regulation of agriculture. This action disappointed the FNSEA, which had been promised much by the government from the establishment of the Common Agricultural Policy, yet the Federation's initial response was cautious. "The difficulties encountered," stated the FNSEA, "are not solely the fault of the French government." However, the FNSEA rapidly became convinced that the fault did indeed lie primarily with the government—a government that continued to show little interest in *concertation* with the FNSEA. In August, Prime Minister Pompidou dismissed brusquely an FNSEA letter encouraging a reopening of the Brussels negotiations, asserting that "international negotiations are the province only of the government." And in September, de Gaulle's press conference made readily apparent the fact that the 30 June rupture had been motivated more by political concern—the desire to impede the development of supranational institutions—than by solicitude for agriculture. The eventual result was that the FNSEA engaged in its last major expression of *contestation* of the Center-Right era. Over the objections of reformers such as Debatisse, who hesitated to condemn formally a government that had launched the structural reform policy, the FNSEA urged Federation members to oppose de Gaulle in the 1965 presidential election. The FNSEA's pressure tactics apparently produced impressive results. Many electoral analysts attributed the failure of de Gaulle to win the election on the first ballot primarily to a decline in his support from the farm sector largely attributable to FNSEA opposition; and, as Yves Tavernier has noted, the attitude of the government in early 1966 seemed to indicate that it agreed with these assessments. A major political figure, Edgar Faure, was appointed minister of agriculture and the government rapidly granted most of the policy concessions which the FNSEA had been demanding for three years.[29]

The success of the 1964–65 show of force by the FNSEA indicated that *contestation* could be effective and seemed to assure its use in the future. Instead, however, it served to eliminate for the duration of the Center-Right era the major factor that had prompted its employment: governmental intransigence. From the time of Faure's appointment and his institution of what one journalist termed "operation charm" through May 1981, the officials of the government never failed to negotiate with the FNSEA in times of crisis, and the FNSEA never resorted to a full-scale "mobilization of troops" against the government.[30]

Crisis and Concertation

From 1965 to 1981 the FNSEA attempted, as all corporatist clients must, to achieve two contradictory objectives. On the one hand, it strove to moderate its demands and restrain its members sufficiently to preserve its status as the privileged agricultural interlocutor of the state. On the other hand, it sought to articulate its demands and mobilize its forces with sufficient vigor to maintain legitimacy and authority in the eyes of the farmers at the *base*. As the following discussion of FNSEA behavior during the crises of 1967, 1969, and 1974 will illustrate, the Federation generally achieved the first objective at the expense of the second.

The year 1967 was marked by a series of violent demonstrations of local origin concentrated in the regions heavily populated by small livestock farmers: the West, Normandy, Burgundy, and the Franche-Compté. The essential demand of these farmers was a revision of the "liberal orientation of French and Common Market agriculture" which would afford increased benefits for the disadvantaged regions and product specializations (e.g., livestock raising).[31]

The FNSEA claimed to support such measures, but many small farmers remained unconvinced. Throughout most of the summer dissident *paysans-travailleurs* forces within the Federation condemned *concertation* as "collaboration" with a state policy designed to eliminate the disadvantaged farmers and called for national demonstrations to manifest the rejection of this policy. Meanwhile, similar demands were made by MODEF and the Comité de Gueret, the two organizations largely responsible for local demonstrations in the Massif Central. Only after MODEF and the Gueret Committee had called for national demonstrations did the FNSEA issue a similar order. When constrained to act on a national scale, the FNSEA emphasized the necessity of moderating the demonstrations and of using them primarily as a lever to assist the national elite in its presentation of demands through *concertation*. Despite the FNSEA appeal for moderation, the demonstrations—executed under the leadership of dissident factions in many localities—proved to be "tragically violent," especially in the West. The demonstrations of 1967 thus seemed to signify a waning of FNSEA authority. As one journalist noted, the FNSEA had begun to appear "imprisoned in the threads of its *concertation* policy" and "deprived of a good part of its freedom to maneuver." Forced to introduce "le serieux" into its demands and "to defend only that which is economically defensible," the Federation had gradually "ceased to support the small farmers in acts, and even in words." As a result, the FNSEA left an "open field" for rival union movements willing—perhaps demagogically—to employ the themes that the FNSEA had used successfully in the 1950s (e.g., the defense of all farms).[32]

In 1969 another, even more significant challenge to FNSEA authority arose following a recrudescence of mass dissatisfaction with the government's agricultural policy. In August and September a series of governmental actions combined to cast a pall over what had been a relatively good year for the agricultural sector. First, the franc was devalued by 12.5%; agricultural prices were held constant for more than a month thereafter, and then were gradually increased to levels that represented a regression of the real price for products such as milk. Second, as part of a general austerity program, medium- and long-term loans for agricultural investment were limited for a period of nine months to 50% of their normal level. The effect of these measures was that while hourly wages increased by more than 11% for the year, agricultural income increased by only 4.3%; moreover, real agricultural income actually declined by more than 2%. Third, the long-term outlook for agriculture—at least for small farmers—began to appear even bleaker than the short-term situation with the publication of the Vedel Report by a government commission. This report, a national version of the Mansholt Plan (formally a "Memorandum on the Reform of Agriculture in the EEC") published by the Brussels authorities in December 1968, suggested that a rational agricultural policy for France would entail the exodus of five-sixths of the present farm population by 1985.[33] To most French farmers, this figure represented a shocking radicalization of the government's goal in modernizing the sector. In 1962, as the Gaullist modernization effort was just beginning, Pisani had—when pressed—given an unrealistic but comforting estimate that only 15–20% of French farms were unviable and could thus be expected to "disappear" through reform.[34]

While mass demonstrations took place under FDSEA or rival union direction in a number of localities (especially in the livestock regions) during August and September of 1969, the FNSEA hesitated to coordinate a national demonstration and urged moderation on the part of its departmental affiliates. No national action was organized until October, when it could contribute to the FNSEA's weight in *concertation*. After scheduling a rendezvous with the president of the Republic for 28 October, the FNSEA organized a national day of syndical action for 17 October. The activities of this day were intended to be no more than a "dignified warning" to the government. Only *cadres* meetings were called for on a national scale, while individual departments were left free to organize (nonviolent) mass demonstrations. The moderate tone which the FNSEA encouraged was symbolized by one of the few departmental activities the Federation chose to mention specifically in its official coverage of the 17 October events; the FNSEA magazine carried a photo of one FDSEA president engaged in a "courteous, but animated" conversation with the prefect.[35]

Even more than in 1967, the FNSEA's moderation and *concertation* in time of crisis engendered widespread discontent at the *base*. Farmers joined in demonstrations organized by rival union movements, while many FDSEA leaders, especially in the more disadvantaged regions, severely criticized FNSEA policy and the continuation of *concertation*. By the time of the meeting with President Pompidou, the challenge to FNSEA authority was serious enough to receive mention—and criticism—in the Federation's official publication. In the discussion with the president, the magazine lamented, "the authority of the FNSEA would have been greater if professional unity were not presently impaired, both by those who are trying to use the agricultural malaise to attract a number of farmers to groupings of a more political than professional character and by those men seeking personal advantage through attempts at [syndical] division."[36]

Despite such criticism and repeated pleas for syndical unity, the challenges to the FNSEA failed to cease and in fact increased drastically after October. Tensions within the FNSEA climaxed in late November 1969 with a tremendous show of rank-and-file opposition to the national elite's persistent moderation. The FNSEA refused to participate in a national *manifestation* initiated by young activists in Brittany as a protest against the imprisonment of three union members for illegal demonstration activities. With reluctance the FNSEA elite sanctioned the CNJA's organization of a demonstration, while urging that it be "prudently" administered. What transpired was not the modest affair favored by the FNSEA elite, but rather a more extensive and vociferous demonstration than the "official" one of October: an estimated 30,000 farmers, including many FNSEA members ignoring the national order, participated in a demonstration that turned into a call for firm opposition to governmental policy and the rejection of *concertation*.[37]

Soon thereafter, in early December, the former leaders of the FDSEA of Indre-et-Loire (which had voted in October to secede from the FNSEA) announced the formation of a new rival union—the FFA—with the ambition of recruiting all farmers opposed to the FNSEA's "collaboration" with the government in the formulation of a policy designed to "*chasser par la misère* the greatest possible number of peasants."[38]

Faced with these signs of unprecedented tensions within the FNSEA, the Federation's national elite was forced to call the first *congrès extraordinaire* in the organization's history. As President Caffarelli admitted in his opening speech on 17 December, the 1969 agricultural crisis had generated a most severe organizational crisis:

> It is necessary to establish contact with that which constitutes the *base* of the FNSEA. There is presently a malaise within the organization. Moreover, a great deal of calumny has been directed at the agricultural leaders. In such a situation the only recourse is to bring together the greatest possible number of members in an extraordinary congress. There is no way that those who defend the farmers will be heard by the government if they themselves are the object of permanent criticism.[39]

In attempting to silence this criticism, Caffarelli was forced to defend both the strategy and the policy of the Federation. On the first point, he noted that many farmers had criticized the FNSEA's relationship with the state as "excessively intimate." Indeed, he continued, since the devaluation there had been a "veritable campaign of disparagement" on this subject. However, he contended, it was necessary for *concertation* to continue (for the reasons discussed earlier) and it was not true that such a strategy compromised the independence of the FNSEA. On the second point, Caffarelli asserted that the policies of the FNSEA were designed to defend the farmers as well as possible within realistic bounds. "Poujadist slogans," he contended, could not lead to meaningful results. The farmers would have to recognize that, like the artisans and small shopkeepers, they were faced with an ineluctable modernization process "without precedent." Rather than ignore this evolution, it was better to "look it in the face and put in place mechanisms which would render it socially and humanly acceptable."[40]

While the *congrès extraordinaire* allowed for the release of some of the tension that had built up within the FNSEA, it hardly served to eliminate the causes of this tension. Constrained in its demands by both conflicts among its disparate members and the desire to retain its corporatist client status, the FNSEA simply could not rally the support of farmers for whom the inevitable economic evolution could not be made "acceptable."

During the summer of 1974 serious challenges to the FNSEA arose once again. Primarily as a result of the oil crisis, the inflation in the price of materials necessary for farm work reached enormous levels by July 1974; the price of fuel had risen by approximately 80% from its 1973 level, while the price of fertilizer had climbed 40% and the price of electricity, animal feed, and other necessities had increased by lesser but still impressive amounts.[41] This inflation, combined with the government's austerity program designed to counter it, produced a staggering impact on the agricultural sector. Agricultural income in 1974 declined by 15.9% from its 1973 level—the greatest yearly decline in the income of any French economic sector since the Liberation.[42]

All summer long, in reaction to the crisis, farmers took to the streets in nearly every region of France. Some demonstrations were organized by FDSEAs, many were organized by rival unions, and many others were relatively spontaneous actions of the *base* without apparent organizational sponsorship. Yet no effort was made by the FNSEA to canalize the greatest agricultural unrest since 1961 and to use it as a tactical lever to force concessions from the government. The FNSEA reacted to the continuing demonstrations in the same fashion in which it had reacted during the crises of 1967 and 1969. With a touch of inadvertent symbolism, FNSEA president Debatisse issued an "appeal for moderation" to the protesting farmers on the same day—23 July—that the minister of agriculture (Christian Bonnet) issued a virtually identical appeal. Debatisse announced that the FNSEA planned no nationally coordinated demonstrations for the summer; the Federation would delay such action until September, at which time the FNSEA would join with other European agricultural organizations in sponsoring a Community-wide demonstration designed to influence the fall meeting of the Council of European Ministers. *Concertation* was to be continued with a 9 August rendezvous of the president of the Republic and the leaders of the agricultural profession. Although no national demonstration was to be scheduled in advance of this meeting, Debatisse announced, the FDSEAs would be free to organize "moderate" demonstrations:

> the actions, whatever they may be, must avoid shocking public opinion and we are ordering our departmental federations to strictly control all of the demonstrations which they organize. In some cases excesses have been committed. We regret it.[43]

Despite this "order" of the FNSEA, mass demonstrations involving violence reminiscent of 1961 continued for more than a month.[44]

The "disobedience" of some FDSEAs, especially in the West, Center, and Southwest, was serious enough to place the topic of the proper use of *manifestations* on the agenda for the FNSEA's March 1975 congress. In one of the congress's major reports, several pages were devoted to reminding Federation members that "direct action is not an end in itself" but rather a means of "reinforcing the position of the union during the course or at the approach of a negotiation"; that all demonstrations, even those at the department level, were to be approved by the FNSEA; and that excessively long or violent demonstrations would "demobilize the farmers" and alienate public opinion.[45] The conclusion of the report manifested the seriousness of the internal organizational tensions which the FNSEA's persistent appeals to "moderation" during the 1974 crisis had engendered. Secretary-General Pierre Cormorèche was forced to acknowledge that the Federation's national elite (the bureau and administrative council) had been "frequently" reproached for the "style of our relations with the *pouvoirs publics*." Reacting indignantly to such criticism, Cormorèche proclaimed:

> As if the function of our union were not first of all to push for a certain number of concrete demands, those which the Congress had defined; how can they be advanced other than through negotiation? As if the great majority of unionized farmers want the FNSEA to become a machine of war in the service of profound political changes! The farmers' union could not become such a machine—its members would desert it.

While contending that the most extreme form of *contestation* would lead to the disintegration of the FNSEA, the FNSEA leaders were forced to acknowledge implicitly that an inflexible reliance on *concertation* threatened to lead to much the same consequence. No change of strategy was promised. Instead, Cormorèche merely reiterated a traditional plea for the maintenance of syndical unity: "What would be grave for all, is if the groups in disaccord decided to constitute [separate] unions. We will not cease repeating that the coexistence of several agricultural unions will weaken the peasant world."[46]

SYNDICAL DISUNITY: THE RIVAL UNION MOVEMENTS

What the FNSEA was reluctant to acknowledge was that several rival union movements already had been constituted, and that they had exploited the spontaneous unrest of the late 1960s and early 1970s—as the FNSEA had used unrest in the 1950s—to demonstrate the representativeness of their organizations and their concern for the plight of the farmers threatened by the government's agricultural policy. The FNSEA may have been justified in dismissing their slogans as demogogic and in arguing that their demonstrations were often less productive than " constructive" negotiations at the summit, but their words and actions clearly reflected the frustrations of many farmers and enabled them to demonstrate that the FNSEA was no longer the favored spokesman for various factions of the farm community.

Since the late 1960s, the FNSEA has been forced to compete with three major rival union movements: MODEF, the *paysans-travailleurs*, and the FFA. Although these rivals failed to receive official governmental recognition until 1981, they have for more than a decade been able to claim significant followings by offering distinctive alternatives to the policy and strategy of the FNSEA.

MODEF

The principal organization to benefit from the growing disillusion with *le syndicalisme officiel* has been the Mouvement de Défense des Exploitants Familiaux. MODEF was founded in 1959 by Communists and Socialists from twenty-three departments, mostly of the South and Massif Central, to provide a means of coordinating rural opposition to Gaullist agricultural policy.[47] Initially the policies of MODEF were essentially identical to those of the FNSEA, though its demands were presented with somewhat more gusto. Since the passage of the reform laws of 1960–62 and their support by the FNSEA, however, the policies of MODEF have assumed a distinctive character. In the words of the Vedel Report, the program of MODEF is the only one that seems devoted entirely to "the interests of the great majority of the farmers of the present generation" and which corresponds "to the old egalitarian dream too strongly anchored in our history to be deliberately ignored."[48]

MODEF has played upon this dream in the popular if unrealistic manner characteristic of the FNSEA in the 1950s. The MODEF leaders claim to be "fully conscious of the exigencies resulting from technological progress" and to be opposed only to modernization "conceived . . . as the inhuman destruction of hundreds of millions of farms."[49] But the MODEF program is essentially a rejection of modernization. It denies all of the uncomfortable realities to which the FNSEA reformers have attempted, however imperfectly and impoliticly, to respond. MODEF views the structural reform program's distinction between "viable and nonviable " farms as "arbitrary," and argues that the rural exodus has been "artificially provoked."[50] It condemns all triage-style efforts to aid some salvagable farms (i.e., those in the FNSEA's second category) as "discriminatory," perferring a policy based on "the old saying that it is better to have two wounded than one dead."[51] In the long run, most of the "wounded" are to be cured through such measures as loans for thirty years at 1% interest for the purchase of land.[52] In the short run, the pains of all of the wounded are to be alleviated through lowering taxes on small farmers, reducing the cost of agricultural equipment (by limiting industrial profits), raising agricultural prices, and reestablishing the indexation of these prices on industrial prices. To the degree that these measures conflict with EEC policy, the regulations of the Common Market are to be revised; MODEF demands a return to purely national price setting and greater freedom for the member nations to take protectionist measures.[53]

The FNSEA leaders have consistently denounced MODEF's program as unrealistic or "poujadist" and have dismissed its claim to be a legitimate rival union with the argument that it is simply an appendage of the Communist Party. It cannot be denied, however, that elements of MODEF's antimodernization program have appealed to many small farmers and that, especially since the late 1960s, the organization's support has not been restricted to Communist activists.

Whereas only twenty-three departments sent delegates to the first MODEF meeting in 1959, sixty-seven were represented at the 1968 congress and more than seventy were represented at the congresses of the 1970s. Moreover, while MODEF was able to present candidates for election to the Chambers of Agriculture in only twenty-nine departments in 1964 and thirty-seven in 1967, by the mid-1970s it was running candidates in nearly seventy departments (see Figure 3.1). Given its lack of the sort of infrastructural support and state subsidies enjoyed by the FNSEA, MODEF's vote totals since 1970 have been impressive. In 1970 it received 41.7% of the vote nationwide in the college for retired farmers, and in both 1970 and 1974 it received roughly 20% of all votes cast (and 30% of votes cast in constituencies where it ran a candidate) in the college of active farmers.[54] Despite the steady erosion of its base of support through retirement and the rural exodus encouraged by modernization policies, MODEF continued to receive the votes of more than 100,000 farmers (about 18% of total vote) at the elections in 1976 and 1979.[55] As MODEF leaders stressed in their repeatedly rejected requests for official recognition from the governments of the Center-Right, these vote totals were higher than those received in comparable professional elections by at least two of the industrial unions (the CFTC and FO) which have long enjoyed recognition.[56] Throughout the 1970s, moreover, MODEF's electoral support was approximately twice as high as that received by the Communist Party from farmers in legislative elections.[57]

The essential reason for the appeal of MODEF is obvious: many within the agricultural sector have long felt that the FNSEA is guilty of supporting a modernization policy that sacrifices the interests of "the present generation" for those of a future generation which will include precious few farmers. The MODEF claim that prosperity could and should be achieved simply by raising prices may be "poujadist" and demogogic, but it strikes a visceral chord among many farmers, and not just the smallest. A 1977 opinion poll vividly confirms this. When asked to give the reasons which best explain the present problems of agriculture, 21% of all citizens mentioned that "farms are too small"; only 1% of the farmers agreed. More than one fourth of all citizens felt that the system through which farmers sell their produce was an important factor, but only 2% of the farmers thought so. For the farmers, the principal explanation for their plight was clear: 83% stated that it was inadequate prices.[58]

Virtually all small farmers have thus supported MODEF's chief policy goal, an immediate improvement in income through significant price hikes and other support measures. But not all "victims of modernization" have viewed MODEF as the best possible vehicle for their defense. As syndical activists and observers have noted, many discontented farmers have been repelled by the degree to which MODEF is controlled by Communists (even in departments where they are much less of a political force than the Socialists, as chapter seven will show, Communists tend to hold a majority on MODEF's executive council and provide most of its salaried staff).[59] However, MODEF's appeal has not been limited solely by such

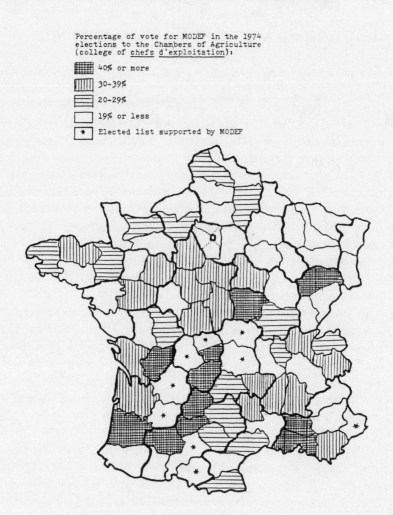

Figure 3.1 Electoral support for MODEF in 1974.

partisan concerns. A good number of younger farmers have found MODEF's leaders to be too old and "sclerotic," its organization too "bureaucratic," its objectives overly defensive and backward-looking, its tactics (protesting against the state for marginal improvements in income, presenting candidates for the Chambers of Agriculture) unimaginative and ineffective.[60] Farmers such as these have tended to reject MODEF in favor of union movements working for a form of socialist modernization.

The *Paysans-Travailleurs*

In the early 1960s, the neo-"poujadist" program of MODEF was the only alternative offered to those alienated by the FNSEA's pursuit of modernization through *concertation*, and it was predominantly older farmers who abandoned the FNSEA. The orientation and complementary laws gave rise to great hopes on the part of most younger small farmers, and with few exceptions they embarked enthusiastically on the course encouraged by the FNSEA and the government: they enrolled in technical education programs, changed the orientation of their production from polyculture to *élevage* (deemed the most efficient style of farming for the *petits*), and borrowed heavily to buy modern equipment and additional land. Dynamic and forward-looking, the younger small farmers worked to achieve "viable farms" and assure their status as *chefs d'entreprise*.[61]

By the mid-1960s, a few of the young modernizers had begun to question whether their efforts would truly be rewarded in the manner promised by the FNSEA. The events of May 1968 contributed greatly to this questioning process. However, as Yves Tavernier has explained, the radical rejection of corporatist modernization was not primarily "the product of a theoretical analysis exterior to the social peasant movement. It was born of a slow *prise de conscience* of the real nature of agricultural policy by those who, after having defended it, were subject to its effects."[62] Even more than May 1968, it was the publication of the Mansholt and Vedel plans that destroyed most remaining illusions as to the prospects for a modernization from which most small farmers could benefit. Criticisms of the Mansholt-Vedel policy covered most of the pages of the first (November 1969) issue of the journal published by what were to become known as the *paysans-travailleurs* (PTs).[63]

In the literature produced by the PTs, the "three agricultures" scheme of the reformers has been portrayed as no more than a "veritable opium" for the "exploited."[64] If administered in a liberal manner, the policy of modernization would eventually lead to the liquidation of even most small farmers who wished to increase their productivity and expand their farms. Moreover, the lucky few who survived, the PTs have argued, would not be the happy and prosperous *chefs d'entreprise* depicted by the reformers. Integration into the capitalist system would make them simply "slaves of their means of production."[65]

To avoid this fate, the PTs have insisted, the farmers must realize that they are workers like those of the industrial sector and that to "obtain mastery of their income and a change of their condition as man and as worker" what is necessary is "a change of the present economic system."[66] What the PTs have sought to achieve is "an agriculture managed by the farmers. In good French that means a self-managed agriculture (*agriculture autogerée*) of the socialist type."[67] Unlike the FNSEA and even MODEF, the PTs have thus acknowledged openly that the realization of their goals necessitates a particular political orientation for society:

> As producers, we have come to the conclusion that we cannot be disinterested in the way our society is organized. Analyzing the present situation, we have come to the conclusion that only a socialist society would be capable of responding best to the objectives which we pursue: equality of opportunity for all, security of employment and income.[68]

In the ideal society envisioned by the *paysans-travailleurs*, the power of banks and multinational corporations would be curtailed in such a way as to allow *agriculture de groupe* to flourish at the commercial and industrial levels as on the farm.[69] The installation of young farmers would be facilitated through financial assistance combined with a system of cantonal *offices fonciers*, or radicalized SAFERs, which would control the land market and prohibit *cumuls d'exploitation* (purchases of land by large farmers or nonfarmers). Income would be guaranteed "within the context of democratic planning" of which *offices par produits*, regulating markets through regional quotas and prices varied according to the volume of production, would be "the pivots." In sharp contrast to the FNSEA and in line with MODEF, the PTs refuse to accept limitations imposed by the Common Agricultural Policy as a serious obstacle to the achievement of their goals. What they have argued is that the government should "quitter la scène à Bruxelles" and "implement its own agricultural policy in a case where their objectives would not be attained."[70]

With these long-term goals in mind, the PTs pursued a strategy of *contestation* very different from that of MODEF throughout the era of Center-Right government. The PTs invested no energy in elections for the Chambers of Agriculture ("the participation of a few *paysans-travailleurs* in this assembly of notables . . . would change nothing")[71] and devoted their time and resources to *action direct* focused on various targets at the local level. Every issue of their journal, *Vent d'ouest*, carried accounts of colorful "commando actions" intended, for example, to pressure a milk cooperative to raise its purchase price, to dissuade a *cumulard* from buying land desired by a small farmer or to frighten away unwanted bidders at an open land auction. Direct action of this intense, often violent and illegal sort accomplished immediate objectives of the PTs while also, allegedly, raising the consciousness of small farmers in regard to the nature of the modernization process under the capitalist system.[72]

The *paysans-travailleurs* have differed from MODEF not only in their policy orientations, strategy, and tactics, but also in their organizational structure. Opposed on principle to representative democracy and bureaucracy, the PTs were for years reluctant to organize themselves formally above the local level. Their *groupes de base* sometimes worked within the departmental branches of the FNSEA or CNJA, but they were nationally united only through informal contacts and the communication proved by *Vent d'ouest*.[73] As the PT ranks expanded beyond their initial Western (and especially Breton) bastion, however, and as more and more PTs were expelled from their respective CDJA-FDSEAs in "socialist witch hunts," the decision was finally made in 1974 to collect fees from local units so as to establish a "minimum of organization" and appear "autonomous" at the national level. Figure 3.2 illustrates the degree to which the PTs had managed by the mid-1970s to achieve some implantation outside of the West, especially in the regions of the Rhône-Alpes and Poitou-Charentes.[74]

While often effective, the ideas and actions of the PTs enlisted the support of only a small minority of the farmers throughout the 1970s for what was intended to be a "syndicat de classe et de masse."[75] Many of the discontented *petits*, of

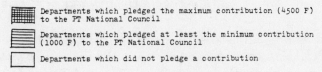

Departments which pledged the maximum contribution (4500 F) to the PT National Council

Departments which pledged at least the minimum contribution (1000 F) to the PT National Council

Departments which did not pledge a contribution

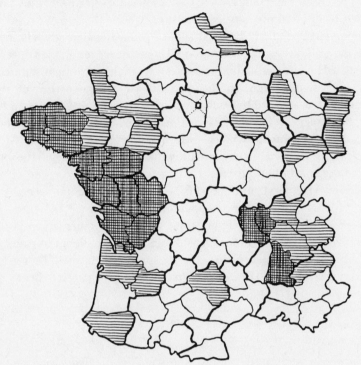

Figure 3.2 Implantation of the *paysans-travailleurs* in 1975.

course, preferred the more staid and traditional programs pursued by MODEF and the FFA. But a more serious problem for the PTs was that, given the divisions of French socialism and the nature of their tactics, they failed to mobilize even all those farmers committed to their vision of socialist modernization. This failure was highlighted in 1975 with the formation of MONATAR, the Mouvement National des Travailleurs Agricoles et Ruraux. As MONATAR's initial manifesto made clear, the objectives of this new organization were virtually identical to those of the PTs. According to the PTs and their principal partisan ally, the small Parti Socialiste Unifié (PSU), the establishment of MONATAR thus simply represented an attempt by the Socialist Party to create its own "agricultural appendage."[76] Most of the founders of MONATAR were indeed members or sympathizers of the PS, but they argued that their organizational effort was less a partisan venture than an effort to mobilize small farmers attracted to the notion of socialist modernization yet repulsed by "the vocabulary" and the tactics of the PTs.[77] MONATAR leaders objected to the "counterproductive purism" and excessive violence or "anarchism" of the PTs, and they attempted to rally small farmers to the cause by employing more restrained forms of direct action in combination with some of the traditional tactics of MODEF, for example, presenting candidates (often on combined MODEF-MONATAR lists) for election to the Chambers of Agriculture.[78]

Although MONATAR did make some organizational progress in the Massif Central and the South, areas where the PTs had never found many recruits, its leaders proved unsuccessful in their effort to build the organization into an independent national force. In the fall of 1977, as the parties of the non-Communist Left attempted to reach a rapprochement in anticipation of the 1978 elections, the leaders of MONATAR decided to merge with a segment of the PTs to create the Mouvement Syndical des Travailleurs de la Terre (MSTT).[79] Nevertheless, the factional struggles within the Left still precluded the formation of a unified organization of Socialist farmers. Only with the election of François Mitterrand in May 1981 and the prospect of governmental recognition was sufficient impetus provided for a serious unification effort. On 4 June 1981 the *paysans-travailleurs*, the MSTT, and four smaller movements joined forces to create the Confédération Nationale Syndicale des Travailleurs-Paysans. Under the leadership of Bernard Lambert, an early spokesman of the PTs, the CNSTP claimed to represent 15,000 to 20,000 members in more than sixty departments.[80]

FFA

At the opposite extreme of the political spectrum lies the Fédération Française de l'Agriculture, the first movement to organize formally as a *syndicat* (MODEF waited until 1975 to do so) in opposition to the FNSEA. The FFA was founded in 1969 when the leaders of the FNSEA's departmental affiliate in Indre-et-Loire decided to secede from the Federation and to mobilize on a nationwide basis all farmers opposed to what they viewed as the official union's support for "a policy of socialization of agriculture."[81] What has set the FFA apart from all other union movements ever since its creation has been its unconditional opposition to all aspects of the structural reform program instituted in the early 1960s. For example, the FFA has condemned the SAFER—viewed by the *paysans-travailleurs* as a timid departure from purely capitalist development—as an invidious hindrance to free enterprise. The FFA's program has thus been unabashedly reactionary, calling not only for a halt to "the liquidation of agriculture" through the state-encouraged rural exodus but also an abolition of all reform mechanisms allegedly designed to result in "agrarian collectivism." For the FFA, the solution to agriculture's problems remains the one proposed by the FNSEA in the 1950s: a dramatic increase in the prices followed by the indexation of these prices on the costs of production.[82]

Although the FFA has a good number of sympathizers among staunchly conservative large farmers within the FNSEA, its efforts to become a major national force have not been very successful. Throughout the 1970s the FFA received only 5–6% of the vote in Chamber of Agriculture elections and managed to present candidates in only fifteen or twenty departments located primarily in the West and the Loire region.[83]

INCOME DECLINE AND INTERNAL FNSEA DISSENT IN THE GISCARD ERA

In the face of pressure from rival union movements and from dissidents within the FNSEA itself, the official union's commitment to corporatist modernization was already becoming politically difficult to sustain by the early 1970s. But during the *septennat* of President Giscard D'Estaing, changes in the political and economic scene rendered the FNSEA's pursuit of *concertation* even more controversial and problematic. From 1974 to 1981, as the parties of the Left moved toward unification and strengthened their bid for power while competition between the Gaullists and the Giscardians became ever sharper, the FNSEA leaders' portrayal of their intimate relationship with the state as an "apolitical" or neutral stand was met with increasing incredulity at the *base*. The credibility of *concertation* was undermined even more seriously however, by the troubled French economy— "severely dislocated" by the energy crisis—and the impact of government economic policies on the agricultural modernization process. Under Prime Minister Raymond Barre, from 1976 onward, the government sought to achieve "three main objectives: to bring foreign trade into balance, to strengthen the franc and to control inflation."[84] In a way that seemed paradoxical to some farmers, but all too understandable to those who viewed the FNSEA as an "accomplice" or tool of the government, agriculture appeared to make the greatest sectoral contribution to the obtainment of these goals while receiving the fewest benefits in return.

The Fruits of Modernization

In his speech at Vassy near the end of 1977, Giscard asserted that French agriculture had "made an immense effort and obtained considerable results" in its drive for modernization and had thus become "a major asset for the future of our country." Indeed, he continued, agriculture had become strong and competitive enough to serve as "le pétrole de la France," producing an annual export surplus sufficient to offset to a great extent the negative impact of oil imports.[85] This assessment was not mere campaign hyperbole. In December 1979, *The Economist* of London published an article entitled "French Farming: Waking Giant" which warned readers to "prepare to tremble . . . the giant is on the move."[86] Two months later the "International Economic Survey" section of the Sunday New

York *Times* titled its article on the French economy "France Looks to Agriculture," referred to agriculture as a "bright spot," and concluded that the sector "is in excellent shape" to produce "green gold."[87]

As the following statistics will illustrate, the bottom line on the agricultural modernization effort was truly beginning to be impressive by the late 1970s. From 1959 to 1977 the volume of French agricultural production increased by 70%.[88] During the 1970s, France's average annual rate of growth in productivity (value added per farmer) surpassed that of all other original EEC members; the French figure was 4.2%, compared to 4.0% for Italy, 1.0% for West Germany, and 2.9% for the entire EEC.[89] With the gains of the 1970s, France rose to third place (on the same level as West Germany and behind only the Netherlands and Denmark) among EEC countries in agricultural productivity.[90] The modernization of agriculture also produced, as Giscard applauded, a dramatic change in the sector's commercial balance (exports minus imports). While agricultural imports always exceeded exports until 1968, the balance became "structurally positive" during the 1970s, despite the negative impact of the oil crisis. As Figure 3.3 indicates, the commercial balance recovered from the serious drought of 1976 (which made its impact in 1977) to record unprecedented surpluses during the last two years of the

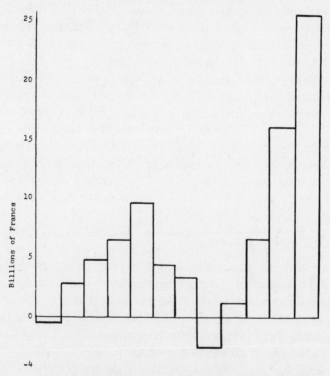

Figure 3.3 France's commercial balance (exports minus imports) for agricultural products, 1970–81. (From *L'Information agricole*, mars 1980, 60, and avril 1982, 24–27.)

Table 3.1   Distribution of Farm Land by Size of Farm

	Small Farms (< 35 ha)	Medium Farms (35–70 ha)	Large Farms (> 70 ha)
1955	64%	21%	15%
1970	50%	26%	24%
1980 [a]	36%	31%	33%
1985 [a]	31%	31%	38%

Source: L'Information agricale, no. 483, Septembre 1977, p. II of the "Connaissance de l'agriculture" insert.

[a] Projections made in 1977.

Giscard era. Remarkably enough, the 1981 surplus of 25.4 billion francs *surpassed* the optimistic goal (20 billion) which Giscard had set in his Vassy speech. The leaders of the export drive have been grains (13.5 billion francs' worth exported in 1979, up from 3.9 billion in 1970), wine and alcohol (12.9 billion in 1979, 2.8 billion in 1970), and milk products (7.2 billion in 1979, 2.8 billion in 1970). By 1979 France ranked third (after the United States and just behind the Netherlands) among all exporters of agricultural products and accounted for 7.5% of the world's agricultural export total.[91]

From the perspective of the government and the nation as a whole, the balance sheet on agricultural modernization was thus clearly positive at the end of the 1970s. The figures looked altogether different, however, when viewed from the perspective of the farmers. The appeal of the FNSEA/CNJA reformers during the "heroic era" had rested on the assumption that "humanized modernization" would impede the "capitalist concentration" of land, save "the maximum" possible number of family farms, decrease the disparities of income within agriculture, and allow all farmers to achieve income parity with the industrial sector. During the Giscard era it became painfully evident that none of these goals had been approached to the degree expected by the reformers.

First, the process of land concentration had scarcely altered its "capitalist" character. As Table 3.1 shows, a dramatic decline in the number of small farms had led to a relatively modest increase in medium-sized farms, but it had also produced a striking increase in large farms. In large part this was due to the underfunding and legal restriction of SAFER activity; from 1970 to 1977 alone the 5,000 largest farms in France succeeded in acquiring a total of 103,000 additional hectares.[92] For those who shared the reformers' goals, the projections for 1985 (made in 1977) painted an even bleaker picture: no increase in medium-sized farms was expected from 1980 to 1985, while the category of large farms was seen as becoming predominant for the first time in French history.[93] By the end of the Giscard era, the mean farm size in France—24 hectares (60 acres)—was almost twice that of 1955 and was the second largest (after the United Kingdom) among the member nations of the EEC.[94]

Second, it had proven to be much more difficult than anticipated to "save" family farms and farmers while encouraging modernization. From 1963 to 1975 alone, the number of French farms declined by more than 27%; moreover, it was projected that the decline from 1963 to 1985 would exceed 40%. In terms of the rural exodus, the percentage of the French work force engaged in agriculture declined from more than 20% to approximately 8% during the first two decades of the Fifth Republic, and the rate of this decline held steady during the Giscard era despite high unemployment levels in the industrial sector.[95]

Third, little progress had been made toward the goals of reducing income inequality within the agricultural sector and providing farmers with income parity with the industrial sector. In the Vassy speech, Giscard proclaimed that modernization efforts had enabled the agricultural sector to achieve "parity with the other modern sectors of national activity: economic parity, social parity, parity in conditions of life, parity in dignity." While Giscard did acknowledge that there were a few "dark spots" in this sunny picture, the Le Monde reporter covering his speech argued that it would be more accurate to speak of "shocking inequalities which it is impossible to ignore."[96] Measured region by region, the inequality of income within the French agricultural sector was, as of 1979, on the order of one to five; in contrast, the regional disparity of income was approximately one to three in the other original EEC states combined. When calculated in terms of individuals rather than regions, the picture looked quite similar. In the early 1970s, according to statistics produced by the Ministry of Agriculture, only 12% of the farmers had an income superior to the parity level, and this 12% accounted for 45% of total agricultural income.[97] As of 1979 the notion of "sectoral parity" was still virtually meaningless given the fact that a typical wheat farmer with more than 50 hectares of land earned a gross income nearly ten times that of a typical éleveur producing meat on a farm of 10–20 hectares.[98]

For a variety of reasons, regional and individual inequalities within the agricultural sector were attenuated somewhat as the decade of the 1970s progressed. From 1974 onward, special subsidies were granted to farmers in the poor mountain regions. Moreover, the poorest farmers, who tend to raise livestock on small plots, were hurt relatively less by the increase in oil prices than the wealthiest farmers, most of whom operate large wheat farms that necessitate the use of vast amounts of fuel and other oil-based products (in constant francs, the gross income per farmer in the élevage sector increased 2.5% during the 1970s, while the grande culture sector registered no increase). Agricultural organizations were careful to point out yet another reason for the slight easing of inequalities during the 1970s: a disproportionate number of the approximately one million farmers who joined the rural exodus during the decade were relatively poor.[99]

By the mid-point of Giscard d'Estaing's septennat, it had become clear to virtually all French farmers that the agricultural modernization process was proceeding in an essentially liberal manner. In an opinion poll of 1977, 70% of the farmers (and 67% of all citizens) interviewed said that the agricultural policy of the government took the interests of *gros agriculteurs* into consideration more than those of the *petits agriculteurs*. At the same time, fully 92% of the farmers felt that French agriculture was presently suffering from "grave" problems.[100] To understand the reasoning behind this figure, it is necessary to examine statistics pertaining to what for most farmers was surely the most legitimate measure of the acceptability of agricultural policy: income.

From the early 1960s until 1973, disillusionment with the character of the modernization process was cushioned by the impressive growth in agricultural income which it produced. During the Giscard era, however, the oil crisis and the government's antiinflation policies combined to produce a steady decline in farm income—a decline which, since it occurred at just the time that the agricultural sector was being applauded as an asset to the national economy, could not help but appear ironic and unfair to most farmers. The central cause of the downturn in income was the fact that, for a modernized agricultural system, oil is more important than soil.[101] The French agricultural sector consumed 39% more fuel and 46% more fertilizer in 1979 than in 1970; the bills for these two products increased from 3.2 to 11.8 billion francs and from 4.2 to 14.5 billion francs, respectively.[102]

From the time of the first oil shock onward, the annual increases in these production costs (*consommations intermédiaires*) consistently outstripped the annual increases in prices for farm products set in Brussels. Whereas from 1960 to 1973 the prices of agricultural products increased an average of 4.4% per year compared with a 3.8% annual increase in production costs, from 1974 to 1979 prices increased by only 6.9% per year while production costs rose at an average annual rate of 10.3%.[103] As Figure 3.4 shows, these developments resulted in a decline in gross farm income and an even more severe decline in net income (gross income minus debt liquidation). While other French sectors were also struggling with income problems during this period as a result of the Giscard-Barre austerity programs, the average French citizen was not suffering as much as the typical farmer. As the latter's income was declining, the former's purchasing power was growing by 2% in 1976 and by 0.6% in the first quarter of 1979.[104]

The economic insecurity of farmers was compounded during the Giscard era by the fact that, as the figures on net income decline reveal, they had accumulated an unprecedented debt burden in the process of modernizing their farms. The indebtedness of the sector increased from 30% of added value in 1960, the year of the first orientation law, to 144% in 1977 (the 1977 figures for West Germany and the Netherlands were 120% and 113%, respectively). By the end of the 1970s, almost 30% of farmers under the age of thirty-five owed debts of more than 200,000 francs.[105]

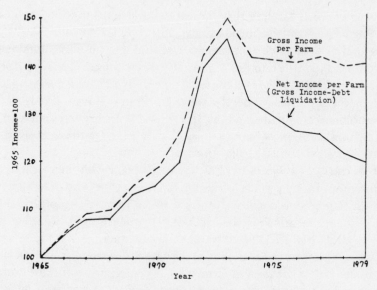

Figure 3.4   Agricultural income in France, 1965–79. (From *L'Information agricole*, mai 1980, 31.)

Tensions Within the FNSEA

In spite of the liberal course of the modernization process and the persistent decline of agricultural income, the leaders of the FNSEA clung tenaciously during the Giscard era to their position that *concertation* with the government was the best means of sectoral defense. At a crucial FNSEA congress in February 1978, for example, the major leaders of the union asserted that it was not difficult to show that *concertation* had achieved a great deal and that, while "much certainly remains to be done," the problems of the sector "can be resolved through *concertation*, once again."[106] The *rapport moral* prepared for this congress went so far as to argue that *concertation* was the "expression of a genuine economic democracy" which allowed individuals to be not mere "administrés" but rather, through their union, participants "in the life of the country". The "essential role" of the FNSEA in this economic democracy, stressed the report, was "to know how to forge compromises without being compromised, avoiding a recourse to excess which engenders further excesses."[107]

The reception that this stirring paean to *concertation* received within the FNSEA revealed the unprecedented degree of the tensions besetting the official union by 1978. For the first time in FNSEA history, the *rapport moral* failed to receive the unanimous backing of the administrative council and was thus not printed and distributed as an official report but rather presented orally as "some *idées forces* intended to facilitate dialogue and later reflection."[108] Many within the FNSEA elite felt that such a portrayal of the FNSEA's relationship with the state was not only excessively rosy but also poorly timed since, coming only a few weeks before the hotly contested legislative elections, it would appear to be an implicit endorsement of the current Center-Right government. Ironically, then, it would make the FNSEA appear to be precisely what the report denied that it was: politically compromised. Other FNSEA leaders objected that such a categorical reaffirmation of the value of *concertation* would be badly out of tune with sentiment at the *base*.[109] An opinion poll administered the year before had shown that only 12% of the farmers felt that "a policy of dialogue and *concertation* with the state" was sufficient for their defense, while 65% said that it was insufficient (22% had no opinion).[110]

Rather than viewing such indices of discontent as reasons to reassert the independence of the FNSEA through a strategy of *contestation*, President Michel Debatisse and his closest advisors decided they would try to alleviate tensions within the Federation by cracking down on the dissidents who had most stridently criticized the policies of the *centrale* and its "collusion" with the government. Debatisse's first targets were the leaders of the Section Nationale des Fermiers et Métayers (SNFM), the FNSEA's association of small renters and sharecroppers. As early as 1977 Debatisse warned the officials of the SNFM, some of whom were Communists, that their call for radical reform of land management policy (entailing, for example, the "democratization" of the SAFER and the rental of land by the state) contradicted FNSEA doctrine and represented an unacceptable flauting of his authority.[111] When the SNFM's president and secretary-general protested against what they termed a political "witch hunt" and attempts to "muzzle" the association, the FNSEA elite tried to arrange their ouster at a SNFM meeting in 1978. This effort failed, but soon thereafter the FNSEA *centrale* fired the SNFM's director "for budgetary reasons" and imposed on the association, without consultation, a half-time director more in tune with the policies of Debatisse.[112]

Another dissident, the national secretary of the FNSEA's Fédération Nationale des Producteurs de Porcs, was dealt with early in 1978. Soon after he delivered a report which was unanimously approved by the general assembly of this specialized association, the secretary was removed from his post—apparently because the *centrale* viewed him as "trop engagé à gauche." His response was to denounce the "conspiracy" prepared by the FNSEA elite for the purpose of "stifling syndical debate."[113]

By far the most important and controversial target of Debatisse's crackdown campaign was the FDSEA of Loire-Atlantique. This Breton departmental federation, the seventh largest of the FNSEA in terms of members, had for years included many of the leaders of the *paysans-travailleurs* movement and thus been a thorn in the side of the national elite. However, given the FNSEA's tradition of according a good deal of autonomy to its departmental branches and its fervent desire to maintain the largest possible membership, the dissidence of the Loire-Atlantique federation had been grudgingly tolerated—even during a number of years when it failed to pay its annual dues to the *centrale*. But events of late 1977 and early 1978 outraged Debatisse and his *équipe* and moved them to reconsider the policy of tolerance and federal flexibility.

In September 1977, all EEC countries began to collect what was termed a coresponsibility tax from milk producers. This new tax, fought for especially by the British as a means to limit the "milk lakes" and "butter mountains" which consumed 40% of the budget of the Common Agricultural Policy, had initially been opposed by the FNSEA. Once it became clear that the alternatives might be a freeze on milk prices or an imposed limit on milk production, however, the FNSEA had agreed to support the tax on the condition that "the profession" be allowed to participate in the management of the milk market and that proceeds from the tax be used for the promotion of milk products. It was with the reluctant blessing of the official union, then, that milk producers were required to pay a 1.5% tax at the point of collection beginning in the fall of 1977.[114]

Despite the fact that the milk lobby within the FNSEA had made its opposition to the coresponsibility tax clear from the outset, the FNSEA *centrale* was surprised and embarrassed by the intensity of protest the implementation of the tax produced. In Brittany, where more than 70% of the farmers specialized in milk production, thousands of farmers took to the streets and drenched the steps of the prefectures with milk. What made the tax appear especially unjust to many was the fact that it penalized most those small farmers who had responded, with costly investments, to the government's call for modernization and increased productivity. "After having systematically pushed for the intensification and expansion of production," proclaimed the *paysans-travailleurs*, "the government now wants to put the excesses on the backs of the farmers and make them pay the consequences of this policy."[115]

Two aspects of the Loire-Atlantique federation's reaction to the coresponsibility tax were viewed in a particularly dim light by the national FNSEA elite. First, it ignored pleas for calm from Paris and worked—along with the *paysans-travailleurs* and MODEF—to organize protest within Brittany and elsewhere. Second, it assumed an important leadership role in a recently formed FNSEA faction (which would later be termed Interpaysanne), a group of approximately twenty dissident FDSEAs opposed to the policies of Debatisse and his *équipe*. With the impetus provided by vociferous opposition at the *base* to the coresponsibility tax, this factional movement strengthened its organizational ties and produced a bulletin, *L'Interdépartemental*, which called for a strategy contradicting that of the FNSEA. "It is possible," the bulletin asserted, "to make the government retreat and to bring a halt to its imposition" of the tax.[116]

By the time of the 1978 FNSEA congress, the actions of the FDSEA of Loire-Atlantique had begun to appear totally unacceptable to the FNSEA's *centrale*. Debatisse thus pushed through the administrative council, in spite of opposition from the FNSEA's Commission on Statutes and Conflicts, a motion to expel the FDSEA of Loire-Atlantique from the Federation. With the concurrence of a majority of delegates at the congress, the dissident Breton

FDSEA became the first to be ousted since the days of the Blondelle purge in the early 1950s.

As the *Le Monde* reporter covering the congress wrote, *le syndicalisme unitaire* was "truly at a turning point in its history." Sharply contrasting views on the proper functioning of the FNSEA were presented by those sympathetic to the Loire-Atlantique, on the one hand, and by the Debatisse *équipe* on the other. Eleven departments signed a motion favorable to the ousted FDSEA, entitled "L'Unité Syndicale Implique le Pluralisme," which included the following lines:

> For some time, the ruling *équipe* of the FNSEA has given the impression of wanting to set aside those expressing views judged nonconformist, rather than pursue syndical debate. . . . Whatever the composition of the government may be, the role of the FNSEA is to defend and to represent all of the farmers, and this entails keeping its distance from the government. At present, the FNSEA objectively plays a relay role in the elaboration and application of agricultural policy.[117]

To such reasoning, Debatisse and his advisors retorted that the "FNSEA does not intend . . . to settle for some procedure of consultation" with the state. "But this desire to participate in the elaboration and management of agricultural policy entails respect for democratic rules within the union." All opinions could be expressed, but it was necessary for all to adhere to "the decisions of the majority. . . . It is for having transgressed these fundamental principles that the departmental federation of Loire-Atlantique has been expelled from the national federation."[118] In line with this logic, Debatisse warned at least two other FDSEAs (those of Allier and Jura) that they too would face the possibility of expulsion unless they altered their behavior. Threats such as these, combined with other facets of the crackdown campaign, led to complaints among the delegates at the 1978 congress that Debatisse was using "dictatorial methods" and imposing a new *centralisme* on the once highly decentralized FNSEA.[119]

It was clear that the FNSEA was indeed functioning according to dynamics quite different from those of the 1950s. The FNSEA elite could no longer allow the sort of disruptive behavior which had flowed from extreme decentralization in the past. To retain the organization's special status as a corporatist client, the FNSEA's leaders had to be able to show state officials that they were able to limit demands articulated to the state, to discipline their forces, and to assure the implementation of policies agreed to in group-state negotiations. Cracking down to achieve these ends would exacerbate internal tensions in a way which would probably have led to scissions or even destroyed the FNSEA in the 1950s. Now, however, these tensions could be contained or offset—as the next chapter will illustrate—through the FNSEA's receipt of tangible and intangible benefits from the state.

If Michel Debatisse's managerial style and devotion to *concertation* were not viewed warmly by dissidents within the FNSEA, they were most definitely appreciated by the Giscard-Barre government. In April 1979, Debatisse announced that he was resigning as FNSEA president to become a candidate for election to the European parliament on the Union pour la Démocratie Française (UDF) list; he noted at the time of his announcement that he had been assured a high enough position on the party list to virtually guarantee election.[120] Debatisse was indeed elected in June and was subsequently selected as vice-chairman of the European Assembly's Agricultural Commission. His tenure in that position was brief, however, for in October 1979 he was brought into the French government as secrétaire d'etat aux industries agro-alimentaires and charged with the task of enhancing the efficiency of the food processing industry, a vital link between the farmers and the export market. The cabinet that Debatisse formed included two of his former associates from the FNSEA.[121] If the leaders of the FNSEA had some misgivings about Debatisse's cooptation into the government, fearing that the move would be taken as a sign that the FNSEA was as compromised and politically linked to the Center-Right as critics had claimed, they were pleased by the fact that his appointment underscored the privileged status of the FNSEA and the government's continued commitment to concertation during troubled economic times.[122]

The process of concertation continued and even intensified during the last years of Giscard's septennat, as the official union and the government worked to draft, push through parliament, and implement a new agricultural orientation law. This new "charter," which Giscard had first proposed in his Vassy speech of 1977, was intended to update the 1960–62 laws so as to guide the sector "through the year 2000." It was also intended, no doubt, to serve a political purpose: to demonstrate that the government and the "profession," especially the official union, were committed to seeking in a cooperative manner a comprehensive solution to the problems of the farm community. In early 1978 seven groupes de travail, composed of state officials and representatives of the profession, began what the FNSEA termed the "long and meticulous preparation" of the orientation law.[123] For the next eighteen months, in the words of the FNSEA secretary-general, "the elected officials of the FNSEA as well as its administrative personnel furnished their collaboration to both many different representatives of the government and the members of parliament," proving in the process that the FNSEA had "clear ideas the combination of which would tend to produce a new agricultural society."[124]

To those farmers principally concerned with income and the stabilization of the agricultural population, the central thrust of the orientation law which the FNSEA helped to shape appeared disconcertingly liberal. In October 1979, not long before the project de loi was to be delivered to the National Assembly, the bill's rapporteur—Maurice Cornette of the Rassemblement Pour la République (RPR)—argued that French agriculture "must acknowledge itself to be a completely competitive sector, able to confront all competition and renounce the temptation for protection." The maîtres-mots of the new orientation law, he asserted, were to be "efficacité, rentabilité, competitivité."[125] Once the projet de *loi* reached the National Assembly in December, Minister of Agriculture Pierre Méhaignerie felt compelled to downplay the bill's neoliberalism somewhat. He stated that the government was committed to a policy of "correcting the handicaps" of the disfavored regions and the mountain zones, explained that the text tried "to reconcile employment and competitiveness," and proclaimed that "our entire policy is based on medium-sized farming . . . what we want is family farms of a very high technical level." Nevertheless, he defined the key principles of the bill in terms very similar to those of Cornette; the trilogy offered by Mehaignerie was "investment, enlargement, and specialization." Moreover, he stressed that the only proper means of improving farm incomes was "to increase the added value per hectare"—in other words, "produire plus et mieux."[126]

Méhaignerie referred to the orientation law as intended to "reussir la seconde révolution agricole" and portrayed it as similar in scope and impact to the laws of the early 1960s, but the new "charter" contained few dramatic departures from the basic principles that had guided agricultural policy in recent years. There was certainly nothing in the new orientation law as innovative or as controversial as the structural reform mechanisms that were the linchpin of the 1960–62 charter. Many critics charged that the new law lacked a "grand design" and that its contents were limited to "minor provisions, without coherence."[127] As a reporter for *Le Monde* quipped, it was not at all clear that the text had "suffisament de souffle pour courir jusqu'à l'an 2000."[128] Perhaps the 1980 orientation law could best be described as a modest reform package designed to tie up loose ends and thereby reinvigorate the liberal *dirigisme* incorporated in the legislation of the 1960s.

The most important sections of the new law were those designed to facilitate the installation or maintenance of young, technically proficient farmers on the land. Among the steps proposed in this regard were the following: (1) several measures were to be taken to provide more capital for the *groupements fonciers agricoles*, financial institutions managed by the Crédit Agricole which enable young farmers unable to meet the ever-rising purchase price of land to rent their land on a long-term basis from groups of nonagricultural as well as agricultural investors; (2) the powers of the SAFERs were to be strengthened somewhat so as to limit further *cumuls d'exploitation*; (3) legal reforms were to be enacted to facilitate succession without the physical division of farm land; and (4) some of the rules pertaining to the IVD (the special subsidy paid to aged farmers on the condition that they retire early and thus make their land available for distribution to the young) were to be liberalized and the amount paid to one category of IVD recipients was to be nearly doubled.[129]

Other sections of the 1980 orientation law were specifically intended to help transform French agriculture into what Giscard termed an "agriculture de conquête."[130] Agricultural productivity and export potential were to be enhanced through such means as an intensified commitment to research and development (focused on such objectives as reducing the costs of production and improving the efficiency of the food processing industry), new measures to encourage the organization of producers, and the creation of a fund for the promotion of agricultural exports. To assist in the coordination and mobilization of support for these new programs, the orientation law also instituted a new *concertation* mechanism: the Conseil Supérieur d'Orientation de l'Economie Agricole et Alimentaire. The CSO, a body composed of representatives of the state, the agricultural profession, the food processing industry, and consumers, was empowered to make recommendations in regard to "the general orientations of agricultural policy" and to help draft regional orientation programs for agricultural development.[131]

To the FNSEA elite, the orientation law of 1980 was on balance "very clearly positive" and represented "a very important stage in the evolution of agricultural policy."[132] The official union not only applauded the general principles of the law, but also welcomed the opportunity which the CSO provided to "participate more actively in the elaboration and the conduct of agricultural policy" and to extend "the *concertation* with the state which the FNSEA has always accepted."[133] The chief concern which the FNSEA manifested from the time of the orientation law's preparation until the end of the Giscard era in May 1981 was that the state would rest content with "verbal solicitude" for the sector, "disengaging financially" from key programs in such a way that the farmers would continue to be "the tired champions of the battle against inflation." If new FNSEA president François Guillaume often expressed his concern more firmly than had Michel Debatisse, he kept the official union on its *concertation* course and never challenged the government with the sort of massive organized protest that would later be used, after the Socialists came to power and began to introduce their new pluralist order, during the winter of 1981–82.[134]

While the FNSEA was continuing to sanction the broad outlines of government policy and increasing its participation in the comanagement of the agricultural sector, rival unions gained a wider audience with their protests against income decline and the dangers of an accelerated modernization process. MODEF categorized the new orientation law as a "mortal blow" to the small farmers and denounced the FNSEA—"le syndicalisme de collaboration"—for supporting "this suicidal orientation . . . , this veritable expropriation" which "is going to redouble its intensity" so as to reinforce the food-processing corporations.[135] Along similar lines, the FFA ridiculed the FNSEA's periodic resort to tough-sounding rhetoric ("déclarations seulement") and condemned the government's new policy as an effort to "comfort the multinationals" which was irreconcilable with the promise "to conserve family farming and to install the maximum number of young farmers."[136] As the Giscard era was drawing to a close, the FNSEA thus struggled to retain its hold over the farmers in the face of what one government official termed "a crisis of confidence between agriculture and the nation" and "among the farmers" themselves.[137]

MOTIVES FOR THE CONTINUANCE OF *CONCERTATION*

It is evident that, contrary to the predictions of reformers in the early 1960s, the strategy of permanent *concertation* produced considerable organizational stress and impaired the FNSEA's legitimacy at the *base* during the two decades after the passage of the first orientation law. It is so evident, in fact, that one is led to wonder why the FNSEA never opted for a *cure d'opposition*, at least during times of crisis. If the FNSEA's leaders were concerned with maintaining the unity of their organization and its authority among the farmers, why did they refuse to engage in *contestation* on occasions when it would have been a popular strategic move? When this question is posed to national FNSEA leaders, the answer given is merely a reiteration of the rationale for *concertation* discussed earlier in this chapter.[138] There would appear to be at least two other plausible explanations, however.

One explanation for the FNSEA's maintenance of *concertation* through May 1981 was quite popular among leaders of rival unions. As one MODEF official asserted in the mid-1970s: "It is the result of political calculations; the reactionaries leading the FNSEA will do nothing to weaken the power of a Right-wing government."[139] This argument is unacceptable in its crudest form, but it does point to an important fact. It may be true, as the FNSEA leaders have argued, that the dependence of the "plight of the farmers" on the *pouvoirs publics* necessarily leads the FNSEA to try "not to oppose uselessly the political parties in power, whoever they may be." But it was hardly coincidental that the FNSEA's dogged adherence to the *concertation* strategy occurred during the tenure in office of a Center-Right governmental majority. In an article of 1974, a key FNSEA official admitted as much with unusual candor. The FNSEA's espoused policy of strict political neutrality (*apolitisme*), he acknowledged, is a "difficult course" for the Federation's leaders to follow. For one thing, "the degree of convergence between [the Federation's] demands and the programs of the different political parties is not the same for all."[140] Indeed, while articles in the FNSEA's publications during the years of Center-Right rule avoided any explicit support for the programs of a particular party, they nevertheless made clear the fact that the FNSEA was skeptical about the agricultural policy proposed by the Left and found more of its positions to be supported by the current majority.[141] Aside from programmatic convergence, the official continued, the FNSEA had another powerful incentive for favoring governments of the Center-Right: "the political votes of [the Federation's] members are not sufficiently diversified for their union organization not to have a tendency to tilt toward a position which their votes direct." According to opinion polls, he noted, 56% of the farmers voted for the Center-Right majority in the 1973 election and an additional 13% voted for the Reformists.[142] More recently, 69% of the farmers voted for Giscard in the 1974 presidential election and nearly as many (67%) voted for Giscard even in 1981; 64% of the farmers voted for the UDF (33%) or the RPR (31%) in the 1978

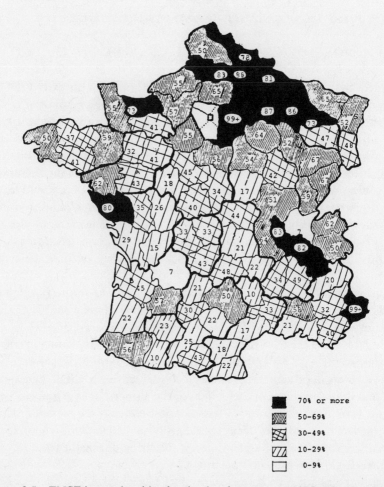

■	70% or more
▨	50-69%
▤	30-49%
▨	10-29%
□	0-9%

Figure 3.5 FNSEA membership density by department, 1975. Membership totals were taken from an official FNSEA document: "Cotisations 1975," 7 juillet 1975, Action Syndicale—FNSEA. The number of farmers eligible for FNSEA membership was estimated from a government document: *Statistique agricole: Enquête communautaire sur la structure des exploitations agricoles en 1967* (Paris: Ministère de l'Agriculture, mars 1969), tableau VII. Neither source allows for an *exact* calculation of FDSEA membership density. National membership figures are impossible to confirm and are not always accurate. For example, Chapter 6 shows that the 1975 Corrèze statistic is significantly exaggerated; the statistics for other departments are doubtless inaccurate as well. To cite but one case—it is improbable that the membership for the department of Rhône remained exactly the same in 1975 as it had been in 1966 (the declared figures were 9,000 for both years); exaggeration of the 1975 figure would explain the apparent anomaly of 83% membership density in this relatively poor department. Moreover, it is impossible to determine exactly the number of farmers who were eligible for FNSEA membership in every department in 1975. No census data are available for 1975. Even if they were, no *exact* determination would be possible; one must estimate the number of eligible farmers from the published number of farms, and many of the smallest of these farms do not support a full-time farmer. It is thus customary to estimate the number of eligible farmers as the number of farms larger than 2 hectares (see Prugnaud, *Les Etapes*, p. 176). Because I

legislative elections, and 60%—the highest percentage of any occupational group—voted for the UDF (28%) or the RPR (32%) even in the Socialist landslide election of 1981 (although farm votes for the Socialists did increase between 1978 and 1981, from 17% to 32%).[143]

What the FNSEA has never admitted publicly is that this membership-induced tendency to support the Center-Right majority was compounded by an organizational factor: the FNSEA's national elite has long been even less politically "diversified" than the agricultural sector as a whole. Ever since Blondelle's purge of the Leftists in the early 1950s, influential positions within the FNSEA have been virtually monopolized by non-Leftists. Some Socialists and even a few Communists (generally delegates from the Section des Fermiers et Métayers or the Southwest region) have held seats on the national administrative council over the past two decades.[144] Since the early 1960s, however, not a single member of the national bureau—the FNSEA's powerful executive body—has been aligned with a party of the Left.[145] Moreover, some of the more outspoken Leftist officials within the organization have, as stated earlier, been ousted through what their sympathizers have termed political "witch hunts."

The dominance of conservative or "moderate" forces within the FNSEA has been sustained through the years not only by skillful political maneuvers on the part of presidents from Blondelle to Guillaume, but also by the rules that govern elite selection and decision-making at union congresses. Departmental federations are accorded votes in proportion to the number of *dues-paying* members they claim.[146] Given this formula, the FDSEAs from Left-leaning departments tend to be doubly handicapped: the number of dues-paying members they can acquire is limited not only by the relative unpopularity of the FNSEA within their respective departments, but also by their inability to attract members with the sort of services/material incentives provided by the FDSEAs in more wealthy (and generally conservative) departments.

The mapping of FNSEA membership density in the 1970s provided by Figure 3.5 manifests a pattern almost identical to that of the 1950s: a greater percentage of eligible farmers join the FDSEAs of the wealthy North and Parisian Basin than join the FDSEAs of the poor regions in the Massif Central and the South. From Figures 3.5, 3.6, and 3.7, as well as the correlations of Table 1.1, one can infer what the case studies of Part II will confirm: this variation in membership density is attributable less to differing levels of FNSEA popularity than to variation across departments in the attractiveness of services offered by the FDSEAs. Of the seventeen wealthiest FDSEAs (those which, as Figure 3.6

---

was forced to use 1967 statistics to estimate the statistics for 1975 (when the number of farms would be smaller in each department), I employed as the 1975 figure the number of farms greater than five hectares in 1967. As a result, the membership density calculations of Figure 3.5 are by no means exact, but are meaningful estimates.

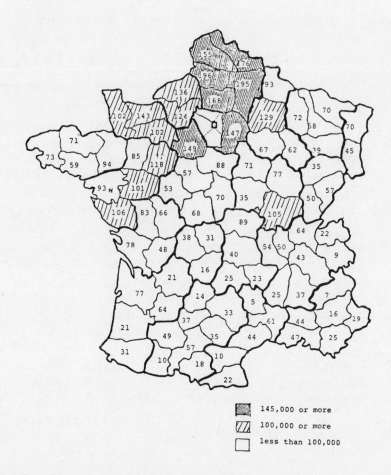

145,000 or more	
100,000 or more	
less than 100,000	

Figure 3.6 Proportional dues paid by each FDSEA in 1975 (in thousands of francs). (From the "Cotisations 1975" document.)

shows, paid wealth-based "proportional" dues of 100,000 francs or more to the FNSEA) as of 1975, the ones that generally provided the most extensive services, 94% received a majority of votes in the 1974 Chamber of Agriculture election and 82% obtained the membership of at least half the eligible farmers. Of the less wealthy FDSEAs, 78% received a majority of chamber votes (only 16% less) but no more than 36% (46% less) obtained the membership of at least half the eligible farmers. Moreover, while 41% of the seventeen wealthiest FDSEAs achieved a membership density of at least 70%, only 9% of the less-wealthy departments achieved this level.

Although internal politics and organizational structure have thus assured the predominance of conservatives or "moderates" within the FNSEA, it must be noted that the partisan leanings of the FNSEA elite did not always produce cordial group-state relations during the era of Center-Right rule; conflicts among the Center-Right factions at times proved to be an obstacle in the path of *concertation*. For example, the anti-Gaullist sentiments of some former Vichy notables were at least a contributing factor in the FNSEA's 1965 decision to oppose de Gaulle's reelection. Such conflict was alleviated after 1966 by the movement of most "centrists" into the governmental majority and by changes in the FNSEA elite.[147] According to one observer, the 1975 election to the FNSEA administrative council was marked by "the regression of the Christian Democratic *tendance* and the elimination of certain leaders who weakly supported the presidential regime."[148] Conflict reemerged, however, as tensions between RPR and UDF factions within both the government and the FNSEA increased in the late 1970s. While Debatisse chose to leave the FNSEA for a UDF post in the European parliament and then joined the French government, others within the FNSEA—including President François Guillaume—were reported to be

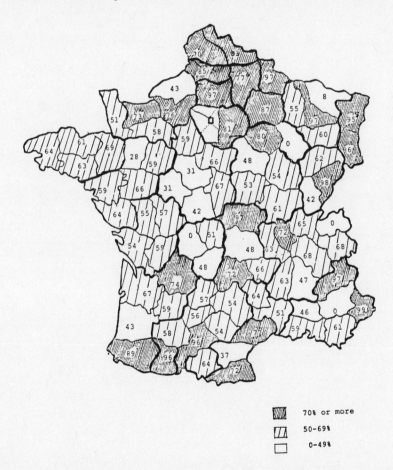

Figure 3.7 FNSEA vote by department: 1974 Chamber of Agriculture elections (college of *chefs d'exploitation*). (These statistics are taken from a mimeographed document produced by the Ministry of Agriculture and obtained for me from the Ministry by the librarian of the APCA: "Elections aux chambres d'agriculture: Colleges des chefs d'exploitation—circonscriptions renouvelables en février 1974.")

dissatisfied with the Giscardian government and to be flirting with the Chiracians.[149]

Despite these tensions, it is clear that the FNSEA leaders had some political motivation for pursuing their strategy of *concertation* during the years of Center-Right government. Yet partisan leanings were by no means the only factor serving to constrain the FNSEA to a *concertation* course. As the next chapter will show, the strategy of permanent *concertation* paid enormous organizational dividends for the FNSEA. Although it entailed considerable "losses" in terms of programmatic appeal at the *base*, it also provided the FNSEA with indispensable "gains" in terms of influence and competitive advantage vis-à-vis rival unions.

4

Comanagement and the Corporatist Bases of FNSEA Hegemony

> The groups which have established close relationships with the administration ...
> are engaged, not in a fight to secure once-and-for-all gain, but in a continuing
> attempt to affect the allocation of resources—or the distribution of power—in their
> favor.
>
> EZRA SULEIMAN[1]

Despite suffering from a decline in popularity, as manifested by the emergence of rival union movements and the results of opinion polls, the FNSEA maintained its hegemony within the agricultural sector throughout the era of *concertation* with governments of the Center-Right. Officials of the Federation noted proudly that the FNSEA remained the only farmer's union of truly nationwide scope, with an affiliate in every department, and that it consistently won nearly 90% of the seats in elections for the Chambers of Agriculture. Moreover, they were able to claim that the membership density of the FNSEA actually surpassed the level achieved during the relatively halcyon days of the 1950s, when the ideal of "syndical unity" faced fewer challenges. Although the number of FNSEA members declined from the mid-1950s to the late 1970s, along with the agricultural population, the membership density of the Federation increased from 33–35% to approximately 44%—a figure higher than that of all French industrial trade unions combined.[2] To a considerable degree, these statistics reflected genuine support for the policies advocated by the FNSEA. As Chapter 8 will make clear, the Socialists would pay a heavy price for underestimating that support when they came to power in 1981.

What was never acknowledged by either FNSEA or government officials during the era of the Center-Right rule, however, was that these statistics provided a distorted image of the Federation's standing in the countryside. As this chapter will show, they were in large part a function of the FNSEA's privileged status within the agricultural sector's corporatist policy-making system. From the time of the Pisani Law onward, the Federation's "professional *appareil* was integrated into the machinery of the state" in a manner that enabled the FNSEA not only to comanage the affairs of France's farmers, but also to enhance its organizational strength.[3] As dissidence within the FNSEA increased, and as rival union movements mobilized more and more disgruntled farmers, the hegemony of the FNSEA rested increasingly on corporatist bases.

In exchange for behaving "responsibly" and suffering the "losses" which a corporatist client must incur, the FNSEA received considerable "gains" from the state—gains not only in influence but also in competitive advantage. In some extreme cases, the FNSEA benefited from the overt repression of "nonofficial" rival unions. But the hegemony of the FNSEA was reinforced primarily through more subtle processes. On a regular basis, the official union benefited from (1) *exclusive or privileged access* to the decision-making centers of the state at the national and the subnational levels; (2) *devolved power* to formulate and implement important aspects of agricultural policy; (3) the *revision of regulations* such as those governing elections to the chambers of agriculture; and (4) *monetary subsidies* intended to further the modernization process. All of these benefits served to reinforce FNSEA hegemony by providing both union elites and rank and file with tangible and intangible incentives to remain active within—or at least stay on good terms with—the official union of the agricultural sector.

EXCLUSIVE OR PRIVILEGED ACCESS

Exclusive Access

Perhaps the most widely recognized benefit granted the FNSEA by the state was the exclusive[4] right to participate in *formal* advisory councils, commissions, and committees. Such participation, as Georges Lavau has argued, provides groups with "invaluable means of accomplishing their objectives" and endows them with "considerable moral prestige."[5] An indication of the utility and prestige value of the right to participate in advisory institutions is the fact that this right was eagerly sought by rival unions, most notably MODEF and the FFA, until it was finally granted by the Socialist government in 1981.[6]

Even before the age of systematic *concertation*, the FNSEA was "invited to send representatives to more than 200 committees, commissions and councils."[7] With the reforms of the early 1960s, however, such institutions increased dramatically in both number and importance. At the *national level* the FNSEA was given the opportunity to exert considerable influence within official administrative councils charged with formulating policy pertaining to, for example, agricultural development (through the Association Nationale pour le Développement Agricole, ANDA), the distribution of subsidies intended to further structural reform (through the Centre National pour l'Aménagement des Structures des Exploitations Agricoles, CNASEA), and state intervention into agricultural markets (through the Fonds d'Orientation et de Régulation des Marchés Agricoles).[8] Legislation of the 1970s expanded this "appareil péripherique d'Etat" by creating such new institutions as the *interprofessions*, a network of national and regional Interprofessional Councils intended to "complete the economic organization of agriculture already put in place by producer groups and cooperatives." Each of the councils, composed of two-thirds professional representatives for the product in concern (pork, wine, etc.) and one-third state officials, was financed through a combination of obligatory dues and state subsidies and was empowered to develop policies on matters such as the orientation of investments and technical research, to enhance the organization of producers, to regulate deliveries of produce to the market, and to promote consumption through advertising campaigns. Like the institutions of the Pisani era, the Interprofessional Councils tended to be controlled predominately by FNSEA delegates, in this case by representatives of the Federation's specialized associations for particular products.[9] It has been estimated that, by the mid-1970s, fully 80% of the state budget devoted to agriculture was managed by *paritaire*-style organisms ranging from ANDA to the *interprofessions*, a degree of "sociopolitical osmosis" unmatched by any other French sector.[10]

From the early 1970s onward, the FNSEA also benefited from its status as the most influential sectoral representative at the highly visible and prestigious Conférence Annuelle, widely viewed as the symbol of *concertation*. Instituted in 1971 at the request of the FNSEA, the Conférence Annuelle was modeled after the "Annual Review" established in Britain in 1947.[11] As it operated during the Center-Right era, the Annual Conference actually consisted of a series of group-state interactions in several stages. First, in the "technical phase," the bureaucrats of the agricultural ministry met for several weeks with the representatives of the FNSEA and the other recognized organizations to "systematically discuss all sectors of agricultural activity and all aspects of agricultural policy." Second, in the "study phase," a certain number of themes were selected "by common accord" as items of the highest priority. In the final "policy phase" these high-priority themes were discussed at the Annual Conference per se: the leaders of the FNSEA and the other professional organizations met for four hours with the minister of agriculture, and then for another four hours with the prime minister. As a rule, the major policy innovations of the year were announced at the conclusion of the conference—a procedure that effectively established a connection in the public mind between the articulation of demands by the FNSEA and their (at least partial) realization by the state. While some measures may in truth have been at least to a degree the response to pressure from nonofficial unions, they were made to appear to be the direct result of FNSEA influence—the fruit of *concertation*.[12]

At the *department level* each FDSEA enjoyed, at least until 1981, exclusive access to a parallel network of formal advisory institutions: councils or commissions that dealt with everything from prices or tax policy to the administration of disaster relief. FDSEA leaders derived prestige and sometimes a great deal more from their seats on bodies such as the *commission des cumuls*, established in 1962 to restrict the activities of so-called *cumulards*— nonagriculturalists who wish to buy land, evict the established tenant, and operate the farm with hired labor. An unfavorable judgment by such a commission could be of enormous consequence for a small farmer—and the possibility of such a judgment often served as a powerful incentive to join or at least stay on good terms with the FDSEA. Organizers for rival unions often cited fear of the "malevolence" of these commissions as a major factor dissuading farmers from abandoning the FDSEA for a nonofficial union.[13]

Privileged Access

Privileged *informal* access to the government and the administration also furnished the FNSEA with gains in both influence and competitive advantage. At the national level, the administration was readily accessible to the FNSEA and assisted it almost daily in the resolution of problems. More important, at the department level the privileged access granted to the FNSEA's affiliates served— perhaps even more than formal access—as a powerful incentive for the attraction of members. Intermediation by FDSEA officials was almost a necessity for the many small farmers who could not understand the workings of the state machine and were hesitant to deal directly with its faceless bureaucrats. In most departments the FDSEA director could telephone the prefecture, speak with an assistant of the prefect, and—often immediately—resolve the particular problems of a farmer. Many FDSEA directors or presidents earned the sobriquet *préfet agricole* by manifesting, among other things, an astounding ability to cut through bureaucratic red tape. In contrast, the leaders of rival unions in most departments had difficulty even obtaining a hearing from the administration until 1981.

DEVOLVED POWER AND *COGESTION*

From the early 1960s onward the FNSEA was not only accorded the means to influence policy through exclusive or privileged access, it was also granted the authority to formulate and implement policy at the subnational level. The power to administer many important aspects of modernization policy was devolved to a network of institutions staffed by representatives of "the profession" and, in most cases, dominated by the FNSEA. The significance of these institutions led one FNSEA sympathizer to conclude that "agriculture appears to be the greatest self-managed (*autogeré*) sector" of the French economy, "even if the form of *autogestion* that we know does not satisfy the theorists of a certain socialism who have still not defined in a clear manner what they mean by *autogestion*."[14] Because of the controversial connotations of "autogestion," FNSEA officials themselves seldom used this term to describe their direct participation in policy-making. They referred to it as simply one aspect of *concertation* or as *cogestion* (comanagement). The most important comanagement institutions were the SAFERs, the ADASEAs, the SUADs, and the Chambers of Agriculture.

The SAFERs

Established by the orientation law of 1960, the Sociétés d'Aménagement Foncier et d'Etablissement Rural are regional agencies designed to ameliorate farm structures by purchasing land as it comes onto the market, implementing necessary improvements (e.g., by consolidating small parcels), and then selling this land selectively so as to render existing farms viable or to create new, viable farms. As of 1975, thirty-three SAFERs were functioning in France with a combined budget of approximately 50 million francs (an average of 1.5 million francs per SAFER).[15] Comanagement of the SAFERs thus provided "the profession" with the power to dispose of a significant sum of money and to make decisions affecting the most vital agricultural interests.

The comanagement of the SAFERs operated in the following manner from the early 1960s through 1981. By statute, each SAFER was defined as an association "constituted . . . by the principal agricultural organizations of the departments concerned and controlled by the state." The participation of the "principal" organizations consisted of their delegation of representatives to a SAFER general assembly which elected an administrative council headed by a president elected from among its members. While this president and the council were empowered to perform the basic functions of the SAFER, their activity was controlled by the state through the *double tutelle* of the Ministry of Agriculture and Ministry of Finance. Two state commissioners, one attached to each of these ministries, had to approve all operations of the administrative council involving more than 60,000 francs or requiring the use of the *droit de préemption* (a right of priority for the purchase of land placed on the market).[16]

Although the comanagement of the SAFERs was said to provide "the profession" with devolved power to control its own affairs, the exercise of this power was restricted to the elites of the "recognized" organizations—especially those of the FNSEA. No statistics are available to illustrate the degree of influence that the FNSEA has enjoyed within all of the thirty-three SAFERs. However, in each of the regions that I studied in depth, the president of the SAFER was—as of 1975—a major FNSEA official: in the Nord-Picardie region the SAFER president was a vice-president of the Aisne FDSEA; in the Aquitaine region, he was the president of the Landes FDSEA; and in the Marche-Limousin region, he was the president of the Creuse FDSEA. A passage in a report of one FDSEA expressed quite well the FNSEA elite's vision of its traditional relationship with the SAFERs: while "not actually a direct branch of the FDSEA," the SAFER "has given an important activity to our organization."[17]

To what degree was the FNSEA's de facto control of the SAFERs an asset in its competition with rival unions? Judging from interviews with both FDSEA and rival union elites, it would appear to have been a definite—albeit limited—competitive advantage. It was an advantage because, especially in departments in which the FDSEA was quite strong, many farmers feared that an expression of opposition to the FDSEA might provoke the "malevolence" of the SAFER (as of the *commission des cumuls*), or at least make a perhaps-crucial marginal difference in its decision.[18] However, this advantage was limited for several reasons. The decisions of the SAFERs affected a relatively small number of the farmers (much less than 1%) each year. Even some rival union leaders expressed the opinion that the *tutelle* of the state limited the degree to which the SAFERs could "systematically discriminate" according to political criteria.[19] One informed, relatively objective observer summed up the significance of the FNSEA-SAFER relationship during the 1970s in the following manner: "many farmers certainly fear abuse [of the SAFER power by the FDSEA], and there are some cases in which there seems to have been abuse, but in general the decisions are as fair as possible."[20]

The ADASEAs

The Associations Départementales pour l'Aménagement des Structures des Exploitations Agricoles were established in 1966 to "furnish the cooperation of the agricultural profession in the implementation" of the various structural reform programs called for in the 1960–62 orientation and complementary laws: the IVD, the subsidies for occupational conversion, migration subsidies, and so on. Before 1981 the ADASEA of each department was controlled by a professional administrative council with a composition that virtually assured FDSEA predominance; in a typical council of 16, the FDSEA itself held 6 seats, the CDJA 3 seats, and the other recognized organizations (which were also generally close to the FDSEA) 7 seats.[21] It is hardly extraordinary, then, that in each of the three departments I examined closely, the president of the ADASEA had always been—like the SAFER president—an FDSEA official.

The benefits which the FDSEAs derived from the ADASEAs during the Center-Right era were far more tangible than those derived from the SAFERs. The ADASEA personnel (a director and one or more counselors) were hired by the FDSEA elite, were subject to its directives, and were often housed in the same building as the FDSEA staff. Furthermore, in most departments the ADASEA-paid personnel worked in close cooperation with "local correspondents" selected from among the elites of the FDSEA's cantonal unions and trained in ADASEA-financed "education and information" sessions.[22] Since most farmers were unaware of the distinction between ADASEA personnel and FDSEA personnel (such confusion was encouraged by FNSEA/FDSEA proclamations that the ADASEA was a "réalisation du syndicalisme"), the former served to enhance the image of the union even in discharging their proper functions—providing information on available subsidies, filling out necessary forms and transmitting them to the state, and so on. Moreover, ADASEA personnel were often utilized for a variety of syndical purposes, such as organizing union meetings, transporting union officials, distributing union literature—even collecting union dues. In effect, then, the ADASEA personnel served more or less as a state-financed adjunct of the staff of the FNSEA's departmental organizations.[23]

The SUADs and Development

Most of the agricultural comanagement institutions were conceived and implemented during the first years of Edgard Pisani's term (1961–66) in the Ministry of Agriculture. The last two years of the Pisani era were largely devoted to the preparation[24] of another extremely important, complex package of *concertation* institutions: those concerning what had traditionally been termed "vulgaris-ation," and what after 1966 would be termed "development." This change in nomenclature was intended to convey a profound conceptual change in this aspect of agricultural policy. Rather than merely serving to disseminate knowledge of technical advances in agriculture, the "development" program was also intended to accelerate structural reforms by "making farmers become conscious of the technical, economic, and social problems" which would have to be solved to assure a prosperous future for their regions.[25]

Along with this change in conception, the new program instituted an important change in the manner through which the state would act to favor development. Up until 1950, throughout what Pisani termed the "first age" of *vulgarisation*, the state had exercised a "quasi-monopoly" of the diffusion of technical knowledge; traditionally it had accorded such activity to the engineers of the administration's *services agricoles*. Because these public efforts were viewed as inadequate by many within the agricultural profession, further private efforts were made to advance the *vulgarisation* process, for example, through the establishment of the CETAs (Centres d'Etudes Techniques Agricoles). The gradual recognition by the state of the utility of these private institutions engendered the "second age" of *vulgarisation* policy: in 1959 the government began to subsidize the CETAs and similar groupings. With the passage of the 1966 development program, a "third age" was initiated: henceforth the state would retain some power over the usage of development funds, but would "grant to the agricultural profession itself the responsibility for the realization of *vulgarisation* and technical and economic progress at all levels."[26]

From 1966 onward the "profession" participated in the formulation of agricultural development policy at the national level and was largely responsible for its implementation at the departmental level. At the national level, representatives of the FNSEA and the other recognized agricultural organizations were accorded 10 of the 20 seats in the *paritaire*-style administrative council of the aforementioned ANDA. This council performed a number of important functions: it advised the agricultural minister on the general orientation of national and regional development programs, regulated the employment and training of development personnel, and managed a national development fund which in 1974 amounted to 229 million francs. Participation in the ANDA council thus provided a wide-ranging source of influence over agricultural policy to the elites of the recognized organizations—and especially the FNSEA. The president of the ANDA council as of 1975 was Gérard de Caffarelli, the immediate past-president of the FNSEA.[27]

At the department level, the "profession" exercised more complete control over development policy. The general orientations of the departmental development program were determined by a *paritaire*-style Conseil d'Etude presided over by the prefect. However, the day-to-day management of the program was entrusted entirely to the board of directors of the SUAD (Service d'Utilité Agricole et de Développement), a board chaired by the president of the Chamber of Agriculture and composed of an equal number of chamber members and delegates from the other principal departmental agricultural organizations.[28]

Although this representational scheme did not accord the FNSEA de jure control of the SUAD, it translated into de facto FNSEA control. Nearly all FDSEAs were assured of a majority on the SUAD board through the combination of seats granted to the official union per se with seats obtained indirectly from FDSEA dominance within the Chamber of Agriculture (and, in most cases, dominance within the other recognized organizations as well). Thus, for example, in each of the three departments that I examined closely the SUAD council contained a vast majority of FDSEA members.[29]

Control of the SUADs served as an immense source of power for the FNSEA's departmental organizations: not only did it enable them to exert great influence over the orientation of the development program, it also provided them with the opportunity to allocate directly—rather than merely solicit—public funds for the subsidization of their organizational activities. This opportunity arose because the SUAD itself was essentially an institution for the coordination of development functions; nearly all of its budget—normally about 2 million francs in 1976—was not spent by the SUAD itself but rather disbursed to a variety of development organisms, many of which were related in varying degrees of intimacy to the FDSEA. For example, in nearly every department (1) the FDSEA's "Women's Section" commonly received a subsidy (e.g., more than

34,000 francs in Corrèze and 20,000 francs in Aisne in 1976) that paid for a counselor or two specializing in farm management and accounting; (2) the CDJA received a subsidy (in *every* department—this was a stipulation of the national ANDA budget) for the employment of two counselors concerned with the technical education and information of the young farmers; this subsidy varied by department but was always significant and sometimes even greater than the entire CDJA budget; (3) the Groupements de Vulgarisation Agricole, which are "sections" of the cantonal unions of the FDSEA, commonly received subsidies of as much as several hundred thousand francs; (4) the EDE (Etablissement Départemental de l'Elevage), which specializes in the development of livestock raising, and the Centre de Gestion et d'Economie Rurale, which assists farmers with management problems such as the preparation of tax returns, both commonly received subsidies of several hundred thousand francs; neither of these organizations was directly controlled by the FDSEA, but both of them were supervised by administrative councils similar to that of SUAD and were thus generally subject to indirect FDSEA control. While a number of organizations with no FNSEA connection also generally received funding, few with overt ties to rival unions such as MODEF ever did.[30]

The Chambers of Agriculture

Established originally in 1924, abolished in 1940 and reestablished in 1949, the Chambers of Agriculture developed during the Fifth Republic into the most important of the "comanagement" institutions of agriculture at the departmental level. This development was unforeseen at the time of their creation under the Third Republic. The essential role of the chambers, as envisioned in that era, was to provide the state with a "consultative organism" representing the local interests of the agricultural profession. To fulfill this role, the chambers were publicly financed (by a special agricultural tax) and their membership was determined by a state-controlled election with suffrage granted to all farmers.

In recent decades, the chambers have become increasingly important through their discharge of what was originally intended to be a secondary role: the creation or subsidization, with public funds, of technical and economic institutions or services in the "collective interest of agriculture." Until 1954, the ability of the chambers to perform this role was severely limited by their meager resources. In 1954, however, and again in 1959, the financial regulations of the chambers were altered in such a manner as to expand greatly their ability to discharge an economic function. From 1954 to 1969, the combined budgets of the departmental chambers increased from just over 7 million francs (roughly 80,000 per chamber) to 156 million francs (roughly 1.8 million per chamber). Since the advent of ANDA and the assignment of the SUADs to chamber control, the budgets of the chambers have been increased even further; as of 1976, ANDA provided most chambers with a subsidy in the vicinity of 1.5 million francs.[31]

This tremendous increase in the financial power of the chambers inspired one observer in the early 1960s to assert that each chamber president was becoming "a second DSA[32] with an all-powerful director commanding . . . several dozen neofunctionaries." Agricultural elites interviewed in the 1970s expressed similar sentiments, referring to particular chamber presidents or directors as the "*préfet vert*" or "*préfet agricole*" of the department. Such assessments were a bit exaggerated. The activities of the chamber elites have been delimited and supervised by the state administration; their program proposals have been subject to the approval of the prefect and their management of the chambers' funds has been controlled by the Cour des Comptes. Nevertheless, the elites of the Chambers of Agriculture have possessed enormous power to affect agricultural policy through their representation on a multitude of institutions (discussed earlier) and their allocation of funds.[33]

A fact not often acknowledged in the literature on French agriculture is that the elites of the Chambers of Agriculture have also possessed enormous power to affect the relative strength of the competing farmers' unions and that, with very few exceptions, this power has redounded to the benefit of the FNSEA. As mentioned in the introduction, the FNSEA has traditionally won approximately 90% of the contested seats in the elections to the chambers. The FNSEA's departmental affiliates have controlled a majority of seats in all but a handful of departments.[34] Some measures of the extent and intimacy of the FNSEA-chamber relationship are provided in Figure 4.1. As of 1975, 72% of the FDSEA presidents were members of their Chambers of Agriculture; 45% of the FDSEA presidents were members of their chamber's executive bureau. In 64% of the departments, the FDSEA and the chamber were housed in the same office building. In 10% of the departments, the FDSEA and the chamber employed the same administrative director—and in a great many more, the director of one of these organizations was the subdirector (and often functioned as the de facto director) of the other.[35]

The FNSEA's control of the chambers during the Center-Right era provided the Federation with manifold organizational benefits. First, it afforded the typical FDSEA even more influence—through the seats allotted to the chamber—over the comanagement institutions and advisory councils just described. In fact, it provided the FDSEA with such a monopoly of power that, as one dissident union activist lamented in the 1970s: "One must work within the FDSEA if one wants to hold any important position and have any influence over policy; if one splits from the FDSEA, one can speak louder—but at the cost of not being heard."[36] Second, control of the chamber provided the typical FDSEA with indirect state subsidization of its infrastructure. While most rival unions were forced to operate with little in the way of an infrastructure, the chamber-dominant FDSEA was able to make use—normally for a small payment if not for free—of the chamber's office building, its equipment (photocopying machines, telephones), its library, and its supplies of office materials. Third, control of the

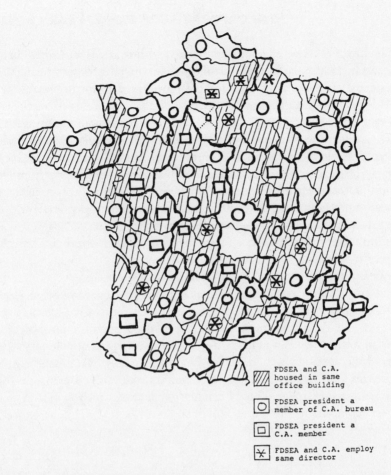

Figure 4.1 Measures of the relationship between the FDSEAs and the Chambers of Agriculture, 1975. (The sources for this figure were two documents obtained in Mont-de-Marsan: "Les Chambres d'agricultures: 1975," Paris: APCA, 1975—this booklet listed the address, membership, bureau membership, and director for each chamber; an untitled FNSEA document listed the address, president, and director of each FDSEA.)

chamber contributed—even more than control of the ADASEA—to the number of administrative personnel at the disposition of the FDSEA elites and thus provided the official union with an extremely important competitive advantage. Whether or not they were formally employed part-time by the FDSEA, nearly all of the chamber personnel—from its director to its cleaning women—performed important tasks for the union on occasion; moreover, in some departments the chamber (and SUAD) staff workers were virtually indistinguishable from those of the union. It was not uncommon for a chamber-paid librarian to be asked to compile a dossier on MODEF activities for use by FDSEA elites during a chamber election campaign, or for a technical counselor employed by SUAD to be asked to drive an FDSEA official to a union rally during such a campaign.[37] Not all chamber personnel were comfortable playing such a dual technical-syndical role, but even those who objected tended to accept it with resignation. As one chamber employee who yearned to be truly "at the service of all the farmers" lamented in an interview: "If I want to work for the chamber, I must also work for the FDSEA . . . the job is an *ensemble*."[38]

The de facto fusion of elites, infrastructure, and personnel almost inevitably led in most departments to improper and even illegal activities. Official evidence of abuses of the chambers by FDSEA elites was presented in a report compiled in 1971 by the *Inspection Général des Finances*. This report, based on a study of the operation of seven chambers, uncovered many "abnormal" or "contestable" aspects of the relationship between the chambers and their respective FDSEAs. Cited specifically in the report were cases in which the interlocking elites of the two organizations channeled "secret subsidies" from a chamber to an FDSEA, for example, by financing with chamber funds most if not all of the cost of newspapers published jointly by the chamber and the FDSEA.[39]

The fate of this particular report is as noteworthy as its contents; it serves as yet another illustration of the preferential treatment generally accorded by the state to the official agricultural union before 1981. Despite the protests of rival unions, the report was never made public; its more essential contents became known only because they were leaked to the press. No effort was made by the state administration or the government to publicize and pursue evidence of the extensive mismanagement of public funds—evidence which could have been highly embarrassing to the official union.[40]

THE REVISION OF REGULATIONS

State action—or inaction—before 1981 also helped the FNSEA to maintain its dominance of the Chambers of Agriculture, the only comanagement institutions the official union gained control of through contested elections rather than state appointments. On several occasions the government altered the regulations for elections to the chambers in a manner seemingly designed to reinforce FNSEA strength. For example, by a decree of 26 September 1969, retired farmers—one of the major constituencies of MODEF—were removed from the college of *chefs d'exploitation* (which has traditionally elected most chamber members—four per electoral district, twelve to twenty in a typical department) and placed in a separate college electing only two chamber members per department. This "reform" reduced the voting power of retired farmers by approximately 71% nationwide: the retired farmers were accorded only one seat per 2,653 voters, while the active farmers were accorded one seat per 722 voters. An immediate result of this measure was the decline of MODEF seats in many of its departmental strongholds; in the case of Landes it produced the defeat of the only MODEF organization that had previously enjoyed a chamber majority. Although it is impossible to prove that the ministry created the retired farmers' college with the intent to combat the increasing influence of MODEF, the inference is certainly plausible (especially in light of some of the facts to be discussed in Chapter 7).[41]

While enacting "reforms" such as that of 1969, the Center-Right government refused to adopt seemingly reasonable regulations which would have weakened the FNSEA's hold on the chambers. For example, the agricultural ministry repeatedly rejected the demand of rival unions for state subsidization of costs incurred during chamber election campaigns, despite the fact that such subsidization had long been given to competitors in elections to the Chambers of Commerce and the Chambers of Industry. In the absence of such subsidization, rival unions were hard-pressed to compete with the FNSEA's departmental branches, most of which benefited not only from larger budgets but also their ability to exploit the resources of the chamber in their campaigns.[42]

State inaction in regard to another issue also served the financial interests of the FNSEA throughout the Center-Right era. Rival union activists repeatedly complained that a number of the Federation's affiliates violated the law by collecting "forced dues," that is, setting up a system whereby friendly officials of cooperatives would automatically deduct from the payments owed to the farmers for the delivery of produce a certain percentage to be forwarded to the FDSEA, normally as a contribution to the *cotisation économique* paid by the FDSEA to the FNSEA's national office. Despite the presence of a good deal of evidence that such practices were indeed widespread in certain areas, state officials refused to investigate. As Chapter 8 will discuss, legal steps to halt this practice would be taken only after Socialists moved into the Ministry of Agriculture in the 1980s.

MONETARY SUBSIDIES

In a special booklet prepared on the occasion of the FNSEA's thirtieth anniversary in 1976, the leaders of the Federation proclaimed: "We want our union to be free, to depend on no one other than the member farmers who comprise it. To finance the union, we have thus chosen a difficult solution: the resources of the union are provided exclusively by the dues of its members."[43] Understandably, the FNSEA was reluctant to publicize the fact that one of the fruits of *concertation* was the union's receipt of monetary subsidies from the state. From the early 1960s onward the FNSEA has received millions of francs per year from various national subsidy programs which, until 1981, provided nary a centime to the rival unions. Throughout the Center-Right era the "nonofficial" unions were systematically excluded from all subsidy programs administered by the "hierarchical-vertical" channel of the governmental system. In some departments, rival unions did succeed (as Part II will illustrate) in gaining a share of the subsidies distributed by the "political-horizontal" channels, that is, the

General Councils.[44] Nevertheless, the amount of subsidization accorded to rival unions was altogether insignificant compared to that received by the FNSEA from two sources: the development program and the *promotion sociale collective* program.

Development Subsidies

As noted earlier, the FNSEA and its affiliates have received a major proportion of the development subsidies distributed at the department level by the administrative councils of the SUADs. In addition, the official union has also enjoyed subsidies allocated at the national level by the directors of the ANDA. In 1979, for example, the FNSEA itself received 1,910,550 francs. The CNJA, charged with the implementation of various development programs for young farmers, received an even greater sum: 4,333,730 francs. The organizational significance of the CNJA subsidy was enormous throughout the 1960s and 1970s. Indeed, Yves Tavernier argued some years ago that the CNJA "only functions at the national and departmental levels thanks to the funds granted by the state." In some years, state subsidies have constituted as much as 92% of the total CNJA budget, with dues accounting for a mere 8%. Development subsidies have also been granted to a host of other organizations under the more-or-less formal control of the FNSEA. One of the best examples of such an organization is the Fédération Nationale des Groupements de Vulgarisation du Progrès Agricole, officially deemed to be a "section" of the FNSEA and headed—as of 1975—by an adjunct secretary-general of the FNSEA; the FNGVPA received 1,172,800 francs from the ANDA in 1974.[45]

Promotion Collective Subsidies

The second major subsidy program from which the FNSEA has benefited is that for *promotion social collective*. This program, one not restricted to agriculture, was initiated by the government in 1959 with the espoused goal of aiding recognized interest groups in their efforts to educate activists who would eventually assume leadership roles and become interlocutors of the state.[46] As FNSEA officials noted in the 1970s, the *promotion collective* subsidy was intended to further the process of *concertation*. Through enabling union leaders to become competent not only in "union techniques" but also in "economic, legal, fiscal and social" matters, this program was to assure that "the union-administration dialogue can build on a base of common vocabulary."[47] Left unstated in FNSEA discussions of this program is that fact that it has also provided the official union with an immense competitive advantage over MODEF and other rival unions.

The funds for *promotion collective* have been distributed in a preferential manner since their inception. Among industrial unions, as shown in the Introduction, the CGT and the CFDT have always received less money in proportion to their membership than have more moderate unions.[48] Among agricultural unions, only the FNSEA and its CNJA affiliate received any *promotion collective* subsidization during the Center-Right era.

The *promotion collective* subsidies granted to the FNSEA and CNJA increased steadily throughout the 1960s. In 1964 the FNSEA received 547,000 francs and the CNJA 750,000 francs—a total of 1,297,000 francs. By 1979 the total exceeded 7 million francs, with the FNSEA and the CNJA receiving approximately 3.5 million apiece. The significance of these figures can be understood by comparing them with the operating budget of the FNSEA's central organization in Paris; in 1970 this budget, composed of the dues of all affiliated organizations, was slightly less than 3 million francs.[49]

Ever since the early 1960s, the *promotion collective* subsidies have enabled the FNSEA to undertake an extensive nationwide program for the *perfectionnement des cadres*, that is, for the education and information of organizational elites and administrative personnel. From 1962 to 1973, 94,206 individuals participated in educational sessions; in 1973 alone, 11,389 individuals participated in sessions lasting an average of several days.[50] These sessions, financed at least 60% by state funds, have varied greatly in their subjects, their participants, and their locales. Sessions have focused on a multitude of subjects, for example, structural reform policy, tax policy, the politics and economics of the European Community and the Common Agricultural Policy, methods for improving productivity, and means of increasing participation in union activity. Some of these sessions—about 4% of the 1973 total—have been national or regional meetings of top-level elites (e.g., FDSEA presidents and administrative directors) initiated and organized by the FNSEA central office. The great majority of sessions, however, have been departmental affairs involving the participation of one or more national FNSEA officials, all of the FDSEA officials, and many of the union's rank and file.[51]

These state-subsidized sessions have served not only to educate and inform the FNSEA's departmental *cadres*, but also to increase the vitality and unity of the union's organization. They have facilitated FDSEA efforts to elicit the participation of members by reimbursing them for travel expenses and providing them with free meals, and they have helped the FNSEA elite maintain contact with the *base* by subsidizing travel from Paris to the localities. Moreover, they have also assisted in the *relance* efforts of weak FDSEAs threatened by rival unions, as funds have been directed toward those departments undergoing intense power struggles. In Landes during the 1960s, for example, extra sessions were held to revivify the FDSEA, and the FNSEA officials whose travel from Paris was covered by a state subsidy stayed after the "education" sessions to organize syndical meetings throughout the department (see Chapter 7).

CONCLUSION

Some of the FNSEA's opponents have charged that the state-supported hegemony enjoyed by the FNSEA during the Center-Right era was reminiscent of the "totalitarianism of the Corporation Paysanne of Vichy."[52] This charge is somewhat misleading, as it fails to acknowledge the fundamental difference between the dynamics of authoritarian corporatism and the dynamics of modern or neocorporatism. In the Vichy corporatist system, the state simply declared that only one "union" had the right to exist. In the neocorporatist system, the state declared that an unlimited number of unions would have an equal right to exist, but treated the official union as "more equal" than the others. Official union hegemony was assured not through a decree, and not primarily through direct repression of rivals, but rather through a more subtle process. According the official union exclusive access to formal councils, privileged informal access to state officials, devolved power to administer important aspects of public policy, favorable reforms of regulations, and substantial monetary subsidies reinforced the FNSEA's hegemony by providing it with enormous competitive advantages vis-à-vis rival unions. Dissident individuals and departmental federations within the FNSEA were often tempted to break with the official union, but few did, for to do so simply meant trying to organize with meager resources against a state-sanctioned machine and—to paraphrase the activist cited earlier—gaining the freedom to speak louder at the expense of not being heard.

If the dynamics of the neocorporatist system differed substantially from those of Vichy's Corporation Paysanne, the modern system did produce a similar outcome. The FNSEA's hegemony of the Center-Right era *was* reminiscent of the Vichy era in that it manifested a successful effort by the state to act as an architect of political order. This is not to say that the FNSEA's organizational strength ever became dependent solely on state supports. The departmental case studies of Part II will show, as the Socialist government was reminded during the winter of 1981–82, that the FNSEA's branches in some regions retained an "independent hegemony" throughout the 1960s and 1970s and that its organization across France was never as much of a state artifact as some of its opponents believed. However, these studies of syndical politics at the grass roots will illustrate that the FNSEA's predominance was "artificial" in some regions and that its nationwide hegemony rested largely—if unevenly and incompletely—on corporatist bases.

II
Syndical Politics and Neocorporatism at the Grass Roots: Three Departmental Case Studies

5

Independent FDSEA Hegemony:
The Case of Aisne

The corporatization of group-state relations in the agricultural sector affected the dynamics of all of the FNSEA's departmental affiliates during the two decades that followed passage of the Pisani Law, but its impact was not equally dramatic throughout France. In most departments the development of the corporatist system made a significant and sometimes vital contribution to the maintenance or even initial achievement of FDSEA hegemony. In such departments, examples of which will be discussed in Chapters 6 and 7, the hegemony enjoyed by the FDSEA from the early 1960s onward was more or less dependent on the organizational supports provided by the corporatist system. In some other departments, in contrast, the benefits of official unionism simply served to strengthen—at some cost—FDSEAs that may be said to have maintained an *independent* hegemony.

For a variety of socioeconomic and political reasons, the most notable cases of independent FDSEA hegemony are to be found in the departments of the North and the Parisian Basin. Here the policies or "purposive incentives" of the FNSEA have possessed a relatively broad appeal, as the region is heavily populated by *chefs d'exploitation* with relatively large and prosperous farms who specialize in state-favored grain (especially wheat) and sugar beet production and tend to be partisans of the Center-Right. In addition, the services or material incentives offered by the FNSEA's affiliates in this region have in general been incomparably attractive. The large budgets of these wealthy FDSEAs have facilitated the development of a wide range of union services capable of inducing the membership of virtually all farmers, including those indifferent to or even—in extreme cases—hostile to the policies pursued by the FNSEA/FDSEA.

Of the independently hegemonic FDSEAs, that of Aisne has probably been the most celebrated. Few if any other departmental organizations can claim to have achieved so much presence and exerted so much influence at the national

Figure 5.1 Aisne and the Picardie region.

level. Two of the seven FNSEA presidents to date have been representatives of the FDSEA—formally known as the USAA (Union des Syndicats Agricoles de l'Aisne)—of Aisne: René Blondelle (1950–54) and Gérard de Caffarelli (1963–71), both of whom served during crucial eras in the development of the FNSEA. While playing a prominent role at the national level, the USAA has also maintained a position of immense and virtually uncontested syndical power within its department; indeed, it has stood as an exemplar of syndical unity. Throughout the 1950s the USAA received nearly 100% of the votes in elections to the Chamber of Agriculture and established a membership density of 80–90%. Since the early 1960s the USAA's candidates for election to the chamber have been challenged on only a few occasions and never received less than 70% of the vote in any district; meanwhile, the USAA's membership density has gradually risen above the 90% level.

Judging from the continuity of these electoral results and membership statistics, the impact of corporatization on the status of the USAA would not seem to have been terribly significant. But the statistics are deceptive. While the development of corporatism in French agriculture may have had a less dramatic impact in Aisne than in many other departments, it nevertheless altered the functions and the status of the FNSEA's departmental affiliate. The very independence of the USAA's hegemony enabled its elites to exploit to the maximum degree the organizational opportunities afforded by the corporatist

Figure 5.2 The cantons of Aisne.

system. Performance of the official union role did, in some ways, render more fragile the USAA's firm hold on the farmers of the department. It implicated the USAA in the programs of the state and thus stimulated unprecedented opposition to the union; for many farmers, the USAA became less an instrument of defense against the state than an adjunct bureaucracy of the state. At the same time, however, it expanded the already impressive resources of the union and increased its influence over the day-to-day life of farmers in what is locally referred to as this "sugar beet-shaped" department; as a result, it provided even dissident farmers with powerful incentives to remain on good terms with the USAA elites and thus stifled the emergence of rival union movements.

The first section of this chapter will discuss the bases of the USAA's independent hegemony. The second section will deal with the adaptation of the USAA to the corporatist system from the early 1960s onward, and the third section will discuss the tensions that arose within the organization during the Center-Right era.

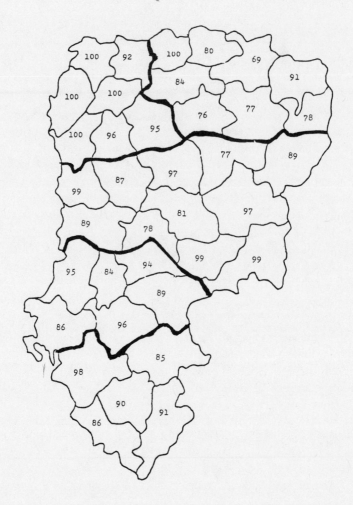

Figure 5.3 USAA membership density by canton, 1974. Membership density (members/farms larger than 2 hectares) for the entire department = 93%.

THE BASES OF THE USAA'S INDEPENDENT HEGEMONY

PURPOSIVE INCENTIVES

There is no need to provide a detailed examination of the USAA's purposive incentives, for in general they have diverged very little from those described in Part I. Throughout the 1950s, with Blondelle for a time serving as president of both the FNSEA and the USAA, the departmental program was identical to that of the national federation. In Laon (the *chef-lieu* of Aisne) as in Paris the union program stressed the identity of all farmers' interests, the consequent importance of price policy for the prosperity of the entire profession, and the strategic necessity for agriculture to act in corporative unity. Appeals for peasant unity in Aisne focused primarily on the common interest of large and small farmers in the price of one product that nearly all of them produced: wheat. Since the early decades of the twentieth century, "the defense of the wheat market [had] always been . . . the major concern" of farmers' unions in the department.[1] An insufficient price for wheat, asserted Blondelle, would mean nothing less than "the death" of agriculture in Aisne. A low price would impede the modernization efforts of all farmers, he argued, producing the "precipitous disappearance of farms between 20 and 30 hectares" and "the acceleration of the rural exodus." In short, it would spell "the end of our dreams of the amelioration of rural living and the transformation of our conditions of work."[2] For Blondelle and his Aisne *équipe*, the only means of averting such an outcome was the unity of the profession against a hostile state dominated by the interests of industrial employers and workers. "Let us be white or red if that is our pleasure," Blondelle once proclaimed to an USAA audience, "but from the professional point of view, let us be a bloc without fissure, a bloc which knows how to resist all violent and insidious assaults; a bloc which will be capable also of attacking to produce the economic and financial pressures necessary for our well being. It is a condition of life or death for our agriculture."[3]

From the early 1960s onward, with the FNSEA's rejection of Blondelle's "prices first" policy and the adoption of a program encouraging reform through state intervention, the USAA's program has diverged somewhat—at least in emphasis—from that of the national organization. In principle, the USAA elites have supported the multifaceted agricultural policy geared to the disparate interests of the "three categories" of farmers discussed in Part I. However, their expression of this program has reflected a continued attachment to some of the traditional liberal notions of Blondelle. While the FNSEA has stressed the necessity to obtain an "equitable income" and "personal and professional security" for the maximum numbers of farmers, the USAA has stressed the necessity to promote individual "freedom."[4] As the USAA president declared in a 1973 report, "Our action is totally oriented toward the defense of free enterprise of a human dimension and the furtherance of personal responsibility."[5] The USAA has thus reacted negatively to most FNSEA proposals to aid small farmers through imposing limits on "free enterprise" and "responsibility." For example, in 1975 the USAA staunchly opposed a Breton scheme to provide small farmers with privileged access to credit and land; and in an extensive critique circulated to all of the FDSEAs, the Aisne union argued that "parity" could only be expected for "farms whose structure permits the full, rational employment of men and material."[6] Elaborating on this principle, the USAA president of the mid-1970s commented in an interview:

> We view the farmers as *chefs d'enterprise*, as businessmen with the responsibility to manage their farms as well as possible. We simply cannot demand, here or at the national level, a good income for a farmer who runs his farm poorly—who spends his time hunting or complaining instead of working. Some things such as selective aids for the improvement of the farm can be demanded of the state, but the essential welfare of the profession must depend on the farmers themselves.[7]

Along the same lines, the USAA has defended the interests of the prosperous "category 1" farmers (see Chapter 3) much more vigorously than has the FNSEA. On the issue of prices, first of all, the USAA has stridently opposed even slight alterations of the hierarchy of prices which would decrease state support for products such as wheat and sugar beets—the basis of Aisne's wealth—and increase the support of products such as beef and milk. The existing system has been defended on a variety of grounds. First, the USAA has argued that the large farmers *need* heavy support because their prosperity is really quite tenuous; although they are relatively wealthy, their high level of productivity has been obtained only through "heavy investment efforts which render their status fragile and very dependent on their creditors."[8] Second, it has argued that the support of category 1 farmers is in the national interest; to claims that wheat and beet supports represent "state aid" for the wealthy, it has responded that "the support of agricultural prices is in fact an exclusively economic measure, indispensable to the security of the consumer as well as the producer."[9] Third, the union has contended that the continued prosperity of category 1 farmers is simply fair: "profit is the just price paid by society to the creativity and progress furnished by the dynamism of the free entrepreneurs that we are."[10]

The USAA has also fought, albeit more ambivalently, for the defense of category 1 farmers on a second vital issue: state intervention through SAFER for the control of the land market. Not until 1974 was the SAFER for the Picardie region established. It would be unfair to portray the USAA as having been the sole cause of this delay, or as having been totally opposed to the purposes of the SAFER. As USAA officials have claimed, the delay could largely be attributed to the anti-SAFER sympathies of neighboring departments.[11] The USAA officially favored the principle behind the SAFER and, before 1974, organized certain "syndical actions" to protect small farmers from losing land to *les gros*; the union paper denounced the selfish and "savage liberalism" of some large farmers.[12] Nevertheless, the USAA never gave the SAFER the enthusiastic and unequivocal support that it received in most other regions. Several members of the union elite admitted in interviews that the passionate opposition of some "savage liberals" forced them to limit their push for the SAFER.[13] This ambivalence is clearly visible in the USAA's pre-1974 public statements on SAFER policy. At the 1971 USAA general assembly, for example, the secretary-general noted that the "presence of a SAFER would have positive aspects" but that, "on the other hand, it could also have negative effects in the sense that it would limit certain individual initiatives."[14] Although the USAA's support of structural reform policy has managed to alienate many of the department's "savage liberals", its policies have thus been significantly more liberal than those of the FNSEA.

Especially given the liberal tone with which it has been articulated by the USAA, it is readily understandable that the FNSEA program of the past two decades has proven to be more popular in Aisne than in the great majority of departments. Few other departments have been as well served by the hierarchy of prices maintained by FNSEA *concertation*. Aisne has stood first among all departments in the production of the two products that have been most generously supported by the state: wheat and sugar beets.[15] In contrast, only about one third of agricultural income in Aisne has been derived from the products that have been least supported: animal products, especially beef and milk.[16] Furthermore, few other departments have been less adversely affected by the "moderation" of the FNSEA's structural reform demands. The farm structures in Aisne are generally among the largest and most efficient in all of France. As Table 5.1 indicates, as of 1967 more than 56% of all farms in Aisne were larger than 20 hectares; in comparison, only 12% of Landes farms, 18% of Corrèze farms, and 26% of all French farms were larger than 20 hectares.

Table 5.1. Farm Structures in Aisne, Corrèze, Landes, and France

	Total Farms	Hectares in 1967					
		1–5	5–10	10–20	20–50	50–100	100+
Aisne	11,579	20.2%	7.9%	15.2%	29.5%	14.3%	12.9%
Corrèze	18,327	18.3%	29.8%	33.8%	16.3%	1.5%	0.2%
Landes	18,234	25.0%	31.2%	31.6%	11.0%	0.8%	0.4%
France	1,689,927	29.6%	18.2%	24.4%	22.0%	5.0%	1.4%

Source: Statistique agricole (Paris: Ministère de l'Agriculture, Mars 1969), tableau VII.

While the socioeconomic structure of Aisne agriculture helps to explain the success of the department's FNSEA affiliate, so does the political coloration of the department's *chefs d'exploitation*. This fact may seem surprising to one familiar only with the global electoral history of the department. Throughout the postwar era, as Juan Linz has noted, Aisne has been a Communist stronghold[17] among the departments that are not "almost completely industrial" (as of 1968 the percentage of the department's population actively engaged in agriculture was only 21.9%, approximately the average for France as a whole—20.5%).[18] However, as Linz points out, it is not the *chefs d'exploitation* (those eligible for USAA membership) within the agricultural population that have provided this heavy Communist vote but rather the *salariés* (farm workers); this latter group, organized by branches of the industrial unions, comprises more than 35% of the Aisne agricultural population (more than twice the departmental average in France).[19] An examination of the 1962 legislative election results lends support to the Linz contention. In the five Aisne cantons with the most *salariés* (an average of 7.56 per farm) the combined Left received 50.4% of the vote compared with 23.5% of the vote for the combined Right; in contrast, the results in the five cantons with the fewest *salariés* (an average of 0.61 per farm) were nearly the opposite—only 23.5% of the vote in these cantons went to the combined Left while 47% went to the Right.[20]

According to several of the union activists interviewed in Aisne, the presence of this large farm worker population has provided a social as well as political reason for small farmers to join the USAA. To many small farmers, association with the USAA has served as an affirmation of social status. "The small farmer who joins the USAA views himself as a free *chef d'enterprise*; to him the opponents of the USAA—both the CGT and MODEF—are agents of the proletarian farm workers, a group he strenuously tries to avoid."[21] Along the same lines, one frustrated socialist commented,

> My socialist friends in Paris think the small farmers should naturally reject the FNSEA and join the rival unions of the Left such as MODEF . . . they think the small farmer should be easily won away from the USAA by pointing to their "objective exploitation"—their low incomes, their indebtedness, their precarious economic position. But this is just not the reality that one finds here. In Aisne, at least, many small farmers are primarily concerned with maintaining their social distance from the farm workers, who are viewed as the lowest class.[22]

Nevertheless, there *are* small farmers who have been hostile to the programs of the USAA/FNSEA. It is hardly surprising that many *petits* would feel uncomfortable having their interests "represented" by an elite which, in the marvelous metaphor of one union member, "is as different from them as a tractor is from a pig."[23] For the fifteen members of the 1975 USAA bureau the average farm size was more than 174 hectares—nearly *four* times the average for all farms in the department. While more than 70% of the department's farms were smaller than 50 hectares, less than 15%—only two—of the bureau's members held farms this small. Moreover, one of these two men was hardly a typical *petit*: Gérard de Caffarelli, a man of some inherited wealth, a Parisian-educated agricultural engineer, former president of the FNSEA, current vice-president of the APCA, and member of the EEC's Economic and Social Committee.[24]

The political as well as socioeconomic composition of the bureau has differed greatly from that of the farm population. According to a variety of union activists, only a few of the most "moderate" Socialists have ever been accepted as members of the USAA bureau. These sources—and some of the bureau members themselves—said in the mid-1970s that it was extremely unlikely that any of the present bureau members had voted for Mitterrand in the 1974 presidential election. Virtually all of the bureau members of widely recognized partisan leanings were either Center-Democrats or Gaullists.[25]

In short, then, the hegemony of the USAA can be explained in part by the attractiveness of the union's purposive incentives. Many farmers in Aisne could be expected to support the USAA/FNSEA for socioeconomic and/or political reasons—but such reasons would hardly suffice for 90% of them, the number which regularly pay union dues. To a great extent, the success of the USAA must be explained by a consideration of the factors to which the discussion now turns.

MATERIAL INCENTIVES

Not even the most committed members of the USAA elite attempt to argue that more than a fraction of the farmers affiliated with the union are actively concerned with its policies and its pressure group activities. Moreover, many USAA activists candidly admit that a significant number of the farmers who regularly pay union dues are in fact hostile toward at least some aspects of USAA/FNSEA policy and favor programs of the sort articulated by rival unions such as MODEF and especially FFA. Several sources estimated that as many as 30–40% of the union's members could be classified as being consistently dissident.[26]

What then has permitted the USAA to obtain the membership of many apathetic farmers and even some dissidents who, in other departments, might have chosen to join rival unions? Judging from observations, interviews, and a study of union documents the principal explanation is quite indisputable: the USAA's ability to offer prospective members an extensive array of highly attractive material services/incentives.

Coordination, If Not Unity

While the organizational mechanisms for the provision of USAA services have for the most part been developed since the origin of the FNSEA, the principles underlying the structure of these services were conceived even earlier, before World War II. It is to René Blondelle, who assumed the USAA presidency in 1938, that most USAA elites attribute the conception of these principles. Blondelle was first elected as president at a time when the USAA was suffering from the effects of both severe political tension and economic crisis. The political divisions prevalent throughout the nation were manifested in Aisne by repeated CGT-led strikes of farm workers and Right-wing demonstration such as one of 1939 at which Henri Dorgères managed to attract 2,000 farmers. Membership in the USAA fell as efforts were made to employ the union as a vehicle for the expression of conflicting political protests.[27] The crises of the agricultural economy also contributed to dwindling union membership; many farmers stopped paying dues yet continued to demand the union's services. The USAA budget was thus under severe pressure, with the union collecting in 1938 only 58% of the dues it had projected for the year.[28]

Upon assuming the office of the presidency Blondelle immediately began to pursue an organizational strategy which, he proclaimed, would allow the USAA to "coordinate, if not unify the peasants." He argued that the "family quarrels" of the USAA could be solved through the deemphasis of diverse political activity combined with an increased emphasis on the development of union services. "The renovated union" would prosper, he contended, only if it increased its efforts to "render to its members tangible, daily services."

I have thought for a long time that an organization like the USAA can only live energetically, properly and easily if it recognizes the necessity to descend from discussions in the high spheres of agricultural and economic theory, to concern itself with the immediate and *terre à terre* interests of the farmers. It is necessary to realize that the farmer . . . lends only a distracted ear to his representatives who fulminate *à juste titre* against this or that disposition, and that he doesn't judge their activity there. To the contrary, it is in the life of each day—in the price of his milk, in the conditions of purchase and the reception of his beets, in the defense of his finances— that he looks for the support of his organization and that he feels the most need of its intervention.[29]

To satisfy the various daily needs of farmers in Aisne and thereby revivify the union, Blondelle and his associates commenced an effort to (1) restructure and centralize the union organization; (2) expand and improve the services offered to union members; and (3) maximize the organizational utility of these services by rendering them unavailable to nonmembers and equally available to all members throughout the department.

The first step taken in the renovation drive was to revise the structure of the union's administrative council so as to establish the USAA as the "centralizing organ of all agricultural activities" in the department and to facilitate the efforts of union leaders to respond to the needs of specific groups within the farming community. The administrators of the USAA were divided into six commissions, each consisting of five to twelve members charged with reporting on the current state of affairs in their assigned areas and suggesting union activities appropriate to these areas.

With this new structure in place, a variety of service innovations and improvements were made. First, an office of agricultural accounting and statistics was established for the region of Laon, modeled after the renowned *office de comptabilité* of Soissons; these offices were among the first of their kind established in France and were to serve, decades later, as an inspiration for the national development of *centres de gestion*. Second, a major effort was undertaken to improve the quality and attractiveness of the union's newspaper, *Le Bulletin*. To make it "more lively" and "both the guide and recreation of the farmer" a number of new features were introduced and union members were offered free announcement/want-ad space in each issue. Next, the USAA commenced negotiations with various tradesmen to arrange cut-rate prices for union members on a host of goods. Finally, plans were made—though not fully implemented until after the war—to hire additional staff personnel who could provide a myriad of personal services to members throughout the department.[30]

Blondelle appreciated the fact that these new services would be of limited utility if not properly monitored. "It is necessary," he argued, "for the union to be at the total disposition of its members; but it is also necessary to prevent the use of its services by free-riders (*resquilleurs*)." At once he ordered that the *Bulletin* no longer be sent to those who had failed to pay their yearly dues. More important, he rationalized the traditional informal and rather chaotic "system" of dues collection. Members of each local union were to be issued a common USAA union card which would signify for one year their good standing and thus their eligibility for the receipt of services. This card system, noted Blondelle, would allow USAA administrators to keep an accurate record of payments and also "permit the refusal of all aid and even all information to a farmer who is not a member."[31]

To finance the new services and make them available to all members throughout the department, the USAA's collection of dues and administration of services were centralized in Laon. Previously, dues were paid to local unions according to locally established scales and services were provided by local unions only to the degree that their own resources would permit. This system served, among other things, to compound the union's difficulties in recruiting small farmers from the relatively poor *élevage* region of Thiérache (in the northeast corner of the department around Vervins). The Thiérachiens paid dues that were meager compared to those of the rich wheat belt (the Soissonais) and could thus sustain only a skeletal administrative structure which was hard pressed to provide any services; the local unions here barely functioned and the small *herbagers* constantly complained that no one cared about them in Laon. Under the new financial system all cantons were to pay dues on an equal progressive scale (with payments hinging on land area held) and the bulk of the money collected by each locality was to be transmitted to the *centrale* in Laon; departmentwide services would then be created and services would be administered in a redistributive fashion.[32]

Vichy and Its Legacy

The renovation of the USAA had only just begun when it was interrupted by the outbreak of the war. This is not the place to recount the full story of the Vichy period.[33] However, the impact of the Corporation Paysanne on the USAA and the organizational legacy of this period both deserve some mention.

Neither the USAA's elite nor its organization was seriously disrupted by the advent of the Vichy regime. Blondelle and most of his associates subscribed passionately to the corporative ideals of the Corporation Paysanne and greeted its institution as "a revolutionary measure" which would enable the agricultural profession to "take possession of its métier" without being "in the hands of the state." However, they eventually cooled on the Corporation as it became clear that it was to function more as an instrument of state *dirigisme*—guided by the occupying German forces—than of professional self-governance. Several USAA officials, including the secretary-general, were killed in the Resistance. Although Blondelle himself served as the regional *syndic* of the Corporation and was branded by some (especially those on the Left) outside of Aisne as a collaborator, he did little to imperil his reputation among the farmers of this department. His claim to have underestimated production so as to limit *impositions* and to have protected young farmers from conscription were credible enough to assure his overwhelming reelection as president of the USAA in the postwar era.[34]

The organizational impact of the Corporation was far from great. Indeed, "the new organization was easily adopted: it was sufficient to change the name of that which existed." Most changes introduced during this period were of only temporary importance. For example, while membership in the Union Régionale Corporative du Départment de l'Aisne was formally voluntary, it was obligatory for all "who wished to benefit from [any] agricultural organization"; thus the USAA as Corporation could claim the membership of the "quasi totality" of departmental farmers as well as 15,000 farm workers. Many of these obligatory members left the organization in the first years after the fall of Vichy while the farm workers joined their own separate unions.[35]

The Vichy period did, however, have some lasting influence on the development of the USAA—influence which led Blondelle to state in 1945 that the Corporation had "continued, improved and amplified the work of Union des Syndicats."[36] The effect of services developed during this period seemed to substantiate the validity of Blondelle's argument as to the utility of material incentives; educational, technical, and economic services attracted to the USAA fold many farmers who had previously refused to join the union. Further, the decentralized administrative structure of the Corporation proved to be extremely effective and was thus retained when the USAA was rebuilt during the postwar era. It was apparent that the appointment of *syndics* for each canton facilitated organizational efforts in regions which were previously poorly mobilized (e.g., Thierache), gave the union a "daily presence" that it had lacked before and provided the *centrale* in Laon with transmission belts capable of illuminating local problems to be handled and of providing union elites with information that improved decision making at the center.[37]

Rebuilding the USAA

The effort to rebuild the USAA into a service-oriented union which could "coordinate if not unify" all farmers began immediately after the union was legally reconstituted in 1945. The USAA charter drafted in May 1945 was heavily influenced by the principle that Blondelle had first proclaimed in 1938: "The union must not only be an *organisation revendicative*, but equally an *organisation constructive*."[38] Most of the charter's sixth article, devoted to the "object of the union," consisted of a long list of services intended to advance the "economic, social and general professional interests" of union members.[39]

To coordinate these services, the USAA elite organized more than thirty special sections or committees within the first few years after 1945.[40] The organization of committees was, of course, much easier than the time-consuming and expensive task of implementing the various services. A number of factors hindered the implementation effort in the first few years following the USAA's rebirth. First, the union was forced to operate with a limited and physically disjointed infrastructure. The union's old office building had been destroyed by the heavy bombing of Laon's lower city in April 1944; union offices and officials were thus scattered throughout the city in temporary locations until a new union building was completed in 1955.[41] Second, the expansion of union service activities entailed the hiring and training of new staff personnel. Third, as one would surmise from Part I, the attentions of many USAA leaders—and especially of the key leader, René Blondelle—were focused largely on Paris and the attempts to establish the FNSEA as well as other agricultural organizations.[42]

As was the case elsewhere in France, however, these organizational problems were offset during the Liberation period by the state's devolution to the USAA of the power to ration many scarce materials vital to the operation of the farm. Aided by two staff assistants provided by the state, USAA appointees controlled the rationing process in the *chef-lieu* in collaboration with local union officials at the cantonal level. It was the USAA's bureaucracy that controlled the distribution of "string, tractors, boots, shoes, machines, tires, bicycles, fertilizer" and other items allotted to the department by the state administration.[43] Given this enormously important power, the USAA had little difficulty in obtaining the membership of almost all farmers in the department; in 1947 an unprecedented and as yet unsurpassed 95.4% of all Aisne farmers paid USAA dues.[44]

When the USAA lost its rationing power, however, the union's membership declined precipitously. By 1953 the USAA could claim the membership of only 72% of Aisne farmers and a continued decline—as occurred elsewhere—appeared likely. Writing at this time, the USAA's official historian lamented that there seemed to be "less faith, less enthusiasm in syndical action" than before and that many cantons were witnessing a "steady diminution" of membership.[45] The dwindling of the USAA's ranks continued in 1954 as the union's membership density reached its postwar nadir, falling below 70%. The budget also registered an all-time low, falling to 359,000 francs from a figure of nearly 500,000 only a few years before.

The next year marked the reversal of the trend toward the diminution of USAA membership. In 1955 the union once again enrolled more than 70% of the department's farmers. A few years later USAA membership hit the 80% level; by the mid-1960s it had reached 90% and by 1974 it had achieved a level of 93%.[46] What factors worked to generate this decisive alteration of the membership trend?

One factor that contributed to syndical revivals in some departments was clearly *not* of importance in the case of Aisne: an increase in the essential structure or intensity of mass participation at the base. Unlike the FDSEA of Finistère studied by Suzanne Berger, the USAA of the 1950s and 1960s did not move toward the encouragement of an *active* membership, one which could control the elites through direct action.[47] The USAA's policies changed only slightly, its elite was not drastically "renewed," and its members continued to play only a *passive* role in the organization. The typical USAA member attended few if any meetings even at the local level. Delegates from the localities to the departmental general assembly exerted little, if any, influence over the composition of the USAA's bureau. Its members were not really elected but rather coopted by the incumbents. Furthermore, USAA presidents were endowed with their "sovereign power" by the general assembly but were invariably hand-picked by their predecessors. This system of oligarchic "indirect democracy" continues to function today and remains predicated on the assumption of a passive membership.[48]

The Service System: Structure and Dynamics

The pivotal pre-1955 period did not, therefore, initiate an expansion of mass participation or a decentralization of union power. What it *did* initiate was a trend toward the expansion and decentralization of *union services*. The farmers of Aisne have been brought into and kept within the union fold through the USAA's provision of manifold services which are vital to the professional life of the farmers and—especially since the early 1960s—its control of many important aspects of departmental policy.

Ironically, the establishment of this "service machine" which Blondelle had conceived in principle began at a time when Blondelle himself was turning away from USAA activity and devoting most of his energies to organizational affairs at the national level. Although he spent less and less time in Laon after resigning the USAA presidency in 1955, Blondelle did continue to have a tremendous indirect influence over USAA affairs. He selected his leading successors on the bureau, President Jacques Thuet and a young secretary-general named Gérard de Caffarelli. And earlier, in 1953, he had chosen the young (thirty-three-year-old) man who would serve for more than two decades as USAA director: Jean-Pierre Prévot. Dynamic and industrious, Prévot had been educated in both the technical and organizational-political aspects of agricultural affairs; he held a diploma as an agricultural engineer and had served from 1949–54 as secretary-general of the CGA's national youth affiliate (the predecessor of the CNJA). More than once during the 1950s Prévot was asked to move to Paris to become the director of the FNSEA; each time he refused, preferring to remain in Laon where he was in charge of structuring and coordinating the most sophisticated departmental farmers' union in all of France—one which an Aisne prefect would refer to in the 1960s as "the strongest organization I have ever seen, with the possible exception of the Communist party." Most of the union elites today credit Prévot above all others with the development of this organization according to Blondelle's design.[49]

In 1954 Prévot and the elected USAA officials commenced a concerted effort aimed at the *expansion* and *decentralization* of the union's organizational network. Expansion was, in the words of Prévot, first and foremost a matter of increasing the budget, that is, of "exploiting the department's wealth for organizational purposes." From the mid-1950s onward, therefore, USAA dues were steadily increased and the financial burden was shifted more onto the backs of the larger farmers. For example, in 1948, according to the union's complex dues scale, a farmer with only 20 hectares was required to pay 9 francs while a farmer with 300 hectares was required to pay 115; by 1972 the dues for the same small farmer had risen to 56 francs, an increase of 520%, but the dues for the large farmer had risen by almost 800%, to 1,020 francs.[50]

A steadily increasing progressive dues scale in Aisne more than offset the impact of a declining farm population and translated into enormous budgetary growth. The USAA lost more than 1,000 members between 1953 and 1974, with its total membership falling from 9,313 to 8,031. Yet between 1955 and 1974 the union's budget increased by more than 700%, from 360,000 francs to 3,034,000 francs; allowing for inflation, the union's real budgetary growth was thus more than 200%. The enormity of the USAA's budget can perhaps be best appreciated through comparison with that of Corrèze: the 1974 general budget of the USAA was more than *twelve* times larger than that of the FDSEA in Corrèze—a department with a larger farm population.[51]

This budgetary expansion has allowed for a commensurate improvement and expansion of USAA services. Since 1954 the USAA has improved its programs for the provision of legal counsel, education, and information pertaining to *habitat rural* and all of the various types of production; moreover, it has added programs pertaining to such matters as group agriculture, the TVA (Value-added tax) and the selection and use of equipment.[52] What really sets Aisne apart from other departments, however, is the degree to which it has expanded the personnel who attend to these programs in Laon and throughout the rest of the department.

Already in 1954 the USAA employed far more salaried staff personnel than most other FDSEAs of that period—or even today. At the time that Prévot was first appointed director the USAA employed thirty full-time or part-time personnel: a legal advisor holding the same advanced degree as the director, about ten specially trained counselors to assist in the activities of the union's social and economic-product sections, more than a dozen part-time counselor-organizers assigned to specific localities, and a number of secretaries working in Laon and several local offices. Meanwhile, in Corrèze the director was the *only* salaried staff worker for the FDSEA! This personnel gap became even greater over the next two decades. While the number of USAA employees had risen to approximately 103 by the mid-1970s, the Corrèze FDSEA staff had also increased . . . to 3.[53] It is little wonder that the FDSEA officials in Corrèze speak in awe of their counterparts to the north. As I was leaving Tulle in 1975 to commence my research in Aisne, the Corrèze FDSEA director made this parting comment: "You will find the riches of Aisne make for a totally different kind of union; our organization is a bicycle—theirs is a Citroën."[54]

While the USAA's organizational expansion proceeded apace, so did its decentralization. Responding to Blondelle's exhortation to "concern itself with the immediate and *terre à terre* interests of the farmers, to enter resolutely into details," the USAA elite established a network of *secrétaires agents techniques de canton*, commonly referred to as cantonal secretaries. Prévot hired approximately a dozen cantonal secretaries in 1954. By 1962, USAA members in all of the department's thirty-seven cantons had access to a secretary: twenty-five were employed full-time by the union, with some serving more than one of the cantons near the central headquarters in Laon. By 1975 several more secretaries had been added, increasing the "secretary corps" to twenty-eight.[55]

Each cantonal secretary serves four basic functions for the USAA. First, he acts as a transmission belt between the center and periphery of the department, keeping the elites of the *centrale* informed on matters of concern to the rank and file. Second, he serves as the administrative secretary for both the cantonal USAA union and the cantonal branch of the Cercle des Jeunes Agriculteurs. Third, the secretary plays a major role in the "animation of union life." Each secretary is charged with a myriad of "animation" duties such as holding information and education sessions on a great variety of issues at localities throughout the canton, organizing the cantonal union's yearly general assembly and the periodic meetings of the cantonal elite, forming commissions to study local problems, acting as a liaison between the local union and other local organizations (this can entail attending several different meetings in a single day), and collecting dues from all individuals who request union services.[56]

The fourth and perhaps the most important function of the cantonal secretary is *promotion individuelle*, that is, the rendering of personal services to members.[57] According to the USAA's activists, it is this function of the secretary that has been the chief factor enabling the union to obtain and retain members. In the words of one cantonal secretary, "Very few farmers are committed enough to the syndical ideal to pay dues if they receive nothing but a newspaper and a few pretty speeches in return; most have a *syndicat-boutique* mentality—they expect some immediate, material benefits from the union, and my job is to provide these benefits."[58]

The typical cantonal secretary is available one or two days a week *en permanence* at an office in his canton. Except for the one or two days per month when he travels to Laon for information and training sessions, the remainder of his time is devoted to calling on farmers who have requested assistance. A secretary generally visits from five to ten farms a day, stopping at each one for an informal chat, a *pastis* or a glass of wine, perhaps lunch, and—only after the obligatory fraternizing has been completed—a serious discussion of whatever problem needs to be dealt with at the moment.[59] As several secretaries joked, the ability to drink six or seven *pastis* a day—sometimes several before 10 A.M.—and still function properly is one of the more important capacities required of a good cantonal secretary.[60]

Aside from serving as a welcome drinking companion and source of local gossip, the cantonal secretary is valued by farmers for the almost infinite variety of services he can provide. These fall into two general categories. First, the secretary serves as the members' chief point of access to the administrative services of the USAA. It is to the cantonal secretary, not to the *centrale* in Laon, that the farmer appeals for information on everything from the laws regarding the construction of farm buildings to the availability of land for purchase through SAFER or the market. Second, the cantonal secretary serves as the farmers' agent in dealing with the vast and—to the typical farmer—wholly incomprehensible agricultural bureaucracy. It is the cantonal secretary who not only provides the forms required for subsidies, but also delivers the completed forms to the appropriate office. It is also usually the secretary who acts when a subsidy seems to be blocked in the bureaucratic machinery; he telephones the appropriate official or even calls on him personally—with his client in tow—to obtain results. This paralegal or agent function of the secretary is invaluable to the many diffident farmers unwilling or unable to face the bureaucracy alone.[61]

Along with these services, the cantonal secretary is also frequently called upon for help with a host of personal matters unrelated to agriculture. When asked what sort of problems they had handled for union members, all of the secretaries gave essentially the same response: "Everything . . . absolutely everything." Each secretary has his own endless supply of anecdotes to substantiate this claim. Cantonal secretaries have dealt with pleas for help with every problem, from fixing a broken gate to preventing a son from being drafted into the army.[62]

With its network of cantonal secretaries, the USAA is able to offer members material incentives unmatched by virtually all other departments, even those equally wealthy neighboring departments of the North and Parisian Basin. The USAA proudly proclaims in one of its official brochures: the "*secrétaires de canton* have, to our knowledge, no equivalent in any other department."[63] The closest thing to cantonal secretaries found in the neighboring departments are the regional (or *arrondissement*) secretaries employed in the Somme.[64] In terms of the delivery of services, the cantonal secretaries are superior even to these personnel in at least three respects: proximity, familiarity, and availability.

Sheer *proximity* is a definite attraction for union members. Several secretaries commented in interviews: "For a small farmer, Laon may as well be on the moon—even a trip to a nearby town to visit a regional office is considered to be a great burden"; "a trip of even a few kilometers, requiring preparation, travel, and waiting in a strange office" seems to many farmers to be more trouble than it is worth; "any time away from the farm is considered so much lost time for a small farmer—for our services to be effective, *we* have to be willing to assume the 'lost time' of travel."[65] The *familiarity* of the cantonal secretaries is also an important aspect of their attractiveness. "The farmers I deal with," commented one secretary, "are positively afraid to bring their problems to someone they don't know; with me they feel at ease—that's a large part of my value to them."[66] Another secretary noted, "Most of the farmers are terrified to speak to someone they don't know, a bureaucrat in an unfamiliar office; what they want is human contact, contact with someone they trust and feel comfortable with—that's the sort of contact only a cantonal secretary can provide."[67]

Availability is the third and perhaps most important quality of the cantonal secretary. No counselor assigned to cover a large section of a department could be expected to prove as available to each of his "clients" as a cantonal secretary. Of course, as the director of the Somme FDSEA stated in an interview, regional secretaries working in cooperation with devoted local union presidents could conceivably match the quality of services provided by the USAA's network of secretaries. To the Somme director the USAA's system appeared "top-heavy," "overly costly," and even "counterproductive," since it assigned to the cantonal secretaries "many of the duties properly performed by a local union president."[68] Such an argument doubtless carries some weight, as some USAA officials admit.[69] However, as has been mentioned earlier, the central concern of the USAA has never been to maximize "participation" or the "active commitment" of its rank and file, but rather to maximize the mobilization of at least passive support for the union throughout the department.

It is important to note that the network of cantonal secretaries does more than make USAA membership seem to be a bargain for most farmers. It also facilitates the USAA's efforts to project an image with appeal for the smaller farmers of the department. While the union's policies are largely tailored to suit the *gros* and most of its elites (including local presidents) tend to be large farmers, its cantonal secretaries are generally hired for their ability to achieve rapport with the *petits* and to deal with their problems; many of the men selected as secretaries are in fact former small farmers from the region which they serve.[70] An example of the degree to which the cantonal secretaries serve to improve the "public face" of the USAA was observed by the author on a day-long visit to one of the cantons in Soissonnais, a large wheat-farming region in the heart of Aisne. Here the local president was the prosperous owner of a 310-hectare farm operated by a *contremaître* and ten *salariés*. Though judged by neighboring small farmers to be an "honest man" with some concern for their problems, his socioeconomic status made him appear to be almost a "different species" and his behavior manifested an upper-class consciousness which alienated even some of the more deferential small farmers of the canton. In contrast, they found the cantonal secretary (a former small farmer) to be amiable, unassuming, and what Americans would term "a regular guy."[71] As a result, most of the union-membership contact in the canton was left to the secretary. One top USAA official categorized the situation this way: "the cantonal secretary *is* the USAA to the *petits* of the canton; thus the president—selected by the central office for his technical expertise—poses no problems for recruitment in the area."[72]

In sum, the enormous budget, extensive services, and vast organizational network of the USAA largely account for the union's ability to maintain organizational hegemony in the department. Especially since the early 1960s, however, the strength of the USAA has been reinforced by a variety of other resources which have been placed at its disposal.

THE USAA AND THE CORPORATIST SYSTEM

> A union official picks up the ringing phone on his desk in Laon: "USAA here . . . Oh, you want the Chamber of Agriculture. Well, Chamber of Agriculture, USAA—*c'est la même chose, quoi!*"[73]

The USAA of the Center-Right era would have been powerful even if it had been detached from all other organizations in the department. But as the phone conversation cited here illustrates, the USAA was absolutely inseparable from the Chamber of Agriculture and from the other semipublic agricultural bodies in Aisne. Furthermore, the USAA enjoyed a most intimate relationship with the local representatives of the state. It is impossible to understand the dynamics of the USAA without appreciating the manner in which it functioned as an official union within the corporatist structure of French agriculture.

Exclusive Membership and Privileged Access

As did the FNSEA at the national level, the USAA held seats on a variety of formal advisory councils, commissions, and committees even before the development of systematic *concertation*. In Laon as in Paris, however, the number and significance of such institutions increased greatly from the early 1960s onward. The USAA of the 1970s sent representatives to approximately forty-six consultative bodies dealing with every conceivable aspect of agricultural affairs within the department, for example, the prices of all major agricultural products, structural reform policy, rural development, tax policy, the prevention of animal diseases, professional education, indemnification of farmers whose land is expropriated for public works projects, the handling of natural disasters, and so on.[74]

Participation on these bodies not only provided the USAA with immense influence over departmental policy but also allowed the USAA to offer what may be termed "specific solidary incentives"—prestigious positions—to a great many of its activists. Because the USAA elite controlled a number of organizations which were allotted seats along with the USAA per se on many bodies, it was able to exercise a tremendous and flexible power of appointment. For example, although the USAA itself was allowed to send only one representative to the Commission Plans de Développement, created in the mid-1970s, it actually selected five representatives: those for the USAA, the CDJA, the Chamber of Agriculture, the ADASEA, and the *centre de gestion*. In 1975 the members of this commission included a USAA vice-president as the delegate of the ADASEA and the president of the USAA's Section Petite Culture as the delegate of the Chamber of Agriculture.[75]

Concertation of the formal variety served to familiarize the union elites with state representatives at the prefecture and elsewhere throughout the department; this familiarity, backed by the impressive membership and resources of the

USAA, paved the way for privileged informal access to the state's decision-makers. Few of the farmers in Aisne during the 1970s were unaware of the fact that the USAA's elites were their best possible source for the resolution of problems pertaining to the state bureaucracy. Many a discussion with a cantonal secretary led to the intermediation of the USAA director or president on behalf of a union member hesitant to approach the bureaucracy on his own. The director's phone would ring constantly with requests for everything from the location of misplaced subsidy checks to the repair of electrical lines downed by a storm. Rendered even more privileged in recent years, the informal access accorded to the USAA by the state thus provided another incentive for Aisne farmers to remain in good standing with the union.[76]

Devolved Power and Responsibility

The comanagement institutions which were established or greatly increased in power after 1960 made the most significant corporatist contribution to the status and strength of the USAA. All of these institutions—the Chamber of Agriculture, the SUAD, the ADASEA, the EDE, and so on—were transformed into veritable branches of the official union in Aisne. In fact, the fusion of these institutions became the source of considerable confusion to many individuals—even those within the agricultural sector. One manifestation of such confusion was a request by the Crédit Agricole of Aisne for a chart that could clarify the "complicated puzzle" of the relationship among all of the *legally* unrelated organizations located in the same *maison* at the Place Edouard Herriot in Laon. Unwinding the intertwined organizations was a "redoubtable task," confessed the USAA official assigned to complete it, but he did succeed in constructing the *organigramme* reproduced in Figure 5.4.[77]

"Nothing would be more false," argued the text accompanying the chart, "than to consider *le syndicat*—the term which the farmers often use to refer to either the whole or one of its parts—as a monolithic bureaucracy centralized in the extreme." Each of the major organizations listed, it is noted, "has a distinct board of directors" and "the holding of multiple presidencies by the same man is very rare." For the most part, the text continued, "the elected leaders constantly control the functioning of each cog of the mechanism."[78]

Despite this effort to establish the functional independence of the various organizations, the text in fact provided considerable information elucidating why the de jure distinctions among them were incomprehensible not only to farmers but also to employees of organizations such as the Crédit Agricole. While the organizations of the *maison* were allegedly not "centralized in the extreme," their "administrative management" was placed under the supervision of a "General Coordination Board" composed of administrators of the major organizations and chaired by their *common* director. This superdirector hired the personnel for all of the organizations, controlled their expenditures (countersigning all of their

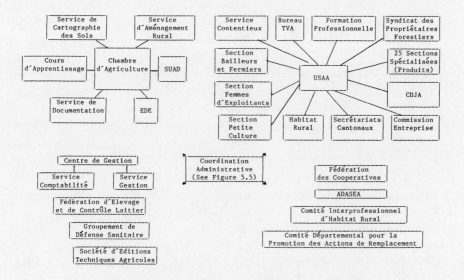

Figure 5.4 The organizations of the Laon *maison*.

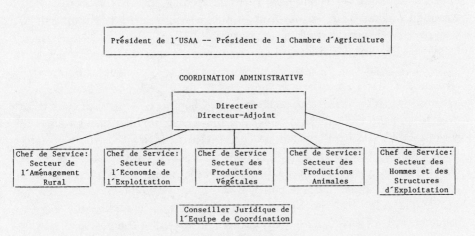

Figure 5.5 The coordination hierarchy in the Laon *maison*.

checks), and supervised their activities. Furthermore, "the administrative personnel often divided their time among several organizations (or services)" and the equipment and supplies in the *maison* were generally shared by all of its residents.[79]

But there is more to the story. As another USAA document explained, the "coordination" of the organizations was not merely administrative. At the top of the Coordination Board hierarchy sat the presidents of the USAA and the Chamber of Agriculture (see Figure 5.5); together they have attempted to define the "common objectives" of the organizational complex, to maintain a *"concertation permanente* on the positions to be taken vis-à-vis the exterior" and to define the "proper mission" for each of the organizations concerned. Given this degree or organizational fusion, the USAA leaders felt compelled to provide the following introduction to a pamphlet distributed to members in the mid-1970s:

> For a long time the bureau of the USAA has wanted to provide the farmers of Aisne with a document giving a complete description of the services which the union offers to its members. But taking into consideration the close coordination existing among the agricultural organizations of the Place Edouard Herriot at Laon . . . this presentation could only be global. In addition, it is often difficult to delimit exactly the place of the union in this ensemble, since with the exception of some technical points, the administrators of these organizations are all devoted to the general policies defined by the USAA. This pamphlet is thus . . . a very concrete testimony to the professional cohesion of our department.[80]

In short, virtually all of the agricultural organizations of the department had been brought under the direct control of the USAA.[81] Despite the union's periodic efforts to demonstrate the independence of each organization, the entire complex was fundamentally—in the words of a top USAA official—"a vertical structure with the power running from the top down." "Perhaps," he added, "the reason I fit so well into the structure is that I was an army officer for several years."[82]

The comanagement institutions were neatly integrated into this "vertical structure" and were thus directly controlled by the USAA elite. To cite but a few examples notable in 1975, the president of the Chamber of Agriculture was a past-president of the USAA; the president of the ADASEA in Aisne as well as the regional ADASEA for Picardie was a vice-president of the USAA; the president of the SAFER in Aisne was a vice-president of the USAA; the president of SUAD was the current president of the USAA. Every member of the boards of directors of these organizations was a member of and most were officers of the USAA.[83]

While control of the comanagement institutions enhanced the USAA's influence over departmental policy, it also contributed to the personnel and the infrastructure at the disposal of the union. To a degree, the USAA enjoyed a similar more-or-less "invisible subsidy" even before the corporatization process commenced. Throughout the 1950s the USAA was able to make some syndical use of its intimate ties to the state-subsidized Fédération des Syndicats d'Elevage et de Contrôle Laitier, a theoretically "independent" organization that employed between twenty and fifty "technicians" hired and supervised by a director (Prévot) shared with the USAA. The USAA also benefited from its ties to the Chamber of Agriculture—but by no means to the extent that it would in later years.[84]

With the new responsibilities it acquired after the institution of the corporatist system, the Chamber of Agriculture budget increased even more dramatically than that of the USAA. From 1958 to 1974 the union's budget increased by almost 500%, from 523,000 francs to 3,064,000 francs; during approximately the same period (1958–75) the budget of the chamber swelled by 2300%, from 226,910 francs to 5,518,442 francs.[85] A rather hefty slice of this budget was employed in various ways that contributed to the operations of the USAA. First and foremost, the chamber paid at least a portion of the salaries of many of the personnel who worked primarily for the USAA. The USAA director, adjunct-director, newspaper editor, many other staff personnel in the *maison* in Laon, and—most important—all of the cantonal secretaries were paid by the chamber as well as the USAA; the chamber's expenditure on the cantonal secretaries alone amounted to more than 500,000 francs in 1975.[86] This "sharing" of the secretaries with the chamber served to ease the strains on the USAA budget—and it did not diminish the role the secretaries played for the union. Although they became part-time SUAD agents, charged with the dissemination of technical information, they continued to perform essentially the same syndical duties that they discharged before the formal "sharing" system began in the mid-1960s.[87]

Second, the chamber financed to a great extent the infrastructure employed by the USAA: the furniture, the photocopying machine, the typewriters, and so forth. It was the chamber, for example, that covered nearly all of the expenses of the impressive library located in the room next to the office of the USAA president; the 15,000 francs' worth of books and documents which it purchased in 1975, as well as the salaries of its two librarians (one of whom is the wife of a USAA cantonal president), came out of the chamber's budget.[88] Third, these librarians and all of the technical experts of the chamber were placed at the constant disposal of the union elites. As an article in the union–chamber newspaper acknowledged: "It is a source of strength for the union to have with it [in the same building] all of the technical and economic research services to prepare dossiers for the general defense" of the farmers.[89] None of these services, quite obviously, were available in the same way to rival union activists in Aisne. Fourth, chamber funds were available to defray the travel expenses of the members of the Chamber of Agriculture—almost all of whom were USAA activists; this item of the chamber budget amounted to 28,000 francs in 1975. As interviews and observations clearly show, much of the travel written off on the chamber also served the purposes of the USAA.[90]

"Invisible subsidies" of the same sort accrued to the USAA from the budgets of the other comanagement organizations as well. Most important, the personnel of these organizations were also "shared" by the USAA. In some cases, this sharing was of a formal nature; for example, the administrative secretary of the USAA's Section Productions Animales also served as the director of the EDE—and the latter paid most of his salary. In other cases the sharing was more informal. For example, the director and counselor for the ADASEA spent much of their time attending to syndical functions and considered themselves employees of *le syndicat*.[91]

In short, the strength of the USAA allowed it to exploit to the fullest the opportunities posed by the network of comanagement institutions. From them it gained power, influence, and what may be termed "invisible subsidies"—not to mention the more visible subsidies to be discussed next.

Direct State Subsidization

From the early 1960s on the USAA received thousands of francs per year from the state through various national subsidy programs. The receipt of these subsidies was never widely publicized by the union; indeed, no mention of them was ever made in the USAA's annual budget. To find an itemization of them one must consult the records of the Chamber of Agriculture, records which have to be complete because they are audited by state inspectors.

The records show that various branches of the USAA regularly received substantial subsidies, most of them derived from the development programs conceived in the 1960s. In 1975, for example, the CDJA and the USAA's Section Femmes d'Exploitants together received 49,985 francs from the ANDA, 4,740 francs from the FAFEA,[92] and another 25,000 francs from Aisne's Conseil Général. The USAA's Service Formation received the largest single grant: 84,499 francs from the FAFEA. Other organizations under the more-or-less formal control of the USAA were granted large sums as well. Direct, "visible" subsidies thus made an important contribution to the USAA's operation, although they were of less vital importance than the "invisible" subsidies discussed earlier.[93]

CORPORATISM AND ORGANIZATIONAL TENSION

Heavily subsidized by the state and intimately involved in the formulation and implementation of many aspects of agricultural policy, the USAA gradually developed into less of an *organisation revendicative* and more of an official union. In fact, it is doubtful that any other FDSEA of the 1960s and 1970s played the role of official union more effectively. Even *Le Monde* made note of this fact at the time of the oil crisis of 1973. For the last few months of 1973, farmers throughout France were faced with a severe fuel shortage; in most departments state officials worked with the oil companies to develop some sort of system for the distribution of the scarce fuel. But in Aisne it was the USAA that assumed the task. The organizational strength of the union and its close ties with the state bureaucracy led to the establishment of a rather remarkable solution to the fuel shortage: a USAA official was given an office in the prefecture and charged with the authority to impose a rationing system on the farmers of the department. "It's amazing what you can do," the official commented in an interview, "when you get on the phone and say you're calling from the cabinet office at the prefecture." Through the distribution and monitoring of rationing coupons by the USAA's cantonal secretaries, few of the department's farmers were left entirely without fuel. As *Le Monde* noted, this system worked quite well in Aisne. Nevertheless, the article continued, "it is not normal" for a union to perform "work which should logically be that of the state bureaucracy."[94]

Indeed, the USAA recognized that the system was neither "normal" nor likely to be very well received by many farmers in the department; thus no mention of the affair was made in the union's newspaper and, in private, officials of the union tried to explain that the rationing task had been forced upon it by state officials unable to cope with the problem. Such arguments failed to establish the propriety of the action in the eyes of some farmers—especially those who, for different reasons, had long opposed the evolution of the USAA toward the official union model.[95]

Although the corporatist system strengthened the union in the many ways described here, it also exacerbated tensions within the organization. Two major dissident factions arose. The first was composed of the small farmers who resented the USAA's role in the implementation of the "moderate" structural reform program which failed to assure them a future in agriculture. One USAA official confessed, "It was easier to convince the *petits* that we supported them in the days when the union seemed to fight the state, when Blondelle called for the preservation of all family farms. 'He defended our beefsteak,' some of them say, 'while now the union tells us about subsidy programs that give us too little—if we are eligible for them.' "[96] Another USAA official distilled the essence of the problem that corporatization had created for the union's image:

> It is our job to explain the new programs and to encourage farmers to go along; but when we do this they blame us for all of the imperfections in the state policies. When I tell them that "parity" means that they will receive an income equal to the SMIC [the minimum wage] they shout: "what are we then, simple workers?" When I tell them they have to attend so many hours of class for technical training to receive a subsidy they cry: "How can we find the time?"[97]

As Table 5.2 shows, it is the farmers with fewer than 20 hectares of land who were least likely to join the USAA. And among those who did pay their dues for some of the reasons discussed earlier, many expressed their displeasure in another way after 1970: by voting for MODEF candidates in elections to the Chamber of Agriculture. In 1974, 23.5% of the voters in Thierache supported the MODEF slate which ran in opposition to the USAA slate headed by Caffarelli.[98]

Table 5.2.   USAA Membership by Farm Size, 1971

Hectares	No. of Farmers	No. Unionized Farmers	Percentage Unionized Farmers
0–1	607	9	1
1–2	553	191	35
2–5	923	424	46
5–10	880	627	71
10–20	1,624	1,470	91
20–50	3,172	3,051	99
50–100	1,545	1,521	98
100+	1,399	1,276	91

Source: "Les Résultats des élections aux chambres d'agriculture: 1955, 1959, 1964, 1967, 1970, 1974, 1976," a document prepared by the chamber librarian.

The second dissident faction within the USAA grew steadily during the 1960s and 1970s and was generally viewed as a greater threat to syndical unity: the "savagely liberal" large farmers (and some Right-wing small farmers) who supported the program of FFA. As Table 5.2 indicates, it was the very largest farmers in the department—those with farms of 100 hectares or more—who were, after the smallest farmers, the least likely to affiliate with the USAA. To a degree, as USAA officials contended, this could be explained by the fact that these farmers were required to pay the highest dues for union membership and often made little use of USAA services (for example, some of them would call a personal lawyer rather than the union's legal service to resolve a tax problem). But the same officials admitted that fewer *gros* had been paying dues in recent years and that more of them had become vociferously critical of the union. These farmers opposed even the moderate structural reform program adopted by the USAA/FNSEA. They objected to the "block to expansion" posed by the SAFER, to the government's subsidizing inefficient *petits* rather than supporting high prices, and to the union's cooperation with the state in the formulation and implementation of these programs. "Few of them are extremely enthusiastic about FFA," remarked one USAA official in 1975, "but if another Dorgères appeared, they would follow him and really split the union apart—that's what I'm afraid of."[99]

During the mid-1970s the USAA took steps to try to combat the dissidence of both the smallest and largest farmers. In regard to the former, the USAA hired a second legal advisor specifically assigned to the problems of the small farmers and began to push more strongly for the Picardie SAFER; it also instituted a campaign to make all small farmers in the department aware of the link between MODEF and the Communists.[100] In regard to the large farmers, the USAA established a special commission—the Commission Entreprise—within the union to provide a forum for the *gros* and especially the "more reasonable" liberals. Furthermore, USAA leaders began to speak out more forcefully at FNSEA congresses in favor of the interests of the most commonly maligned *gros*, the wheat and sugar beet growers.[101]

Such efforts failed to eliminate the tensions generated by corporatist modernization. In 1979, for example, FFA-style conservative forces were moved for the first time to present a list of candidates for the Chamber of Agriculture and received 30% of the vote in a contest with a USAA list headed by Gérard de Caffarelli.[102] Nonetheless, rival union activists continued to have difficulty making much headway in Aisne. As one national MODEF organizer despaired (with only slight exaggeration): "A few of our men armed with pamphlets are not going to have much success in competition with a machine which employs one hundred staff workers, controls two hundred more and effectively *makes* agricultural policy in the department."[103]

6

Dependent FDSEA Hegemony: The Case of Corrèze

Corrèze lies only an afternoon's train ride from Aisne, but in many socioeconomic respects it is an altogether different world. The Picardie region, which includes Oise and Somme along with Aisne, ranks first among France's twenty-one regions in per capita agricultural productivity; the Limousin region, encompassing Haute-Vienne and Creuse along with Corrèze, ranks next to last.[1] While Aisne is a department of vast, prosperous commercial farms operated largely by *salariés*, Corrèze is the department of "family farming par excellence"; as of 1967, 82% of its farms were smaller than 20 hectares and virtually all were operated directly by *chefs d'exploitation* with only familial assistance.[2] Whereas Aisne specializes in products that have been heavily supported by the state, Corrèze derives 78% of its agricultural income from the type of production that has been least favored: livestock raising (*élevage*), three fourths devoted to meat production and one fourth to milk production.[3] Not only are the farmers of Corrèze relatively poor and *petits*, they also tend to be older than those of Aisne and most other departments. As of 1970, only 6% of the *chefs d'exploitation* in Corrèze were younger than thirty-five and fully 65% were fifty-five or older.[4]

The farmers of Corrèze also differ from those of Aisne in their political behavior. A profoundly "de-Christianized" region, Corrèze has been a bastion of the anticlerical Left since 1848. Although it is now perhaps best known as the department of Jacques Chirac (more on this later), it has long been and remains a stronghold of peasant communism. With *chefs d'exploitation* providing much of its support, the Communist Party received almost 40% of the votes in the 1945 legislative elections. More recently, on the first ballot of the 1973 legislative elections, the Communists received lesser but still impressive totals in each of the three districts of the department: 32% in Tulle, 28% in Ussel, and 24% in Brive.[5]

In short, Corrèze is heavily populated by the types of farmers who have manifested the least satisfaction with the programs of the FNSEA. Not

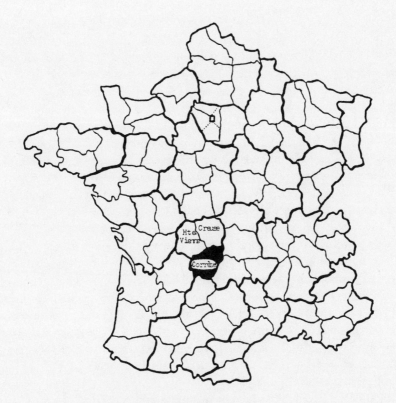

Figure 6.1 Corrèze and the Limousin region.

Figure 6.2 The cantons of Corrèze.

surprisingly, the FNSEA has thus been unable to monopolize farmers' unionism in Corrèze as it has in Aisne. The Corrèze FDSEA has been forced to contend with at least one rival union since the early 1950s and with two since 1974. As measured by the vote in elections to the Chamber of Agriculture, the opposition to the FDSEA was quite significant in the 1950s and has become even more notable in recent years. In 1952 the FDSEA received only 60% of the ballots cast in the three electoral districts combined. Despite the exodus of many marginal farmers, FDSEA electoral support declined in two of the electoral districts throughout the 1960s. And in 1974 the FDSEA slate was defeated for the first time in one of the districts (Brive), receiving only 46.6% of the vote. By 1974–76, the FDSEA's share of the vote in the department as a whole had declined to a mere 51.9%.[6]

Judging from these electoral results, one would expect to find that the FDSEA of Corrèze has been able to claim only slightly more than half of the unionized farmers in the department and that it has been forced to engage in rather stiff union competition for influence over agricultural policy. But this has not been the case. Ever since the early 1950s the FDSEA has been able to organize 70–75% of the unionized farmers in Corrèze. Moreover, since the 1950s and especially since the mid-1960s the FDSEA has enjoyed a virtual monopoly of union influence over the formulation and implementation of all aspects of departmental agricultural policy.

Although the FDSEA has held hegemonic status among the farmers unions of Corrèze, it has by no means enjoyed a stature equal to that of the USAA in Aisne. As will be discussed in the first section, the FDSEA has been quite limited in its programmatic appeal and extremely poor in terms of material resources; its dominance over its union rival(s) has always rested on rather tenuous bases. Its organizational hegemony in the department, as the second section will show, has long been maintained through exogenous resources and has, for the past two decades, been dependent on the corporatist system.

THE TENUOUS BASES OF FDSEA DOMINANCE

PURPOSIVE INCENTIVES

Except for a brief period at the end of World War II, the FDSEA of Corrèze has never succeeded in articulating a program with appeal for all farmers of the department. Two essential factors have hindered the development of "syndical unity" in Corrèze. The first and by far the most important factor has been intense political conflict; ever since the early 1950s the FDSEA has been, for the most part, limited to the recruitment of non-Communist members. The second factor has been the persistent tension between the FDSEA's effort to respond to the socioeconomic concerns of the department and its desire to remain on good terms with a national federation which has not always defended these concerns with great enthusiasm; the FDSEA has had difficulty in recruiting many disadvantaged farmers while refusing to denounce the "moderate" policies of the FNSEA.

Political Conflict

The "national and republican" sentiment of the Resistance in Corrèze served, for a short period after the war, to bring together all of the political factions that had been divided into separate agricultural organizations during the Third Republic.[7] When the FDSEA was born in 1945 its bureau included a Communist president along with representatives of every other major political force.[8] In the euphoric atmosphere of the Liberation, FDSEA congresses were entertained with speeches such as the following:

> . . . we have called on men coming from all political horizons, without worrying whether one was of the Right or another was of the Left. We have requested the cooperation of all ardent unionists, knowing that the efforts of all of us would be required to give to the métier of peasant the place that it merits. Apples are neither radical nor socialist, pigs are neither red nor white and the sweat of all peasants is the same color.[9]

But such rhetoric soon proved incapable of overcoming the recrudescence of political tension. Immediately after Henri Queuille—a native Corrézien—had formed a government in 1948 grouping the Radicals, MRP, and SFIO, and isolating the Communists, FDSEA bureau members began to disagree over the proper response to the state's agricultural policies. And relations within the bureau were strained even further when, later in the same year, the FNSEA moved—for transparently political reasons—to expel FDSEA president Champseix from his post on the Commission Nationale de Conflits.[10]

Open conflict between the FDSEA's Communist and non-Communist factions continued throughout 1949 and into 1950. In April 1949 Champseix was reelected FDSEA president by a vote of 17 to 16 in the federal council; soon thereafter his opponents appealed to the FNSEA conflict commission, charging that the election's results had been affected by highly questionable procedural maneuvers. During the months in which the case was pending, Champseix continually denounced the efforts of his opponents to "destroy the unity" of the union. His attacks became even more passionate when the non-Communist faction refused to participate in several violent union actions, actions for which Champseix was eventually fined and briefly imprisoned by order of the local correctional tribunal. In November 1949 half (seventeen) of the FDSEA's federal council members met, following a directive of the FNSEA, and elected one of Champseix's major opponents—M. Chassain—the new FDSEA president. Champseix responded by filing his own appeal with the FNSEA's national conflict commission. Finally, in March 1950, the faction fights were resolved by the national federation: "The Congress of the FNSEA decreed . . . the exclusion of the Champseix faction and recognized in Corrèze only the organization headed by Chassain."[11]

The 1950 FNSEA decree has proven to be of lasting impact. For the last three decades the excluded faction has been organized as a separate union, the FCSEA (Fédération Corrézienne des Syndicats d'Exploitants Agricole)—known since 1959 as the FCSEA-MODEF.[12] Although not formally affiliated with the Communist Party, the FCSEA-MODEF has been directed by an elite composed almost entirely of PCF activists. Its presidents and secretaries-general have always been members of the party and its bureau has opened few places to nonparty members; in 1973, for example, six of the eight bureau members were Communists.[13] There can be little doubt, moreover, that the members and supporters of the FCSEA-MODEF have primarily been recruited from among the department's Left wing and especially Communist farmers. Not only interviews but also aggregate data support this contention.[14] For example, Left votes by canton in the 1962 legislative elections and FCSEA-MODEF votes by canton in the 1959 Chamber of Agriculture election yield a correlation coefficient of 0.734; furthermore, for the same elections, Communist votes and FCSEA votes correlate to a remarkable degree: 0.908. In recent years the FCSEA-MODEF has remained popular in most of its traditional strongholds, but has also succeeded— while presenting a common slate of candidates with a new union movement, the MADARAC (Mouvement d'Action et de Défense pour l'Amélioration du Revenu des Agriculteurs Corréziens, a MONATAR affiliate)—in winning more electoral support throughout the department. As a result, Left votes in the 1973 legislative election and FCSEA-MADARAC votes in the 1974–76 Chamber of Agriculture elections yield a correlation coefficient of only 0.479; even more striking, the correlation between Communist votes and FCSEA-MADARAC votes in these same elections is a mere 0.104.[15]

As one would expect, the elites and supporters of the FDSEA have since 1950 been drawn disproportionately from the Center-Right. The political leanings of many of the major FDSEA leaders have been manifested through their efforts to obtain political office. André Treuil, the FDSEA president from 1951 to 1956, ran for deputy as a candidate of the RPF in 1951 and the Independents in 1956; Pierre Deprun, the FDSEA president from 1956 to 1974, ran for deputy as an MRP candidate in 1946; Jules Barry, an FDSEA treasurer during the 1950s and president of the Chamber of Agriculture from 1952 to 1972, ran as a Radical in 1946; Damien Jos, an FDSEA vice-president in the 1950s, ran as a—virulently anti-Communist—candidate of the SFIO in 1946; Charles Ceyrac, an FDSEA administrator and president of the Crédit Agricole, was elected as the *suppléant* for the UDR's Jean Charbonnel in 1968; René Malmartel, director of the FDSEA since 1951, has run for *conseiller général* on several occasions under various "moderate" labels.[16]

Although the FDSEA has been more successful than the FCSEA in attracting support from the Center-Left, both its members and its electoral backers have clearly been drawn heavily from the Right. Once again, aggregate data as well as interviews confirm this contention. Right votes in the 1962 legislative elections and FDSEA membership by canton in 1963 yield a correlation coefficient of 0.431. Ten years later, in 1973, the correlation between votes for the Gaullists and FDSEA membership by canton was 0.443. An intense membership drive in 1974, following the FDSEA's first loss of a Chamber of Agriculture district election, served to increase FDSEA membership in twenty-eight of the department's twenty-nine cantons—but especially in those more favorable to the Gaullists. After the drive was complete the correlation between 1973 Gaullists votes and (1974) FDSEA membership had risen to 0.538. The correlation between Right votes and FDSEA votes in chamber elections has been roughly similar to these vote–membership correlations: 0.491 was the correlation between Right votes in 1962 and FDSEA votes in 1959, while 0.456 was the correlation between Gaullist votes in 1973 and FDSEA votes in 1974–76—with the correlation in Jacques Chirac's district being higher than in the other two.[17]

This particularly strong statistical relationship between the popularity of Gaullist leader Chirac and that of the FDSEA is a reflection of the intimate personal and political relationship that Chirac has enjoyed with the FDSEA elite since his rise to prominence. While all of the FDSEA leaders claim to have pursued a strictly "apolitical" policy through the years, many of them freely stated in interviews that Chirac has been—as a deputy, as minister of agriculture, and as prime minister—"a good friend of ours," a politician who had "never forgotten to defend the farmers of Corrèze" while in Paris.[18] A perusal of the FDSEA's newspapers indicates that the "apolitical" union did not hesitate to publicly praise Chirac the minister in a manner that could serve his interests as well as those of the union. For example, an issue of the FDSEA paper—*L'Union Paysanne*—which appeared just before the 1976 Chamber of Agriculture election could not have been better designed to appeal not only to the political instincts of the Corréziens, but also to their fabled *mentalité assisté*, that is, their recognition of the fact that, in the words of one scholar, "Corrèze is too poorly endowed economically to improve its condition without considerable financial assistance—thus without its finding adequate means to weigh on the politico-administrative apparatus."[19] The front page of *L'Union Paysanne* for 30 January 1976 echoed Chirac's slogan for the legislative elections: "Vote Well, Vote *Utile*" (emphasis added). Directly beneath this exhortation was a concrete illustration of what voting "usefully" meant. Chirac, at that time both prime minister and president of the Corrèze Conseil Général, was shown in a photograph cutting the ribbon to open the newly, beautifully refurbished home of the Chamber of Agriculture and the FDSEA; standing next to him was Pierre Deprun, president of the chamber and immediate past-president of the FDSEA. The caption above the photo read, "'An act of faith in Corrèze agriculture,' declared J. Chirac at Tulle." Inside on

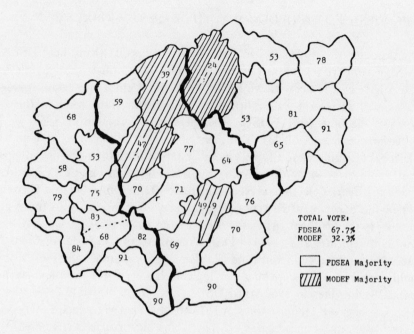

Figure 6.3 FDSEA vote (percentage by canton) in the 1959 chamber election.

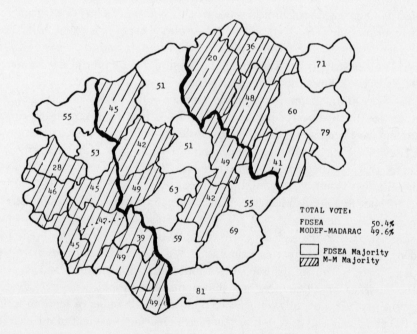

Figure 6.4 FDSEA vote (percentage by canton) in the 1974–76 chamber elections—college of *chefs d'exploitaion*.

page three was another photo of Chirac and the following description of his brief speech: "Chirac's address . . . proved once again that our former Minister of Agriculture is not only exceptionally familiar with the *dossier agricole*, but is perfectly conversant with the daily realities of the rural milieu and, despite the high functions which are presently his, has them constantly in mind." [20]

Manifesting at least an informal tie with the political "majority" may have convinced some farmers to support the FDSEA during the 1960s and 1970s, but it also alienated a good number. In fact, it contributed in 1973–74 to the first union scission since 1950. The scission was not precipitated by politics alone, however. It also represented a reaction to two other related issues: FDSEA-FNSEA relations and the nature of the corporatist system. These two issues must thus be discussed before turning to an analysis of the recent schism and the general nature of current tensions within the FDSEA.

Socioeconomic Concerns and FDSEA-FNSEA Relations

The policies advocated by the FDSEA of Corrèze have never diverged substantially from those advocated by the FNSEA. However, the Corrèze program—like that of the USAA—has differed from the national program in tone and emphasis, reflecting the special socioeconomic concerns of the department. The history of relations between the FDSEA and the FNSEA may be categorized

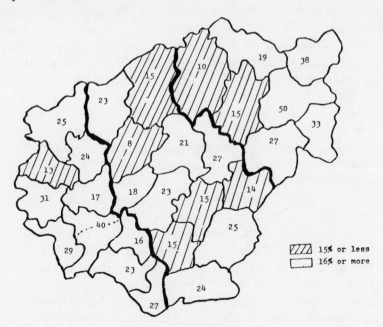

Figure 6.5 FDSEA membership density by canton, 1974. Membership density (members/farms larger than two hectares) for the entire department = 23%.

as falling into three rather distinct periods: a somewhat tense era from the early 1950s to the early 1960s, a most harmonious period from the time of the former Jacistes' rise to power until approximately 1974, and an essentially harmonious but more troubled period from 1974 to the present.

The FDSEA's relationship with the FNSEA was quite ambivalent throughout the period in which the national organization pursued its traditional "prices first" policy under the leadership of predominantly Northern elites. On the one hand, the Corrèze elite felt compelled to recognize publicly the relatively disadvantaged status of small farmers, especially *éleveurs*, and to push the FNSEA for a more vigorous defense of "the South"; such a line was particularly necessary in a department in which a rival union often engaged in demonstrations and ascribed the plight of the Corréziens as much to the "gros agrariens" of the FNSEA as to the "antipeasant" policy of the government.[21] FDSEA assemblies thus often featured criticism of the national organization, criticism sometimes harsh enough to necessitate the "defense" of Blondelle and his associates by visiting representatives of the FNSEA.[22] More important, the FDSEA elite participated fully in the meetings of the Comité de Gueret. In fact, throughout the 1950s one of the more Left-wing leaders of the Corrèze FDSEA—Damien Jos, an SFIO member—served as vice-president of the Comité.

On the other hand, the FDSEA leaders retained their loyalty to the FNSEA elites who had ruled in their favor during the disputes of 1949–50 and with whom they were more politically sympathetic than many of the Gueret activists. During periods of agricultural crisis and agitation in the Centre region, the Corrèze FDSEA consistently worked to "moderate" protests and emphasized the necessity of maintaining national "syndical unity." For example, throughout the tumultuous crisis of 1953–54 the Corrèze elites urged that all regional actions be coordinated with the *centrale* in Paris and that demonstrations be restrained and nonviolent.[23] Moreover, they specifically condemned those who sponsored the organization of an independent Comité Général d'Action Paysanne, and they gave assurance of the "confidence of the department of Corrèze in the national federation." "We will do nothing," proclaimed Jos, "to encourage a movement advocating the division of the union organizations."[24] Largely because of this loyal stand, the FDSEA of Corrèze was one of the few in the "South" to maintain a seat on the FNSEA's administrative council from the early 1950s (1954) until the end of what may be termed the Blondelle era.[25]

Though FDSEA-FNSEA relations were relatively cordial during the 1950s, they became much more harmonious with the dawn of the 1960s and the conquest of the FNSEA by former Jacistes such as Debatisse. This development can hardly be viewed as surprising. Many of the major FDSEA leaders of this era, including President Deprun and Director René Malmartel, were themselves products of the Jaciste movement and had long been close collaborators of the increasingly famous Debatisse of neighboring Puy-de-Dôme. With the FNSEA now advocating structural reforms and generally devoting more attention to the problems of the less developed regions, the Corrèze FDSEA began to support the national organization with unprecedented enthusiasm.[26]

Several events of 1964–65 signaled the formal beginning of this new FDSEA-FNSEA relationship. First, the Corrèze FDSEA severed its traditional relationship with the Comité de Gueret. More precisely, the FDSEA found that it had been abandoned by the committee. At a session of the FDSEA Federal Council in July 1964, Deprun announced that the committee had held an important meeting without inviting Corrèze, despite the fact that Jos still held his post of committee vice-president. In response to questions, Deprun explained that the Corrèze FDSEA "had been reproached" for manifesting "excessive discipline in regard to the FNSEA."[27] Later Deprun argued, not entirely without reason, that the committee had become "too politicized," infiltrated by "MODEF types" and employed as a "tool of the Communists in their battle with the FNSEA."[28] Second, within months after the Gueret affair, the Corrèze FDSEA initiated its association with a new "establishment" regional organization. In March 1965, Deprun was elected president of the recently formed FRSEA (Fédération Régionale des Syndicats d'Exploitants Agricoles) du Massif Central; serving as the secretary-general on the FRSEA bureau was none other than Michel Debatisse.[29] Third, at the 1964 FNSEA congress a major figure of the Corrèze FDSEA—Deprun—was for the first time elected to a seat on the bureau of the national federation.[30]

For the next decade the Corrèze FDSEA continued its virtually unconditional support of the FNSEA, and in fact developed into one of the most powerful Southern cogs in Debatisse's renovated FNSEA machine. While continuing to hold the presidency of the FRSEA, the Corrèze FDSEA also obtained the presidency of the CRJA (Centre Régional des Jeunes Agriculteurs) du Massif Central. And at the 1975 FNSEA congress, the FDSEA of Corrèze became one of only eight FDSEAs—and the only one in the Massif Central—to hold two seats on the national administrative council.[31]

While most of the FDSEA leaders have remained ardent supporters of the FNSEA *centrale*, rumblings of dissent have appeared in recent years. As in most other departments, some disillusionment with the national structural reform policy became evident as early as the crisis of 1967. Rank-and-file criticism of the FNSEA during the crises of 1969 and 1974 was strident enough to lead some FDSEA figures to voice concern over the Federation's apparent "indifference" to the fate of the less-developed regions, and to demand more coherent programs of assistance for the *éleveurs*. Declining membership totals, disappointing results in chamber elections, and pressures from below combined to produce a move toward a harder line in 1974: Pierre Deprun resigned the FDSEA presidency, ostensibly to devote more time to his presidency of the chamber, and was replaced by a more outspoken man—Georges Chapelle—who had been reproached by Deprun in

1969 for publicly denouncing Debatisse. Once again, therefore, the FDSEA began to diverge—if perhaps less than in the 1950s—from the program of the *centrale* in Paris.[32]

Both political divisions and socioeconomic problems have thus served to limit the FDSEA's recruitment efforts in Corrèze. Of course, as was shown in Chapter 5, even a most successful FDSEA such as that of Aisne cannot hope to attract all farmers with its purposive incentives. Unlike the USAA, however, the FDSEA of Corrèze has been ill-equipped to attract the hostile or even the indifferent farmers with an array of material incentives.

MATERIAL INCENTIVES

It was with considerable nostalgia that spokesmen at FDSEA assemblies in the 1950s recalled the days of the Liberation when "it was necessary to call on the president of the local union to obtain a ration coupon for tires and other goods."[33] Armed as were all other FDSEAs with the power to control rationing and thus to provide "material advantages" to prospective members, the FDSEA of Corrèze enrolled 90% of all farmers in 1946.[34] But this figure plummeted within the next few years. By 1950 the FDSEA had lost *half* of the 22,000 members it had registered in 1946; between 1950 and 1957 FDSEA membership declined from 11,000 to 6,500; by 1963 FDSEA membership had been reduced to 4,351; and by 1973 to 2,746—a mere 18.2% of all farmers in the department.[35]

To a great degree, of course, the initial reduction in FDSEA membership can be attributed to the political divisions within the department and the emergence of the rival FCSEA. Since 1950 the FDSEA has been faced with a divided membership market and has been hard-pressed to recruit Communists and their sympathizers. Given this factor, one could hardly expect the FDSEA to have maintained a membership density as high as that of the USAA. It must be noted, however, that the FDSEA has been strikingly unsuccessful in recruiting members even *within* its own "market." One vivid manifestation of this fact is provided by a comparison of FDSEA membership statistics and the votes received by the FDSEA at elections to the chamber. In 1959, for example, FDSEA membership was only slightly more than 30% of the number of FDSEA voters; in 1974 the FDSEA membership represented somewhat less than 30% of its electoral supporters.[36]

More than anything else, the FDSEA's recruitment difficulties can be attributed to the union's failure to develop the sort of services found in departments such as Aisne. The union elites have certainly been aware of the organizational utility of such services/incentives. The minutes of FDSEA meetings, especially in the 1950s, are full of passages such as the following: "M. Merpiller speaks of the difficulties encountered in collecting dues. It is necessary in his opinion that the local unions have an economic activity and provide material advantages for their members."[37] And the 1955 Activity Report of the union proclaimed that "a lively local union is . . . one which provides services."[38] However, like most of its counterparts throughout the less-developed regions of France, the FDSEA of Corrèze has suffered from an acute shortage of the endogenous resources necessary to translate such an awareness into a functioning network of services.

An examination of FDSEA budget statistics for the last thirty years vividly illustrates why the Corrèze union has been unable to match the activities of organizational "Citroëns" such as the USAA. In 1957 the budget of the FDSEA was a mere 39,600 francs, approximately one thirteenth of that for the USAA. During the next sixteen years the FDSEA budget grew by a factor of more than five, reaching 211,000 francs in 1973. Yet the Corrèze budget remained paltry in comparative terms, roughly one twelfth that of the USAA. More remarkable still was the gap between the two unions' expenditures on personnel: in 1973 the USAA spent almost *forty* times more money (1.6 million francs) on staff personnel than the Corrèze FDSEA (about 40,000 francs).[39]

With such budgetary limitations, the FDSEA has obviously been unable to develop anything like the USAA's extensive network of cantonal secretaries. In fact, it has scarcely been able to maintain even a skeletal staff operation. In the early 1950s the FDSEA functioned with only *one* full-time employee, Director René Malmartel. Assisting Malmartel were two part-time employees, a secretary and the operator of the FDSEA's Service de Désinfection des Etables. Beginning in 1956 Malmartel himself became at least formally a "part-time" FDSEA employee, as half of his salary was picked up by the Chamber of Agriculture. From this point until the 1970s the union functioned with a full-time secretary, the half-time Malmartel, and the Stable Disinfection Service operator. Early in the 1970s the latter was dropped, and in 1974 a full-time adjunct director was hired to assist Malmartel. The composition of the FDSEA's "staff" has thus altered somewhat over the years, but it has never included more than three individuals.[40]

To many farmers in the department, Malmartel has long been the veritable personification of the FDSEA. While Director Prévot of the USAA has essentially served as a chief executive, merely supervising the actions of a legion of specialists, Malmartel has been compelled to perform a multitude of diverse tasks. Aside from coordinating the activities of the FDSEA elites, he has served as the union's legal advisor, newspaper editor, and technical consultant to the social and product sections; moreover, it is he who has generally acted as the members' intermediary with the state bureaucracy, while also—unlike Prévot—sometimes filling in for elected union officials at meetings of various commissions. The only service that Malmartel himself did not administer over the years was the Stable Disinfection Service; one man was paid to drive a truck throughout the department, spraying the stables of members for a fee roughly 25% less than that charged to nonmembers.[41]

Elected FDSEA officials have, of course, assisted Malmartel in the provision of union services—but to no great extent. Members of the Federal Council have organized activities for the specialized sections, and local union presidents have attempted to provide the sort of assistance to members—advice on tax payments, help in applying for subsidies and dealing with the bureaucracy, and the like—which cantonal secretaries generally provide in Aisne. But as one local union president confided in an interview, "We can only do so much . . . we have families and cattle to care for . . . even those of us with understanding wives have only so much spare time to devote to the union; my mother lives with us, and she even complains when a member comes by the house to use the telephone." And in the words of another official, "All of our elected officials are interested in the union's welfare, but few of them are passionately committed . . . the union is seen as important, but not as the central interest in life."[42]

Several union leaders contended in interviews that local elites had not been sufficiently inspired to work for the organization and that much of blame for this could be attributed to Pierre Deprun. The FDSEA could have attracted more members, they argued, if Deprun—president from 1956 to 1974—had spent less time in Tulle and more at the *base*, encouraging local presidents and assisting the rank and file. Indeed, the replacement of Deprun by the younger and more dynamic Georges Chapelle seemed to make a significant difference in organizational affairs. After the FDSEA's embarrassment in the 1974 Chamber of Agriculture elections, Chapelle devoted himself to the revivification of long dormant local unions, the recruitment of new elites, and the expansion of membership. At least partially as a result, membership rose in virtually all of the cantons and increased throughout the department from roughly 2,700 in 1973 to more than 3,400 in 1974.[43]

Nevertheless, there were limits to what could be accomplished by a renovation and reinvigoration of elites. Even with the efforts of 1974, FDSEA membership increased from only 18% to 23% of all farmers in Corrèze.[44] Little progress was made—without the exogenous resources to be discussed later—in instituting the sort of services that could assure a long-term increase in the stability of membership. The FDSEA remains an extremely weak union, too poor to provide the sort of *capital-intensive* (salaried staff-operated) services found in Aisne and insufficiently inspirational to provide the sort of *labor-intensive* (elite-operated) services—derived from political commitment—which Chapter 7 will show to be employed by the MODEF affiliate in Landes.

Despite its organizational problems, the FDSEA has managed ever since the 1950s to maintain a larger membership and more influential position than its FCSEA-MODEF rival. No exact depiction of the FCSEA's status is possible, given its unwillingness to make public membership and budget statistics. Informed estimates suffice, however, to provide a meaningful portrayal of its evolution. When the FCSEA first split from the FDSEA in 1950, its membership was approximately 3,800—slightly more than one third that of the FDSEA.

Roughly the same FCSEA/FDSEA membership ratio obtained for the next two decades, with the FCSEA claiming slightly less than one third as many members as the FDSEA in the 1970s; as of 1975, the FCSEA-MODEF could claim the membership of only about 6% of all farmers in the department. Moreover, the FCSEA's recruitment record within its own membership market has been even worse than that of the FDSEA; in the 1970s the number of members recruited by the FCSEA represented only about 10–15% the number of voters who supported it in elections to the chamber.[45]

One explanation for the FCSEA's weakness relative to the FDSEA is that it has suffered, in the words of a rather sympathetic observer, from leadership "sclerosis." It has retained essentially the same elite that emerged at its formation in the 1950s, and this group has manifested "even less dynamism than Deprun." Moreover, the three major leaders (Boucheteil, Champseix, and Lacassagne) have remained "quite Stalinist," difficult for even Left-wing socialists to deal with.[46]

But few of the agricultural elites interviewed in Corrèze felt that this was the major reason for the FCSEA-MODEF's failure to approach the membership and influence levels achieved by the FDSEA. To understand the FDSEA's hegemony in the department, one must appreciate the degree to which the FDSEA has benefited from a privileged relationship with the state and the exploitation of the corporatist structures of French agriculture.

CORPORATISM AND DEPENDENT FDSEA HEGEMONY

"If the Chamber of Agriculture were eliminated tomorrow, the FDSEA would simply stop functioning." "For our union the essential fact of life is poverty; the Federation lacks the material means to do anything by itself—it is just not mature, not adult enough to have an independent existence." "The simple fact is that the union doesn't have the resources for a *vie propre*."[47] These comments were made in 1975 not by FDSEA opponents, but by past and present members of the union elite: a former CDJA vice-president, a current FDSEA vice-president, and a former FDSEA bureau member. The assessment of the FDSEA's status by the FCSEA-MODEF president was similar, but more succinct: "Sans subventions, c'est fini."[48]

From the 1950s onward the FDSEA's hegemony in Corrèze has been dependent on its access to exogenous resources that have been unavailable to its union rivals. These resources remained quite limited during the first decade after the 1950 scission, but they nevertheless "considerably facilitated" the development of the FDSEA's meager organization. From the Conseil Général, which considered the FDSEA to be the "only representative of the peasant world in Corrèze," the union received modest subsidies as well as exclusive seats on advisory committees.[49] But the principal source of support was the Chamber of Agriculture, entirely controlled by FDSEA elites after 1952.

Rather poor itself during the 1950s, the chamber could afford the FDSEA only small direct subsidies. Its "indirect" subsidies, however, made a vital contribution to the union's operation. The FDSEA and the chamber were effectively merged, sharing the same office building and the same personnel. Two events of 1956 more or less formalized the de facto merger. First, FDSEA Director Malmartel was named an "assistant" of the chamber, the immediate effect of which was to relieve the FDSEA of the burden of paying one half of his salary.[50] Malmartel was given the title of "adjunct director" of the chamber, but from 1956 until 1976—when he was formally named director—he served as its de facto director. While the de jure director performed rather mundane tasks,[51] Malmartel assumed most of the important duties discharged by Prévot in Aisne. Second, the chamber assumed a formal role in the publication of the FDSEA's newspaper L'Union Paysanne; two pages of chamber news were added to each issue and the paper's subtitle was changed to the "Organ of Information of the FDSEA and the Chamber of Agriculture of Corrèze."[52] This development was doubly beneficial for the FDSEA. The chamber began to contribute one third— or even more, according to some observers—of the paper's publication and distribution costs. Furthermore, the inclusion of chamber news—including technical information, price reports, and so on—helped to increase the paper's circulation and to augment its advertising revenue.[53] Without this sort of chamber subsidy, the newspaper of the FCSEA folded in 1959 and the rival union was reduced to publishing a short column in MODEF's national paper, L'Exploitant familial.[54]

With the advent of the corporatist system in the 1960s, the FDSEA began to receive privileges and benefits of much greater significance. Through 1981, while membership and chamber vote totals manifested its declining popularity, the status of the FDSEA was bolstered by its enjoyment of the sort of corporatist favors outlined in Chapter 4.

Exclusive Membership and Privileged Access

As mentioned earlier, the FDSEA was the only union deemed by the state to be "representative" of the farmers of Corrèze in the 1950s. Despite its declining membership, its dwindling majorities in chamber elections, its defeat in the district of Brive in 1974, and the emergence of a second rival union, the FDSEA remained the only union allowed to serve as an official intermediary between the farmers and the prefecture during the Center-Right era.

The FDSEA exercised a great deal of influence over agricultural policy in Corrèze through its exclusive membership on more than thirty councils, commissions, and committees, for example, the commission des cumuls and the (produce) prices committee.[55] The union gained additional influence and prestige through its participation in the department's monthly agricultural conference. In this official conference at the prefecture, the leaders of the FDSEA and the other "recognized" agricultural organizations met with the prefect and his staff for a wide-ranging discussion of the progress and problems of agriculture throughout the department.[56]

Important though this formal FDSEA-state interaction was, the FDSEA derived its greatest influence through the privileged *informal* access accorded it by the prefecture. Farmers with problems pertaining to all aspects of agricultural policy regularly filled the chairs outside of Director Malmartel's office, anxious to gain his intermediation with officials of the state. Small farmers were invariably impressed by Malmartel's ability to pick up the phone, dial the prefecture, speak for a few moments with one of the chief assistants of the prefect, and obtain a promise of immediate attention to the problem at hand.[57] Indeed, Malmartel's power was such that his friends and enemies alike referred to him as the "préfet agricole de la Corrèze."[58]

No such informal access was granted to the leaders of rival unions such as the FCSEA-MODEF and MONATAR. When asked in the 1970s how readily the rival unions were received at the prefecture, the prefect's chef de cabinet responded, "Oh, we agree to talk with them whenever they wish to make an appointment . . . after all, we also meet with CGT leaders as you have seen today."[59] However, as the FCSEA president retorted when he heard this statement, "Sure, he will agree to speak with us if we persist, if we wait two weeks for an appointment and then don't mind waiting in the hall of the prefecture for an hour or so . . . often we can't even get by the secretary on the phone . . . meanwhile, Malmartel and Deprun spend half of their time in the prefect's office."[60] Obviously this assessment was somewhat exaggerated, but it did seem to be essentially valid. When asked to name the major agricultural leaders in the department, the *chef de cabinet* responded: "M. Deprun, M. Malmartel, M. Papin . . . Georges . . . what's his last name? Oh yes, Georges Mantes . . . You see, we are on such good terms that I call many of them by their first names." But he did not refer to any of the FCSEA-MODEF or MONATAR leaders by their first names; in fact, he did not mention them at all.[61]

Just how important was this privileged formal and informal access? According to one rather objective observer, it definitely contributed to the FDSEA's competitive position in membership recruitment: "The farmers know where the power is . . . this may not lead them to pay their FDSEA dues, which some can't afford, but it does make them think twice about becoming known as a supporter of the MODEF."[62] A former FDSEA bureau member who left to form MADARAC complained that it could dissuade union elites from rejecting the official union: "One must work within the FDSEA if one wants to hold any important position and have any influence over policy in the department; if one splits from the FDSEA, one can speak louder—but at the cost of not being heard."[63]

Direct State Subsidization

During the 1950s the FDSEA received some subsidies from the state, but these were generally limited to rather meager sums—several thousands of francs—granted by the department's Conseil Général. In later years the FDSEA continued to receive modest subsidies from the Conseil; in 1975, for example, it received 12,000 francs along with an additional several thousand granted to the CDJA. The Conseil also awarded smaller sums—6,000 francs—to each of the rival unions, the FCSEA–MODEF and MADARAC–MONATAR.[64] These were the only subsidies received by the rival unions—but they were by no means the only ones accorded to the FDSEA.

Throughout the era of "strong corporatism," the FDSEA received generous subsidies from a number of sources. The official union often received, as it did in 1975, as much as 20,000 francs from the *promotion collective* fund.[65] From the mid-1960s onward, however, the major source of subsidies in Corrèze, as elsewhere, was the "development" program. In 1976, for example, the FDSEA's Women's Commission received a SUAD grant of 34,307 francs and an additional several thousand from the Conseil Général. That same year the CDJA received a subsidy of 91,140 francs, only slightly less than one third as much as the entire FDSEA budget generated by dues payments.[66] As important as these sums were to the maintenance of the organization, they were much less significant than the "indirect" or "disguised" subsidies which the union received.[67]

Devolved Power and *Cogestion*

"In union and professional matters," argued an FDSEA editorial of 1976 attacking the rival unions, "it is above all realism and thorough technical study of the dossiers that counts . . . and not demogogic and ultimately scarcely credible demands (*revendications*)."[68] What the editorial did not mention, as one rival union leader noted in an interview, was that the FDSEA's brand of "realism" and its thorough "technical study of the dossiers" were possible only because of its control of the executive boards, infrastructure and personnel of the publicly financed *cogestion* institutions.[69] From this control the official union derived not only considerable power but also a variety of "disguised" subsidies.

While rival unions in Corrèze were able to influence agricultural policy only through the expression of "demands" via letters to the prefect and mass demonstrations in the streets, the FDSEA exercised power directly through its exclusive seats on the boards of the multitude of corporatist institutions. As of 1975, the president of the Chamber of Agriculture and the SUAD was the immediate past-president (Deprun) of the FDSEA; the president of the ADASEA was the current FDSEA president; the president of the departmental SAFER was the current FDSEA secretary-general (previously the president of the regional SAFER had also been a member of the Corrèze elite, Damien Jos).

Along with these key institutions, the FDSEA also controlled a number of other publicly financed bodies regularly portrayed as branches of the union. In the FDSEA's 1971 *Compte Rendu d'Activités*, for example, the Bureau TVA—a counseling service financed entirely by the chamber—was described simply as having been "put in place by the union" and "headed by our secretary general"; the Comité d'Etude Interprofessionnel de la Noix et du Noyer du Bas-Limousin—a service for nut producers financed primarily by the chamber—was described as having "its headquarters at our Federation"; in addition, the ADASEA was described as an "association created through the impetus of the union, presided by President Deprun."[70]

While the development of the corporatist system thus contributed greatly to the influence and the status of the FDSEA, it also served to expand the infrastructure and personnel at the disposal of the union. The chamber had accorded such "indirect subsidies" to the FDSEA even in the 1950s, but after 1960 these subsidies increased enormously. The budget of the chamber was never more than a few hundred thousand francs in the 1950s—by 1976 it had risen to roughly 4 *million* francs.[71] Moreover, whereas the salaried staff of the chamber consisted of two employees in 1952 and only eleven as recently as 1964, by 1975 it had increased to *thirty-eight*. Most of this increase was attributable to the creation of SUAD, the employer of twenty-six of the chamber's personnel in 1975.[72]

In terms of infrastructure, the contribution of the chamber to the operation of the FDSEA was indeed formidable. In the first place, it enabled the FDSEA to enjoy office accommodations qualitatively different from those of its rivals. The FCSEA-MODEF was forced to work out of a tiny one-room office accessible only by an alley entrance in a dilapidated cooperative warehouse, and the "head-quarters" of MADARAC-MONATAR was merely the home of its president; meanwhile, the FDSEA utilized several spacious offices, a large conference room, and the library of the refurbished three-story Chamber of Agriculture building located less than 50 yards from the prefecture. Although FDSEA director Malmartel claimed that the FDSEA "pays its share" of the building's expenses, very few in the department believed it. According to several informed sources, the chamber paid virtually all of the rent as well as such expenses as the "telephone, heating, and cleaning women."[73]

In terms of personnel, the chamber contributed a great deal more than cleaning women to the FDSEA. An exposé published by several former FDSEA activists in 1976 alleged that at least ten employees of the chamber devoted all or most of their time to FDSEA activities.[74] There was little reason to doubt the validity of the charge. It was openly acknowledged that both the FDSEA director and his secretary had long been paid largely by the chamber. Moreover, unpublished minutes of FDSEA meetings recorded discussions such as the following concerning the "sharing" of personnel. In a 1973 meeting the president of the FDSEA's Commission Féminine asked chamber President Deprun to "specify the conditions in which the technical personnel of SUAD could be placed at the disposal of the union for the assistance of its specialized sections." In response, Deprun "reassured Mme Chezalviel." "There will be no problem in this area," he stated; "the union sections and the Commission Féminine in particular will be able to work in *bonne collaboration* with SUAD and its personnel."[75] Again at a 1974 FDSEA meeting, Deprun remarked that three of the women employed by SUAD "work *d'une façon permanente* with the Commission Féminine of the FDSEA." Furthermore, he explained to new FDSEA president Chapelle that four other SUAD technicians were assigned to work "en liaison" with the product sections, although they did have a good deal of work to do for SUAD per se and thus could devote "only a part of their time to the animation of the sections."[76]

Not all of the SUAD technicians utilized by the FDSEA were comfortable playing their dual role. One admitted, "Frankly, my sympathies are with MADARAC . . . but I am never assigned to help with their activities. If I want to work for the chamber, I must also work for the FDSEA . . . the job is an *ensemble*. My salary is paid by all of the farmers, including those of the FCSEA and MADARAC, and in theory my job is to be 'at the service of all of the farmers' . . . but you can see to what degree I am only at the service of the FDSEA." By coincidence, I encountered this same man almost a year later while doing research in Landes. The technician had been sent there to help implement a major FNSEA program to manifest the solidarity of all French farmers: the Operation-Paille. Conceived during the drought of 1976, this program entailed the shipment of hay from the least affected departments to those—such as Corrèze—which had been hard hit by the lack of rain. After exchanging greetings at the FDSEA headquarters in Mont-de-Marsan, the SUAD technician joked, "You see, Malmartel sends me to the four corners of France as a symbol of syndical unity."[77]

The Suad technicians were not the only chamber employees utilized freely by the FDSEA. Indeed, I must acknowledge the degree to which my research in Corrèze benefited from this, one of the fruits of corporatism. Several secretaries employed by the chamber were directed by Malmartel to assist me in finding stacks of FDSEA documents scattered throughout the basement of the FDSEA-chamber building. Discussions with these women revealed that they were always asked to perform FDSEA duties as a routine part of their job.[78] By the same token, the chamber-financed librarian routinely assumed tasks for the FDSEA, some of a more questionable nature than others. For example, at the request of Deprun and Malmartel, the librarian devoted a great deal of time to compiling a file on MODEF activities for use during the chamber election campaign of 1976—a curious activity indeed for someone paid to advance the interests of "all farmers in the department."[79]

Although some FDSEA activists expressed concern about the propriety of the FDSEA-chamber "merger" before 1974, it was not until after the chamber elections of that year that the issue was ever broached in public. At the chamber's first session of 1975, the four newly elected representatives of the FCSEA and MADARAC mounted an effort to challenge the legality of the organizational "confusion." In refusing to approve the budget for 1975, MADARAC leader Yves Terrieux proclaimed that his group of four found the chamber not to be "at the service of all farmers who contribute to its budget." It seemed, he argued, "that the farmers were not all equal (*sur le même rang*), especially in regard to the aid granted to agricultural organizations within the department." It was not proper, he continued, that the chamber pay the "housing and administrative expense" as well as the "salaries of some personnel" utilized only by selected organizations. "Things should be made clear," he asserted, and "there should be no overlapping of the Chamber of Agriculture and the FDSEA, or at least the other unions should not be forgotten." A ruffled Deprun retorted that "Corrèze had not innovated in this matter," that "in all departments the building of the chamber also houses the FDSEA, the CDJA, the Centre de Gestion, etc., and that numerous services are common to these organizations." Moreover, he continued, the services of SUAD were in truth "at the disposal of all farmers" and all unions were eligible to apply for subsidies from the chamber. When this retort met with objection by Terrieux, Deprun said that he could only repeat once again "the state of affairs which has existed for many years."[80]

Rebuffed in their effort to challenge the official union system through the Chamber of Agriculture, the rival unions decided to use their political ties to muster a challenge in the Conseil Général. In the Council's meeting of 9 January 1976, several Communist councillors close to the FCSEA and several Socialists— especially François Daurat, a MADARAC leader and one of the four dissident members of the chamber—combined to question granting a subsidy of 180,000 francs to SUAD. "I vote against this subsidy," proclaimed Daurat. "I did not approve the budget of the Chamber of Agriculture [either], because I feel that these technicians have many things to do besides engaging in *action syndicale*, which is not their role." Several of the councillors unfamiliar with the workings of the chamber asked for an elaboration of this criticism, noting that the SUAD dossier described its activities as "very specialized work" intended to provide "technical assistance" to the farmers. Daurat responded that a good many of the "technicians" devoted most of their time to *animation syndicale* for the FDSEA, and that he could give a specific objectionable example from firsthand observation:

Two years ago, when we—my colleagues and myself—were candidates for the Chamber of Agriculture, the incumbent President of the Chamber of Agriculture decided—as was his right—to come hold a meeting in Juillac [Daurat's canton]. And he was accompanied by two of his technicians. I think they would have been more useful *sur le terrain*. That's an example; I could give you many others. When the technicians are solely at the disposal of the farmers, then I will vote a subsidy for SUAD.

The spokesman for the Communist group seconded Daurat's objection, demanding that the nature of the SUAD technicians' employment be studied so as to assure that the FDSEA—which had been granted a direct subsidy—was not being accorded an extra and even larger "subvention déguisée."

After this debate the vote was taken on the SUAD subsidy. It passed, but only by the slimmest of margins: eleven in favor, ten opposed, and three abstaining.[81] Seemingly, a warning had been issued: in a department in which the FDSEA could not claim organizational and political power held, for example, by the USAA of Aisne, its exploitation of the opportunities posed by the corporatist system would be closely monitored.

CORPORATISM AND ORGANIZATIONAL TENSION

Although the establishment of the corporatist system strengthened the FDSEA of Corrèze in a variety of ways, it also served to exacerbate tensions within the union. Criticism of the FDSEA/FNSEA's intimate collaboration with the state in the formulation and implementation of agricultural policy was not prevalent in the early 1960s, during the hopeful days after the passage of the Pisani Law. From the mid-1960s onward, however, a succession of agricultural crises—most of which hit the *éleveurs* of the Massif Central especially hard—served to generate increasing discontent.

During the crisis of 1967, heated debates occurred within the councils of the FDSEA over the proper response to the policy of the government. After the "moderate" FNSEA demonstration of 2 October, many of the FDSEA's leaders reported in a bureau meeting that a good number of the farmers "wanted to cause more commotion"; that they "came away disappointed, they wanted to go further . . . they had begun to block the road in front of the *salle de fêtes* before the meeting, but afterward they left with their hands in their pockets." Malmartel regretted that they had favored such action and argued that they should spend less time criticizing and more time offering "concrete propositions." Although the majority refused to join in further demonstrations sponsored by the FCSEA-MODEF and the Comité de Gueret without an order from the "national organization," a sizeable minority wished to do so. It was thus decided to allow members to participate in these demonstrations, but to refrain from according them official FDSEA sanction.[82]

Even greater divisions were engendered by the crisis that ensued in 1969 after the devaluation of the franc. Once again the national federation was strongly criticized by the *base*, and one FDSEA bureau member went so far as to condemn the FNSEA openly to the press, charging that many farmers felt "it is not sufficiently concerned with the farmers of our region." Although he was criticized for not "washing his dirty linen *en famille*," many of the other union leaders supported him in private debates. Several urged that the union undertake a "grève de participation" at meetings scheduled with the administration and the representatives of the government. Again, however, the bureau majority favored "moderation." Deprun and others rejected the idea of a strike, contending that the interests of the farmers could only be defended through participation in official commissions and committees. Cooperation with the Comité de Gueret was also rejected, despite the expressed fear that many farmers—and especially the young—were becoming "indifferent" to the union and that "one risked seeing them leave and even go toward other organizations."[83]

This prediction proved to be prescient. Over the next five years the FDSEA lost almost 25% of its members, more than 800 in all.[84] But this was only the prelude to what would occur with the onset of the crisis of 1974: for the first time since 1950, the FDSEA suffered a major scission. Two of the FDSEA's Federal Council members, one of them also a bureau member, decided in late 1973 to form a dissident "association"—MADARAC—within the FDSEA. For a short time their internal opposition was tolerated; however, when it became known that they planned to work with the FCSEA-MODEF for the election of a slate of chamber candidates opposed to the policies of the FDSEA, they were expelled from the Federal Council by a vote of 24–7, with 6 abstentions.[85]

The decision to form MADARAC was motivated by a number of factors. Politics was definitely an important one; both of the initial organizers, one of whom was Daurat, were Socialists opposed to the increasingly intimate relationship that had developed between Debatisse-Deprun and Jacques Chirac. Indeed, when MADARAC leader Elie Bousseyrol was interviewed before the 1974 chamber elections, he charged that "Le leader syndical actuel c'est M. Jacques Chirac."[86]

Politics was not, however, the only motivation behind the division. The MADARAC leaders, who soon joined a group of like-minded farmers in other departments to form MONATAR, voiced many criticisms of the FNSEA/FDSEA which had considerable resonance at the *base* of the FDSEA. They charged that the "official" union could no longer "play the role which is proper to it"; constantly engaged in the implementation of agricultural policy, the FDSEA had become "la courroie de transmission du pouvoir" and thus was not in a position to push strenuously for the defense of the farmers. Its policy of "permanent compromise" seemed not to be resolving the problems of the Corréziens, but rather promising the "désertification du départment." Moreover, they charged, the FNSEA of Debatisse could no longer be viewed as the champion of the less-developed regions. In the words of Bousseyrol, "the FNSEA does not defend the interests of the farmers of our region . . . the FNSEA cannot at the same time defend the *gros* farmers of the Parisian Basin who have 500 to 1,000 hectares and more, and the *petits* farmers of Corrèze who have from 15 to 40 hectares. The FNSEA has made its choice, and I have made another one."[87]

The appeal of such a critique of the FNSEA was manifested on several occasions during the crisis year of 1974. First, despite a massive electoral campaign employing the chamber-subsidized newspaper[88] and the assistance of many chamber personnel, the FDSEA lost—for the first time ever—a Chamber of Agriculture election in one of the department's three electoral districts: 53% of the voters in Brive, the largest district, rejected the FDSEA slate in favor of one featuring two representatives of each of the rival unions. Furthermore, the MODEF-MADARAC slate received 49% of the votes in the other district in contention, Ussel, losing by a mere 93 votes. For the FDSEA, an ominous sign for the future was the fact that its support was shown to be weaker among the younger than among the older farmers of the department. The farmers over age sixty-five, moved into a separate electoral college in 1970, had voted 59.9% for the FDSEA in 1970 and would support it to the tune of 58.5% in 1976; in contrast, only 50% of the farmers under sixty-five supported the FDSEA in 1974 and only 54% (in the district of Tulle) did so in 1976. Corrèze, whose oldest farmers seem to vividly remember the Communist-sponsored scission and street fights of 1949–50, stands as one of the few departments in which the FDSEA is supported more by those over than by those under sixty-five.[89]

Second, the MADARAC critique was shown to appeal even to some of the FDSEA leaders who chose to remain within the official union. At the January 1974 meeting of the Federal Council, several speakers accused the FDSEA, as well as the FNSEA, of being "politically too close to the current government."[90] Similar comments were made by a number of other speakers at the union's general assembly in March. The most virulent criticism was voiced by the cantonal delegate of Brive, Roland Meyjonade. After analyzing the current crisis, he proceeded to blame it on the leaders of the government and several FNSEA officials who seemed to be "in their pocket." "We contend," Meyjonade continued, "that the combative spirit of our President Debatisse has been seriously dulled (*émoussé*) by his intimate contact with the ministerial antechambers. . . . It is necessary not to confuse proposition . . . with submission and devotion."[91] A few months later anti-FNSEA speeches were again to be heard, this time at another Federal Council meeting. Several delegates voiced their regret "that the FNSEA is not taking a harder line," and urged stepped-up demonstrations at both the departmental and national level. To this Deprun could only respond, "It is unthinkable to doubt the combativeness of the national leaders."[92]

In response to the FNSEA's continued support for an increasingly liberal modernization policy and its politically compromising pursuit of *concertation*, however, a good many Corréziens were compelled to think the unthinkable as the 1970s progressed. In 1979, at a time when cooperation between Communists and Socialists was difficult to sustain, the Corrèze affiliates of MODEF and MONATAR again presented a common list of candidates for the Chamber of Agriculture and received 46% of the total vote.[93] With the plurality electoral system then in effect, the rival unions failed to receive a single chamber seat for their efforts (and lost the four seats they had held in the Brive district). Nevertheless, they successfully conveyed the message that the FDSEA's legal monopoly of power within the department was a very distorted reflection of the balance of syndical popularity in the countryside.

7

Artificial FDSEA Hegemony:
The Case of Landes

The department of Landes, situated in the Aquitaine region of the Southwest, is similar to Corrèze in at least two important socioeconomic respects: it is populated almost entirely by small farmers engaged primarily in livestock raising and it is among the poorest of French departments.[1] However, two other features of Landes lend it a character quite different from that of Corrèze and of virtually all other departments. First, nearly half of the farmers in Landes, compared with only 13% nationwide, engage in part-time work off the farm. The principal reason for this is that, as Figure 7.2 shows, the northwestern two thirds of the department are occupied by forest land; this section of Landes contains the largest and most heavily wooded forest in all of France, responsible for more than half of the national production of pine resin (*gemme*). In the forest region, approximately three fourths of the farmers work only part time on tiny plots covering an average of from 3 to 7 hectares; most of these are *paysans-gemmeurs* who devote several months of the year to the collection of resin in commercial forests. Even in the southeastern "agricultural" section (containing 71% of the department's agricultural population), part-time farming is common. The average farm size here is only 12–18 hectares, and 35–40% of the farmers augment their incomes by working either in the forests as *gemmeurs* or in the factories of forest-related industries (e.g., lumber and paper production, chemical processing).[2]

The second distinctive feature of Landes is that it contains far more former and current *métayers* (sharecroppers) than any other area in all of France. Sixty years ago nearly all of the farmers in Landes were at least partially engaged in *métayage*; in 1929 fully 55% of the Landais in agriculture worked entirely as *métayers*, while only 20% of the farmers did so in the department—Gironde—in which *métayage* was second most prevalent.[3] At the end of World War II, more than 75% of the Landes farmers were still at least part-time *métayers*. This percentage dropped precipitously after the passage in 1946 of the Statut de

Figure 7.1 Landes and the Aquitaine region.

Fermage, a bill facilitating the transformation of *métayage* into *fermage* (the renting of land for a fixed sum not directly tied to the harvest). As late as 1955, however, 31.7% of the farms in Landes were still under *métayage*; in contrast, the figure for France as a whole was a mere 3.2%.[4] The movement away from *métayage* has proceeded apace during the last three decades—only 11% of the farms in Landes were under *métayage* as of 1970.[5] Nevertheless, there are few farmers in the department who are not either former *métayers* themselves or the children of former *métayers*.

Both part-time work off the land and *métayage* have profoundly affected the nature of political and syndical behavior throughout the history of Landes. While working as *gemmeurs*, many of the peasants of Landes were exposed to socialist doctrines and the organizational methods of the CGT even before the turn of the century; thousands of them participated in CGT-sponsored demonstrations against forest landowners in 1907 and 1909.[6] Furthermore, as *métayers*, thousands more of the Landais proved receptive to the overtures of the CGT's agricultural branch as early as 1919. The notorious demands of landowners—including, in early years, even the insistence on a feudal *corvée*—met with violent CGT-sponsored demonstrations on a number of occasions; the mass actions and bloody repression of 1920, 1938, and 1950 (when landowners resisted the implementation

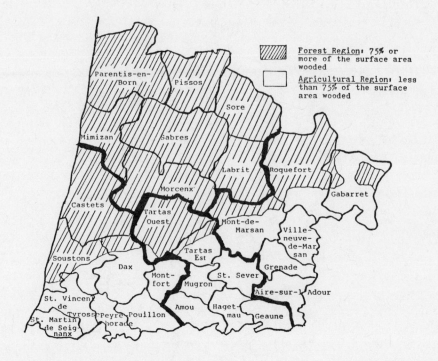

Figure 7.2 The cantons of Landes.

of the Statut de Fermage) are still vividly remembered first- or secondhand by most Landais.[7]

As Juan Linz has noted, *métayage* provides much more occasion for conflict—and for the development of a genuine class consciousness—than any other form of tenure on the land. It is not surprising, then, that Linz's study of ecological data in France and Italy manifested at least a "possible connection between leftism and *métayage*."[8] Such a connection is certainly evident in Landes. On the one hand, Landes has proven to be a predominantly Leftist department since 1902–14; most of its deputies have been Socialists elected at the second ballot with considerable help from first-ballot Communist voters (the Communist vote was 15–20% in 1951, 12–17% between 1967–73).[9] On the other hand, the only section of Landes that has consistently resisted this Leftist trend is the southeastern corner (the agricultural region of Tursan, encompassing the canton of Geaune and portions of the cantons of Hagetmau, Saint-Sever, Grenade, and Aire-sur-l'Adour), the one area of the department in which *métayage* has never been a common mode of land tenure. Of the three Landes *circonscriptions*, only the one covering this region elected a non-Socialist (a Center-Democrat) to parliament in each of the elections from 1967 to 1973.[10]

As one would expect, the FNSEA has historically experienced a great deal of difficulty in recruiting the farmers of this department far removed—geographically, socioeconomically, and politically—from the prosperous wheat fields of Aisne. Indeed, from the early 1950s through the mid-1960s, the FDSEA of Landes was arguably the weakest in all of France. When it split from the Leftist "CGA des Landes" in 1951, the FNSEA's departmental affiliate could claim the membership of only a tiny fraction of the farmers; by 1963 its membership density stood at only 12.7%, while its rival—now the CGA-MODEF—enrolled 46% of the farmers on its membership lists. The inferiority of the FDSEA was most embarrassingly manifested in 1964, when Chamber of Agriculture elections were contested for the first time in the department: the FDSEA received only 35% of the votes in the college of *chefs d'exploitation* and lost *all* of the directly elected seats. The secretary-general of MODEF, a Communist, proudly assumed the role of president of the Chamber of Agriculture.

The 1964 electoral fiasco did not auger well for the FDSEA. From the mid-1960s through the 1970s, however, the FDSEA enjoyed a remarkable improvement in status relative to its MODEF rival: it more than doubled its membership density (to 29%), increased its electoral support and—in 1970—won control of the Chamber of Agriculture. As will be discussed in the first section, this progress of the FDSEA can be attributed in part to a renewal of its elite, a change in its program, and the expansion of its organizational activity—combined with the disproportionate exodus from the land of MODEF supporters. But as the second section will demonstrate, the advance of the FDSEA must be attributed primarily to the benefits it received from the state following the advent of the corporatist system. The impact of corporatization in French agriculture was more dramatic in Landes than in virtually any other department: while the FNSEA's affiliate managed to achieve hegemony in Landes, it was an extremely dependent or even *artificial* hegemony.

THE BASES OF THE FDSEA'S INFERIORITY VIS-À-VIS MODEF

PURPOSIVE INCENTIVES

The program of the FNSEA/FDSEA has never enjoyed wide appeal in Landes. At the time of its founding in the syndical scission of 1951, the organization recognized as the FNSEA's departmental affiliate could claim the support of only a small minority of the Landais. Since 1964 the FDSEA has changed its policies and its image in such a way as to increase somewhat its popularity among its nontraditional constituencies. Nevertheless, from the 1950s to the present the purposive incentives of the FDSEA have essentially restricted the union to the recruitment of the more politically conservative and socioeconomically advantaged farmers of the department.

From SLIR to the FDSEA

As did farmers all over France, most Landais hoped that the new CGA-FNSEA established during the Liberation period could bring syndical unity to their department. In Landes, however, these hopes were soon dashed by the emergence of serious political and socioeconomic divisions within the agricultural sector. The first tensions appeared in March 1945, when the initial CGA-FDSEA election produced a union bureau composed almost entirely of *métayers-fermiers* known to be Communist and Socialist activists; landowners and more conservative farmers, many of whom had been powerful during the era of the Vichy Corporation, found themselves excluded from the union's elite.[11]

Union tensions were exacerbated after the passage, in 1946, of the Statut de Fermage. Prepared in 1945 by Tanguy-Prigent, the Socialist minister of agriculture, this bill was pushed through parliament by a *rapporteur général* from Landes—an SFIO deputy, Charles Lamarque-Cando. The Statut de Fermage, which stands in retrospect as "one of the principal agricultural bills of the Fourth Republic," greatly increased the rights of *métayers* and *fermiers*. The law facilitated the transformation of *métayage* into *fermage*, decreased the share of the harvest owed by *métayers* to their landlords, lengthened the term of land leases held by *métayers-fermiers* to nine years, limited the ability of landowners to evict their tenants, and gave tenants the right to remuneration by the landowner for improvements that they might make on their farms.[12]

In Landes the Statut de Fermage represented nothing short of a legal revolution in socioeconomic relations. The years from 1946 to the early 1950s were understandably replete with conflict between landowners and *métayers-fermiers* attempting to assert their newly granted rights. In this veritable class struggle, there was no doubt as to the side taken by the CGA-FDSEA: union leaders mustered the full force of the organization to support the small farmers, publicizing abuses by the landlords and organizing demonstrations in favor of victimized *petits*. The most famous "great battle" took place in Marosse during January and February of 1950. For more than a month, masses mobilized by the union confronted the riot police—witnessed by a large contingent of the Parisian press—in protest over the expulsion of several *métayers* from their plots. Many of the landlords charged with violating the letter or spirit of the new laws were barred from the union at its assemblies between 1945–50.[13]

It was primarily these expulsions that led in turn to the CGA-FDSEA's expulsion from the FNSEA in February 1951. Meeting in Paris with the same Commission Nationale des Conflits that had ruled against the Communist leaders of the FDSEA in Corrèze (and elsewhere) the year before, the representatives from Landes repeated their charges against the landowners who had been expelled. After hearing testimony from the landowners, the commission delivered its ruling: the CGA-FDSEA des Landes had "become a Communist cell," had violated the statutes of the FNSEA, and would thus be expelled from the national federation.[14] Soon thereafter the commission granted official FDSEA status to a small rival "union" which had been formed in 1949, the SLIR (Syndicat Landais d'Initiatives Rurales). As will be discussed later, however, the old CGA-FDSEA—operating as the "CGA" during the 1950s and as the CGA-MODEF after 1959—did not lose its popularity along with its official name.

The organization accorded FNSEA sanction after 1951 was profoundly different from the old CGA-FDSEA. Led by a deeply religious small farmer from Meilhan (Tartas-Est), René Lafourcade, the new FDSEA preached the corporative gospel of social peace and class unity within the agricultural sector. Upon organizing SLIR in 1949, Lafourcade announced that its intention was to "fill a void." The CGA was not, as a true farmers' union should be, working to "educate the mass of the *paysans landais*," to solve the urgent "technical problems" of production. For the CGA, he contended, only "one thing counts": "Faire de la lutte des classes, dresser l'une contre l'autre deux categories d'agriculteurs." As an alternative Lafourcade offered the farmers an organization in which "one does not engage in politics, but . . . treats only professional questions."[15]

Lafourcade and the SLIR-FDSEA elite rejected the notion that "the class struggle," "social agitation" or "la voie revendicative" could solve the problems of the *métayers-fermiers*. The plight of all farmers, they contended, could be improved only through "la voie constructive": the advancement of the entire profession through individual initiative ("Aide-toi, le ciel t'aidera") and sectoral unity. The "men blinded by politics" promised the masses a "utopian dream" and flattered them by "exaggerating" their rights, argued Lafourcade. But "one cannot always speak of rights, one must also think of duties." "Duty," he continued, "consists . . . of subordinating the particular interest to the general interest . . . the happiness of all resides in union, in the implementation of a constructive program of education and the continual improvement of our production." In place of the CGA's promise of victory for the *métayers-fermiers*, Lafourcade offered his own—corporative—utopian dream:

> We must work to see that the *paysans landais* some day abandon their ideologies of diverse colors, which divide them, and move toward the union of all in the village, toward an atmosphere of trust, goodness and peace. What could be more beautiful, indeed, than a village in which all of those who earn their living from agriculture were united in a single union possessing its sections for landlords (*bailleurs*), tenants (*preneurs*), *proprietaires-exploitants*, . . . its local cooperative, . . . its specialized sections for wheat, for corn, for wine, for meat, for milk, etc.

Thus all would be united in a "common movement toward progress," assured of the enjoyment of "the true prosperity" measured not in money but in the proper "virtue" available to all classes.[16]

Throughout the 1950s the FDSEA of Landes loyally supported the programs of the FNSEA while its leaders—and especially Lafourcade—continued to espouse their corporative ideal of class unity and to condemn the incursion of "politics" (read "Communists") into the agricultural sector. No fundamental change in FDSEA principles accompanied the rise to union power of new, younger leaders in the 1960s. But they did bring to the union a significant change in tone—less religiously anti-Communist, more pragmatic. Reflecting on the role played by Lafourcade in the union's development, the young FDSEA director stated in 1976: "he was a tireless worker and a good honest man who built the foundations of this organization . . . but his philosophy belonged to the eighteenth century."[17] Yet even with this rejection of Lafourcade's zealotry and—as will be discussed later—a tremendous expansion of the FDSEA's organizational activity, the FNSEA's affiliate in Landes has been unable to expand its appeal far beyond the constituencies receptive to Lafourcade's sermons in the 1950s.

The Political Bases of Division

Just as in Corrèze, the syndical division in Landes has neatly reflected the department's political polarization ever since the early 1950s. In Corrèze the political factor has contributed to the maintenance of a tenuous FDSEA dominance: Socialists in that department have traditionally been unwilling or unable to cooperate with the Communists, and until quite recently most of them have thus supported the "moderates" of the FDSEA (see Chapter 6). In Landes, however, the political factor has worked in favor not of the FDSEA, but of the CGA-MODEF. As evidenced by the SFIO's sponsorship of the pro-*métayer* Statut de Fermage in 1946, the Socialists in Landes have traditionally allied with the Communists on the most important socioeconomic issues of the department. Throughout the last three decades both the "moderate" political parties and the FDSEA in Landes have suffered from the solidarity of the Left: in the political realm, the Communists have continually supported Socialist candidates on the second ballot of legislative elections; in the syndical realm, the Socialists have—with relatively few reservations—cooperated with a CGA-MODEF dominated by Communist activists.[18]

As Lafourcade and his successors in the FDSEA have often been eager to point out, there can be no doubt that the elite of the CGA-MODEF has always been predominantly Communist. The union's bureau has consistently contained a majority of Communist activists. Its president and secretary-general have always been not only members of the Communist Party, but also members of the party's federal bureau for Landes. Moreover, the administrative staff of the CGA-MODEF has been composed almost entirely of Communists, and the union's director for the past thirty years—Jean Bourlon—has also served as a member of the Communist Party's federal bureau. The Communist members of the MODEF elite have by no means been hesitant to openly manifest their political affiliation. Indeed, the MODEF president as of 1976 (Franck Marcadé) had been the Communist candidate for *deputé-suppléant* in the second *circonscription* of

Landes at each of the last several legislative elections—and both the MODEF president and senior vice-president (Marcel Sintas) were Communist members of the department's Conseil Général.[19]

Although the elite of the CGA-MODEF has been dominated by the Communists, it is misleading and inaccurate to portray the organization as simply a "Communist cell" or a "branch of the Communist Party." If anything, the CGA-MODEF has been a "branch" or "transmission belt" for the united Left in Landes. At the elite level, Socialists have always exercised a good deal of influence. In the 1976 bureau, for example, five of the eleven members were prominent Socialists—one of them (André Cantiran), a MODEF vice-president, was presently serving as a *deputé-suppléant* for the Socialist Party in the department's first *circonscription*. During the 1960s, one of the MODEF vice-presidents (Fernand Secheer) served for a time as an SFIO deputy. And a Socialist has traditionally been chosen as president of the union's influential Association des Fermiers et Métayers.[20]

At the rank-and-file level of the CGA-MODEF, Socialists or Socialist sympathizers have greatly outnumbered Communists. This contention of the union's elite seems to be substantiated by available ecological data. For example, Left votes by canton in the 1962 legislative election and MODEF votes in the 1964 Chamber of Agriculture election yield a correlation coefficient of 0.395; in contrast, the correlation between Communist votes and MODEF votes in these two elections was merely 0.178. The data for more recent years yield similar results, while demonstrating that the progress of the FDSEA has limited MODEF support more to strongholds of the Left. Left votes in the 1973 legislative election correlated with MODEF votes in the 1974–76 chamber elections to the tune of 0.641; for the same elections, the Communist-MODEF vote correlation was 0.423.[21]

Because its strength has been dependent on the support of both Socialist elites and members, the CGA-MODEF has seldom if ever been employed as a tool of strictly PCF propaganda; Socialist as well as Communist activists affirm this in interviews. However, the CGA-MODEF has never claimed to be an "apolitical" union. Especially in recent years, with the Left often functioning in relatively united fashion at the national level, MODEF has undertaken a variety of political activities. Since the agreement on the Common Program, for example, the union has organized yearly study groups to explain the nature of the pact. And in 1974 the union assisted avidly in François Mitterrand's presidential campaign within the department.[22]

In contrast, the FDSEA *has* claimed to be completely "apolitical" ever since the days of Lafourcade. Nevertheless, as one would expect, both the elites and the supporters of the FDSEA have always been drawn predominantly from the Center-Right. None of the union's leaders in the 1950s ran for public office or explicitly manifested a political affiliation in any other way; yet interviews with two of the original FDSEA bureau members (elected in 1951) confirmed that the union's elite of this era consisted entirely of MRP supporters and other "moderates." One man who was said to have been on the "Left wing" of the SLIR and early FDSEA boasted that "only the width of a cigarette paper" had separated him from the "moderate Socialists."[23]

Since the renewal of the FDSEA elite in 1964, some "moderate Socialists" have been recruited as union leaders and administrators. Nevertheless, the political complexion of the union's elite has not changed considerably.[24] Indeed, on at least one occasion—at the time of the 1967 legislative elections—the allegedly "apolitical" union has been openly linked with one of the Center-Right parties. Long-time FDSEA vice-president and (since 1964) director Jean Ducourneau ran in 1967 as the Center-Democratic Party's candidate for deputy in the department's first *circonscription*. Moreover, he made little effort to avoid giving his candidacy the appearance of formal FDSEA sanction. On the ballot he listed his occupation as "director of the FDSEA" (in contrast, MODEF candidates for political office have never listed their union affiliation on the ballot, describing themselves simply as "agriculteur" or "cultivateur"). More important, Ducourneau employed the FDSEA headquarters as his de facto campaign center—in fact, boxes of his party pamphlets and letters from such party leaders as Jean Lecanuet are still stored in the FDSEA archives (as I discovered by chance in the process of research). After years of being castigated by the FDSEA for "mixing politics and union affairs," the CGA-MODEF responded to the Ducourneau affair with an amusing if sardonic article entitled "M. Ducourneau: La Politique et le Syndicalisme." With "the campaign headquarters of the Center Democrats . . . installed at the home of the FDSEA," the article concluded, "MM. Ducourneau . . . et consorts auront beau crier qu'ils ne font pas de politique!"[25]

As for the rank and file of the FDSEA, it is clear that they have also consistently been recruited primarily from among the conservatives of Landes. As Figure 7.3 shows, the farmers older than sixty-five in 1976—those who had been initially recruited in the 1950s—voted for the FDSEA at a rate higher than 45% in only three cantons, all located in the "moderate" southeast corner of the department. FDSEA votes in the Chamber of Agriculture election of 1964 and Right votes in the 1962 legislative election yield a correlation coefficient of 0.365. And the FDSEA-Right vote correlation was even higher for the 1974–76 chamber elections and the 1973 legislative election: 0.626.[26]

Socioeconomic Divisions

A former secretary-general of the FDSEA interviewed in 1976 despaired that, while the CGA-MODEF enjoyed a reputation as the "defender of the small farmers," the FDSEA since the 1950s had been unfairly branded as the "union of the *hautes propriétaires*."[27] Such a categorization is not entirely unjust, however; the socioeconomic divisions of Landes agriculture have been reflected in the

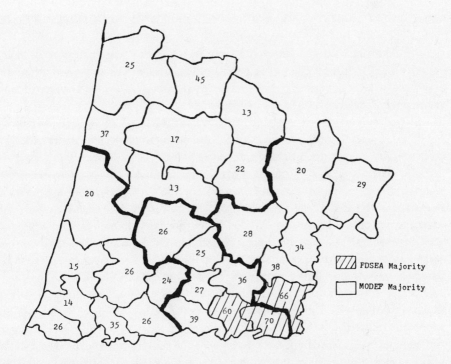

Figure 7.3 FDSEA vote (percentage by canton) in the 1976 chamber election—college of *anciens exploitants*.

composition of the FDSEA and CGA-MODEF elites and membership rolls ever since the union scission of 1951.

The FDSEA of the 1950s was not controlled exclusively or even primarily by large landowners; Lafourcade, its major spokesman, and the majority of its bureau members were small farmers devoted to the corporative ideal discussed earlier. Nevertheless, the FDSEA's bureau and administrative council did contain some prosperous *propriétaires* along with those of modest means from the Tursan region. Moreover, in line with Lafourcade's vision of the "ideal village" of class unity, the FDSEA operated a Section des Bailleurs consisting of the sort of landlords drummed out of the CGA in 1950–51. It was not untill 1964, on the other hand, that the FDSEA made a serious attempt to organize a Section des Fermiers et Métayers.[28] In sharp contrast, the CGA bureau of the 1950s and early 1960s was composed entirely of small farmers—most of them *fermiers-métayers*. Furthermore, the CGA refused to accept *bailleurs* as members while operating the largest Section des Fermiers et Métayers in all of France.[29]

As of 1976 the socioeconomic divisions of the scission era were still clearly reflected in the contrasting compositions of the two unions' elites. The FDSEA bureau members were, within the Landes context, a most privileged group. The farms held by the nine bureau officers covered an average of 83 hectares—more than six times the size of the average departmental farm. Four of the nine officers operated farms of at least 100 hectares, while less than 1% of the farms in Landes were this size or larger. Moreover, while only 7% of the farmers in Landes employed any *salariés*, almost 80% of the bureau members did so.[30] Although they were by no means among the most disadvantaged farmers of the department, the MODEF bureau members of 1976 were modest in means compared to the FDSEA elite. The farms of the MODEF officers covered an average of only 27 hectares, with the two largest covering 70 and 40 hectares. Furthermore, none of the MODEF bureau members employed *salariés*.[31]

There are no data available from which to derive a detailed comparison of the socioeconomic status of the two unions' rank and file. However, from the results of elections to the department's Tribunaux Paritaires de Baux Ruraux (special courts established at the time of the Liberation to adjudicate legal disputes between *fermiers-métayers* and their landlords) it is at least apparent that the two unions have appealed quite unequally to the most and least prosperous of the Landais. Since the 1950s the FDSEA has presented a slate of *bailleurs* for election to the Tribunaux—a slate uncontested by the CGA-MODEF. Not until 1973, however, did the FDSEA present a slate of *preneurs* (*fermiers-métayers*) in opposition to that of the CGA-MODEF. The results of the 1973 election underscored the limited following of the FDSEA among the relatively disadvantaged farmers. For the department as a whole, the FDSEA received only 17% of the *preneurs*' votes. The FDSEA did not even present candidates in the southwestern Dax region, the area of MODEF's greatest membership density and popularity. In the northeastern section around Mont-de-Marsan, the FDSEA tallied 24% of the vote. Only in the southeastern corner of the department—the conservative Saint-Sever district, including the cantons of Geaune and Hagetmau—did the FDSEA elect its two candidates, with 55% of the vote. To the FDSEA, this single victory symbolized "a terrible contre-coup to the words and writings of MODEF," which had long claimed to be the sole representative of the *preneurs*—but the election hardly challenged MODEF's status as their favored union.[32]

To a great degree, therefore, the recruitment efforts of the FDSEA in Landes have been limited by its inability to appeal to the predominantly Leftist and disadvantaged farmers of the department. But the efforts of the FDSEA have long been hindered as well by its inability to match the material incentives for membership offered by the CGA-MODEF.

MATERIAL INCENTIVES

The *Syndicalisme de Sentiment*

By the end of 1963 the FDSEA had evolved into a stagnant union headed by aging elites resigned to the agricultural sector's domination by MODEF, or what they still termed the "ex-CGA." More than a decade after the 1951 scission, the FDSEA could claim only slightly more than one fifth of the department's unionized farmers: 2,365 (12.7% of the farmers) compared to 8,593 (46%) for MODEF.[33] The FDSEA had become what one official would later term a "*syndicalisme de sentiment*," reaching the Landais almost exclusively through Lafourcade's corporative and anti-Communist sermons in the union's biweekly paper *Le Réveil Landais*. The union was hardly an organization at all. Its budget of about 35,000 francs was only one fifth as large as that of the relatively poor FDSEA of Corrèze and only one third the size of that of its MODEF rival— moreover, more than half of the meager budget was consumed by the costs of Lafourcade's newspaper. The FDSEA functioned with *no* salaried administrative personnel, while MODEF had a staff of five; the FDSEA held no regular *permanences* outside of Mont-de-Marsan, while the staff and elite of MODEF were available weekly in virtually every canton to handle the problems of members. The "specialized sections" of the FDSEA functioned only in the southeastern corner of the department—indeed, as Figure 7.4 shows, the union could claim only a sprinkling of members elsewhere. The FDSEA played a role in the Chamber of Agriculture only because the leaders of MODEF had never presented separate slates of candidates for election. Because its limited budget had made it appear to be of only modest importance, and because it had long been headed by a politically "independent" president capable of arbitrating between the two unions, the CGA-MODEF had always agreed to present "united lists" of chamber candidates according the FDSEA a good deal of representation.[34]

But the FDSEA received a tremendous jolt in 1964. Three weeks before the chamber elections of 1964, the leaders of MODEF announced that they would break with tradition and present partisan lists of candidates in the three most populous (the "agricultural" rather than forested) districts of Landes. The MODEF decision was predicated on the realization that the increasingly wealthy and influential chamber had become "a prize worth fighting for" and the assumption that the FDSEA could be easily beaten.[35] Faced with this well-calculated power play, the FDSEA leaders professed shock and protested vehemently. Lafourcade denounced MODEF for deciding to "politicize" what should be a "purely professional" institution and announced that the FDSEA would refuse to conduct—as MODEF planned—a "political-style campaign" in support of its candidates. "Honest, strictly professional elections," declared Lafourcade in *Le Réveil Landais*, "do not require such propaganda." Meanwhile, however, Lafourcade issued a confidential memo to all of this cantonal presidents urging that the electoral contest be presented in the most simplistic political terms:

> In nearly all of the colleges two lists are opposed. One defends the principles of the FNSEA, of which the motto is "The profession first; no politics with the union." All *tendances* are represented within the FNSEA. The other union fights against the national federation to divide it. It is patronized by the Communist Party and the CGT. The unspoken goal of its leaders is to lead the peasants toward their party.

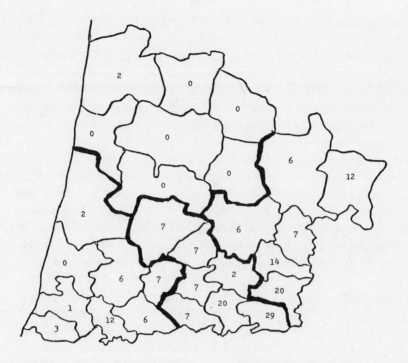

Figure 7.4 FDSEA membership density by canton, 1963. Membership density (member/farms larger than 2 hectares) for the entire department = 12.7%.

With them the party is always more important than the profession. Their union is the agricultural section of the Communist party.[36]

Lafourcade's allegedly "apolitical" attack on the "ex-CGA" was a bit more restrained in his public articles, but it was no less explicit. He argued that the "ex-CGA" could be equated with the Communist Party and claimed that it would be opposed by "all of the true *syndicalistes*, of all classes and origins, Socialists, Radicals, 'MRPists,' Centrists, Gaullists, even 'conservatives,' not to mention the large mass who form the majority: the *non-politistes*."[37]

The result of the FDSEA's years of organizational stagnation combined with its "purely professional" campaign was an unmitigated fiasco, the reverberations of which reached as far as Paris and the FNSEA *centrale*. The FDSEA lost all three of its direct confrontation with the "ex-CGA," received a mere 35.3% of the total vote, and found itself virtually excluded from the chamber. Only its two candidates from the "united list" for the forested district and its three uncontested candidates in the college for *bailleurs* made their way into the twenty-eight seat chamber. Within the next few months the MODEF secretary-general, Marcel Sintas, was elected chamber president by a vote of 22–0, with 6 abstentions. MODEF assumed full control of the chamber and, when a new chamber office building was constructed a year later, installed its union headquarters in this seat of official agricultural power.[38]

"We have received a *belle piquette*," wrote FDSEA vice-president Ducourneau in the first postelection issue of *Le Réveil Landais*, "Why hide it? Everyone knows about it." Ascribing the loss to the deception of the "ex-CGA" and the enormous number of nonvoters (45.7%), Lafourcade could only vow: "not at all discouraged, we must commence at zero and plan a robust counterattack. Remember my prediction: When one hits bottom one must inevitably rise again."[39]

Building a *Syndicalisme d'Intérêt*

Beginning almost "at zero," the FDSEA would indeed "rise" within the next ten years—to a position of organizational strength without precedent in its history. By 1970 the FDSEA obtained control of the Chamber of Agriculture, and by 1974 it increased its membership to 3,706—a membership density of 29%, still considerably less than that of MODEF but more than double its 1963 figure.[40] This "rise" of the FDSEA must be attributed largely, as will be discussed in the next section, to the direct assistance it received from the state through the structures of the corporatist system. However, it also entailed a considerable revivification effort on the part of a renewed FDSEA elite—assisted by the FNSEA *centrale* in Paris.

"In light of the grave situation provoked by the elections to the Chamber of Agriculture," Lafourcade asserted in a 1964 memo to his administrative council, important fundamental decisions will have to be taken to "chart a new path for the future."[41] The members of the FDSEA council agreed—but ironically, one of the first fundamental decisions they made in charting their new path was that the sickly, sixty-year-old Lafourcade should resign the presidency of the union he had founded. Pressuring Lafourcade to resign, the younger members of the FDSEA elite felt that the essential orientation of union activity would have to change. They disagreed neither with his politics nor with his loyalty to the FNSEA and its policies; what they rejected was his missionary zeal and his lack of attention to organizational dynamics. "He was simply too pure," one young FDSEA official commented years later. "He continued to think that the peasants could—and should—be attracted to the union by his moral and political arguments. His was a *syndicalisme de sentiment* . . . what we needed was a *syndicalisme d'intérêt*."[42]

The man chosen to replace Lafourcade as president and to coordinate the building of a *syndicalisme d'intérêt* was Jacques Castaing, a dynamic thirty-five-year-old farmer from Hagetmau who had briefly served as the union's vice-president. Castaing was pragmatic, less concerned with abstract moralizing and more concerned with the sort of union approach that Blondelle had instituted in Aisne: he believed that the union must establish close contact with the *base*, intensify its activity *sur le terrain*, and give the farmers a "material interest in joining the union."[43] What this meant, noted one of the new members of the

Castaing *équipe*, was that "we had to become the pupils (*élèves*) of MODEF . . . the fight under Lafourcade was like a rugby match between great athletes and a bunch of missionaries . . . we had to start playing the game their way, working hard, holding *permanences*, giving services."[44]

One of the first steps taken by the Castaing *équipe* was to contact FNSEA officials in Paris and to request their support in the *relance* effort. In March 1964 the head of the FNSEA's Service d'Action Syndicale, M. Delorme, traveled to Landes to discuss means of improving FDSEA activity in the department. Delorme offered several basic suggestions for revitalizing the union: (1) hire some staff personnel who could devote themselves full time to union activities; (2) work to develop socioeconomic services that could attract members to the organization; and (3) make every effort to increase the budget and to use it wisely. On the one hand, he suggested economy measures such as ceasing to publish such a costly union newspaper; within two years the FDSEA thus halted publication of *Le Réveil Landais* and began to share the costs of the paper (*Le Sillon*) sponsored by the FDSEA of a neighboring department, Basses-Pyrénées. On the other hand, he promised both indirect and direct financial assistance from the FNSEA: the FDSEA would be allowed to pay only a portion of its national dues for the next few years while remaining on good terms with the *centrale*, and the FDSEA would be accorded a significant subsidy out of the *promotion collective* fund that the FNSEA received from the state.[45]

Over the next few years the FNSEA assisted the FDSEA of Landes in the planning and implementation of a great many union functions subsidized with thousands of francs from the *promotion collective* fund. In 1964, for example, the FDSEA sponsored several major "information and education" sessions in various localities, each featuring as guest speaker a member of the regional or national union elite.[46] The next year, in December of 1965, six "Journées d'Etude" were organized in Dax—the heart of MODEF country—under the auspices of the FNSEA's Service de Perfectionment des Cadres. Most of these sessions were concerned at least ostensibly with technical-economic topics, but their central purpose was indubitably to revivify the FDSEA.[47] After the sessions were initially proposed by the FDSEA, FNSEA president Gérard de Caffarelli wrote to suggest two schemes which could render the "education" sessions "an aid for the Landes Federation in its effort of *relance syndicale*." First of all, Caffarelli instructed the FDSEA to plan, in conjunction with the normal sessions, a *vin d'honneur* to which the department's leading notables (both in and outside of agriculture, including political figures) would be invited; the reception was to be financed entirely by the FNSEA, but the FDSEA was to play the role of "puissance invitante." Second, "the presence of the administrators of the FNSEA at Dax" was to be exploited so as to allow "a national participation in the . . . effort of *relance syndicale*." Thus on the day preceding the "education" sessions, the national figures—whose travel to Landes was covered by the *promotion collective* subsidy—were to attend local union meetings in ten different cantons.[48] As is recorded in the correspondence of

FDSEA leaders, the "Journées d'Etude" proved to be a great success for the union—a success funded indirectly by the state. Such sessions were repeated in the following years, each receiving subsidies of 4,000 francs or more.[49]

Meanwhile, the FDSEA proceeded in its efforts to expand its staff and its membership. Two months after the Delorme visit, in May 1964, Castaing appointed the FDSEA's first salaried administrative director: Jean Ducourneau, union vice-president since the early 1950s.[50] By the end of the year a second full-time organizer and administrative secretary, François Barets, had been appointed. The Barets appointment epitomized the effort to create a new FDSEA image and stimulate its activity: he was the son of a *métayer*, known to be "moderately" Leftist, and at the age of twenty-four was energetic and willing to work "fourteen hours a day."[51] Over the next few years, the Castaing *équipe* and the new staff personnel concentrated their attention on three basic tasks: (1) creating new local unions in cantons that had previously been written off as the territory of MODEF; (2) expanding personal services to members through *permanences*; and (3) expanding collective services through the organization of the union's special socioeconomic sections.

Creating Local Unions

The new union elite systematically attacked the problem of expanding the FDSEA's network of local unions. Barets and others studied commune-by-commune results of the 1964 chamber election and made note of localities in which the FDSEA seemed to possess a large number of sympathizers who could be transformed into members. Each of the communes in which FDSEA implantation seemed possible were then "sounded out" through contacts with local notables. Two networks of contacts were employed. First, confidential memos were sent to the presidents of FDSEA unions in neighboring communes, requesting the "names and addresses of farmers [in the target commune] . . . likely to join our FDSEA." Though this effort was not always successful, it did produce some excellent results. Many presidents responded with expressions of enthusiasm and lists of thirty or forty potential members.[52] One of the more detailed negative responses indicates the enormous difficulty of attempting to form FDSEA local unions in the MODEF heartland:

> At Nerbis [in Mugron] we have only a single farmer on whom we can count . . . with him we have discussed the union situation at Nerbis and there is nothing that can be done for the moment. The mayor . . . is an administrator of the other Federation, his son is the cantonal president for the other Federation's youth branch, and both are *animateurs* of the CUMA [Coopérative d'Utilisation du Matériel Agricole] and all other local activities. In principle everything is based on them and no one would dare try to *sortir de leurs sillages*.[53]

A second sort of contact alluded to in this letter was also employed in the implantation campaign: politically sympathetic mayors. Consulting local officials and newspapers, the FDSEA staff compiled a notebook with the names and political affiliations of all mayors in the department. Those who were known to be Communists or "pure Socialists" (sometimes referred to in the notebook as "Communist Socialists") were avoided in favor of the union contacts mentioned earlier. But all of the other mayors were contacted via letters. This tactic produced some results, but it was often an abysmal failure. The mayor of Saint-Vincent-de-Tyrosse, for example, responded to the FDSEA request for organizational assistance in the following icy language:

> I regret to inform you that it is impossible for me to engage in the constitution of a farmers union. There are others who are more qualified for that, but I believe that I must point out to you that another union already exists to which, if the information which has been given to me is correct, almost all of the farmers belong.[54]

As this letter and the preceding one clearly reveal, the task of challenging a solidly implanted farmers' union can be formidable indeed—but the task would be even more formidable if not impossible for a minority union (such as the MODEF in Aisne) unequipped with the sort of corporatist supports discussed later in this chapter.

Permanences and Personal Services

Officials of both unions in Landes recognized in 1964 that one of the major sources of MODEF strength in Landes through the years had been its extensive network of regular permanences—well publicized "office hours" kept by staff and elected officials at convenient locations (a café, a mairie, the office of a cooperative, etc.) throughout the countryside. To the permanences a host of MODEF members would come to request precisely the same sort of personal services asked of the cantonal secretaries in Aisne—everything from assistance in obtaining subsidies to help in reading and understanding tax laws. The permanences allowed the MODEF leaders to keep in contact with their rank and file, to pass along union information and—in the words of one official—"to give the members the feeling that their union cards are worth something."[55] As of 1964 the CGA-MODEF activists provided members with regular permanences in fifteen different villages and towns of fourteen different cantons.[56]

Before 1964, the FDSEA had held no regular permanences—even in the chef-lieu, Mont-de-Marsan. According to one FDSEA official, the union was simply not capable of doing so: "We were at a disadvantage. They had more money from dues to pay staff personnel, but more importantly . . . they had more motivation—they were doubly motivated, devoted not only to their union ideals but also to their political ideals."[57] After the ascension of the Castaing équipe a major effort was made to establish permanences. Armed with more motivation to work "at the base" and assisted for the first time by paid staff personnel, the

FDSEA leaders announced in 1964 that members could consult with union representatives daily in Mont-de-Marsan and once weekly at several other locales.[58] These service sessions were expanded throughout the 1960s with the assistance of publicly financed ADASEA personnel.

The Socioeconomic Sections

The new FDSEA elites also made a major effort from the mid-1960s onward to create or reinvigorate the union's socioeconomic sections. First priority was given to the establishment of an FDSEA Section des Fermiers et Métayers; although such a section had long existed on paper, it scarcely functioned at all as of 1964. Ever since the early 1950s, the Lafourcade bureau had written off any chance of recruiting *fermiers-métayers* in competition with the CGA-MODEF. But Castaing and his associates decided that the organization of a rival section would be crucial to the *relance* effort, for two reasons. First of all, the absence of an FDSEA section served to reinforce the notion that the FDSEA was simply "the union of the *bailleurs*." And the FDSEA leaders were convinced that a significant number of *fermiers-métayers* were sympathetic to the principles of the FDSEA, but were virtually forced to join the MODEF section for the services it could provide—especially paralegal defense of their rights before the *tribunaux paritaires* (one MODEF official in particular, Albert Juste, was famous for his presentation of cases before the *tribunaux*).[59]

In its effort to organize a section, the FDSEA staff employed techniques similar to those used in organizing new unions. A circular was sent to each local union marked "very urgent and confidential." The local presidents were requested to send to union headquarters the names and addresses of the three "most serious" *fermiers-métayers* in the commune. Informed by the FNSEA that only two members (a president and treasurer) were required for the establishment of each local section, the staff acted quickly to form sections from which could be derived a departmental bureau. Indeed, the staff acted so quickly that it managed to alienate some of the section's few veteran members. When the "delegates" of the local sections met in January 1965 to name representatives for a national meeting in Paris, some local "presidents" found out about the proceedings only by reading *Le Sillon*. As one irate "president" complained in a letter to Ducourneau, the lack of a well-publicized convocation made it evident that "without doubt the *section des preneurs* is run by one or two men; the others count only on paper."[60]

While the section may have been established with undue haste, serious efforts to appeal to the *fermiers-métayers* soon followed. Special weekly *permanences* were scheduled for the *fermiers-métayers* of the conservative Tursan region, where the greatest recruitment success was expected; one of the new staff members, Barets, was assigned the task of defending clients à la Juste before the *tribunaux paritaires*; and, in a patent imitation of MODEF's newspaper, a "Coin des Preneurs" column began to appear regularly in *Le Reveil Landais* (and was continued in *Le Sillon*).[61] The new FDSEA section proved to be a moderate success, although it stood no chance of overtaking its MODEF counterpart. A decade after its formation, the FDSEA *section des preneurs* still existed only on paper in most of the communes of the MODEF heartland. Moreover, as noted, the FDSEA was able to attract only 17% of the departmental vote for its slate of *fermiers-métayers* candidates in the *tribunaux* elections of 1973—but it did win seats on the *tribunaux* for its representatives from the Saint Sever (Tursan) district.[62]

FDSEA energies were also devoted to pumping some life into two other social sections that had been virtually moribund during the 1950s: the *section féminine* and the CDJA. In 1965 the wife of a former FDSEA secretary-général was "elected" president of the Women's Section; within a few years, aided by subsidies from SUAD similar to those discussed in Aisne and Corrèze, this section had inaugurated a program of activities for women focusing on such issues as accounting and the obtainment of scholarships for children.[63] SUAD subsidies also contributed to the activities of the CDJA, as its two *animateurs* worked with the elected officials to develop various *vulgarisation* programs.[64] The public image of the Landes CDJA was given a significant boost when, in the years after the 1964 chamber election, its leaders were consistently selected for national office. CDJA President Michel Simon was first elected to the CNJA administrative council, and then, from 1968 to 1970, served as the national president of the CNJA; when Simon stepped down in 1970, the new president of the Landes CDJA—Laurent Damestoy—was elected adjunct secretary-general of the CNJA.[65] The election of the young leaders from Landes served both to increase the status of the FDSEA-CDJA within the department and to provide the CNJA with "dependable" (i.e., non-Leftist) elite representatives from the "South."[66]

Attention was also given to the organization of specialized economic sections (again with the help of some subsidies to be discussed later), producer groups for various products and a SICA (Société d'Intérêt Collectif Agricole) "Foie Gras des Landes."[67] All of these activities served to demonstrate the FDSEA's newfound commitment to "concrete action" and "material interests" rather than stale moralizing.

For the most part, the organizational activities designed to strengthen the FDSEA were concentrated in the heavily populated "agricultural" southeastern third of the department. However, in the mid-1960s, the union also began to devote considerable attention to the sparsely populated forest region of the northwest. For years this Grande Lande region had been experiencing a slow but steady transformation of both its economic and its demographic character. On the one hand, the miserable quality of the *paysan-gemmeur* life had led to a tremendous rate of exodus from the land—by far the greatest rate within the department; more than 40% of the part-time farmers abandoned their tiny plots between 1955 and 1970. On the other hand, a new sort of farm and farmer had been appearing; the government's Compagnie d'Aménagement des Landes de Gascogne was consolidating small plots, clearing land, and encouraging men to settle on new farms of 70 hectares and more similar "to those which the *défricheurs* of Aisne" had established in the last century.[68] The ever-increasing *gros* of the Grande Lande—many *pieds-noirs*, most newcomers to the department, and all relatively prosperous—seemed to be likely prospects for FDSEA membership. Before 1968, however, few of them joined the union; FDSEA activities touched only the densely populated southeast and none of its services were tailored to meet the special needs of the few farmers in the forest region.

In 1968, however, one of the Grande Lande residents—Maurice Marrocq, a native Landais and a friend of Lafourcade from his Jaciste days—made convincing arguments for the devotion of organizational energies to his region. First, these few departmental *gros* could contribute significantly to the FDSEA's hard-pressed budget; as of 1968 the union's budget (86,000 francs), while twice that of 1964, was still only one third of MODEF's (and less than half of the Corrèze FDSEA's).[69] Second, the support of these wealthy and influential farmers could be of assistance in the effort to win the district's seats in the forthcoming (1970) chamber election.[70]

With the assistance of the FDSEA elite, Marrocq thus proceeded to organize an intercantonal union: the Syndicat des Exploitations de la Grande Lande (SEGL), headquartered at Marrocq's home in Solferino. Since 1968 the SEGL has served both as an intradepartmental regional federation and as the functional equivalent of the Commission Entreprise in Aisne. In the words of Marrocq: "Our raison d'être has been to overcome the isolation which is a fact of life for us, to attend to problems that the *petits* of the South don't have and don't even realize we have." Aided by FDSEA staff personnel, the SEGL has held information sessions regarding problems related to *main d'oeuvre*—important because most of the members employ from three to ten *salariés*; provided assistance with the completion of tax forms, complicated here by deductions for investment in irrigation equipment, losses due to frequent forest fires, and so on; organized a CUMA for irrigation equipment and provided technical information on advances in irrigation; and organized an association to combat forest fires.[71]

As of 1976, the formation of the SEGL had definitely made its intended membership, budgetary, and electoral contribution to the FDSEA. Beginning in 1968 with thirty-two members, the SEGL had grown to ninety-two members by 1976; moreover, its members had helped to create regular FDSEA unions in four cantons never before organized. In financial terms, the impact of SEGL had been even greater: while its members accounted for only 2% of total FDSEA membership in 1976, they provided 10% of its dues payments (31,630 francs in all, or more than 3,500 francs per member—compared to a 60-franc contribution for a farmer with 15 hectares in the South). Moreover, the SEGL made an important contribution to FDSEA victories in the district's chamber elections of 1970 (won by 77 votes) and 1976 (won by 164 votes).[72]

The formation of the SEGL has been an unqualified material benefit for the FDSEA, yet it has also been somewhat detrimental to the union's effort to portray an image as a valid representative of the department's small farmers and especially the *fermiers-métayers*. The SEGL members' employment of *salariés* on vast farms (averaging 135 hectares) has by no means escaped the attention of MODEF. Many articles in the MODEF paper have alluded to the contradiction between the interests of these "gros patrons" and the *petits* of the South.[73]

Nevertheless, the SEGL and the many other organizational efforts of the FDSEA since 1964 have served to improve tremendously its stature within the department. Between 1963 and 1974, as Figures 7.5 and 7.6 show, the FDSEA increased its number of local unions from 122 to 179, its membership from 2,365 to 3,706, and—with the decline in departmental farmers—its membership density from 12.7% to 29%. During the same years, moreover, the FDSEA increased its budget by a factor of ten (from 35,000 to 340,947 francs) and its salaried staff personnel from zero to seven. Finally, the FDSEA won control of the Chamber of Agriculture in 1970 and has maintained it ever since.[74]

But the FDSEA has remained the minority farmers' union in Landes. Although it has failed to keep pace with the growth of the FDSEA over the last decade, the CGA-MODEF has maintained its superior hold over the department's farmers. In fact, between 1963 and 1974 its budget increased by a factor of almost nine (from 84,020 francs to more than 700,000 francs) and its paid staff personnel increased from five to twelve. Moreover, while its membership total suffered slightly from the rural exodus (falling from 8,593 to 8,561), its membership density increased from 46% to more than 66%. Although FDSEA officials argue that the MODEF membership figures are inflated by the inclusion of part-time farmers primarily engaged in factory work (and ineligible to vote in chamber elections), they acknowledge that the majority of the Landais are still affiliated with their rival.[75]

How then is one to account for the FDSEA's control of the Chamber of Agriculture and the preponderant influence over the making of agricultural policy that it has enjoyed? Neither the answers to these questions nor the growth of the FDSEA can be understood without a consideration of the impact which the corporatist system had on the department of Landes during the 1960s and 1970s.

CORPORATISM AND THE CREATION OF ARTIFICIAL FDSEA HEGEMONY

To a great degree, the rise of the FDSEA is a testament to the power of the central government within the French political system. From the early 1960s onward, government officials in Paris and Mont-de-Marsan successfully pursued a policy of creating artificial FDSEA hegemony in Landes. On the one hand, they

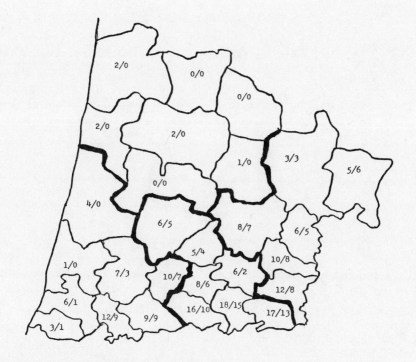

Figure 7.5 FDSEA local unions, 1974/1963.

influenced the composition of the Chamber of Agriculture through "reforms" favorable to the FDSEA and granted the FDSEA the sort of corporatist favors dispensed in other departments. On the other hand, the state acted on several occasions to impede the activities of the superior MODEF organization.

A study of the attempt to impose FDSEA hegemony in Landes also illustrates, however, the limits to the power of the centralized French state. Prefects in Landes were forced to make concessions to the very real—if "illegitimate"—power of MODEF. Moreover, the efforts of the state were counteracted to a degree by MODEF's influence within the "political-horizontal" channel of the French political system: the Conseil Général.

STATE ACTION IN FAVOR OF THE FDSEA

"Reform" of the Chamber

After the electoral fiasco of 1964, the new FDSEA elite resolved to devote considerable effort to improving the union's performance at future elections. Aside from working to expand its membership and popularize its image, the Castaing *équipe* also decided to engage in a full-scale "political-style" campaign for each election. Electoral campaign committees of four to six members were formed in each canton to check registration lists; raise money for campaign expenses through a special subscription; distribute posters, handbills, and free

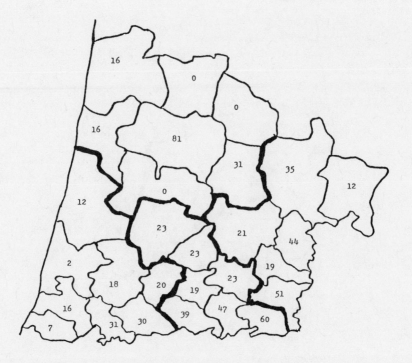

Figure 7.6 FDSEA membership density by canton, 1974. Membership density (members/farms larger than 2 hectares) for the entire department = 29%.

issues of *Le Sillon*; contact "political friends and influential persons" to "request their support or to warn them about the diverse maneuvers of our adversaries"; help turn out FDSEA voters on election day; and monitor the tabulation of votes and report any irregularities to local officials and union leaders.[76]

As mentioned previously, Ducourneau proclaimed in 1964 that it was not the "ex-CGA" but rather the "abstentionnistes" who had caused the FDSEA to lose the election. The FDSEA leaders expected that increasing the electoral turnout would significantly improve their chances. As a result of the intensive campaigns after 1964, this assumption was put to a test, for turnout increased with every election and rose from just over 50% in 1964 to more than 80% in the late 1970s. And indeed, the assumption proved to be correct. Table 7.1 shows that the FDSEA vote has increased in every district at every election (with the exception of the minute decrease in Saint-Sever in 1976).[77]

However, only the 1967 FDSEA victory in Mont-de-Marsan district I was achieved without the benefit of an enormously significant change in the electoral laws instituted before the 1970 election. In September 1969 the Ministry of Agriculture announced that in all future elections the retired farmers would be removed from the college of *chefs d'exploitation* (which until 1983 elected sixteen of the thirty-four members in Landes) and placed in a separate college electing only two chamber representatives. It is impossible to prove that the ministry decreed this "reform" specifically to combat the national influence of MODEF;

Table 7.1   Chamber Election Results (FDSEA Vote)

District	1964	1967	1970	1974	1976
Mont-de-Marsan I	United list	—	52%	—	57%
Mont-de-Marsan II	42%	52%	—	55%	—
Dax	28%	32%	—	37%	—
Saint-Sever	40%	—	49.6%	—	49%

but this inference is certainly plausible. The Ministry of Agriculture was no happier than the FNSEA with the MODEF victory in Landes in 1964 and the nationwide surge in MODEF support—and it was widely recognized that MODEF support was disproportionately strong among the older voters both in Landes and across the nation.[78]

There was certainly no doubt in the minds of the Landes MODEF leaders that the "reform" had been designed to reduce their influence. As a MODEF article commented after the 1970 election, "the *pagaille* created by the . . . decree of 26 September 1969 . . . has, as if by chance, favored certain candidates. . . . An attempt is being made to find a formula in which the vote for MODEF will not count at all."[79] Whatever the intention of the electoral reform, its effect was to aid the FNSEA. Without the reform, the FDSEA—which received only 30–35% of the retired farmers' votes in 1970, 1974, and 1976—would have lost every district in each election from 1970 onward. With the retired farmers' votes added to those of the active farmers, the FDSEA would have received only 47.5% of the 1970 vote and only 42.4% of the 1976 vote for Mont-de-Marsan district I, and only 49.9% (2,750–2,765) of the vote in Mont-de-Marsan district II in 1974.[80] A confidential FDSEA memo acknowledged in 1974, "It is evident that the creation in 1970 of the college anciens exploitants permitted us to obtain very good results in the balloting of the *chefs d'exploitation*."[81]

FDSEA control of the Landes chamber was virtually assured by this reform enabling it to receive 8 of the 16 directly elected seats. For as in most other departments, the FDSEA was always capable of winning the great majority of the indirectly elected seats. Of these 18 seats, 7 were impossible for MODEF to contest: they were reserved for the "propriétaires-usufruitiers" (3) and the representatives of the Centre Regional de la Propriété Forestiere (4). Furthermore, another 6 (increased from 4 in 1970) were reserved for "representatives of agricultural organizations" such as the Crédit Agricole and the Mutualité; these seats were selected by rather prosperous "notables," and the FDSEA thus won all 6 of them in 1970 and 1974 and 4 of the 6 in 1976.[82] Three statistics illustrate clearly the degree to which the complex, multicollege electoral

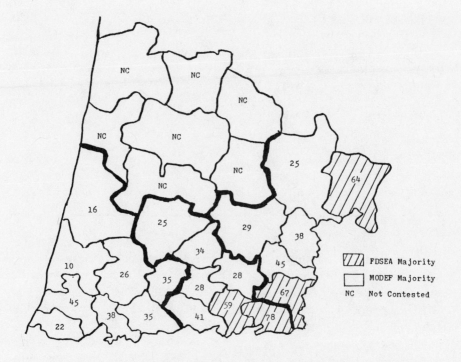

Figure 7.7 FDSEA vote (percentage by canton) in the 1964 chamber election.

system skewed the composition of the chamber in favor of the FDSEA: in the elections of 1974 and 1976, the FDSEA received only 42.6% of the votes cast by all of the farmers in the department's four districts—but it won almost 65% (22 of 34) of the seats and controlled 100% of the bureau posts, selecting Jacques Castaing as chamber president.[83]

Privileged Access

Despite its minority status, the FDSEA of Landes was granted privileged formal and informal access to the state throughout the Center-Right era; the leaders of MODEF were never granted seats on the various departmental commissions and committees in their capacity as representatives of the nonofficial union. However, the MODEF leaders were, on occasion, reluctantly accorded seats in *other* capacities, for example, as representatives of the Chamber of Agriculture, as general concillors, or as "technical experts" on specific matters. The political power of MODEF—expressed at times in the voting booth and at other times in the streets—made it difficult if not impossible for the prefect of Landes to fully implement the government's corporatist policies.

Between 1964 and 1970, the leaders of MODEF obtained seats on departmental commissions through their control of the Chamber of Agriculture. Even during this period, however, they were unable to convince the state to grant them additional seats as the department's dominant union. As a result, the

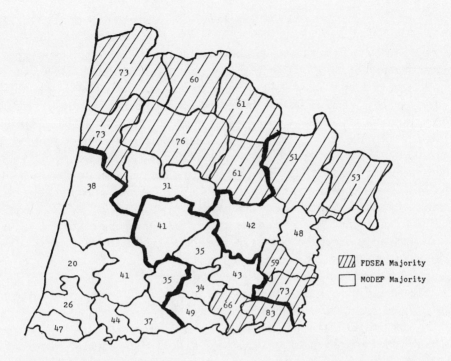

Figure 7.8 FDSEA vote (percentage by canton) in the 1974–76 chamber elections—college of *chefs d'exploitation.*

FDSEA and its supporters controlled all of the formal decision-making bodies (other than the chamber itself). For example, on the Commission des Structures the official union obtained a majority of seats through the appointment of representatives for the FDSEA, the CDJA, the ADASEA (discussed later), the Crédit Agricole, and the Mutualité. The MODEF leader present as the representative of the chamber repeatedly protested against the policy of ignoring the CGA-MODEF and its youth affiliate (the Cercle des Jeunes Agriculteurs), but to no avail. Articles in the MODEF paper thus reminded the prefect and the DDA that although they could deny "the true representatives" of the farmers seats on formal commissions, "the farmers will find other means to make themselves heard and understood."[84]

The use of such "other means" became a necessity after the election of 1970 turned control of the chamber over to the FDSEA. From 1970 until 1975 the prefects of Landes attempted to adhere faithfully to the government's nationwide policy of according a representative monopoly to the FNSEA's departmental federation. No seats were granted to MODEF leaders on most commissions; MODEF was not even informed about, let alone invited to, formal cantonal meetings between state officials and representatives of the recognized agricultural organizations; moreover, the prefecture pursued a policy of strictly denying even requests for informal meetings between state officials and MODEF delegations.[85] The initial MODEF response to this "policy of discrimination" was limited to formal protests and a steady stream of threatening articles in the union newspaper. With the onset of the agricultural crisis of 1974, however, the MODEF leaders decided to back up their verbal protests with mass demonstrations. From mid-1974 to early 1975, MODEF mobilized its membership for a series of demonstrations at the most vulnerable *sous-préfectures* (such as that located in its bastion of Dax) and at the prefecture itself. These efforts reached their climax on 3 February 1975 when, after receiving another refusal of a request for consultations with the prefect, 250 MODEF members stormed the prefecture and occupied it for two hours, thundering protests through a portable loudspeaker system; the demonstration ceased only after a clash with the riot police. "The Government has just demonstrated once again in Landes," exclaimed the next issue of the MODEF paper, "how it conceives of dialogue with MODEF . . . through the intermediation of the CRS."[86]

Soon after this disruption of the peace, the prefect was replaced by another man seemingly more aware of the maxim cited by one of the subjects of a recent study of French public administration: "To be a good Prefect you have to appreciate 'the art of the possible.' "[87] Within a few months the new prefect acknowledged that the practice of this art in Landes would entail at least the de facto recognition of MODEF. From 1975 onward the leaders of MODEF were accorded some seats on most commissions as representatives of nonunion organizations (e.g., cooperatives) or as "consulting experts" on the specific matters of concern. Moreover, delegations of MODEF were readily received at the prefecture. As MODEF articles lamented, however, the nonofficial union continued through the 1970s to be rebuffed in its requests for de jure seats—and the FDSEA thus retained control of all the formal decision-making bodies.[88]

Devolved Power and Indirect Subsidies

While the prefecture responded to the 1975 demonstration by appointing MODEF leaders to some departmental commissions, it left the comanagement institutions entirely in the hands of the FDSEA elite. As in Corrèze and Aisne, in Landes the FDSEA was the only union accorded seats on their administrative councils during the 1970s. Furthermore, as of 1976 major FDSEA figures held the presidency of each of the principal institutions: the president of the chamber and of SUAD was the immediate past-president of the FDSEA, Jacques Castaing; the president of the ADASEA was the FDSEA's secretary-general, Raoul Massetat; the president of the departmental and regional SAFER was the current FDSEA president, Michel Simon. And FDSEA activists also held the presidency of such key institutions as the EDE (the "Maison de l'Elevage"). There can be no doubt that FDSEA control of these institutions enhanced the union's prestige as well as influence; indeed, in 1976 the MODEF president complained that some of the younger farmers in the department were attracted to the FDSEA by "arriviste" ambitions, viewing the official union as a "trampoline to power."[89]

The FDSEA did not hesitate to exploit its control of the comanagement institutions to develop its image as *the* power within the agricultural sector. One example of such exploitation occurred in October 1974 when the government declared that all livestock raisers could receive a subsidy (*prime*) for each steer sold before 1 February 1975. In most neighboring departments the application forms for these *primes* were distributed by the public livestock agency (the EDE) to mayors' offices, cooperatives, and numerous other agricultural organizations. In Landes, however, the FDSEA-controlled Maison de l'Elevage announced that the Landes FDSEA had been empowered to distribute these forms and that all farmers wishing to procure them should apply to the headquarters of the FDSEA. To this MODEF responded with an article entitled "La FDSEA des Landes se croit tout permis" and demanded that the application forms be made equally available to MODEF. Chamber president Castaing reacted to this protest by offering a compromise solution: the forms would be distributed only by the Maison de l'Elevage. Given the FDSEA's control of this agency, MODEF denounced the step as a "purely formal" compromise and yet another example of the "abusive privileges" granted by the state to the official union.[90]

Like the FDSEAs of other departments, the Landes FDSEA also obtained an indirect subsidy—the free use of publicly financed personnel—from its control of the comanagement institutions. In regard to the Chamber of Agriculture-SUAD, however, such "disguised subsidies" were relatively limited by the power and presence of MODEF. In at least two important respects, the Landes MODEF was much more able than rival unions elsewhere to monitor the FDSEA-chamber relationship and to prevent abuses. First, because MODEF controlled the chamber during the mid-1960s when a new Maison de l'Agriculture was constructed, it was the nonofficial union rather than the FDSEA that had its office in the chamber's residence; although FDSEA officials "investigated ways to correct" this anomaly, it persisted, providing MODEF with a splendid vantage point. Second, because MODEF continued to be represented in the chamber by a sizeable delegation—more than 30% of the members—well-informed about the workings of the institution, the nonofficial union was able to scrutinize the budget and restrict questionable allocations of funds for personnel. As a result of these two factors, the FDSEA enjoyed nothing like the de facto merger with the chamber that one found in departments such as Corrèze. In fact, the chamber personnel interacted with those of both unions in a rather formal manner quite unlike that witnessed in either Corrèze or Aisne. Nevertheless, with the FDSEA elite in control of the chamber, SUAD technicians and others devoted a disproportionate amount of their time to the "animation" of activities for branches of the official union, such as the Women's Section.[91]

In contrast to the chamber, other comanagement institutions almost exclusively served the FDSEA after their establishment in the mid-1960s. The most notable case in point is the ADASEA. Controlled by state-appointed FDSEA directors, the ADASEA was described in official union literature as a "réalisation du syndicalisme" and its *permanences* were listed next to those of the FDSEA in the same column of *Le Sillon*. Because of the extensive need for structural reform services in Landes—the department which has dispensed the largest number of IVDs—the ADASEA employed a large staff: four counselors and three secretaries as of 1976. All of these ADASEA personnel were hired and supervised by the FDSEA elite and worked closely with the staff of the official union on a daily basis. The FDSEA-ADASEA relationship was so intimate, in fact, that MODEF encouraged its members to obtain IVD information from its union staff and refused to publicize the activities of the publicly financed ADASEA.[92]

Direct State Subsidies

Largely because of the factors just discussed, direct state subsidies to the FDSEA were a bit more limited in Landes than in departments such as Corrèze during the 1960s and 1970s. Nevertheless, they made a substantial contribution to official union activity. In 1975, for example, the CDJA received a subsidy of 60,000 francs—50,000 from SUAD and 10,000 from the Conseil Général—to further its "educational" function. The FDSEA's Women's Section also received a sizeable portion of the 76,500 francs allocated from SUAD funds for "education" sessions devoted to accounting practices.[93]

STATE HINDRANCE OF MODEF ACTIVITY

Aside from refusing to accord MODEF seats on departmental commissions and to receive its delegations, state officials in Landes acted in a number of ways to hinder MODEF's organizational activities and to restrict its power during the Center-Right era. One example which particularly outraged MODEF leaders occurred in January 1975. The president of the Cercle des Jeunes Agriculteurs-MODEF requested the use of an amphitheater in the agricultural school of Dax for its departmental congress; such requests had been routinely granted in previous years. This time, however, the Cercle president received a letter from the prefecture informing him that "M. the Minister of Agriculture has specified in a very precise manner . . . the conditions governing the utilization of public educational establishments for meetings . . . only meetings requested by professional organizations which maintain official relations with the Ministry of Agriculture [are to be permitted]." The Cercle was left with no recourse other than to protest this ruling to the prefecture and—through the mediation of a sympathetic Socialist deputy—to the ministry.[94]

The most important case of state restriction of MODEF power took place seven years earlier, at the time SUAD was established. When asked by the prefect to propose a six-member board of directors for SUAD, the president of the chamber—Marcel Sintas, secretary-general of MODEF—did precisely what his counterparts in other departments had done: he proposed a board composed exclusively of members of his own union. Upon consultation with his superiors in Paris, the prefect learned that such a board would simply not be acceptable. Faced with a contradiction between his duty to implement governmental policy and his duty to maintain order in the department, the prefect was obviously placed in a most difficult situation. "Everyone at the ministerial level," he noted months later in a meeting of the Conseil Général, thought that the resolution of this dilemma would be an "impossibility." The "union dualism" of Landes rendered the constitution of the SUAD board "an extremely laborious operation." His solution to the problem may not have been perfect, he noted, but he added—rather wistfully—that such a solution would not have been necessary at all "if I were in a department like the majority of rural departments in France, where the problem is not posed in the same conditions."[95]

The compromise "solution" was the following: along with the six MODEF members designated by the chamber president, the SUAD board was to include six FDSEA members—appointed by the prefect—and four members of the Conseil Général who would participate in a "consultative role" at all board meetings. While the prefect admitted that this solution was largely the result of pressure from the "ministerial level," he justified his action essentially by arguing that "SUAD would not be able to function unless an accord were reached among all of the union *tendances* existing in the department." Only if he could "establish an equilibrium" among the *tendances*, he asserted, would the programs of SUAD be efficiently and properly implemented.[96]

The MODEF and its supporters in the Conseil Général objected to the "solution," but were forced to accept it when told that no SUAD funds would be forthcoming otherwise. In noting his reservations, one general councillor expressed the "hope" that the prefect would also "follow the policy of equilibrium in choosing directors for the Maison de l'Elevage" and other comanagement institutions (such as the ADASEA) which were controlled exclusively by the FDSEA.[97] This "hope" was never fulfilled, however. In fact, the "policy of equilibrium" was soon revealed to have been little more than a sham even in regard to SUAD. After the FDSEA won control of the chamber in the 1970 elections, the new chamber-SUAD president—Jacques Castaing—was allowed to appoint a board composed entirely of FDSEA activists. With the SUAD board now safely in the hands of the official union, the prefect (after, one would assume, breathing a sigh of relief) discarded the "policy of equilibrium" and—despite vehement MODEF protests—refused to appoint a single member of the rival *tendance*.[98]

THE CONSEIL GÉNÉRAL'S CHALLENGE TO
THE CORPORATIST SYSTEM

Despite the presence of a most formidable MODEF organization, the corporatist system had thus been implemented almost completely in Landes by the early 1970s. The artificial hegemony of the FNSEA's departmental affiliate remained essentially intact throughout the Center-Right era. However, the nonofficial union's ability to mobilize its membership for mass demonstrations created headaches for the prefects and forced a few concessions from the state. Moreover, the MODEF forces continued to challenge the official union's "monopoly" and achieved some gains through exercising influence in the Conseil Général.

As noted earlier, the largest subsidy accorded directly to the official union was that received by its youth affiliate—the CDJA—through the channel of SUAD. Beginning in 1967, the supporters of MODEF in the Conseil Général annually made an issue of the SUAD subsidy when considering the sums to be accorded by the Conseil to the CDJA and the Cercle-MODEF. They argued that "equal treatment" for the two youth groups must necessarily entail the granting of a larger sum to the Cercle, which has received no "manne du Fonds de vulgarisation."[99]

Such arguments fell on deaf ears through 1971. In 1972, however, the MODEF supporters achieved a significant breakthrough. Armed with documents showing that the SUAD subsidy to the CDJA was now quite generous (35,000 francs) and that the Cercle could claim a far larger membership, the pro-MODEF councillors proclaimed that the state policy served to create an "iniquité vraiment revoltante." One union was being punished, they continued, simply because it failed to hold "political opinions in accord with those of the government." Backed by a MODEF pressure campaign at the cantonal level, this logic led to the acceptance by the Conseil of the *principe du rattrapage*. From 1972 onward, the Conseil attempted to reduce the inequality of subsidies accorded to the two unions by providing the Cercle with a sum designed to offset the CDJA's SUAD grant. Table 7.2 displays the degree to which the Conseil's policy gradually improved the balance of union subsidies during the 1970s.[100]

Table 7.2   Subsidies Granted to the CDJA and Cercle-MODEF (in francs)

	Conseil-Cercle	Conseil-CDJA	SUAD-CDJA	Total (Cercle/CDJA)
1967	2,000	2,000	20,000	2,000/22,000
1970	1,800	1,800	25,000	1,800/26,800
1972	20,000	2,000	35,000	20,000/37,000
1974	30,000	10,000	40,000	30,000/50,000
1975	40,000	10,000	50,000	40,000/60,000

With each passing year, the debates on the CDJA-Cercle subsidy issue became more heated and lengthy—they filled only five pages of the Conseil's minutes in 1967, but by 1975 they consumed no less than twenty pages. Emulating their opposition, the CDJA activists mounted an extensive cantonal campaign in 1975 urging the councillors to cease their "discriminatory" policy. The pro-CDJA councillors (all of the Center-Right) were thus moved to call for "justice" for the CDJA and to contend that the "equalization" policy had merely contributed to "a veritable war between two professional organizations." To this the pro-MODEF councillors retorted that the SUAD-inflated CDJA subsidy was still larger than that of the Cercle, and that they were thus forced to work "against the injustice created by a government which recognizes only one category of unions, despite the fact that this is an antidemocratic position. . . . *C'est un scandale!*"[101]

In the end the pro-MODEF forces emerged victorious: the political power of MODEF and a small Left majority in the Conseil combined to produce a decision not only to retain the *principe du rattrapage*, but to attempt in the future to provide the Cercle with a subsidy *equal* to that received by the CDJA from SUAD and the Conseil. One "moderate" councillor objected that this policy amounted to a "revolt against the Government . . . and the Administration"—and he was right. The Conseil Général of Landes had succeeded where its counterpart in Corrèze had just barely failed. Given the centralization of the French political system, it could do no more than put a dent in the machinery of the corporatist system. But it provided a vivid reminder of the extent to which the nationwide hegemony of the FNSEA rested on corporatist bases.

III
The Politics of
Decorporatization in
Mitterrand's France

8

The Politics of Decorporatization:
Reform, Revolt, and Retrenchment

> In the case of a mandate that has emerged from a particularly heated controversy, the interests who fought unsuccessfully to prevent the program from being authorized . . . expect to have a say and may even expect, or at least hope, to win back in the implementation game—particularly in the writing of regulations and guidelines—what they lost in the policy-adoption game.
>
> Eugene Bardach[1]

For the farmers' unions which had long struggled to compete for members and influence with *le syndicalisme officiel*, the outcome of the May–June 1981 French elections generated enormous excitement. Both President François Mitterrand and the solid Socialist majority in the National Assembly were pledged to introduce the sort of agricultural reforms that the Leftist rivals of the FNSEA had promoted for years. Moreover, the new minister of agriculture manifested a commitment to institute not only this reorientation of economic policy, but also a dramatic change in the structure of relations between sectoral interest groups and the state. In her first major speech, Edith Cresson declared that her ministry would strip the FNSEA of its privileged status within the policy-making process while providing equal rights for the rival farmers' unions which governments of the Center-Right had steadfastly refused to recognize. "It is the victory of democracy," exulted one of the newly recognized unions, "the end of the monopoly of the FNSEA and its CNJA satellite."[2] Cresson's adoption of a pluralist interest intermediation policy impressed scholarly observers as well. One commented that the government had "ended the corporatist ties" of the agricultural sector with remarkable "ease," while another noted that Cresson had seemingly "unravelled almost instantly" the "elaborate construction" of corporatist group-state relations developed over two decades.[3] As this chapter will show, however, such judgments were premature. Much to the consternation of the FNSEA's rivals, the Socialist government has managed to achieve only a modest degree of decorporatization, leaving most aspects of the traditional group-state system essentially intact.

Before examining this case study of the politics of decorporatization, let us briefly consider the issue in more general terms. As Bardach and other analysts of policy-making have shown, it is altogether possible for the losers of the policy adoption game to emerge as the battle-scarred winners of the implementation game. It seems logical to assume that such an outcome will be especially likely in cases where the policy adopted is one of decorporatization opposed by a long-established client group. Schmitter has noted that, despite the contradictions and intragroup tensions which the maintenance of corporatist arrangements entails, decorporatization "from below" should be expected to be relatively uncommon. Corporatist systems should tend to manifest a "resilience unmatched by more pluralist arrangements," he has argued, because "the sunken institutional costs" for the client group are considerable. Such a group might at times feel it necessary to opt for a *cure d'opposition* and withdraw "from a particular negotiation or forum," but it would be unlikely to push for a process of decorporatization entailing the sacrifice of a host of organizational benefits.[4] By the same token, a number of factors would seem to militate against the adoption—or, as in this case, the thorough implementation—of a policy of decorporatization "from above." On the one hand, where a well-developed corporatist system exists, the sunken institutional costs of the state are as considerable as those of the client. Severing the complex ties between the state and an established client will logically entail all of the costs typically associated with bureaucratic reorganization: (1) a cost of time, as scores of government personnel must be assigned the task of devising alternative policy-making structures rather than pursuing other priorities; (2) a cost of efficiency, as traditional patterns of group-state relations will be disrupted and adjustments to new patterns must be made; (3) a cost of money, as resources must be devoted to the liquidation of old structures and the establishment of new ones; (4) an increased burden on top officials, as they must continually be alert to the possibility that bureaucrats accustomed to the traditional mode of group-state relations may not be committed to the development of new procedures.[5] For these reasons alone, then, the implementation of decorporatization may prove to be so disruptive as to be counterproductive.

On the other hand, an established client can be expected to possess and employ formidable means of resistance. Even if a new government were willing and politically able to terminate immediately all of the forms of state support which had traditionally flowed to a privileged client group, it could only hope to weaken that group over a period of years. In the short run, the erstwhile client should continue to manifest a degree of state-enhanced organizational strength derived from the benefits delivered under the former regime. For a new government intent on implementing sweeping reforms of both policy and the decision-making process, therefore, an established client should be expected to represent a potent obstacle, a sort of *obstructionist legacy* of the old regime. Moreover, an established client can strive to combat decorporatization not only through *negative* means (active resistance), but also through *positive* means. If a client manifests a willingness and ability to cooperate, that is, to discharge some of the functions for the new regime that it performed under the old one, it would seem to stand a chance of deflecting the government from its decorporatization course.

The agricultural policy-making process in France from 1981 through the summer of 1984 exemplifies this sort of dynamic. In the face of FNSEA resistance, external constraints, and competing priorities, the Socialist government has been compelled to attenuate its drive for reform of both economic policy and interest intermediation policy within the agricultural sector. Moreover, since 1983 the government has made a concerted effort to secure social peace and stabilize the policy-making process by cultivating FNSEA cooperation, establishing an increasingly stable "moderate corporatism" system which has provoked cries of treason by dismayed activists within the rival unions of the Left.

REFORM: SOCIALIST AGRICULTURAL POLICY IN 1981

For the Socialists, the fundamental flaw of what they termed the Center-Right's "schéma productiviste" was that it manifested insufficient concern for the human traumas entailed in the relentless process of agricultural modernization. As party spokesmen stressed in the 1979–80 debates over Giscard's agricultural orientation law and again during the 1981 electoral campaign, the survival of small- and medium-sized farmers had long been jeopardized by a policy that perpetuated sectoral inequalities and produced successive annual declines in real income.[6] It was this dark side of the government's "green oil" venture that motivated the Parti Socialiste (PS) to organize, in February 1981, a National Convention on Agriculture devoted to condemnation of current policy and the presentation—by presidential candidate François Mitterrand—of a comprehensive reform program intended to assure agricultural "recovery" and the "promotion . . . of family farms." Pierre Joxe, a Socialist expert on agriculture, argued at the convention that the problems created by the current majority were "so enormous that even the most rapidly applied measures will take time to reverse the tendency." However, he pledged, the PS would go so far as to commit itself to a policy of "no longer losing a single active farmer."[7]

Achieving the Socialists' goals, Mitterrand acknowledged, would require a wide-ranging reform effort at home in combination with a reorientation of EEC policy in Brussels. Many of the dozen measures which he proposed for internal reform had been included in the 1972 Common Program of the Left, and all of the key points had been discussed at length in the book *Projet socialiste* prepared by the Socialist Party in 1980.[8] Mitterrand's restatement of these ideas was viewed as politically important, however, for it seemed to signal a serious commitment to agricultural reform on the part of both the PS and its presidential candidate, neither of which was commonly perceived as placing a high priority on the affairs of this sector.[9]

The most important and controversial planks of the reform platform proposed by Mitterrand were those calling for the creation of *offices par produits* and *offices fonciers*, agencies inspired by the *office du blé* which had been established by Leon Blum's Popular Front government in the 1930s.[10] The *offices par produits* (produce agencies), which would replace the privately managed *interprofessions* developed over the years with state support by the FNSEA and other agricultural organizations, were to be charged with organizing the various produce markets (and possibly controlling imports) so as to provide a guaranteed minimum income for small farmers. The precise mode in which these offices would operate was not stipulated, but Mitterrand stated that they would deliver a guaranteed income by providing farmers with "assured" (and relatively high) prices for a *quantum* (fixed proportion) of their produce; beyond the *quantum*, prices would continue to be determined by the free play of the market within limits imposed by the EEC. To those who argued that the *offices par produits* would contravene EEC regulations, Mitterrand and the Socialists offered a dual response. On the one hand, they argued, the *offices* would be tolerated as representing a national adjustment of European policy no more problematic than others which had been approved in the past. On the other hand, they pledged to fight for the institution of a European offices system modeled after that to be created at the national level.[11]

The *offices fonciers* (land agencies), which would replace the SAFERs established in the 1960s, were to be granted new powers to control land speculation (and hence prices) and maximize the ability of marginal farmers to acquire the increments of land desperately needed to render their operations viable. The specific powers to be accorded these *offices* were not enumerated by Mitterrand, but he did highlight a structural difference between them and the traditional SAFERs. While the SAFERs operated at the regional level under the control of farmers delegated by the FNSEA and other officially recognized organizations of the profession, the *offices* were to function at the departmental and cantonal levels and were to be controlled by farmers chosen through direct (sectoral) elections. Critics had long charged that such *offices* would be far more subject to local pressure than the SAFERs had been and would only serve to distribute land in a politicized and inefficient manner. For the Socialists, however, the *offices fonciers* seemed to represent progress toward a rural form of *autogestion*. "We are not afraid," proclaimed PS spokesman Bernard Thareau at the 1981 convention, "of a real local democracy."[12]

At the European level, aside from promising to push for adoption of the *offices par produits* scheme, Mitterrand pledged to abandon what he characterized as Giscard's policy of "submission . . . to the pretentions of Madame Thatcher" and to pursue a hard line in Common Agricultural Policy negotiations. This would involve, first of all, "mobilizing opinion so that the French government could hold out against its European partners" and obtain a general price increase of 15%, "without which our agriculture would be drained of its substance." Second, it would mean demanding that "the Treaty of Rome be strictly applied." Efforts by Britain and others to scuttle the Common Agricultural Policy would thus not be tolerated, argued Mitterrand, and the "play of influences . . . outside the Community"—that is, the United States, which had pressured Brussels to decrease its protectionism—would be combated.[13] No effort was made by Mitterrand or other participants at the 1981 convention to explain precisely how such results were to be sought or to assess how, realistically, a Socialist government could be expected to bring home better deals from Brussels than the Giscardians had delivered.

While the Socialists thus challenged the fundamental principles of the Center-Right's agricultural policy at the convention of February 1981, they refrained from issuing an explicit call for the dismantlement of the symbiotic FNSEA-state relationship upon which that policy had in large part been predicated. Nevertheless, a curtailment of the FNSEA's privileged status was implicit in the plans for both the *offices par produits* and the *offices fonciers*. Moreover, Mitterrand had hinted as early as 1974 that he favored certain changes in the structure of sectoral group-state relations, and a number of Socialist spokesmen at the 1981 convention manifested sufficient animosity toward the FNSEA to leave little doubt that the Federation would fare poorly under a government of the Left.[14] Bernard Thareau denounced FNSEA president Guillaume for presenting his rank and file with a distorted view of the Socialists' program, especially the *offices par produits*. Whereas Guillaume had charged that it was "demogogic and dangerous" to propose a *quantum* system enforced by such agencies, Thareau retorted that the FNSEA favored retention of the present price-setting system "because it perpetuates inequalities."[15] Pierre Joxe went so far as to level personal attacks at the FNSEA's leaders, using words such as "braggart," "liar," and "trickster" to describe Guillaume and his predecessor, Michel Debatisse. It was curious, Joxe argued, that the FNSEA could persist in portraying itself as an "apolitical" organization while its immediate past-president was holding a post in the government and its current president was scarcely concealing his support for Jacque Chirac's presidential campaign.[16] This vitriolic verbal sparring of February 1981 was but a foreshadowing of the hostility that would characterize relations between the Socialists and the FNSEA after the elections of May–June.

Despite the Socialists' rhetorical commitment to reform, it seemed plausible, even as François Mitterrand was moving into the Elysée Palace in May 1981, that the new president and his government might well opt with some reluctance for a policy of continuity in the agricultural sector. After all, the Socialists' highest priorities focused on other areas such as nationalization, decentralization, and industrial relations. The financial and political costs of pushing ahead with reform projects in those key spheres would surely be considerable, one could reason, so perhaps discretion would prove to be the better part of ideological valor in the agricultural sphere. Such logic seemed all the more seductive when one added the fact that, unlike most of their compatriots, the farmers had not given the Socialists even a slim mandate for reform in the elections; indeed, they had provided both Mitterrand (33%) and the Socialist Party (32%) with less electoral support than any of the other occupational groups.[17] To obviate a potentially disruptive political confrontation, what was needed at the rue de Varenne (the site of the Ministry of Agriculture) was an experienced and politically deft minister familiar with the agricultural dossier.

Enter Cresson, Stage Left

Once Mitterrand unveiled his initial cabinet it became clear that he had rejected the logic of caution in favor of an effort to fulfill his principal reform promises even at the expense of confrontation. His choice for minister of agriculture was Edith Cresson, in many ways the antithesis of the sort of politically "safe" minister just described. Cresson was not only the first woman in French history to be appointed minister of agriculture, reason enough for eyebrows to be raised in the countryside, but was also the kind of woman guaranteed to generate a negative response from the traditionalistic agricultural community: an attractive Parisian feminist with a taste for fine clothes and "extravagant" jewelry.[18] Throughout her twenty-two months in the agricultural post she would consistently ignore her associates' advice to tone down her flashy image, dismissing her critics (many of whom referred to her with such sobriquets as "la parfumée") as "prehistoric animals." When a *Paris-Match* survey of January 1983 showed that Cresson was one of the twenty women (and the only politician) with whom French men would most like to have an affair, one could only wonder how many disgruntled farmers had named her as a way of making a barbed political statement.[19]

Setting aside the issue of her sex, some more important characteristics of Cresson made probable the development of tense relations with the leaders of the FNSEA and other established interlocutors. As one observer noted, her air of assurance and her "brutal candor" sometimes gave "her initiatives the appearance of a provocation."[20] And most significant of all, she was among the least experienced of the ministers appointed by Mitterrand. Whereas virtually all of her colleagues had served for years in the National Assembly, the only elected posts which Cresson had held by the time of her appointment were those of mayor in a small town (since 1977) and deputy in the powerless European parliament (since 1979).[21] Her experience in agricultural affairs consisted of having written a doctoral thesis (in demography) on the problems of women in rural France and having often "visited farms and stables" while a mayor in Vienne.[22]

As the FNSEA elite noted with some trepidation, Cresson's rise to power had been based primarily on her work within the Socialist Party organization. Since 1975 she had been a member of its *comité directeur*, and she had earned a reputation as "one of the species of militants always ready to relaunch the debate when the smoke and fatigue" had begun to wear on others.[23] Cresson took party doctrine seriously and was sustained by a passionate faith in socialism. A book of her reflections published in the mid-1970s underscored this fact; she derived its title (*Avec le soleil*) from Jean Jaurès's assertion that since the enemies of socialism "struggle against the most radiant ideal," they are "like an army forced to fight with the sun in their eyes."[24] Clearly this was one minister who could be expected to strive for the implementation of the party's ambitious reform proposals.

In reflecting on why Mitterrand had selected Cresson for the agricultural ministry, the *Nouvel Observateur* speculated that he had deemed it "necessary to have at this post a militant, pugnacious minister rather than an expert technician," because he calculated that "the FNSEA would be sure to adopt an oppositional and political stance" when faced with a Socialist government committed to reform.[25] To help prepare her reform legislation and to assist in coping with expected FNSEA resistance, Cresson surrounded herself with a highly politicized cabinet, the core of which had long served in the National Agricultural Commission of the PS. One of her cabinet members had served as an official of an FNSEA product association until he was ousted from the post for his dissident views.[26] As one would expect, Cresson's chief associates in the National Assembly also shared her conviction that the reform effort was vital and her perception of the FNSEA as an obstacle. After the June elections, one of the Socialist deputies who would serve as a major ally of Cresson and a key player in the policy-making process (as *rapporteur* for the agricultural budget) was Yves Tavernier, a professor from the prestigious Institut d'Etudes Politiques de Paris who had published a plethora of articles criticizing the agricultural policies of the Center-Right and debunking the FNSEA's claim to be the legitimate spokesman for the entire farm community.[27]

If the leaders of the FNSEA viewed the appointment of Cresson as a portent of trouble, they soon learned that their fears had been justified. In her first speech as minister of agriculture, Cresson alluded to the system of group-state relations which had developed over the past two decades and issued what might be termed an anticorporatist manifesto: "It is necessary," she proclaimed, "to end the confusion between the role of professional organizations and that of the state. The former must negotiate and contest if they feel it necessary; the state must make the decisions."[28] Within a few days she made it clear that her interest intermediation policy would consist not only of stripping the FNSEA of its "right" to comanage the sector, but also depriving the Federation of its status as the only officially recognized union representative for agriculture. Announcing that she was merely acknowledging "the union pluralism which exists in reality," Cresson terminated the FNSEA's traditional "monopoly" by according official recognition to three additional unions: MODEF, the FFA, and the CNSTP (Confédération Nationale Syndicale des Travailleurs-Paysans). As noted in previous chapters, MODEF and the FFA had been present on the agricultural scene for years. In contrast, the CNSTP was an amalgamation of six Socialist-leaning movements created on 4 June 1981—the day after Cresson's inaugural speech.[29]

Understandably, the imposition of this new pluralist order was viewed as an affront and even a grave threat by the FNSEA. Cresson's decision to launch this revolution in group-state relations was definitely one of the major factors that provoked the FNSEA to instigate a wave of peasant protest some months later. For this reason, many analysts would retrospectively view Cresson's termination of the FNSEA's monopoly as an enormous political gaffe. It is crucial to note, however, that for Cresson this was not a gaffe which could easily have been avoided, but rather an important and carefully calculated step in the Socialist effort to democratize French politics and enhance equity in the agricultural sector. "It is necessary," she argued, "to open the process of *concertation* to other professional organizations" which can claim a following in the countryside.[30] The FNSEA's union rivals had a "right to live," and the Socialist government—unlike the regime of the Center-Right—could not be expected to "destroy union rights, since it was we who invented them!"[31]

Within limits, the logic of Cresson's argument was incontestable. Opinion polls and professional elections had repeatedly shown that the FFA and especially MODEF could claim to represent significant segments of the farm community. Governments of the Center-Right had accorded official recognition to industrial trade unions of lesser importance, and their stubborn refusal to incorporate the FFA and MODEF into the policy-making process had obviously been a political gesture in favor of the FNSEA. In righting these wrongs, however, Cresson took at least two steps that severely weakened her claim to be acting simply in the name of democratization. First, the granting of recognition to the CNSTP was a move as blatantly partisan as the Gaullists' and Giscardians' support of the FNSEA had been. The article of the Code du Travail that spells out criteria for recognition by the state specifically cites "experience and length of service" as a factor to be considered, and yet the CNSTP—the Socialist-oriented union—was recognized within hours of its creation.[32] Second, soon after assuming office, Cresson met with leaders of a dissident and predominantly Socialist faction of the FNSEA— Interpaysanne—at the ministry, apparently to discuss the possibility of their splitting from the FNSEA to join the new CNSTP.[33] This move was most certainly a gaffe, for it enabled the FNSEA to score political points by portraying Cresson as less a devout democrat than a clumsy Machiavellian. "A government should not attempt to encourage division within a union organization," fumed FNSEA president Guillaume at a press conference, adding "that is not democracy."[34] *Le Monde*, which generally manifests much more sympathy for the Socialist government than for the FNSEA, tartly criticized Cresson's action as an infringement of the union rights which she had pledged to protect and expand:

> Imagine how M. Séguy would react if the Minister of Labor were to receive a group representing a minority within the CGT. One would instantly hear something like "an intolerable intervention into the affairs of a democratic organization." Why should something which would be unthinkable for an industrial trade union not be for a farmers' union?[35]

In short, this move enabled the FNSEA to seize the moral high ground which Cresson had otherwise managed to claim for her own.

What the Interpaysanne affair and the premature recognition of the CNSTP made patent was that Cresson and her associates were eager to use the levers at their command to alter the balance of syndical power in the agricultural sector and thereby create conditions conducive to the achievement of their economic policy goals. During the Gaullist-Giscardian era, efforts to create a farmers' union allied with the Socialist Party had failed repeatedly in the face of sectarian divisions within the Socialist movement and predictable hostility on the part of the FNSEA (and its governmental patrons) as well as MODEF, which claimed to represent all Leftist farmers. With the PS ensconced in power, however, it now seemed feasible and politically expedient to foster development of a Socialist *relais* in the countryside. For the success of this venture, and for other purposes as well, it appeared vital to abrogate the *droits acquis* of the FNSEA. Maintaining the traditional comanagement system seemed likely to prove counterproductive in *policy* terms, for the FNSEA could be expected to oppose the Socialists' initiatives at the legislative stage and to sabotage them at the implementation stage.[36] Furthermore, allowing the FNSEA to retain its traditional status and privileges promised to be counterproductive in *political* terms, as the Federation could exploit its state-derived resources to rally agricultural opponents of the Socialist government. From the perspective of Cresson and her associates, therefore, imposition of the new pluralist order thus seemed to be an indispensable first step toward launching the drive for agricultural reform. At the same time, the step did not appear to them to be terribly risky. There was some chance that decorporatization might spur the FNSEA to mobilize farmers in a manner politically threatening for the regime, but most within the Cresson team doubted that the "ex-official union" could succeed in doing so. The experts on agricultural politics who were close to Cresson tended to view the FNSEA as a very fragile organization, a sort of "giant with feet of clay" that would be severely weakened by the loss of its monopoly status.[37]

During the first six months of the Socialists' reign, while Mitterrand enjoyed what he termed his "*état de grâce*" (honeymoon period), Cresson and other government figures did make some effort to appease the FNSEA and its allies by stressing that their economic initiatives would include measures designed to benefit all farmers, large as well as small. In regard to Brussels negotiations, for example, Cresson emphasized that the government "intends to pursue a policy of greater firmness in regard to its partners and the commission when the fundamental interests of the producers appear to be threatened." "The era of bad compromises in Brussels has ended," she insisted.[38] Mitterrand played on this theme as well; a hard line was not difficult to maintain during these months, as no major decisions were scheduled to be made at the European level until 1982. Cresson and Mitterrand also tried to convince the farm community that their campaign to reduce sectoral inequalities would be accompanied by a continued effort to improve agricultural productivity, and that they were no less concerned than Giscard with furthering the *vocation exportatrice* of French agriculture. In a speech redolent of the former president, Mitterrand proclaimed that agriculture was "a determinant force for the assurance of national independence" and that France must be "a great agricultural nation." To underscore the seriousness of his commitment to the "international vocation" of the sector, the president delivered this address at his political base in Nevers before an assemblage of ambassadors, including those from the United States and the Soviet Union.[39]

Against this reassuring backdrop, however, the government began to implement the more controversial components of what Mitterrand termed simply the "new agricultural policy."[40] In June, Cresson announced that the government would depart from the tradition of providing "undifferentiated assistance" to farmers; henceforth "selective assistance" would be the guiding principle of special state credit programs, with aid reserved for those most in need.[41] The first program tailored in this fashion was unveiled in August, as Cresson instituted a plan to help "farmers in difficulty." Credits were to be distributed selectively, on a case-by-case basis, with state bureaucrats at the department level making the final allocation decisions. In line with the government's turn away from corporatism, moreover, the FNSEA was not allotted an official role in the administration of the program.[42]

More important initiatives were introduced, in accord with custom, at the sessions of the Annual Conference on agricultural policy held in October and December. It was at these meetings that the FNSEA was forced most painfully to come to grips with its newly downgraded status. Policy departures were not prepared in *groupes de travail* composed of FNSEA and state officials, as in the past, but instead were drafted solely by bureaucrats of the ministry after brief consultations with all of the competing farmers' unions. At the formal meetings with the prime minister and the minister of agriculture, moreover, the FNSEA's input was limited in an unprecedented manner by the participation of representatives from the CNSTP, the FFA, and MODEF as well as the unions of agricultural employees. Whereas the government portrayed this new policy-making process as an "enlargement" of *concertation*, Guillaume dismissed the October meeting as "a succession of monologues" and announced after the December meeting that "*concertation* no longer exists at all."[43]

While the new policy-making process generated discontent on the part of the FNSEA, the economic reforms discussed at the Annual Conference meetings provoked even more tension. At the October session Cresson announced that the government fully intended to go forward with its plans to create *offices par produits* and *offices fonciers*. The ministry was currently in the process of preparing bills for each of these agencies, said the minister, and they would be ready for delivery to the National Assembly by the spring of 1982. However much it may have been anticipated, this news was a blow for the FNSEA. The Federation had vigorously opposed both reform schemes and had fought especially hard to convince the government that the produce offices would be bureaucratically unwieldy in their operation and economically deleterious in their impact.[44]

The coup de grâce was delivered at the final session on 8 December when Prime Minister Pierre Mauroy presented the government's plan to compensate the farmers for the 3.1% fall in income (9 billion francs) which it was estimated the agricultural sector had suffered in 1981, the eighth consecutive year (by most measures) of income decline. Mauroy's compensation package totalled 5.5 billion francs, 4 billion of which would aid the farmers indirectly in the form of increased budgets for various "economic" and "structural" programs administered by the Ministry of Agriculture. The other 1.5 billion francs were to be paid out directly to the farmers according to a formula which, in reflecting the government's commitment to progressive "selective assistance," departed dramatically from traditional practice. Unlike the Giscardians, who in 1980 had distributed income support checks to *all* farmers in amounts *proportionate* to their turnover (*chiffres d'affaires*, or c.a.), the Socialists proposed to provide "national solidarity" assistance only to those most in need and to allocate the money in *inverse relation* to turnover: 3,000 francs for each farm with a c.a. below 50,000 francs; 2,500 for each farm with a c.a. of 50,000 to 100,000; 2,000 for each farm with a c.a. of 100,000 to 250,000; nothing for those with a c.a. higher than 250,000. "I am not saying that [those who are to receive no direct support] are privileged," said Mauroy, "but we must reserve our credits for the most modest, those who are struggling on their farms, [so as to avoid] the continuation of the rural exodus and the concentration of enterprises."[45]

For the FNSEA, already profoundly disturbed by the processes and policies of the Socialist government, this income support plan seemed to provide proof positive that "social justice" as conceived by the new regime "rapidly finds its limits in the world of the peasantry."[46] The Federation condemned every aspect of the Mauroy plan: the *amount of funds* allocated for the total package, which represented compensation for only a little more than half of the 9-billion-franc decline in income; the *mode of financing* the package, which entailed—in an unprecedented move—employment of 2.7 billion francs drawn from the capital surpluses of the farmers' cooperative bank, the Crédit Agricole (only slightly more than half of the total package was thus to be funded by the state budget); and the *mode of distribution*, which left more than one-third of the full-time farmers without any direct income assistance.[47]

To the government's consternation, even the farmers' unions of the Left—whose participation in the Annual Conference had been expected to counterbalance the ineluctable opposition of the FNSEA—reacted in an essentially negative fashion. "The orientations are good," declared Bernard Lambert of the CNSTP, "but the volume of social assistance is insufficient. Before, one had either a scooter or a Rolls; today, one [who receives aid] is starting off again on a scooter." As Lambert and other critics noted, the fact that checks were to be allocated on a *per farm* rather than per capita basis meant that the actual amount received by the typical farmer in the poorest category would only be 1,500 francs, for generally wives (and sometimes older children as well) worked along with their husbands on small farms. Even with the government's assistance check, therefore, most family farmers would still suffer a decline in income in 1981. This appeared to be a grave injustice in light of the fact that the government had recently announced a 21.3% increase in the minimum wage. Moreover, as the FNSEA's rivals on the Left noted dolefully, it seemed to substantiate the FNSEA's charge that the Socialist government was interested only in "ouvriérisme" and simply did not care much about the plight of the farmers.[48] The Socialists' *état de grâce* was now about to end in the agricultural sphere: the stage had been set for a full-fledged peasant revolt.

REVOLT: THE FNSEA AND THE HOT WINTER OF 1981–82

As a spokesman for MODEF pointed out at the conclusion of the Annual Conference, the government's provision of only meager assistance to the small- and medium-sized farmers was a "political . . . and psychological mistake," for it seemed certain to "push them to rejoin *les gros*." This mistake was compounded when, to the embarrassment of the CNSTP and MODEF, Mauroy and Cresson sought to portray the FNSEA as the only farmers' union truly opposed to their initiative. What the government's representatives did not seem to realize, commented a reporter for *Le Monde*, was that their castigation of the Federation for its hostility toward an extremely unpopular program would merely "reinforce the power of the FNSEA" and "facilitate the unity of action against [the government] *sur le terrain* . . . the government is going to propel the farmers out into the streets and into the courtyards of the prefectures."[49]

These words proved prophetic, as the FNSEA seized with alacrity the chance to manifest its willingness and ability to mobilize the farmers. Ironically, a government seeking to weaken the FNSEA through its interest intermediation policy managed, through its economic policy, to impair the credibility of its union allies and hand the Federation a golden opportunity to strengthen its status among the farmers by proving itself the most potent vehicle for their defense. After many years in which the FNSEA leaders' commitment to "combat" had been essentially rhetorical, with their freedom to protest constrained by their privileged involvement in the policy process and their client obligations, they relished the chance to act in a way that would simultaneously challenge a hostile government and enhance their image with the *base*.

Antigovernment demonstrations began three days after the conclusion of the Annual Conference with angry farmers in Strasbourg chanting "l'hiver sera chaud," and the the winter did indeed prove to be hot. Not since 1961 had such an extensive and violent series of protests exploded in the French agricultural sector. With encouragement from Guillaume and other national leaders, virtually all of the FNSEA's departmental branches organized local *manifestations* at some point from December to February, with other farmers' unions often joining in the fray. Groups of farmers ranging from several hundred to several thousand paraded through the provincial capitals and other major cities waving placards and shouting slogans, many of which exploited the presence of a woman at the rue de Varenne, such as "Edith sexie . . . agriculture frigide!" and "Edith, nous t'espérons meilleure au lit que Ministère!"[50] All across France the prefectures were bombarded with rocks and manure, official cars were overturned, and highways were blocked by tractors. In a widely publicized incident near Perpignan, farmers ripped up 800 meters of railroad track (causing damage estimated at a million francs) and deposited several meters of track at the main entrance to the prefecture. So many riot police and armored vehicles were deployed in some cities that, in the words of Le Figaro Magazine, France almost seemed to be in a "state of siege." Although no deaths were reported, scores of protesters and police were injured in bloody confrontations verging on riots.[51]

Faced with what the press was beginning to call "la révolte paysanne," Cresson felt compelled to proclaim that "the government does not want war." The demonstrations had been provoked not by the government, she argued, but rather by "the policy of disinformation now being used for political purposes by a handful of FNSEA militants."[52] As the Socialists' weekly paper reported, some of Cresson's advisors actually began to fear that the FNSEA was striving not merely to alter agricultural policy, but to destabilize the Socialist government as the truckers' union had done a decade before in Allende's Chile.[53] Meanwhile, the administrative council of the FNSEA issued a communiqué that restated the union's grievances against the government, voiced approval of the demonstrations organized "to express [the] profound disappointment" of the farmers, and denounced "police provocations . . . which constitute a regrettable incitation to a chain of violence."[54]

As the "manifs" continued week after week, it became clear to the government that steps would have to be taken to defuse the crisis and move toward a rapprochement with the FNSEA.The seemingly interminable rural disturbances, which received a great deal of media coverage, were beginning to tarnish the image of the regime and to embolden its opponents at a time when debates over other crucial issues—the nationalization of industries and the implementation of a thirty-nine-hour work week, for example—were reaching a very sensitive stage. On 20 January Cresson announced a shuffling of her cabinet, the most extensive in any ministry during the first year of Socialist government, thus attempting to appease the FNSEA by reassigning some of the officials the Federation had found most objectionable.[55] At the same time, she reiterated the government's hard line on EEC negotiations and appealed to the FNSEA to "work hand in hand" with her in preparing for the Brussels price talks due to begin near the end of the month.[56] When the response to these overtures proved to be disappointing, President Mitterrand decided to intervene personally. In late January it was announced that the president would meet privately with the FNSEA's Guillaume on 2 February in an effort to "dissipate the peasant malaise" and establish the bases for group-state dialogue.[57]

Only hours before Mitterrand was scheduled to receive Guillaume on 2 February, the peasant revolt reached a symbolic climax. On a visit to a farm in Calvados, Edith Cresson was surrounded by 1,200 protesters (many of them women) hurling eggs and insults. As the frenzied mob made it impossible for her to leave by limousine, Cresson was forced to run across a meadow with her outnumbered guards and leap into a helicopter summoned by the *gendarmes mobiles*. Dramatic scenes of the beleaguered minister fleeing from "her" farmers were broadcast into millions of homes, providing what to many seemed a vivid demonstration of the Socialists' waning popularity and capacity to govern.[58] No one could remember when a minister of agriculture had been treated more rudely, although Cresson made an awkward effort to downplay the incident by insisting that her reception had actually been worse a few days before in Poitiers (the major city of her political base, Vienne), where she had suffered "an extremely violent blow to the back and another behind the head."[59] Cresson and her supporters charged that the "ambush" in Calvados had been carefully staged by the FNSEA to strengthen Guillaume's hand in his discussions with Mitterrand and, more pointedly, to demonstrate the need for Cresson's dismissal. The FNSEA denied the charge, but Guillaume lent it credibility by refusing to apologize for the assault and dismissing it brusquely with the words "It has happened to other ministers, and it will happen again. Those are the risks of the profession." One thing, at least, was crystal clear. As *Le Monde* commented, the helicopter incident served as a "spectacular symbol [of] the divorce consummated between the government and the most powerful of agricultural organizations."[60]

When Guillaume and Mitterrand met on the afternoon of 2 February, this "divorce" was at the top of the agenda. Two thirds of their sixty-minute discussion was reportedly devoted to the FNSEA's grievances over Cresson's policies, especially what Guillaume termed "systematic efforts to destabilize" his organization. Guillaume received no promises of change from the president. Indeed, he was given the unwelcome news that Cresson would remain as minister of agriculture, and that a reform of the Chamber of Agriculture's electoral laws which she had proposed (and which, as discussed later, Guillaume recognized would mean a reduction in the FNSEA's chamber seats) would be supported by Mitterrand.[61] Nevertheless, the tête-à-tête at the presidential palace did provide Guillaume with some solace, and in retrospect it stands as a major turning point in relations between the government and the FNSEA.[62] The FNSEA chief asserted in an interview a few days later that Mitterrand, unlike Cresson and many other Socialists, seemed to have "a real rural sensibility which could permit him to understand the problems of the peasant world. . . . He recognizes the importance of the FNSEA. I think he understood that one cannot seek to weaken and humiliate this union without consequences."[63] As he would do again some months later following a rendezvous with the Prime Minister, Guillaume thus attempted to make the point that the FNSEA was not in fact bent on undermining the government and that, with a more accommodating minister at the rue de Varenne, the Federation would be willing to deal in a cooperative fashion with the Socialists.[64] The wave of violence began to abate, and at the end of February a somewhat chastened Cresson appeared at the FNSEA's annual congress in Touquet to express the government's desire for renewed *concertation.* "The government is extending you its hand," she proclaimed, and "hopes to go beyond impassioned debate to employ the language of reason in dealing with the farmers."[65]

The drama of the 1981–82 peasant revolt was nearly over, but a denouement remained to be enacted. Despite the soothing words of Mitterrand and Cresson, the FNSEA continued to perceive the government as a threat to its organizational interests and its policy concerns. At the Touquet congress, therefore, the leaders of the Federation announced plans for what they hoped would be an eye-catching display of the FNSEA's power: 100,000 farmers were to be mobilized for a demonstration in Paris on 23 March. Calling for such a *manifestation* entailed considerable risk on the part of Guillaume and his associates. Not since 1973 had more than 40,000 farmers been assembled by the FNSEA, and never had such a massive peasant rally been staged in Paris.[66] The logistical problems and the cost would be staggering, and if the turnout proved to be unimpressive, the government officials still skeptical of the FNSEA's authority would be encouraged to continue their reform effort and decorporatization campaign. Moreover, there was always the possibility, especially given the events of the past few months, that the demonstration might lead to violent actions which would turn public opinion against the farm community. As *Le Monde* commented, the FNSEA was making an "enormous bet."[67]

Seldom has such a wager been so convincingly won. Thousands of FNSEA activists began to pour into Paris by car and train beginning a few days before the "historic event" was to take place. On the morning of the twenty-third, FNSEA members stationed at all of the major subway stops distributed 200,000 copies of a pamphlet entitled "Paris, The Peasants Are Coming to Meet You" to startled Parisians on their way to work. A few hours later, a horde of demonstrators (estimates of their numbers varied from 60,000 to 120,000, equivalent to 10–20% of all FNSEA members) brought traffic to a halt as they marched behind thirty tractors along a 3-mile-long route from the Place de la Nation to the Porte de Pantin, where they gathered to hear speeches by FNSEA representatives. Throughout the day, a special FNSEA security service composed of 5,000 union members managed to prevent any violent disturbances of note. All in all, the events were remarkable enough not only to make front-page news all across France, but even to receive extensive coverage in the New York *Times* and to be shown on the evening news programs of American television. As the FNSEA leaders stated, they had succeeded in delivering a "solemn warning" to the government of what could be expected if the FNSEA's demands were ignored and if the "governmental projects marked more by the stamp of doctrine than by realism" were not reconsidered.[68]

RETRENCHMENT À LA CRESSON:
MODERATING THE REFORM CAMPAIGN

In the words of a rival union official, the FNSEA's stunning show of force "shocked and scared the pants off the Socialist government."[69] Just as the massive Versailles demonstration directed against the Savery education bill would do in June 1984, the peasant protest of March 1982 applied a "coup d'arrêt" to the government's reform effort.[70] Not long after the Paris events, Cresson pledged publicly that reforms "will not be imposed against the will of the farmers."[71] Her choice of words marked a major political change, for she had previously ridiculed Guillaume's equation of "the will of the farmers" with "the will of the FNSEA." This sea change was not overlooked by the Leftist unionists, who naturally continued to reject such an equation and were greatly disillusioned by the government's change of heart. In the face of resistance from "the conservative Right," despaired the CNSTP, "the government is hesitating, President Mitterrand is appeasing, the reform projects are lagging and . . . the farmers are suffering."[72]

Though the FNSEA-led resistance of the farmers was no doubt the most visible and powerful brake on Cresson's drive for agricultural reform, it must be noted that other factors which emerged in early 1982 also compelled the government to begin opting for "realism" over "doctrine." By April the general economic indicators "were no longer at orange—they were scarlet." The inflation rate was rising rapidly (while it was falling in most other industrial countries), pressure was building for a second devaluation of the franc, the budget deficit for 1982 was projected to be almost a third higher than it had been in 1981, and the trade deficit was edging toward record levels. On 16 April the government thus initiated a "second phase of change"—a phase of pragmatic moderation—in the industrial sector, and two months later it was forced to go even further, imposing a general economic program of austerity ("rigueur").[73] In this context the Socialists' enthusiasm for potentially costly and disruptive reforms waned significantly. From the spring of 1982 through the end of Cresson's tenure at the Ministry of Agriculture in March of 1983, economic and political constraints— sometimes reinforced by the institutional constraints of the EEC—combined to produce an era of retrenchment. Although Cresson and others at the rue de Varenne retained their commitment to reform, they were forced to moderate some plans for change and to abandon others. The retrenchment process can perhaps best be illustrated through an examination of developments regarding what were to have been the twin pillars of the Socialist economic policy for the agricultural sector, the *offices fonciers* and the *offices par produits*, as well as the initiatives related more directly to decorporatization.

The *Offices Fonciers*

When the Socialists assumed power in 1981, it was expected that they would make reform of the traditional farm land management system one of their highest priorities within the agricultural sphere. Such reform had been a central enough concern to be included on the list of "110 Propositions for France" which Mitterrand distributed during his election campaign.[74] Party officials had long argued that the land management agencies—the SAFERs—established by the Gaullists in the early 1960s were seriously flawed and should be replaced by *offices fonciers* which would transform land from "an object of speculation" into an "instrument of labor" available to those "producers who have the most need of it."[75] The *offices* were to function in a more decentralized and "democratic" manner than the SAFERs, with cantonal and departmental boards staffed by directly elected representatives of the farmers (and local government officials) rather than by FNSEA delegates. Moreover, the *offices* were to be accorded far greater control of the land market than the SAFERs had been allowed to exercise. While a narrowly defined "right of preemption" and a limited budget had prevented the SAFERs from purchasing even 20% of the land placed on the market each year, the *offices* were to be armed with sufficient rights and funds to purchase all of the available land. In allocating this land to needy farmers, furthermore, the *offices* were to be empowered not to sell parcels—as the SAFERs had done—but to rent them, thus making it possible for young farmers without much capital to acquire viable farms.[76]

It did not take the Socialist government long to realize that translating the abstract conception of *offices fonciers* into acceptable legislation would be a formidable task. Opposition to the scheme emerged on two fronts. Within the agricultural profession, the FNSEA and its allies objected to both the mode of governance and the extended powers planned for the *offices*. Placing control of them in the hands of elected farmers and politicians at the local level would, they argued, not only politicize the land management process but also generate tremendous personal conflicts. More important, granting the *offices* all of the powers envisioned by militant Socialists would undermine property rights and represent an intolerable first step toward nationalization of France's farm land. "If you want to have an effective land policy," cautioned one FNSEA official, "be sure to consider what the farmers will accept and support."[77] Along with these objections from the farm community, proponents of the *offices fonciers* scheme also found themselves confronted by skepticism within the government. Some officials who remembered that even the creation of the SAFERs had generated controversy were reluctant to risk conflict over the sensitive property rights issue, and many were wary of the expense that the *offices* venture would entail.[78]

Faced with these political and economic complications, the Ministry of Agriculture produced a draft bill for the *offices fonciers* in February 1982—only a week after Cresson's helicopter incident—which was "more moderate than anticipated" by most observers and a crushing disappointment for Socialist farmers such as those affiliated with the CNSTP. The bill called for the creation of *offices* at the cantonal and departmental levels, but it described their composition in vague terms and accorded them powers far more limited than originally planned: the cantonal *offices* were to play only an advisory role, and their departmental counterparts were to be given control only over the allocation of land. The crucial functions of land acquisition and management were to be left in the hands of the interdepartmental SAFERs, whose boards of directors would be only slightly "democratized" and whose powers would continue to be restricted to selling rather than renting land. Several vital questions, including the degree to which the SAFERs' "right of preemption" was to be extended, were left to be dealt with at a later date.[79] A disillusioned CNSTP mocked the proposed reform, asserting that if the agencies were to perform such derisory functions they "had no need for the pompous title of *office*."[80] Meanwhile, President Mitterrand sought to reassure not the young Socialist farmers, but rather those who, like the FNSEA leaders, felt the proposal was excessively radical. "There is no question of imposing the *offices* without the consent of the farmers," he declared. "If the cantonal *office* appeared as some means of administrative and bureaucratic pressure, it is an article of my program which would be dropped."[81]

From the spring of 1982 through the end of Cresson's tenure at the agricultural ministry, the handling of the *offices fonciers* bill amounted to a veritable comedy of indecision. Buffeted by contradictory protests from the Left and the Right, and confronted with a worsening economic crisis, the government repeatedly proved incapable of deciding how to formulate the bill's many controversial and complex elements. A polished version of the bill was initially scheduled to be deposited with the National Assembly by April 1982, but in May farm leaders were complaining that "no one knows where, in which ministry, the bill can be found."[82] Edith Cresson announced publicly in June that the bill was "practically ready," but three months later the CNSTP was complaining that it had apparently "disappeared in smoke:"[83] In November Cresson assured the legislators that the bill would be in their hands "before the end of December."[84] In the middle of that month, however, Cresson was forced to confess to impatient militants that the bill continued to be "stuck" somewhere in the governmental machinery.[85] By March 1983, when Mitterrand's cabinet shakeup removed Cresson from the rue de Varenne, the bill had still not materialized. As *Le Monde* commented on this occasion, the land agencies were "*les grands absents* of these twenty-two months." It seemed, remarked the CNSTP, that the bill had been "forgotten in the back of a [locked] drawer and someone had lost the key."[86]

The *Offices par Produits*

The government did manage to establish the other pillar of Socialist agricultural policy during the Cresson era, but it was a rather wobbly pillar bearing little resemblance to that which had been promised by the PS during the 1981 election campaign. As Cresson herself acknowledged, the *offices par produits* legislation sponsored by the government failed to incorporate many of the most important proposals of the *Projet socialiste*. What it represented, she argued, was an effort to go "the farthest possible" given the political opposition of the farm community and the constraints posed by the EEC's Common Agricultural Policy.[87]

Seventeen different versions of the *offices* bill were considered by the government from the fall of 1981 through June 1982, when a *projet de loi* was finally presented to the National Assembly.[88] At each crucial step along the way, with the clamor of demonstrating farmers and the concern of EEC partners increasing, the successive drafts of the *offices* bill diverged further from the model conceived by Socialist militants. The most ardent proponents of the produce agencies were gravely disappointed as early as March 1982, for the text of the initial draft bill then made public included no references to the *quantum* or the possibility of controlling imports and proposed no mechanism for assuring a guranteed minimum income. Only the preamble of the bill retained a semblance of the radical tone prevalent a few months before, and the vague promises therein presented were accompanied by an extremely important caveat: "*To the extent that European regulations will permit it*, [the *offices*] will guarantee to agricultural producers the prices paid for their produce within the limits of a certain volume of production and they will participate in the implementation of a modulation of subsidies . . . and taxes" (emphasis added).[89] With this clause the government made clear, to the dismay of the extreme Left, that it did not intend to push forward with a national reform that might provoke EEC partners and thus jeopardize the status of the Common Agricultural Policy.

However objectionable the "liberal capitalist" CAP might be, with its restrictions on national pricing policy and its requirement that imports from other EEC countries not be obstructed, it was impossible for the government to ignore the fact that the CAP continued to provide France with a net budgetary gain of more than a billion francs per year—indeed, in most years a larger gain than that received by any other EEC member.[90] Not surprisingly, such calculations were altogether objectionable to the Leftist farmers who had long heard the PS in opposition condemn the Center-Right's practice of justifying certain policies through invocation of "the Brussels alibi." At a meeting between Cresson and CNSTP officials devoted to discussion of the *offices* bill, the government was thus hoisted with its own rhetorical petard: the minister was attacked for "hiding behind European regulations."[91] Clearly, then, in the absence of a sweeping reform of the CAP, which the government promised to fight for but which no one could reasonably expect, the *offices* would thus not be allowed to pursue the most ambitious goals once envisioned for them.

Before the draft *offices* bill was presented for approval by the Council of Ministers on 2 June, the government retreated still further from its original reform scheme. Under pressure from the conservative farm organizations, President Mitterrand personally intervened to edit some of the bill's more controversial passages. "I have looked over this text," he told a group of farm leaders, "and I have crossed out everything that could be considered as statist (*étatique*)." In the process, Mitterrand produced what the FNSEA termed "some definite improvements"—modifications that a spokesman for the Leftist farmers condemned as having "expurgated [the bill] of all of its contents."[92] What the *toilettage* of Mitterrand accomplished, for the most part, was to assure that the *interprofessions* developed over the years would continue to play an important role rather than being supplanted by the *offices*.[93] Whereas the March draft had stipulated that the *offices* (whose boards were to include only a minority of farmers, with a president and director appointed by state decree) were "to organize the producers" and "to organize relations among the diverse professions" concerned with the various types of produce, the June draft reduced the role of the offices to "encouraging" such activities. Where the *interprofessions* were deemed to be playing an effective role, it was implied, the intervention of the *offices* would be minimal. Most important, the June draft explicitly downgraded the degree to which the *offices* could exercise administrative *tutelle* over the *interprofessions*. While the March draft had said that the professional bodies would be required to submit their annual budgets and programs to the *offices* for approval, the draft edited by Mitterrand stated that the *offices* were simply to be "consulted each year" on such matters.[94] As it had done in the case of the aborted *offices fonciers* bill, the government thus opted for a significant measure of continuity in formulating the *offices par produits* legislation; like the SAFERs, the *interprofessions*—which minority unions viewed as being "undemocratically" controlled by the forces of the FNSEA—would remain in place and perform much the same role they had played in the past.[95]

The *offices par produits* bill which the government maneuvered through the National Assembly from 29 June to 1 July was thus "an empty shell" to many on the Left and, in most respects, a relief to the conservatives. As Cresson acknowledged to the deputies, the government had sought to "make a tabula rasa neither of the past, nor of international commitments, nor of the organizations created by the farmers themselves."[96] When promulgated in October, the *offices* law created not a mechanism to assure a guaranteed income for the farmers, but merely a set of agencies that would enable the state to play a somewhat increased role in organizing producer markets—especially those (such as the one for low-grade wine) which had not been effectively regulated by an *interprofession* committee.[97] The FNSEA, which only months before had been gravely concerned that the government might impose a system of "offices à la mode de

1936," could find little in the bill to complain about except the mildly radical wording of the preamble and numerous ambiguities regarding the way in which the "couple interprofessions-offices" was to function once all of the implementing decrees had been issued. Indeed, the major complaint voiced by FNSEA president Guillaume was that confusion would be generated by the fact these agencies heralded by the Socialists as a dramatic innqvation seemed to have no real purpose. "Scarcely cooked," he observed, "the soufflé will fall quickly." It appeared that Cresson had persisted in pushing through at least a simulacrum of an *offices par produits* law, concluded Guillaume, merely to avoid "losing face and to save what little credibility she still possesses."[98]

The Decorporatization Campaign

In a study of public policy implementation, George Edwards commented "perhaps the only public policy that executes itself is the [American] president's decision to recognize a foreign government. . . . If a president recognizes a foreign country, diplomatic relations with it are thereby established. Most policies, however, require an intricate set of positive actions on the part of many people to be implemented."[99] The error that some observers of the French agricultural scene committed in concluding that Cresson's recognition of the minority unions in 1981 meant the instantaneous destruction of the corporatist system and the FNSEA's privileged position was to equate that recognition with the sort described by Edwards. In fact, if it were truly to entail decorporatization, the "recognition" of the FNSEA's rivals was a policy whose implementation would require "an intricate set of positive actions on the part of many people." All that the June 1981 "recognition" policy accomplished, in and of itself, was to create what the introductory chapter termed an "unstable" corporatist system. It signaled that the new government was unwilling to engage in traditional *concertation*, and it assured that the FNSEA would reciprocate, but it did not instantly terminate either the FNSEA's privileged role in the complex machinery of sectoral policy-making or the material benefits the Federation had always enjoyed as a consequence of that role. As for the minority unions, the "recognition" decision merely provided what one CNSTP activist termed a symbolic "permis d'exister."[100] The minority union leaders understood fully that institution of the promised "new pluralist order" (actually, in the terms of the introduction, a system of "structured pluralism") would necessitate a vast and complicated implementation process. Their expectation at the dawn of the Cresson era was that implementation would occur quickly and completely. In this policy area as in the others discussed so far, however, they were to be disappointed. A need to devote time to formulation of the economic reform bills, a concern to avoid excessive disruption of the policy-making process, an uncertainty as to what criteria should be employed in allocating seats on certain commissions, a measure of disenchantment with the Leftist unions, and (especially after the onset of the "hot winter") a fear of provoking even more intense resistance by the FNSEA—all of these factors contributed to governmental delay and retrenchment on the decorporatization front.[101]

To gauge the extent to which the structures of corporatism were (or were not) altered during the Cresson ministry, let us employ the categories introduced in Chapter 4's discussion of the state-derived bases of FNSEA hegemony under the old regime: exclusive or privileged access, devolved power, monetary subsidies, and revision of regulations. In regard to access to the decision-making centers of the state, traditional practice was indeed changed significantly, but much less than one might assume. At the national level, Cresson invited the minority unions to participate in the Annual Conference and a few other formal functions such as the Etats Généraux du Développement Agricole, a special conference organized by the ministry in February 1983 for an exchange of views concerning the past and future of agricultural development policy (the FNSEA knew that most of the scheduled speakers at this affair could be expected to deliver diatribes against the programs that it had supported for the past two decades, and thus boycotted all three of its sessions).[102] In stark contrast, however, the minority unions were *not* granted seats in any of the important official administrative bodies, such as the ANDA and the CNASEA, and these thus continued to be dominated by the FNSEA as in the past. As for informal access, the FNSEA was received less warmly and frequently at the ministry than in earlier days, and rival union representatives now found themselves able to obtain audiences with officials, but the latter sometimes felt that they were treated with less respect than the "ex-official union." The CNSTP leaders, for example, complained that they were dealt with in a condescending fashion by some top bureaucrats who dismissed their ideas as utopian and rushed them out of the office.[103] By the same token, all of the minority unions were dismayed to discover that they were unable to obtain audiences with the president of the Republic or to persuade the minister of agriculture to appear at their annual congresses; in these respects the FNSEA retained its privileged status, for Mitterrand did find time to meet with Guillaume, and Cresson continued the ministerial tradition of delivering a speech at the annual conventions of both the FNSEA and the CNJA.[104]

The politics of access at the departmental level mirrored the national practice. While the minority unions were in principle granted the right to equal informal access to state officials, they were generally accorded less time than their FDSEA counterparts. Moreover, the newly recognized unions were not granted seats on any formal *paritaire*-style bodies in most departments, and elsewhere they were invited to send delegates "on a consultative basis" (i.e., with no voting rights) to only a few committees.[105] Understandably, their reaction was resentment and impatience. In our case study department of Landes, for example, where the MODEF branch could claim a larger following than virtually any other Leftist union in the country, the MODEF leaders were shocked that the

government which they supported repeatedly denied their requests for representation. By October 1982 the MODEF leaders were frustrated enough to declare
that it was impossible "to accept the ostracism to which [our organization] is
subjected in numerous commissions, where everything happens as if the tenth of
May 1981 had not intervened."[106] In similar terms, many farmers who attended a
PS agricultural conference in December 1982 demanded that "union pluralism
be made a reality *sur le terrain*" and expressed outrage over the fact that the
"Guillaume *locaux*" had essentially been allowed to retain their official
monopoly.[107]

This situation arose because Cresson and her advisors found it very difficult
to reach agreement on a short-term solution to a political dilemma involved in
implementing the new pluralist order: given that the minority unions were of very
uneven strength from department to department, and totally absent in many, how
were the few (usually 4–6) seats available on official departmental committees and
commissions to be divided among the competing unions? The minority unions
demanded that they be given seats in all departments, but the ministry deemed
this to be both impractical and politically unviable. During 1981 and 1982,
therefore, the ministry stopped short of instructing the *commissaires* (formerly
prefects) and local agricultural officials to provide seats to the minority unions, but
rather left them free to decide whether the local balance of union power
necessitated a change of traditional policy. At the same time, Cresson attempted to
assuage the impatient minority unions by promising (in private) that they would
be accorded representation in formal committees at both the national and
departmental levels after the January 1983 Chamber of Agriculture elections, the
results of which would be employed as the criterion for seat allocation.[108]

From the perspective of the minority unions, the situation was even worse in
regard to the comanagement institutions which had traditionally provided the
FNSEA with devolved power to administer important aspects of agricultural
policy at the subnational level. From 1981 through the end of Cresson's ministry,
the SAFERs, the ADASEA boards, the Chambers of Agriculture (and the SUAD
boards controlled by them) remained just as firmly as ever in the hands of FNSEA
officials; no short-term effort was made to impose a change in either their
composition or their behavior. Minority union activists complained that the
employees of many chambers continued to act as the "servants and recruiting
agents of the FNSEA and the CNJA," and that union competition was thus still as
skewed in favor of the FNSEA as it had been under the old regime.[109] Once again,
Cresson could only pledge that this situation would be changed in the wake of the
next chamber elections.

Judging from published statements and interviews, it appears that the
minority unions were disappointed more than anything else by the government's
reluctance to alter radically the traditional subsidization programs controlled by
the Ministry of Agriculture. Some within the ministry wanted to do so, but
Cresson—under pressure from her superiors to avoid steps that might exacerbate

tensions in the countryside—was constantly reminded by the FNSEA that "watering the little unions with money in a futile attempt to make them grow" would be considered a casus belli of the first order.[110] While the newly recognized unions were provided with some state funds, the FNSEA and its youth branch thus continued to receive the lion's share of ANDA and *promotion collective* subsidies—17,171,000 francs in 1982, for example, nearly 84% of the total allocated to farmers' unions (see Table 8.1).[111] As the minority unions knew well, these figures were only "the tip of the iceberg," for the FNSEA-CNJA continued to receive an even larger percentage of the SUAD subsidies allocated at the department level, to exploit "hidden subsidies" derived from control of the Chambers of Agriculture, and to benefit indirectly from grants to nonunion "technical" organizations. The cash-poor rivals of the FNSEA were astonished and bitter that the government would continue to subsidize so heavily its determined foes while refusing to help its putative friends more. At a meeting with Cresson in April 1982, the CNSTP leaders categorized the situation as

Table 8.1　*Promotion Collective* and ANDA Subsidies (in francs)

Union	1982			1983		
	Prom. coll.	ANDA	Total	Prom. coll.	ANDA	Total
FNSEA	3,640,000 (37.4%)	3,845,000 (35.6%)	7,485,000 (36.5%)	4,100,000 (36.4%)	4,038,000 (33.4%)	8,138,000 (34.8%)
CNJA	3,640,000 (37.4%)	6,046,000 (56.0%)	9,686,000 (47.2%)	4,100,000 (36.4%)	6,475,000 (53.5%)	10,575,000 (45.3%)
FNSEA-CNJA Total	7,280.000 (74.8%)	9,891,000 (91.7%)	17,171,000 (83.7%)	8,200,000 (72.8%)	10,513,000 (86.9%)	18,713,000 (80.1%)
CNSTP	1,100,000 (11.3%)	300,000 (2.8%)	1,400,000 (6.8%)	1,100,000 (9.8%)	530,000 (4.4%)	1,630,000 (7.0%)
MODEF	800,000 (8.2%)	300,000 (2.8%)	1,100,000 (5.4%)	900,000 (8.0%)	530,000 (4.4%)	1,430,000 (6.1%)
FNSP [a]	300,000 (3.1%)	0 (0.0%)	300,000 (1.5%)	800,000 (7.1%)	0 (0.0%)	800,000 (3.4%)
FFA	240,000 (2.5%)	300,000 (2.8%)	540,000 (2.6%)	260,000 (2.3%)	530,000 (4.4%)	790,000 (3.4%)
Total	9,720,000 (100%) [b]	10,791,000 (100%)	20,51,000 (100%)	11,260,000 (100%)	12,103,000 (100%)	23,363,000 (100%)

Source: Pays et paysans! novembre 1984, p. 9.

[a] The FNSP began to receive ANDA subsidies in 1984. The CNJA received 7,263,000; the FNSEA 4,557,000; the FNSEA-CNJA together 11,800,000; the CNSTP, MODEF, and FFA 550,000 each; and the FNSP 400,000.

[b] This column and some others total slightly more or less than 100% due to the fact that the percentages were rounded off to one decimal place.

"scandalous" and demanded the financing to which they had a "just claim." A year later in an interview, a leader of another minority union lamented:

> A lot of people heard Cresson's speeches and thought she did a lot to assist us, but the truth is that most of the time her words weren't followed by action. She was constrained by the government, but I also think she was a little naive—she put us in a difficult situation. What she did was to attack the FNSEA verbally, which helped it to gain support from farmers unhappy with the government, while leaving the structures of the old system almost intact. What we needed was more money and rights, not good words and broken promises.[112]

In a few cases, at least, the departmental branches of the minority unions found that their new official status did help them to obtain more money from a source discussed in Part II: the Conseil Général. For example, MODEF of Landes was accorded 150,000 francs from the Conseil in May 1982 for improvement of its Accounting and Management Service.[113]

In at least one important area, that of regulations governing elections to the Chambers of Agriculture, the Cresson ministry did deliver on promises made to the minority unions. A decree of 3 August 1982 set the next chamber elections for the end of January 1983 and altered the rules of the electoral game in several ways guaranteed to increase the representation of the minority unions (and, more generally, the forces of the Left) at the expense of the FNSEA: (1) the plurality system (with multimember districts) traditionally used to allocate seats in the largest and most politically important college, the one for active farmers, was to be replaced by a list proportional system; (2) within limits, the campaign expenses of all unions whose lists received at least 5% of the vote in that college or one seat in any college were to be reimbursed by the chamber; and (3) the number of seats in two colleges which the FNSEA or its allies had traditionally dominated was reduced (from 2–6 to 2 in the college of owners of rental land, from 2–4 to 2 in the college of local unions), while the number of seats in the two colleges of salaried workers was increased (from 1–4 to 3–8 in the college of farm workers, from 1–2 to 4 in the college of employees of agricultural organizations).[114] Predictably, the FNSEA condemned these reforms and charged that they represented a blatant partisan move to "handicap" the FNSEA and strengthen the "groupuscules politisés" sympathetic to the government.[115] Pleased though the minority unions were with the central thrust of the reform, they too were dissatisfied with certain aspects of it. Their major complaint was that the government, after having confided that it intended to eliminate the college of local unions, decided at the last minute to yield to FNSEA pressure and retain it, albeit with fewer seats in some departments. All three of the Leftist unions signed a press release branding this move as "an inadmissible concession to the FNSEA" that "risks [the perpetuation of] an absolute monopoly in some departments." They also protested that the electoral reform should have been accompanied by a stipulation that chamber minorities were to be proportionally represented on the committees and boards that wielded almost all of the institution's power. As cases such as Landes and Corrèze had illustrated in the past, mere representation within the chamber was no guarantee against the retention of a near monopoly of power by the FNSEA.[116]

On balance, then, the Cresson ministry moved far more slowly and incompletely in implementing the decorporatization effort than many observers and union activists had expected. Two major reasons for this, no doubt, were a fear of excessively provoking the FNSEA and a concern to avoid a total disruption of the policy-making process. But a third crucial factor was also involved: Cresson and others within the government lost some of their enthusiasm for the new pluralist order venture as it became clear that the effort to create a Socialist *relais* in the agricultural sector was fated to produce very discouraging results. From June 1981 through the summer of 1982, the CNSTP managed to enlist only a few thousand supporters (to the surprise of the government, many Socialist farmers chose to remain within the FNSEA and even participated in the March 1982 Paris demonstration), suffered from sectarian divisions and grew increasingly hostile to the government as more and more Socialist campaign promises were broken. Once the reform effort was derailed by the "hot winter," the CNSTP began to deride Cresson for her timidity, to castigate "President *Rassurand*," and to fill the pages of its monthly publication with headlines unflattering to the government: "Disappointments vs. Promises," "Things the President Has Forgotten," "The Arbiter Has Changed—The Game Remains to Be Played," and "Tactique Adroite" (with the double entendre quite intended). In addition, the CNSTP publicly denounced the government's efforts to persuade its would-be ally to play the role of a supportive client, declaring that "the CNSTP will not be an 'FNSEA of the Left.'"[117] The government was encouraged by the fact that the Interpaysanne faction of the FNSEA finally decided to split from the Federation in April 1982, but this development too had its negative side: fewer dissidents than expected decided to break away, and they proved unable to engineer a merger with the CNSTP. A second Socialist-oriented union thus emerged, the Fédération Nationale des Syndicats Paysans (FNSP), manifesting the intensity of divisions within the Left and complicating the government's attempt to cultivate a useful interlocutor in the countryside.[118] In short, the government's effort to exploit its power for the development of a Socialist *relais* met with many problems reminiscent of those which had frustrated the similar venture undertaken forty years before by Pierre Tanguy-Prigent, the Socialist minister of agriculture of the Liberation epoch.[119]

When the first Chamber of Agriculture elections employing the new electoral laws were held in January 1983, the failure of Cresson's campaign to weaken the FNSEA and bolster the Socialist forces in the countryside was vividly illustrated. The minority unions employed their state subsidies to mount more extensive campaigns than ever before, and the three Leftist unions managed to agree on common lists of candidates in a score of departments. However, the FNSEA responded to the challenge with a campaign effort unprecedented in the history of French professional elections. In the style of a candidate for the presidency of the Republic, François Guillaume flew from department to department in a rented jet, rallying his troops and reinforcing the FNSEA's image as—in the words of one journalist—"an empire within the state."[120] Turnout at the elections increased from the 54–57% of the 1970s to more than 70%, and more competing lists were presented than ever before. Table 8.2 shows how these factors significantly affected the pattern of FNSEA electoral support. Compared with 1974, support for the Federation was more heavily concentrated in the departments whose FDSEAs possessed high membership densities; this probably reflected both a disproportionate ability of those strong organizations to turn out the pro-FNSEA vote, and—as Table 8.2 also indicates—a relative decline in FNSEA support among farmers in the poorer, Left-oriented departments.[121]

Table 8.2   The Correlation Between FNSEA Vote 1974–83 and Indices of Departmental Wealth, Political Orientation and FNSEA Membership

	Agricultural Income per Capita	Crédit Agricole Loans per Capita	Vote for Giscard 1974	Vote for Left 1978	Vote for Mitterrand 1981	FNSEA Membership Density
% FNSEA vote, 1974 chamber election	.200	.165 [a]	.042 [a]	−.103 [a]	−.054 [a]	.230 (1975)
% FNSEA vote, 1983 chamber election	.326	.353	.191	−.286	−.264	.504 (1981)

Sources: The sources for agricultural income per capita and Crédit Agricole loans per capita are the same as those listed for Table 1.1. The sources for FNSEA membership density in 1975 are the same as those listed for Figure 3.5. The source for "vote for Giscard 1974" (on the second ballot of the presidential election) is Howard Penniman, ed., *France at the Polls: The Presidential Election of 1974* (Washington, D.C.: American Enterprise Institute, 1975). The source for "vote for Left 1978" (on the first ballot of the legislative elections) is J. R. Frears and Jean-Luc Parodi, *War Will Not Take Place: The French Parliamentary Elections, March 1978* (New York: Holmes and Meier, 1979). The "vote for Mitterrand 1981" (on the second ballot of the presidential election) data are taken from Didier Maus, ed., *Textes et documents relatifs à l'élection présidentielle des 26 avril et 10 mai 1981* (Paris: Documentation Française, 1981). FNSEA membership density in 1983 was calculated on the basis of data included in "Le Financement public du CNJA et de la FNSEA et le nombre réel de leurs adhérents," *Nouvelles Campagnes*, novembre 1982.

Note: N = 75; Corsica, the Paris region, and the ten most urbanized non-Parisian departments were excluded. A plot of these data revealed that five northern departments (Aisne, Ardennes, Marne, Meuse, and Somme) were "outliers"; all of these departments have large populations of salaried farm workers, who tend to vote disproportionately for the Left. When these five outliers are excluded, the correlations between the political variables and FNSEA vote increase, e.g.: .271 for Giscard vote/FNSEA vote 1983, and −.363 for Left vote 1978/FNSEA vote 1983.

[a] Not significant at the .05 level.

To the surprise and dismay of Cresson's ministry, all three of the Left's unions combined received only 23% of the vote, with the CNSTP claiming a mere 6.0%, the FNSP 5.4%, and MODEF 8.8% (a decline over previous years attributable mainly to competition from the newly formed unions); the ultraconservative FFA received 6.0%. Although the FNSEA was somewhat embarrassed by the fact that a number of its affiliates presented competing lists, manifesting personal as well as political divisions within the Federation, Guillaume and the national elite were delighted with the results. By official ministry calculations, the FNSEA received 63.9% of the vote (70.9% according to the FNSEA) in the college of active farmers; the FNSEA estimated that it received 95% of the vote in the college of local union organizations (where the loosely organized rival unions were poorly placed to compete) and 93% of the vote in all of the other colleges except for those of salaried workers.[122]

Once the new Chamber of Agriculture members had met to select their presidents and executive committees, the extent of the FNSEA's victory became even clearer. Although the changes in the electoral law and college composition did vastly increase the number of seats held by the minority unions and by salaried workers of the Left, they were insufficient to alter the chamber majority in more than a handful of departments. Of the ninety chambers, only twenty-one chose new presidents, and informed observers calculated that seventeen of these (including Michel Debatisse, who won a close election in Puy-de-Dôme with the help of an FO representative) were members of the FNSEA camp.[123]

The outcomes in our three case-study departments reveal just how limited the impact of the electoral reform was. In Aisne, the FFA (9.3% of the vote, 2 seats) and an alliance of Left unions (16.3%, 4 seats) together received over a quarter of the vote in the college of active farmers and thus won seats for the first time, but the USAA won 16 of the seats in that college and all 21 in the other nonemployee colleges; the traditional USAA elite was thus assured of complete control of the chamber, for it possessed 67% of the 55 total seats, 12 of which were held by salaried workers.[124] In Corrèze, an alliance of MODEF and MADARAC (now affiliated with both the CNSTP and the FNSP!) received 40.4% of the vote and won 9 seats in the major college, but the FDSEA won 13 seats therein and 11 of the 17 seats in the other agricultural colleges. The FDSEA elite thus controlled 52% of the 46 total seats, 7 of which were held by salaried workers (4 FO, 2 CGT, and 1 CFDT).[125] In Landes, MODEF received 48.5% of the vote and 11 seats in the college of active farmers, but the FDSEA won 11 seats in that college and 11 of the 17 seats in the other agricultural colleges. While the FDSEA elite's control of the chamber was less secure than in the other two cases, with the FDSEA claiming only 44.8% of the 49 total seats, the traditional majority retained its hold with the help of votes from a number of the moderate salaried workers.[126] In these three cases, as in virtually all other departments, the forces of the chamber minority were accorded no representation on the executive council and were given none of the chamber's posts on departmental commissions.[127] All three of the chamber presidents in our case-study departments were former FDSEA presidents as of 1983 (and by coincidence, they were the three individuals elected vice-presidents of the Assemblée Permanente des Chambres d'Agriculture in 1983).

Income and the EEC

It is probable that the 1983 chamber elections would have produced even worse results for the Socialists had the farmers not benefited, during 1982, from a reversal of the downward trend in income that had plagued the agricultural sector since 1974. According to preliminary estimates released by the Ministry of Agriculture in November 1982, gross agricultural income for 1982 rose by 2.9%; the average farmer's purchasing power, which had fallen by 14% in 1980 and another 5% in 1981, increased by 2.5%. Moreover, the preliminary calculations indicated that the inequality of income distribution within the sector was reduced somewhat during 1982, for the gross income of farmers with less than 20 hectares of land increased by an average of 4–6%, while that of farmers with more than 50 hectares declined by 1%.[128] The news would become even better months later, after Cresson's departure from the rue de Varenne, as final calculations revealed a gross income increase for 1982 of more than 8% and even revised the 1981 figure from a decline (one which had helped to touch off the "hot winter") to an increase of 3.5%.[129]

Edith Cresson reacted with understandable exultation to the preliminary statistics for 1982, citing them as evidence that "socialism is working in agriculture."[130] Given the meager progress the government's reform effort had made by the end of 1982, however, most observers dismissed this assessment as ministerial hyperbole. "C'est pavoiser un peu vite," remarked a disgruntled CNSTP official. Nearly all analysts agreed—and the farmers recognized—that the single most important factor which generated the income upturn for 1982 was one over which the government had no control: the weather. Excellent weather produced abundant harvests for most crops (the volume of production increased by the largest figure in years, 8.7%), leading one farm official to quip that "the Good Lord has been with François Mitterrand."[131] Without the happy accident of bumper crops, no income improvement could have been achieved, for the average increase in produce prices for 1982 (11.2%) once again failed to keep pace with the increase in production costs (11.5%).[132]

It should be acknowledged, however, that the government did deserve some credit for the positive income figures of 1982, for three reasons. First, the partial price freeze instituted in June 1982 helped (along with a decline in world oil prices) to limit the increase in production costs. Second, the controversial income assistance program—intended to compensate for the (apparent) income decline of 1981—which was implemented in 1982 contributed to the reduction in sectoral inequality.[133] Third, and most important, the EEC price hike which the government negotiated in May 1982 did represent an improvement over that of the previous year (11.2% compared with 10.3%), although it fell below the 15% figure that Mitterrand had once claimed to be necessary. As the Socialists had promised, the French government refused to yield to Margaret Thatcher's pressure for a far more modest increase. Indeed, the French and six of their EEC partners used an unprecedented tactic to overcome British opposition: they pushed the 11.2% price increase through the Council of Ministers with a "qualified majority" vote, thus departing from the EEC tradition (which, ironically, had been imposed by de Gaulle) of acting only by unanimous consent on important matters. This French-led coup left the British government in a state of "stunned disbelief" and, for once, earned Cresson at least some muffled applause from the farm community.[134]

RETRENCHMENT À LA ROCARD:
SERVING OLD WINE IN NEW BOTTLES

In March 1983, when Michel Rocard replaced Edith Cresson as minister of agriculture, a new stage of retrenchment began. Whereas Cresson had been passionately committed to reform, and had switched to a course of moderation and retreat only under enormous pressure from her government and the FNSEA, Rocard was universally recognized to be "a man of pragmatism, moderation, and dialogue" (or, in the disparaging phrase preferred by more doctrinally pure Socialists, a representative of "the American Left").[135] "Après le diable, le Bon Dieu"—those were the words with which Le Monde summed up the FNSEA's view of the transition at rue de Varenne.[136] Moreover, as one minority union noted with despair, it was evident that the central mission assigned to Rocard by President Mitterrand was the antithesis of the one originally undertaken by Cresson: establish "peace in the countryside (don't irritate Guillaume)."[137] "Michel Rocard told us clearly," lamented the CNSTP leadership after a rendezvous at the ministry in April 1983, "it is firmly decided that agricultural policy will be comanaged with M. Guillaume. Daily events confirm this well. We can only hope all the same that agricultural policy will not be purely and simply dictated by the FNSEA."[138] As a top official at the ministry confided in the summer of 1983, the Rocard équipe was committed to the principle that "politics is the art of the possible" and felt that "there is no alternative to comanagement in this sector."[139]

But as the FNSEA soon learned, the policy of the Rocard ministry was to be one of retrenchment rather than roll-back. Over the past eighteen months, in the face of FNSEA demands to "de-recognize" the rival unions and revert to the status quo ante, Rocard has stressed to the Federation's leaders that "he has an inheritance" which he—under pressure from fervent reformers within the Socialist Party—must respect and which they have no choice but to accept.[140] At the same time, however, he has implemented policies launched by Cresson with "a logic of rectification" sufficient to preserve the essential privileges of the FNSEA, to reconfirm the Federation's special role in the policy-making process and to elicit once again, within limits, its concertation with the state.[141] What the Rocard ministry has produced, in short, is a sort of synthesis of the pre-1981 group-state system and its Cresson-era antithesis which, in terms of our theoretical framework, could be termed an increasingly stable "moderate corporatism" system. An examination of initiatives undertaken in the Rocard era will show why the FNSEA, though still yearning for a complete reconstitution of the old sectoral regime, has been willing to applaud the ministry for "faithfully trying to reestablish *concertation*"—and why the minority unions have condemned as "treason" the government's "flirtation with the FNSEA."[142]

The *Offices par Produits*

Although their powers were limited, the new produce agencies instituted by Cresson at least represented for the minority unions a means of achieving some role in the market management process long monopolized by FNSEA forces through the *interprofessions*. Cresson had left no doubt that some of the positions on the executive councils of the *offices* would be accorded to nominees of the FNSEA's rivals. One of the first tests of Rocard's commitment to the new pluralist order (and, indirectly, to economic reform) thus arose in July 1983 when the ninety-two agricultural representatives on the *offices* for milk, meat, fruits and vegetables, and wine were selected by the ministry. Wary though the minority unions had been, they were still shocked by the degree to which Rocard failed the test: not a single one of the nominees of MODEF, the FNSP, the CNSTP, or the FFA was chosen, and nearly all of those who were given seats were members of the FNSEA's produce associations. Furthermore, among the four executive council presidents chosen were an FNSEA vice-president and a former FDSEA president. "Who is going to represent the interests of the small farmers . . . in these *offices*?" queried a MODEF spokesman; it seemed that the government was "turning its back to the policy of reducing inequalities." And as an FNSP leader stated, the new councils appeared to be the first tangible manifestation of "the resumption of *cogestion* . . . by the state-FNSEA *couple*." Rocard thus showed that the new institutional bottles introduced by Cresson could be used to serve the old corporatist wine, watered down though it might be.[143]

The *Offices Fonciers*

Another important manifestation of retrenchment à la Rocard was the agricultural land reform bill presented to the National Assembly in April 1984. Unlike the various versions prepared in the Cresson era, Rocard's reform bill was one that the FNSEA could deem "generally positive." Most of the bill's provisions called for nothing more than small technical changes in the law related to the control of agricultural structures and the rights of renters, and in fact most of them had been supported by the FNSEA for a number of years. Ironically, as *Le Monde* commented, the strongest words of opposition to the bill were voiced by the Left majority. A Communist deputy expressed regret that the bill did nothing to

"democratize" the SAFERs, and a Socialist deputy complained that the bill
would "disappoint . . . some who expected more." The Socialist *rapporteur* for
the bill focused on the chief source of disappointment for the Left, the absence of a
provision creating *offices fonciers*, and explained simply that they reflected a
"different logic" from the one at the heart of this bill and "would require financial
means which it would be difficult to mobilize in this period of economic
recession." As the debates continued, the comedy of indecision notable during the
Cresson era surfaced once again. The issue in concern was an article of the bill
which gave the *commissaires* the power to create, in "difficult cases," an ad hoc
cantonal commission charged with providing an opinion to the departmental
commission empowered to allocate land purchased by the SAFER. A number of
the Socialist deputies demanded that such commissions be created on a
permanent basis in every department, as stipulated in Cresson's version of the
offices bill, while Rocard and others refused to agree, noting among other things
that the FNSEA objected even to the ad hoc commissions (viewing them as seeds
from which genuine *offices* might be allowed to grow). After a lengthy session of
private intraparty negotiations, it was decided to delete the controversial article
from the bill and attempt to arrive at mutually acceptable language to be inserted
at one of the later readings. Needless to say, the experiences of the past few years
gave no one much hope that this circle would ever be politically squared, and it
was not. The law approved by parliament during the summer of 1984
incorporated an article virtually identical to that which Rocard had proposed in
April.[144]

Decorporatization Derailed

Tension between Rocard and more militant Socialists quickly emerged, quite
predictably, over general decorporatization policy as well. Cresson had managed
to deflect criticism of her reluctance to implement the new pluralist order by
promising that action would be taken soon after the 1983 Chamber of Agriculture
elections, but Rocard—who moved to the rue de Varenne two months after the
elections had been completed—was obviously unable to use this ploy. Within
weeks after Rocard arrived at the ministry, minority unions were noting that "the
government has already lost precious time in not taking into immediate
consideration the results of the chamber elections" and demanding that steps be
taken to assure their rights. When it became clear that Rocard was less than eager
to respond to their demands, the Leftist unions exerted pressure for action
through their contacts at Matignon and the Elysée as well as the ministry.[145] In the
face of intense counterpressure from the FNSEA, however, Rocard announced
that a further "délai de réflexion" would be necessary before "this explosive
dossier" could be resolved.[146]

　　The key decision involved setting a threshold of chamber votes at which the
minority unions would be deemed eligible for representation in the many

commissions and committees at the department level. Table 8.3 illustrates how the alternatives considered entailed vastly different effects on the system of representation. The ministry and all of the farmers' unions recognized that the stakes were very high, for access to the department-level bodies was a means not only of exerting influence and obtaining information, but also of establishing credibility as an effective union. The recruitment efforts of FNSEA rivals in the pre-1981 era had been seriously hindered by the fact that they offered activists the chance "to speak louder, but at the expense of not being heard." The recognition of the minority unions in 1981, and the expectation that they would soon be granted full participation rights, had already precipitated FDSEA scissions in several departments and elsewhere had enhanced the minority unions' ability to attract members. Both the FNSEA and its opponents were convinced that if the right to participate were extended broadly, the balance of union power could be profoundly affected.[147]

Table 8.3   The Effect of Alternative Representation Thresholds

| | No./% Departments in Which Minority Union(s) Would Receive Seats if Representation Threshold Set at: | | | |
	10%	15%	20%	25%
MODEF	37 (41%)	20 (22%)	13 (14%)	6 (7%)
CNSTP	22 (24%)	9 (10%)	1 (1%)	0 (0%)
FNSP	16 (18%)	11 (12%)	8 (9%)	5 (6%)
FFA	27 (30%)	13 (14%)	5 (6%)	2 (2%)
Alliance[a]	15 (17%)	11 (12%)	6 (7%)	3 (3%)
Total with at least one	80 (89%)	51 (57%)	31 (34%)	16 (18%)

Source: The table was derived from data in "Resultats officiels de l'élection aux chambres d'agriculture du 28 janvier 1983," a four-page mimeo distributed by the Ministry of Agriculture.

[a]   In a number of departments, including Aisne and Corrèze, two or even all three of the minority unions of the Left formed an electoral alliance and presented a common slate of candidates. When the ministry announced that 15% would be the threshold, it also stipulated that alliances which had reached this figure would be accorded representation (in most cases, however, the alliances would be given only one seat, so only one of the allied unions would be represented). The actual figures for MODEF, the CNSTP, and the FNSP will thus all be slightly higher than reported here.

After having come to grips with the fact that Rocard was unwilling to accept its position that none of the minority unions was worthy of recognition, the FNSEA lobbied intensely for a threshold of no less than 25%, a figure that would give seats to only a single minority union in 18% of the departments. The CNSTP, which knew that it would receive no seats at all with this formula and would suffer the most from any threshold above 10%, argued vociferously that *all* of the nationally recognized unions should be accorded seats in *all* departments; in support of their position, the *paysans-travailleurs* noted that nationally recognized trade unions had long been accorded the right to have a delegate even in enterprises where they had no organizational presence. While sympathetic to this hard line, the other minority unions confided that they could accept a threshold of 10%, a figure which would provide seats to several unions in many departments and at least one non-FNSEA union in 89% of them. During the summer of 1983, ministry officials informed a disappointed FNSP delegation that Rocard viewed this figure as politically unacceptable and was tilting toward a threshold of 20%.[148]

It was not until the end of October 1983, seven months after he assumed office, that Rocard finally issued an official ruling: the threshold was to be set at 15%. The FNSEA leaders publicly denounced this decision, which they knew reflected a partial concession to last-minute pressure by Socialist deputies and other militants; Guillaume complained that "the minister is feeding the little mutts who nip at our heels." However, he and his associates also recognized that Rocard had strongly resisted demands for a lower figure and that the outcome could have been much worse; with this threshold minority unions would receive seats in just over half the departments, only MODEF would hold seats in as many as twenty departments, and the FNSEA would retain a majority of seats nearly everywhere. For these very reasons, the minority unions and many PS officials were outraged. CNSTP spokesmen protested that "the 15% rule makes a mockery of pluralism" and announced that, with the support of the Syndicat des Avocats de France and other legal rights groups, they intended to file an appeal with the Conseil d'Etat. Meanwhile, a large segment of the Socialist delegation in the National Assembly "hotly contested" Rocard's decision and demanded that the FNSEA not be allowed to continue exercising its "monopoly of comanagement of agriculture."[149]

Despite this pressure from within his own party, it is not the minority unions but rather the FNSEA which Rocard has sought to appease since the announcement of the 15% rule. In February 1984 the ministry revealed that it would issue a decree stipulating that, on two of the most important local *paritaire*-style bodies (the development planning commission and the land commission which serves as a link to the regional SAFER), the FNSEA's and CNJA's departmental branches were each to receive one seat *in addition* to those to which they were entitled on the basis of chamber votes. While the FNSEA applauded this decree as a sign of the ministry's recognition that policy could not be effectively administered without its cooperation (since even popular branches of the minority unions were often poorly organized as well as hostile), the rival unions naturally found it "inadmissible" and unjust. "What would one say," argued one anti-FNSEA activist, "if the Socialist Party had supplementary representatives on the General Councils under the pretext that it holds a majority at the national level?" Others pointed out that the implications of the decree were bizarre in some cases. In Loire-Atlantique, for example, it led to a distribution of seats that bore no relation at all to the chamber vote: FDSEA-CDJA, 3 seats for 28%; FNSP, 1 seat for 42%; FFA, 1 seat for 24%.[150]

While Rocard has thus severely limited minority union access to official bodies at the department level, he has completely excluded these unions from commissions and committees and the national level. When pressed to explain how such a policy squares with the official doctrine of union pluralism, Rocard and other officials at the ministry have stated that the policy process necessitates a distinction between *"lieux de réflexion"* and *"organes de gestion."* In the former, such as the Chambers of Agriculture and special conferences at the ministry, every organization has a full right to participate because "there must be a place for nonconformist ideas." But in the latter, where the government must work on a daily basis to manage the affairs of the sector, only "those who represent the greatest number" and have the organizational capability to make *cogestion* effective merit a place.[151]

This interpretation of the significance of "recognition" is, quite clearly, drastically more narrow than what Cresson and her supporters had in mind. Furthermore, it has been applied in a manner that has reduced minority union access even further: the national-level *lieux de réflexion* have been virtually eliminated, as Rocard has at least temporarily discontinued the tradition of the Annual Conference (viewed by the FNSEA as worthless in its pluralist form, and opposed as a symbol of compromising *cogestion* by the CNSTP) and has held no extraordinary conferences as significant as Cresson's Etats Généraux.[152] In terms of informal access, the Leftist minority unions have continued to fare better than they did before 1981, mainly because some of the committed reformers brought to the ministry by Cresson have remained on the scene. However, they have complained of receiving a frosty reception from the top officials in Rocard's cabinet (some of them, an FNSP activist has charged, "seem more like *Chiraciens* than Socialists"), while the FNSEA has saluted these men for their commitment to the resuscitation of traditional *concertation*. Rocard himself has not only respected most of the FNSEA's traditional privileges, such as attending its annual congress while declining to appear at the meetings of minority unions, but has stated publicly that the FNSEA's "capacity to comanage. . .is decisive for the effective functioning of the institutions. . .of agricultural policy-making."[153]

Not surprisingly, then, the Rocard ministry has failed to follow up on Cresson's pledge to break the FNSEA's monopoly of devolved power at the local level and to decrease its privileges substantially in other regards. Since mid-1983, the pages of minority union publications have been replete with complaints about the refusal of FNSEA majorities in the Chambers of Agriculture to include their opponents on committees or to stop "brainwashing the peasant world with public funds" by disseminating vital information only in the pages of newspapers jointly published by the chamber and the FDSEA, and the denial by SAFER officials of a right to minority positions on these vital land management agencies.[154] Moreover, the hopes which the Etats Généraux raised for a change in development policy have been dashed by the ministry's refusal to include minority unions on the SUAD boards.[155] On the subsidization front, the ministry has announced that it will accord the minority unions "identical access" to ANDA and *promotion collective* funds, but as long as such payments are made on a basis of the capacity of the unions to stage educational sessions and perform technical services, the small unions poor in infrastructure will continue to receive much less than the FNSEA; in addition, the latter will continue to benefit from what the CNSTP has termed its "piracy" in the Chambers of Agriculture.[156] One of the few areas in which minority union and Socialist Party pressure has yielded at least a ministerial pledge for change is that of regulation enforcement. In response to numerous complaints from the FNSEA's rivals and written questions by Left deputies in parliament, Rocard has promised to send agricultural field agencies a circular requiring the cessation of "forced dues collection" (the practice which some FNSEA-allied cooperatives have followed of deducting a percentage of payments due to farmers and forwarding that sum to the union).[157] Nevertheless, given the current climate of group-state relations and the inherent difficulty of assuring compliance with such an order, it would seem that minority unions should expect to be disappointed in this regard as in many others.

Income, the EEC and Systemic Stability

To what extent has Rocard's cultivation of close ties with the FNSEA succeeded in recreating a *stable* corporatist system, that is, one in which the group favored by the state seeks to secure its status by manifesting a willingness not only to cooperate in the policy-making process but also to play the crucial client role of moderating demands and restraining members during periods of sectoral unrest? The first eighteen months of the Rocard era have provided ample opportunities to gauge the stability of the emerging "moderate corporatist" system, for they have featured a series of economic problems and one major sectoral crisis. What the FNSEA's behavior during this period has shown is that the system is becoming increasingly stable, for the FNSEA elite has acted in a fashion strikingly reminiscent of the 1970s, resisting pressures for the sort of antigovernment *contestation* directed against Cresson and seeking to preserve social peace in the countryside. Ironically, but understandably, it is the minority unions most closely affiliated with the Socialist Party which, during the Rocard era, have sought most fervently to exploit crises to mobilize their troops and thus challenge the Socialist government.

Whereas Cresson's first eighteen months in office featured a hard-won victory on the Brussels price front and (after release of the figures eventually proven to have been excessively pessimistic) good news in regard to agricultural income, Rocard's first year and a half have yielded quite different results, but also a very different reaction from the FNSEA. In May 1983, just before the completion of the EEC price negotiations, the FNSEA's Guillaume asserted in a press conference that an 11.7% price hike was necessary and that in its absence it would be justified to expect another wave of demonstrations.[158] Two days later, when an increase of only 8% was announced, Guillaume branded the deal as "insufficient" but stopped short of encouraging an organized response, and the FNSEA's line of "moderation" continued throughout the summer.[159] In late September 1983, Rocard revealed that—for the second year in a row—the agricultural budget for the coming year would increase by less than the overall budget. The FNSEA complained that this showed "the government . . . no longer considers the development of the agricultural sector as a national priority," but once again it failed to respond with mobilization.[160] Then, in November, the government made public a report which estimated that agricultural income for 1983 would register a decline of 3.8%, a figure larger than that released by Cresson in 1981.[161] To this news, the FNSEA responded not as it had done during her ministry, but rather as it had normally done when faced with similar "provocations" before 1981: the national council of the Federation listed its grievances, categorized the situation as one of "mounting peril," and announced plans to organize routine demonstrations in December intended to pressure the government on the eve of the next EEC talks in Athens.[162] Two developments on 1 December served to illustrate the degree to which the traditional dynamics of group-state relations had been restored. On the one hand, the FNSEA's Guillaume was received by Mitterrand at the presidential palace for a discussion of the issues—such as the admission of Spain and Portugal to the EEC, a step opposed by the FNSEA—to be raised at the Athens summit. On the other, the FFA concluded its congress by complaining about the intimate relationship between the government and the FNSEA, and declaring itself to be "in a state of resistance."[163] The FNSP echoed these themes some weeks later, condemning as "treasonous" the government's "flirtation with the FNSEA" and calling for allied actions with other Leftist unions against a majority which "today no longer has a plan" for reform.[164]

A far more significant test of systemic stability arose during the first six months of 1984 with the onset of a major political crisis, one that almost certainly would have generated an explosion of FNSEA-led violent protests during the Cresson era. On 13 March, Michel Rocard announced the signing of an EEC accord with profound implications for the agricultural sector. As finalized some weeks later, the package of EEC agreements included not only a meager price hike (5% for French farmers, 2–3% less than the expected inflation rate for the year) almost guranteed to produce another year of sectoral income decline, but also an extremely controversial program intended to limit the spiraling cost of the Community's subsidization of milk producers. The government agreed to reduce French milk production for 1984–85 to 3% less than the figure for 1983, and to do so by (1) providing 30,000 current milk producers with 600 million francs in special subsidies to retire earlier than planned or to switch from milk production to another form of activity; (2) increasing the coresponsibility tax on milk (which the Socialists in opposition had pledged to eliminate) from 2% to 3%; and (3) instituting a graduated "super tax" to be imposed on farmers whose dairies have already collected an annual quota to be set by the state. In presenting this milk program, Rocard asserted that "France has a right to say to its farmers that their interests were well defended," but even he—who had chaired the European Council of Ministers during the negotiating sessions—felt compelled to acknowledge that the solution to the milk problem was "difficult, painful" and that the "bitter pill" had been accepted only because the likely alternative was "the collapse of the Community."[165]

As *Le Monde* commented, "the quotas revolution" represented a "historic disruption in the economic life of our country since, for the first time, [the government] is limiting the right of production for thousands of entrepreneurs."[166] The impact of the program would be broad, for more than 40% of the farmers produce at least some milk, and it would be especially pronounced in protest-prone Brittany, for 70% of that region's farmers specialize in milk production. These facts alone were enough to make the program politically problematic, but several others were certain to compound the effect. The plan seemed to penalize most the many small farmers who had invested heavily to increase their milk production and thus render their operations economically viable; it would exacerbate the regional inequality of agricultural income, as a large percentage of milk producers were concentrated in poor areas; and it would hasten the exodus from the land of small farmers whom the government had promised to save. All things considered, it seemed reasonable to expect "a real outburst of anger from the farmers . . . a *guerre du lait*."[167]

In the short run, the highly unpopular milk plan did severely strain relations between the FNSEA and Rocard's ministry. At an appearance before the FNSEA annual congress just after the announcement of the program, Rocard's speech was often interrupted by hisses, catcalls, and derisive laughter. FNSEA president Guillaume harshly criticized every aspect of the EEC accord, asserted that the Federation's confidence in the minister had been shaken, cautioned that "if necessary, the farmers will go up to Paris again," and then, in a press conference after the session, sought to deny any complicity in the milk plan by proclaiming "*concertation* doesn't exist."[168] A few weeks later Guillaume intensified his rhetorical assault, asserting that the farmers were "violently disappointed" with the Brussels accord and urging the milk cooperatives to refuse to administer the quota system for the government.[169]

Even at this point, however, the FNSEA stopped short of organizing a wave of violent protest actions like those of the "hot winter." In late March the Federation orchestrated a one-day demonstration in the provincial capitals, but the 40,000 farmers who participated were urged to avoid incidents and journalists noted that the atmosphere was "calm" virtually everywhere. Indeed, the FNSEA elite's restraint displeased dissident activists in Brittany, where the president of the Finistère FDSEA complained that "the FNSEA doesn't really defend us" and stated that "the Bretons must count only on themselves."[170] A month later the FNSEA organized a demonstration in the largely milk-producing Loire, attracting roughly 20,000 farmers, but again the protest was restrained and only a single violent incident was reported.[171]

On 29 May 1984, as Rocard hosted a meeting of the EEC ministers of agriculture in Angers (Maine-et-Loire), the "milk war" reached a climax whose political dynamics were strikingly different from those of the "hot winter." Two separate incidents in western France symbolized the dramatic changes that the orientations of the farmers' unions had undergone since the Cresson era. First, a coalition of CNSTP, FNSP, and MODEF militants from the northwestern departments carefully planned and executed a protest action even more spectacular than the FNSEA's ambush of Cresson in 1982: a small group of them kidnapped the director of the Office National du Lait, François Ranc, as he stepped off a train in the Breton city of Rennes and forced him to accompany them to a farm where, for several hours, fifty activists angrily "explained *sur le terrain* the consequences of the implementation of the milk quotas for a recently installed young farmer." This "visit" was interrupted when eighty police arrived, along with (once again!) a surveillance helicopter. But the drama continued, for several of the young farmers escaped with Ranc and proceeded to hold him hostage; meanwhile, another group of *paysans-travailleurs* telephoned the prefecture and announced that Ranc would be released only if Rocard agreed to meet with them and also to schedule a "round table" on the milk issue in June. When the demands were refused, Ranc was held until evening and then "dropped off" at the prefecture in Rennes. Fifty-six Leftist militants were later questioned, and both the president and secretary-general of the Ille-et-Vilaine branch of the CNSTP were arrested. At a press conference in Angers, Rocard condemned the incident as "an act which discredits French agriculture" and declared that it would "modify profoundly the nature of the relationship which the state could maintain with organizations that permit this sort of thing." In a reversal of the state of affairs during the winter of 1981–82, the press now noted the emergence of a "divorce between the farmers of the Left and the government of the Left."[172]

While the Ranc kidnapping strained relations between the Leftist unions and the state to the breaking point, the second incident of 29 May manifested the FNSEA elite's renewed willingness to play the traditional client role and served to reinforce the Federation's status in the eyes of Rocard. A peaceful demonstration of 20,000 FNSEA-CNJA activists assembled in Angers was nearing its conclusion when, all of a sudden, several beer bottles were hurled at the riot police, who responded by firing teargas shells. "At this moment," wrote the *Le Monde* reporter on the scene, "everything could have come unhinged. But a solitary silhouette . . . rushed through the smoke toward the police entrenched behind their armored car: 'Don't fire, in the name of God!' It was François Guillaume, the president of the FNSEA. With several gestures . . . he ordered his troops to restore order in the ranks." One of the farmers protested that "we are big enough to settle our affairs alone," but the crowd dispersed and further violence was avoided. When Rocard heard about the incident, he decided to "pay just tribute" to the FNSEA by arranging for Guillaume and other FNSEA leaders to meet with the EEC ministers. After this meeting, Rocard expressed support for Guillaume's proposal to institute a European annual conference modeled after the traditional French conference system, and the EEC ministers accepted an FNSEA invitation to do what François Ranc had been forced by the Leftist militants to do: visit the farm of a young Frenchman to observe firsthand the difficulties of coping with the current crisis.[173]

The twin dramas of May 1984 seemed to illustrate that the system of agricultural group-state relations, destabilized for several years by the government's policy of decorporatization, was approaching a new equilibrium in many ways similar to that of the pre-1981 era. Subsequent events have been consistent with such a conclusion. For example, the FNSEA has assisted, albeit reluctantly, in the implementation of the "milk quotas" scheme while the minority unions have remained disgruntled and on the margins of the policy-making process, and Rocard (whose reappointment to the Ministry of Agriculture was supported by the FNSEA when a new government was formed in July 1984) has publicly reaffirmed the "responsibility of the government" to work with social "partners capable of committing themselves to implement consensual decisions."[174] At the same time, however, there have been reminders that the new system is not the "strong corporatism" of the past. Some FNSEA and CNJA officials have repeatedly voiced opposition to the principle of quotas, have continued to complain about the government's failure to reinstitute the monopolistic comanagement system of the 1960s and 1970s, and have stressed that "the traditional cooperation between the government and the agricultural world instituted by . . . Edgard Pisani" rested on an "unwritten pact" whereby the official union's *concertation* was contingent on the government's delivery of an acceptable agricultural policy.[175] As long as the degree of group-state consensus on political and policy goals remains less impressive than it was during the former regime, it seems evident that both the FNSEA and the state must learn to live with the structures and behavior of a "moderate corporatism" system whose stability will remain vulnerable to jolts from both "above" and "below."[176]

CONCLUDING REFLECTIONS ON DECORPORATIZATION

This study of the evolution of relations between the state and the farmers' unions from 1981 to 1984 has provided, on one level, a sectoral "window" revealing many of the more politically significant particularities of contemporary French politics. The specific trajectory of the decorporatization campaign has been affected by such factors as the ambitious and somewhat naive initial vision of the prospects for reform on the part of a Socialist Party which, when it assumed office in 1981, had been locked out of national power for twenty-three years; the instinct for caution and retreat in the face of resistance on the part of president François Mitterrand, a man who has said that the unknown burial site of deposed Chilean president Salvadore Allende is an "obscure spot [that] haunts my dreams"; the heterogeneity of a ruling party that encompasses individuals as different in their commitments to Socialism and styles of authority as Edith Cresson and Michel Rocard; the tenuous nature of the links between the French Socialists and their putative allies among interest groups; the instinct for resistance and even revolt on the part of interest groups whose *droits acquis* are threatened; and the complexity of public policy implementation in what remains arguably the most centralized of democracies.[177]

On another level, however, this study also serves as a fruitful case from which to derive some general propositions regarding the dynamics of decorporatization. Given the perils of generalizing from a single case, the propositions are necessarily merely suggestive, but they should be of some use for specialists on corporatism, especially since very little has yet been written on the topic of decorporatization. First, *decorporatization is a complex and costly process.* However profitable decorporatization "from above" may appear to a government, for both policy and political reasons, it thus seems likely—as noted in the first pages of this chapter— to be a policy that will seldom be attempted (an explanation for the dearth of case studies on the issue) and, when attempted, will commonly be incompletely implemented. Second, *decorporatization is likely to engender resistance from the client group targeted for deposition.* That resistance should probably not be expected to be as dramatic or as effective in most cases as it has been in the case discussed here, given the peculiarities of French political culture, but it seems almost certain to emerge as a source of political costs and a factor tending to prompt reconsideration or moderation of the decorporatization drive on the part of the government.

Third, for the reasons cited earlier and for another one as well, *decorporatization is unlikely to yield an outcome as extreme as what we have termed "strong pluralism" or even "structured pluralism."* The additional reason is that, as noted in the Introduction, well-developed corporatist arrangements tend to emerge in particular sectors not merely because of the political affinity of the government and its client but also because of the Herring-Shonfield law, that is, the state's need for sectoral cooperation in the administration of policy in sectors where state intervention is especially pronounced and difficult. The desire to depose an established client viewed by the government as potentially problematic should thus not be expected to entail a desire for the thorough elimination of corporatist-style collaboration by the state with sectoral groups. In the case discussed here, for example, Cresson clearly intended to supplant the FNSEA-state relationship with some sort of alternative tie between the state and a Socialist *relais*. The failure of Cresson to seduce the CNSTP into playing the role of "an FNSEA of the Left" significantly reduced the already slim chances for a thorough deposition of the FNSEA. Fourth, *a strategy of decorporatization "from above" can be reversed not only by resistance "from below" but also by (perhaps unexpected) cooperation "from below."* Once the FNSEA's leaders made it clear that they were not intent on destabilizing the Socialist government for partisan reasons, but were willing— even in the face of unwelcome economic policies—to play a modified client role in exchange for the retention of structurally biased influence and competitive advantages valuable for organizational maintenance, the government's incentives to continue the decorporatization campaign were diminished and a group-state rapprochement became possible. While other groups and governments cannot be expected to behave precisely like those discussed here, there is good reason to believe that their "sunken institutional costs" would incline them toward a similar mode of behavior.

Conclusion

Agricultural Corporatism in Comparative Perspective

For the development of corporatist theory, an enterprise concerned with producing and explaining statements of regularity in group-state relations, the importance of the foregoing analysis of agricultural corporatism in France lies chiefly in its usefulness as what Harry Eckstein has termed a heuristic case study. Such case studies can play a vital role in the process of theory building, for they "stimulate the imagination toward discerning important general problems," serve as a source of "theoretical puzzles and insights" and, most important, suggest prelimary theoretical constructs or "clue[s] to a valid general model." In this chapter, an effort will be made to tap the heuristic potential of our national case study of agricultural corporatism. The first section will extract the central theoretical puzzle posed by the French case and present a hypothesis and general model designed to solve that puzzle. In the second section, the validity of the hypothesis will be tested with four "comparative crucial case studies" drawn from other democratic polities. The final section will present some concluding reflections on the potential utility of our model of the corporatization process in the agricultural sector.

THE CORPORATIST IMPERATIVE IN AGRICULTURE: TOWARD A GENERAL MODEL

Simply stated, the central theoretical puzzle suggested by the previous chapters is as follows: why has corporatization developed more fully in the agricultural sector than in other French sectors? Should this development be viewed as a curious anomaly explicable solely in terms of particularities of the French case? The inattention to the agricultural sector in the theoretical and comparative literature on neocorporatism implicitly suggests such a conclusion. Moreover, at least one of the principal authors within this literature has argued explicitly that "organized agriculture" has tended to be excluded from the "corporatist pattern" and thus "largely confined to the classical pluralist 'pressure politics.'"[2]

Various findings of this study suggest, however, that the converse may be true—that certain distinctive features of agriculture render this sector unusually prone to a relatively high level of corporatization. The discussion of the Fourth Republic era illustrated that a weak government, a low degree of group-state consensus, and a would-be client reluctant to assume an extensive role in the administration of public policy could combine to restrict corporatization, but even during that period the level of corporatization in the French agricultural sector (an advanced version of "structured pluralism") was significantly higher than that of the labor sector and in some respects higher than that of the business sector. Since the emergence of the "strong corporatism" system in the 1960s, FNSEA officials have consistently attempted to silence critics of *cogestion* by alleging that agricultural policy-making entails a sort of corporatist imperative. More recently, as Chapter 8 noted, officials of the Socialist government have echoed this line as a defense for their decision to minimize decorporatization within the agricultural sector. What logical and empirical bases are there to support this contention?

As the French case indicates, such a claim must be tempered at the outset by an important caveat. The level of corporatization achieved within the agricultural sector of a liberal democratic polity is in part determined by two factors which can be expected to vary quite significantly from case to case: *the capacity of the state* to cultivate ties with prospective clients, a capacity which itself is determined by such factors as political culture (more or less conducive to formal, corporatist group-state relations) and governmental structure; and *the degree of group-state consensus.* Given the importance of these variables, one would not expect to find that all polities manifest a uniformly high level of corporatization in the agricultural sector. However, it seems reasonable to hypothesize that there exists a more limited form of "corporatist imperative" in agriculture, that is, that *there is a tendency, at least within industrialized democratic polities, for this sector to achieve a level of corporatization higher than that of other sectors such as labor and business.* As the model of Figure C.1 shows in schematic form, a plausible explanation for this tendency would rest on the assumption that, within the agricultural sector, two other important factors are generally conducive to the development of a relatively high level of corporatization: *the degree of state need for a client* in facilitating intervention and achieving policy goals, and *the capacity of groups* to mobilize and discipline members.

The State's Need for an Agricultural Client

While there is good reason to interpret skeptically the claims of both FNSEA and government officials, it should be noted that support for their contention can be

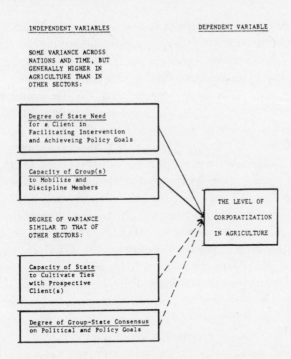

INDEPENDENT VARIABLES

DEPENDENT VARIABLE

SOME VARIANCE ACROSS
NATIONS AND TIME, BUT
GENERALLY HIGHER IN
AGRICULTURE THAN IN
OTHER SECTORS:

Degree of State Need
for a Client in
Facilitating Intervention
and Achieveing Policy Goals

Capacity of Group(s)
to Mobilize and
Discipline Members

DEGREE OF VARIANCE
SIMILAR TO THAT OF
OTHER SECTORS:

Capacity of State
to Cultivate Ties
with Prospective
Client(s)

Degree of Group-State Consensus
on Political and Policy Goals

THE LEVEL OF

CORPORATIZATION

IN AGRICULTURE

Figure C.1   A model of the corporatization process in agriculture.

deduced from what we have termed the Herring-Shonfield law: "The greater the degree of detailed and technical control the government seeks to exert over [private] interests, the greater must be their degree of consent and active participation."[3] If one accepts the essential validity of this "law," then one should expect that—ceteris paribus—the level of corporatization in the agricultural sector will be unusually high, for this sector has in most polities featured an uncommonly high degree of state intervention. *"In all countries of the world,"* noted a 1972 FNSEA report, "recognizing especially the consequences of economic evolution and the disequilibrium of international markets, the state has been compelled to play an extensive role in the agricultural domain. . . . Vis-à-vis the other [economic sectors], the role played by the state is much less extensive."[4] In the case of democratic capitalist systems, the pronounced necessity for state intervention in the agricultural sector has fundamentally stemmed from what V. O. Key once referred to as "the perverse refusal of the economic system to solve [agriculture's problems] in accord with the rules of classical economics."[5] Within market economies, the prices of most agricultural products have tended to suffer from chronic instability, for two reasons. First, the supply of products fluctuates drastically while the demand for them remains relatively inelastic. Second, agricultural producers—millions of small, dispersed, and uncoordinated production units—tend to overreact to market changes. Thus, for example, an increase in price often leads to a sharp expansion of output followed by a collapse in prices and a concomitant excessive contraction of output. Such large and unpredictable price fluctuations hinder the farmers' ability to plan their operations, discourage them from undertaking risky technical improvements, and—an extremely important political fact—undermine the security of their income.[6]

Given the economic and political inadmissibility of such an outcome, the states of all democratic capitalist regimes have intervened in an attempt at least to "iron out" wide and erratic fluctuations in agricultural production, price, and income. The goal of stability has, moreover, led in virtually all national cases to a policy of agricultural subsidization, as "the state comes under strong pressure to aid farmers when times are bad without imposing any balancing charges at other times." The "peculiarly vulnerable" nature of agriculture, the strategic import-ance of food production, and the political power of the farm vote (magnified by its diffusion and by the overrepresentation of rural areas in many electoral systems) have thus generally combined to produce state intervention with the espoused goals of maintaining not merely price stability but also income parity.[7]

This secular trend toward state intervention in agriculture was accelerated during the world wars, when the rationalization and expansion of production became a principal concern everywhere.[8] Since World War II the trend has been sustained—not just in France, but in nearly all polities—by the technologically induced necessity of developing more modern and efficient agricultural struc-tures. On the one hand, governments have felt it necessary to provide farmers with information regarding advances in equipment, biology, accounting, and produc-tion techniques. On the other hand, as agricultural modernization has reduced the quantity of labor needed within the sector and has lessened the viability of small farms, governments have been pressured to "ease such painful changes as the flight from the land."[9]

Here it should be noted that the likelihood of a tendency toward agricultural corporatization can be deduced not only from the Herring-Shonfield law, but also from what could be termed a *corollary* of that law: *the more difficult an interventionist scheme is to administer within a sector, the more the state must seek the collaboration of interest groups.* Administrative difficulty is a function not only of the extent of intervention, but also of the structure of the sectoral economy. A theme common to the literature on agriculture in many different polities is that state intervention in the sector poses "forbidding administrative . . . problems," for no other economic domain features production units so *numerous, small,* and *inaccesible.*[10] It may be true, as Beer has asserted, that "no ministry engaged in economic control can have staff large and specialized enough to enable it to make policy and administer it without the [cooperation] of the producers in the sector concerned," but the dilemma facing an agricultural ministry is one of special severity.[11] Unlike the largest steel factory, even the largest farm produces an insignificant proportion of total sectoral output; moreover, state officials charged with making on-site inspections can visit no more than a few farms in a single day. Anyone who has driven around the countryside with such officials can attest that their ability to contact farmers is even further restricted by such mundane problems as the fact that finding a specific farm is more difficult than finding a factory. As the case studies of Part II illustrated, interaction between state officials and farmers is rendered even more difficult by the fact that the latter, generally less well educated and more isolated than most citizens, often view the former as intimidating and alien; the contrast with the *pantouflage*-prone business sector could not be more striking.

Organizational Capacity of Agricultural Groups

As our examination of the labor, business, and agricultural sectors in France illustrates, another variable which plays an important part in determining the prospects for corporatization is the capacity of sectoral interest groups to play the client role. A sector that features several groups with low membership densities is unlikely to prove fertile ground for corporatization. In a case such as that of labor in France, for example, even a concerted effort by the government to promote group-state cooperation through subsidization (for example, the *promotion collective* program) and increased institutional access (for example, the "New Society" experiment of Chaban-Delmas and Delors) may yield little progress in the face of groups both highly competitive and organizationally weak. What reason is there to believe that the agricultural sector, in contrast, should tend to feature groups of an uncommonly high organizational capacity conducive to corporatization?

The case of French agriculture suggests at least two factors that could be expected, in other democratic polities, to facilitate the emergence of the sort of hegemonic (or even monopolistic) and high-density agricultural unions capable of serving as effective clients. First, one would assume that *farmers' unions in other nations could manage, as has the FNSEA, to rally the support of disparate farmers by employing the argument that sectoral "unity" is a necessity for a declining sector in an industrial society increasingly dominated by urban interests.* An examination of other West European cases shows that such a "purposive incentive" is indeed commonly employed. In West Germany, for example, the leaders of the dominant Deutschen Bauernverband (DBV) have long sought to solidify their position and fend off the emergence of rival unions by promoting consciousness of the fact that agriculture is a "marginal group" in danger of becoming a "hopeless minority" in advanced industrial Germany; the particular interests of the farmers must be sublimated to the common sectoral cause, it has been argued, now that "one can truly say: *Feinde ringsum!*" (We are surrounded by enemies).[12] In Great Britain, where the agricultural sector has long been the smallest in Western Europe, much the same theme has been exploited by the dominant National Farmers' Union (NFU). Some farmers in Britain, as in France and West Germany, have contested the alleged value of defensive unity, but a number of studies have confirmed that the idea of "farmers' solidarity" has genuine appeal. "The agricultural interest tends to think of itself as engaged in a desperate many-fronted struggle for stability and prosperity. In this context unity seems all-important, since farmers are heavily outnumbered by vaguely identified 'urban interests' which are thought to be ignorant and ill-disposed." Many of the NFU's arguments have been "directed to the dangers of division," and most farmers have supported the notion that they must "speak with one voice, that they might be heard at all."[13] The predominant farmers' union of Italy, the Coltivatóri Diretti (National Confederation of Direct Cultivators, or Coldiretti), has commonly invoked the theme of an agricultural sector engaged in a "battle" against urban interests less vaguely defined than in Britain. As Giuseppe Ciranna notes, the leaders of the Coldiretti have relied heavily on "ideological cement" to unify the disparate farmers, portraying them as a socioeconomic category whose "unità" derives from universal adherence to "ruralità," or traditional rural values. It is the Confederation, they have argued, which has served as the "in-surmountable wall" protecting the farmers' common interests against assaults by their "implacable enemies," especially the Communists.[14]

The prevalence of this "impulse" for sectoral unity can be expected to discourage the organization of rivals for the dominant farmers' union, thus enhancing the prospects for monopolistic or at least hegemonic representation. Moreover, to some extent it can be expected—through rendering the union's cause an apparently urgent one—to facilitate the dominant union's efforts to achieve a high membership density. A study of the British NFU, for example, contends that it was the minority status of agriculture and "the strength of groups representing other sectors of the population, ultimately traceable to the development of trades unions, which gave British farmers the incentive to organize."[15] Such an argument has been made in regard to the German DBV as well.[16] Plausible though this notion may seem, it must be viewed with considerable skepticism. As incentive theorists have contended, and as our analysis of the FNSEA has confirmed, high membership densities are more likely to be explicable in terms of selective material incentives. Is there reason to believe that agricultural unions are more capable than other socioeconomic organizations of recruiting and retaining members through utilization of such incentives?

The French case suggests that *farmers' unions may indeed be uncommonly capable of such incentive-based mobilization, for it demonstrates that farmers manifest a vast range of needs to which unions can respond with services delivered in the form of selective incentives.* In other words, it suggests the following as a general principle of incentive theory: the capability of an organization to recruit members through services/selective incentives is to some extent a function of the range and degree of need for services on the part of prospective members. How do the service needs of farmers compare with those of, for example, industrial workers and businessmen? Industrial workers clearly have a variety of needs to which trade unions have attempted to respond for recruitment (and other) purposes. Along with insurance, welfare benefits, and the handling of grievances against employers, "a few labor organizations have provided low-cost housing for members and their families; others offer credit unions, recreation facilities, free legal services, family counseling, or old-age homes. Many provide trained community counselors who advise members on their eligibility and rights under social legislation or point out the proper community agency or government office to visit in case of personal difficulty."[17] Although such services have contributed to the organizational efforts of trade unions, they have seldom sufficed to produce a high membership density. Whenever legally possible, therefore, trade unions have relied on "compulsory membership" (through union security agreements) and "coercive picket lines" rather than positive selective incentives.[18] One might argue that the relatively modest success of trade unions in attracting members through selective incentives should be attributed at least in large part to limits on organizational resources rather than worker needs; nevertheless, it is evident that the work-related needs of the industrial employee are less numerous than those of the typical farmer. As the FNSEA never tires of repeating, the farmer is not an employee but instead a *chef d'entreprise* who must engage in a wide range of business activities: purchasing land, machinery, seeds, fertilizer, and other materials; obtaining loans and insurance normally involving larger sums than in the case of the industrial worker; planning and accounting for production; coping with unanticipated problems such as drought and disease; managing hired hands (in many cases); selling produce; interacting with the state bureaucracy; and, so as to pursue these other activities, obtaining a steady flow of information.

The multifarious activities of the farmer thus create a range of service needs at least equal to that of most businessmen, but here the similarity between the two types of *chef d'entreprise* ends, for the typical farmer is less equipped to cope with such needs in the absence of organizational assistance. Farmers tend to possess lower levels of education and income than the members of other sectors, and as noted previously, their enterprises are invariably relatively small and isolated.[19] Given these facts, one would expect to find farmers' unions in most polities capable, even without exogenous resources derived from the state, of exploiting the many opportunities for recruitment through services/incentives and thereby achieving relatively high levels of membership density. A survey of union activities in selected Western democratic polities will illustrate that there is a good deal of evidence to support this assumption.

West Germany

Important though its purposive appeals may have been, it is clear that the DBV could not have achieved its remarkable membership density—roughly 90%, with regional variation from 80% to 100%—without the provision of an impressive array of selective incentives. All observers agree that the DBV's mobilizational success can be attributed largely to the fact that each regional branch employs a network of officials who, like the cantonal secretaries of Aisne, provide members with "technical information on agricultural production, and advice on legal and tax matters—services that are often of vital importance for small and medium-sized farms." Another factor that has contributed to the DBV's recruitment efforts is its intimate relationship with the Deutsche Raiffeisenverband (German Federation of Cooperatives), a large cooperative organization on which virtually all German farmers rely for a wide range of economic services on both the input side (e.g., the financing of farm machinery purchases) and the output side (e.g., the sale of agricultural products) of the productive process. Although the cooperative organization is legally separate from the farmers' union, officials of the latter play a major role in directing the former and, at the state and local levels, the phenomenon of *Personalunion* seems sufficient to render the distinction imperceptible to farmers.[20] It is logical to assume that, in at least many localities, DBV membership is marketed along with Raiffeisenverband services or is assumed by farmers to be a prerequisite for their obtainment. It also seems likely that, at least in some instances, the DBV benefits from the sort of "forced dues" extracted by cooperatives for unions in France.[21]

Great Britain

Like the DBV, the National Farmers' Union of Britain has obtained an impressive membership density figure (nearly 80%) in large part through the delivery of useful and even indispensable services. At the local level, county secretaries and their assistants provide members with "legal guidance on literally thousands of matters each year" as well as advice on taxation issues and a wide range of technical matters.[22] As one study notes, the NFU has reminded its constituency that many disputes involve one farmer against another, and that if only one is a member "the other might find himself with the great weight of the Union against him." Over the years, as state intervention has increased, the perceived utility of the NFU's intermediation services has been enhanced by the farmers' need to deal almost constantly with "the complex governmental machinery on which they so greatly depend." In a typical week, for example, an NFU secretary of the 1960s "gave advice on a contemplated farm purchase, the settlement of a claim against a potato dealer, a rent dispute, an accident claim, a contemplated partnership, a company formation, a mortgage difficulty . . . and a rail damage claim" as well as responding to "the ordinary every-day calls" related to deficiency payments claims, form filling, insurance, electricity supplies, compensation through the Town and Country Planning Acts, water charges, and National Service deferments.[23]

Another important material incentive which the NFU has long employed to attract members is cut-rate insurance. After a period during which the county branches negotiated reduced premiums for their members, the union leadership decided in 1919 to establish an NFU Mutual Insurance Society. "Only members of the union are eligible to insure with the Mutual, and this service contributes much to the Union's hold on its membership." In addition, the Mutual serves indirectly to enhance the union's ability to provide other services. The insurance company contributes to the funds of the county branches, pays part of the county secretaries' salaries, and also yields commissions for the NFU's field men, who are the only authorized agents for the Mutual within their respective areas. "Without this assistance," it has been concluded, "the Union could not maintain anything like its present extensive local organization."[24]

Italy

Studies of the Coltivatori Diretti acknowledge that the dominant farmers' union in Italy owes its organizational success, reflected in a membership density of approximately 80%, not only to the "charismatic personality and brilliant organizational and political skills" of its founding president—Paolo Bonomi—but also to its ability to provide its members with "a wide spectrum of services." As Joseph LaPalombara has observed:

> Services performed for members touch on every conceivable interest. At the local level, special units organize youth and women; where land reform has resulted in the assignment of land to peasants, special divisions are created to help the new proprietors confront their many new problems; at the provincial level there are special units that offer the landowner assistance regarding social insurance, trade-union matters, fiscal problems, developments in technology, and so on; throughout the organization there are educational units that not only aim at raising the level of literacy but also examine the myriad problems that confront the farmer in an era of changing technology and rapid urbanization.[25]

Along with these services, the Coldiretti has also employed a wide variety of other common means to attract members. While it does not directly operate an insurance company in the fashion of the British NFU, it controls, through an interlocking directorate, a private insurance firm (the Fonda Assicuratuvo Tra Agricoltori) which offers special terms to its members.[26] In addition, it controls a network of "essentially private" agricultural consortiums which, like the German Raiffeisenverband, "are of immediate economic importance to the farmers within a particular district who are its members."[27] Given the public functions which these consortiums discharge, a more detailed discussion of them will be reserved for the next section.

United States

The system of services developed over the years by the American Farm Bureau Federation (AFBF) is so impressive that it has become one of the standard examples cited by theorists, such as Olson and Moe, concerned with demonstrating the utility of selective incentives. By all accounts, it is the Farm Bureau's "supermarket of services" which—at least in the postwar era—has been the major factor enabling the AFBF to become the first farm organization in American history to achieve "a large, stable, nationwide membership."[28] With "one of the largest business empires in the United States," the AFBF's membership has been steadily rising in recent years as the number of farms has been declining, and its membership density—which comes close to 100% in some states—now approaches 35% nationwide.[29]

The key to the Farm Bureau's success in recruiting members has been the nationwide development of the "Kirkpatrick-type" cooperatives or business organizations which were originally conceived in Illinois. These organizations are legally separate from the Farm Bureau, but are controlled by the parent organization and generally restrict their benefits to its members. Thus, for example, the Farm Bureau's mutual casualty insurance companies sell their product only to members, while its marketing and farm supply cooperatives pay a patronage dividend—often amounting to far more than annual union dues—to members.[30] Insurance is the "cornerstone" of the Farm Bureau's business operation; as of 1968 its network of fifty-five insurance companies held total assets of more than 1.5 billion dollars. Although less well known, its cooperative network accounted in 1968 for 200 million dollars in assets and 500 million dollars in sales, figures surpassed by less than forty retail chains. Offering savings of as much as 25–30% on such products as tires, chemicals, baling twine, feed, and fertilizer, the marketing program has thus provided "a strong incentive for new and continued membership."[31] In some states, the Farm Bureau also acts as a marketing agent for its members, "buying and selling what the latter produce."[32]

While serving as sources of material incentives for members, the Farm Bureau's vast array of business operations—which includes real estate holdings and travel agencies along with agricultural units—also produces revenue which is employed directly or indirectly (e.g., through the payment of rent for office space) to support the organization's infrastructure and pay its staff.[33] Like the insurance company owned by the British NFU, therefore, the business dealings of the AFBF facilitate the maintenance of a personnel network capable of providing legal and technical advice to individual members.

Agriculture Versus Labor: A Comparison

Perhaps the simplest way to illustrate the impressive nature of the membership densities achieved by agricultural unions is to compare them with those of labor unions. As Table C.1 shows, in France and every one of the cases examined earlier, the membership density of *the largest* farmers' union alone is significantly higher than that of *all* labor unions; indeed, on average, the membership density of the former is almost *twice* that of the latter. To the extent that membership density is an accurate measure of organizational capacity, and that organizational capacity is an important variable affecting prospects for corporatization, these

Table C.1   Membership Densities in the Agricultural and Labor Sectors 1970–80

	Membership Density of all Labor Unions	Membership Density of the Largest Farmers' Union	Farm Edge Over Labor
France	23%	44–65%[a]	+21–42%
Britain	50%	76%	+26%
Italy	33–40%	80%	+40–47%
West Germany	40%	90%	+50%
USA	24%	35%	+11%
Mean	35%	67%	+32%

Sources: The labor union statistics are taken from Klaus von Beyme, "Neo-Corporatism: A New Nut in an Old Shell?" *International Political Science Review* 4:2 (1978), 182. Similar but unidentical figures (France, 22%; Britain, 50%; Italy, 50%; West Germany, 43%; United States, 21%) are given in Gerard Adam, *Le Pouvoir syndical* (Paris: Dunod, 1983), p. 42. The non-French farmers' union figures are taken from, or calculated on the basis of data cited in, the following: Paul Ackermann, *Der Deutsche Bauernverband im Politischen Kräftespiel der Bundesrepublik* (Tubingen: Mohr, 1970); Samuel R. Berger, *Dollar Harvest: The Story of the Farm Bureau* (Lexington, Mass: Heath, 1971); Percy Allum, *Italy: Republic Without Government?* (New York: Norton, 1973); Graham K. Wilson, *Special Interests and Policymaking: Agricultural Policies and Politics in Britain and the United States of America, 1956–70* (London: Wiley, 1977).

[a] The FNSEA membership density of 44% cited in earlier chapters was based on the number of dues-paying members (537,000) given in a confidential union document (of 1975) intended only for internal use. For public consumption, the Federation—like many other organizations—tends to give a significantly inflated figure, e.g., 750,000 (1975), 700,000 (1976), or even 850,000 (1982); see note 2 of Chapter 4 for the sources of these figures. If calculated on the basis of the mean of these three numbers, the FNSEA's "official" membership density would be 65%. That figure is included in this comparative table because the membership densities of the non-French farmers' unions are generally based on "official," and probably inflated, membership statistics.

figures thus lend support to the hypothesis that the agricultural sector should be expected to achieve a relatively high level of corporatization. These figures can, of course, be viewed in another way as well; to some degree, such relatively high membership densities may be an *effect* of corporatization. From either interpretive angle, these statistics seem to support the "corporatist imperative" hypothesis.

TESTING THE CORPORATIST IMPERATIVE HYPOTHESIS

In his classic article on the theoretical utility of case studies, Eckstein argues cogently that carefully selected case studies may, if properly employed, serve not only as "plausibility probes" but even as valuable tests of candidate theories. "One can use a well-constructed experiment," he notes, "conducted to stimulate as closely as possible the specified conditions under which a law must hold, and compare its results with that predicted by the law." By the same token, a "well-chosen case"—what he terms a "crucial case"—can also be used to test a theory:

The fact that a point [representing a particular case] falls, or does not fall, on a curve . . . is not at all insignificant. If the curve is not constructed to pass through the point but *preconstructed* to represent a theory, and if, given the nature of a case subsequently examined, we can predict, according to the theory, that it must fall on, or very near, the curve at a specified location, the fact that it does so is of the utmost significance, and its location far from the predicted point will impeach the theory no less than the tendency of several points to describe a divergent curve. At any rate, this is the case if the bases for predicting the location of an unknown point are really compelling—which is the object of a crucial case study. In such a case study, the compelling instance "represents" a regularity as, in comparative study, a sample of individuals "represents" a population.

A "crucial case," Eckstein continues, "is a case that *must closely fit* a theory if one is to have any confidence in the theory's validity . . . it must be extremely difficult, or clearly petulant, to dismiss any finding contrary to theory as simply 'deviant.'" Further, he argues, it is conceivable that "the most powerful study of all for theory building" consists of "comparative crucial case studies." Although he insists that the utilization of multiple cases is not necessary if any one case is truly "crucial," he acknowledges that it will provide an even more compelling test.[34]

The purpose of this section is to test the corporatist imperative hypothesis through employing the methodology suggested by Eckstein. It must be acknowledged at the outset that the model or theory from which this hypothesis is derived allows for only a rough prediction of the points where our "crucial case studies" should fall. As noted earlier, the model includes two variables—the capacity of the state and the degree of group-state consensus—which, in some cases, could yield an outcome out of line with that predicted. However, it does enable one to assume that such "deviant" outcomes are probably due to the effect of those variables. Second, the model is not refined enough to predict with great precision. Nonetheless, it does predict that the level of corporatization in the agricultural sector will be higher than that achieved in other sectors (or equal, if those sectors are at the "strong corporatism" level). It seems reasonable to assume that the agricultural level will be between one and two levels higher; hence Figure C.2 actually includes not one curve, but a maximum and minimum curve. One other caveat must be noted here related not to our model, but rather to the data on which our predictions will be based: although it is hypothesized that the level of corporatization in the agricultural sector should be higher than that of both labor and business, the agricultural level will be compared only with that of labor, as shown in Figure C.2. This restriction is necessary because the secondary literature includes no rankings for business. Fortunately, rankings for labor—on a scale similar to the one used throughout this book—have been presented by Gerhard Lehmbruch, and it is these which will be employed for our comparative purposes.[35]

Before proceeding to test our hypothesis with case studies drawn from other

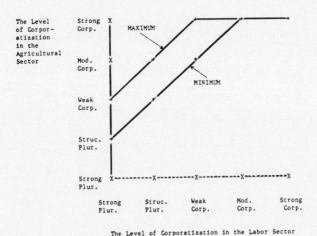

Figure C.2 The curve(s) postulated by the corporatist imperative hypothesis.

polities, let us conduct a preliminary test with our French "cases," that is, those that can be taken from a longitudinal comparative analysis of group-state relations in France since the era of the Fourth Republic. Figure C.3 plots the "predicted" and actual points at which the agriculture/labor comparisons fall during three different periods: the 1950s, the 1960s–70s, and the 1980s since the advent of Mitterrand's Socialist government. The results are encouraging: in each case, the level of corporatization achieved in the agricultural sector is higher than that of the labor sector. It must also be noted that the result for the 1960s–70s is somewhat sobering. The fact that the point for this period falls above our "maximum" curve serves as a reminder that our model can provide only rough predictions. However, this "deviance" is at least explicable within the terms mentioned earlier. Given the detailed analysis of Part I, it seems safe to attribute the uncommonly high level of agricultural corporatization during the 1960s and 1970s to the extreme effect of the two more "unpredictable" variables: the capacity of the state (extremely high) and the degree of group-state consensus (very high in the agricultural case, very low in the labor case).

Let us turn now to the test based on non-French cases. Four national cases will be examined: West Germany, Great Britain, Italy, and the United States. It should be acknowledged that, to some extent, this selection of cases rests on pragmatic grounds: all four of these polities are large and important enough to have been discussed in a body of secondary literature sufficient for at least a rudimentary analysis (even in these cases the literature, including that in German and Italian, fails to deal with some points one would like to see covered). Primarily, however, these cases have been selected according to theoretical criteria: all are (at least since the end of World War II) liberal democratic polities, the sort to which our model is expected to be relevant; they represent a range of

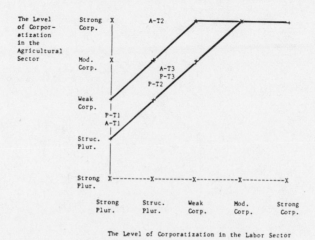

Figure C.3 "Predicted"/actual locations of France—1950s (T1), France—1960s–70s (T2) and France—1980s (T3) on the curve(s) of Figure C.2.

rankings on the labor scale (moderate corporatism in West Germany; weak corporatism in Britain and Italy; strong pluralism in the United States), and thus should produce a range of points along our curve(s); and they are cases in which relatively high degrees of state need for a client and/or organizational capacity have been demonstrated, not merely assumed. It thus seems acceptable to consider these as "crucial case studies." If one is to have confidence in the validity of our model and the corporatist imperative hypothesis, these cases *must fit*. At the same time, it would be extremely difficult in these cases to dismiss as simply deviant a finding contrary to our hypothesis—especially a point representing a lower level of corporatization in agriculture than in labor. Figure C.4 gives the predicted location of each of these cases within our postulated curve(s).

To test our hypothesis, let us now determine the actual location of each case by examining—to the extent allowed by the available data—the level of agricultural corporatization indicated by the role of the state in shaping the pattern of interest intermediation, the nature of group-state interaction in the public policy-making process, the nature of intragroup relations, and the nature of intergroup relations.

West Germany

By all accounts, the system of interest intermediation in the West German agricultural sector has been of the predicted "strong corporatism" variety since the early years of the Federal Republic. During the first two decades of this regime, the Deutscher Bauernverband became "one of the most powerful groups in the nation" not only by obtaining the membership of virtually all farmers, but also by exploiting its partisan ties to the ruling Christian Democratic party.[36] In the mid-1950s, DBV members accounted for nearly 10% of the Christian

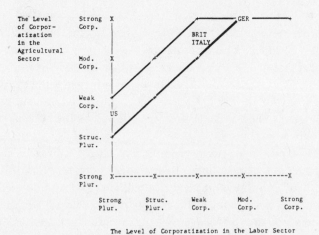

Figure C.4   Predicted location of case studies on the curve(s) of Figure C.2.

Democratic delegation in the lower house of parliament, and throughout the 1950s the minister of agriculture was "usually a member of the DBV."[37] At this time the DBV gained recognition as the sole official representative of the agricultural sector and began to enjoy a degree of privileged formal and informal access to the state which the FNSEA would not achieve until the 1960s.

At the national level the DBV has long wielded a good deal of influence within the agricultural committees of parliament, but it has devoted much more attention to the utilization of contacts within the government and especially the bureaucracy of the Ministry of Agriculture.[38] The ministry has viewed the DBV's unified, centralized, and moderate representation of agricultural interests to be highly "functional" and has collaborated with its leaders and staff so intimately that some observers have characterized this group-state relationship as one of "symbiosis," while others have referred to the ministry as a *Verbandsherzogtum* (interest group duchy) ruled by the DBV.[39] While the DBV has thus thus benefited from a degree of informal access matched by few if any interest groups in other sectors, it has also enjoyed exclusive sectoral representation within formal bodies such as the Import and Storage Boards and the Economics Ministry's Konzertierte Aktion committees. In addition, the minister of agriculture has traditionally met on a regular basis, usually once or twice a month, with the DBV president.[40]

The DBV has also received privileged access to the *Länder* governments and bureaucracies. At the subnational level, however, the DBV derives much of its influence over policy-making from another source: control of the *Landwirtschaftskammern* (Chambers of Agriculture), comanagement institutions similar in structure and power to those of France. The DBV leaders, in cooperation with the Christian Democratic government, founded the chambers in the late 1940s and have dominated them ever since. As Paul Ackermann has argued, "one must not ... view the DBV in isolation" from the *Landwirtschaftskammern,* for they serve as one of the principal bases of its organizational monopoly within the agricultural sector. While they provide the DBV's regional branches with less direct subsidization than the French chambers give the FDSEAs, they provide a similar sort of infrastructural support and also enhance the status of the DBV leaders who control their executive boards; in Ackermann's words, these DBV figures are endowed by their chamber posts with "an aura of official authority."[41]

The DBV's privileged status vis-à-vis the state, its control of the chambers and its close ties (including interlocking elites) with the Deutsche Raiffeisenverband have no doubt contributed, along with the union's endogenously supported services, to the DBV's ability to enroll nearly 90% of all German farmers as members and to avoid serious organizational challenges to its sectoral hegemony. It was not until the early 1960s that a notable attempt to organize another national farmers' union was made. Between 1961 and 1964, large farmers primarily from northern regions formed the Notgemeinschaft Deutscher Bauern (Emergency Association of German Farmers, NDB), a movement which, like the French FFA, opposed structural reforms and criticized the dominant union for its readiness to compromise with the state. The NDB did succeed for a time in pushing the DBV toward a more conservative and assertive stance, but it failed to attract many members and disappeared from the scene within a few years.[42] Another more important effort to launch a rival to the DBV was made in the early 1970s. In 1972, after the German government had adopted a "Green Plan" which excluded many small and part-time farmers from eligibility for subsidies, a group of disgruntled farmers rejected the DBV as a means for their defense and formed the Deutscher Bauernverband der Landwirte im Nebenberuf (German Union of Part-Time Farmers, DBLN). However, as one would expect given its lack of the status and selective incentives available to the DBV, the DBLN has attracted few recruits and has scarcely represented a threat to the official union. Following a policy similar to that pursued by French officials before 1981 in regard to the FNSEA's rivals, the German Ministry of Agriculture has shown no inclination to "exploit divisions within the farm community" by granting recognition to the DBLN.[43]

One might have expected the DBV to suffer significantly from the defeat of its Christian Democratic allies in 1969 and their consequent exclusion, for more than a decade, from the federal executive. However, two political factors prevented the CDU/CSU's misfortune from imperiling the DBV's privileged status. First, throughout the tenure in power of the SPD-FDP coalition, the Ministry of Agriculture was in the hands not of the Social Democrats, whose links to the DBV are quite weak, but rather the Free Democrats, a party that was solicitous of DBV interests in an effort to pry farm voters away from the Christian Democrats. Second, the dominant SPD (which regularly received a mere 10% of the farm vote) had no organizational ally in the agricultural sector and was thus neither tempted nor pressured to grant official recognition to a rival of the DBV. Although DBV influence with the government may have waned somewhat during the 1970s, therefore, its status within the agricultural sector and its importance for the ministerial bureaucracy were not significantly diminished.[44]

Great Britain

As a host of scholars have testified, the dynamics of interest intermediation in the British agricultural sector have long been the highly corporatized sort predicted by our model. The rise of the NFU to its position of near monopoly among British agricultural organizations was greatly facilitated "by its recognition by the Government as sole spokesman for the general interests of farmers," and the NFU has traditionally enjoyed a relationship with the state categorized by various authors as "probably unique in its range and intensity" (Self and Storing), "the most intimate and powerful . . . of all the quasi-corporate relationships between the Government and interest groups" (Lieber), "a model for a new style of indirect government" (Alderman), and "the classic case of incorporation" (Grant).[45] This group-state "partnership" has lifted the NFU "above the level of party warfare and enables it to function, as Union leaders sometimes point out, almost as an arm of the state."[46]

It was the state's increased intervention into the agricultural sector, especially during the two world wars, that established the bases for the position which the NFU would hold in the contemporary era. During World War I the government enacted unprecedented measures to regulate and increase food production, and in doing so it felt the need to step up consultation and cooperation with the industry. "Almost accidently," note Self and Storing, "the Union found itself a major force in agricultural politics as it was called upon to play a major role in policy formation and execution." Not coincidently, "its membership leaped from 20,000 in 1913 to more than 100,000 in the early 1920s." A second jump in membership, from 125,000 in 1939 to 210,000 in 1953, accompanied the union's response to the government's need for its renewed "assistance in the conversion of agriculture to a wartime basis." It was the pattern of interaction established during World War II that proved decisive. The NFU moved away from what had been an ineffective strategy of attempting to influence parliament and focused its attentions on building ties with the bureaucracy, shouldering "widening responsibility for the agricultural policy in exchange for an increasing measure of influence over it."[47]

The NFU's partnership with the state was formalized early in the postwar era with the passage of the 1947 Agriculture Act obligating the government to consult "such bodies of persons who appear to them to represent the interests of producers in the agricultural industry."[48] In practice, this vague phrase has been interpreted—until very recently, as will be discussed later—in such a way as to grant the NFU exclusive access to the government. On the national level, during periods of both Labour and Conservative government, the NFU has traditionally been the sole agricultural spokesman accorded seats on dozens of advisory committees and included in the Annual Price Review, an institution established by the Agriculture Act of 1947 and the one after which the French Annual Conference was modeled.[49] Like farmers' unions of other countries, moreover, the NFU has played what is in some ways an even more influential quasi-official role at the local level.

One of the chief innovations of the 1947 Agriculture Act was the institution of County Agricultural Committees (CACs), bodies intended to assure "the large measure of voluntary co-operation necessary to the success of many agricultural programs." Although the CACs serve many purposes identical to the French Chambers of Agriculture, their members are not popularly elected and are formally expected to behave as "agents of the Minister." A typical CAC consists of twelve members, seven nominated by agricultural groups (three by the NFU) and five more directly appointed by the Ministry of Agriculture. In practice, about 75% of the CAC members have usually been farmers, a majority of which are union members. In some counties, as Self and Storing note, the committee members have tended "to think of themselves as a kind of special subcommittee of the county branch of the National Farmers Union" and, in general, Farmers Union-County Committee cliques have not always been "easy to avoid." In some cases, the county branch of the NFU has "automatically added all farmer members of the committee to its own executive body."[50]

Through participation in the CACs, the NFU and the farmers have "not only accepted extensive programmes of regulation and subsidy but shared in their administration." Indeed, in a tone similar to that of the FNSEA, the NFU has claimed that its indirect yet official role within the CACs has put agriculture "in the proud position of being the only great industry that is self-governing." Hyperbole aside, it is clear that the NFU has derived both intangible and tangible organizational benefits from the CACs. NFU leaders who also hold committee posts, like the DBV leaders prominent within the *Landwirtschaftskammern*, have been bestowed with an aura of official authority. In addition, the NFU-CAC officials have been in a position to wield a good deal of power as they inspect farmers' methods of milk production, count their subsidized sheep, punch the ears of their subsidized calves, and check their subsidized corn acreage. Prudent farmers have been well-advised to remain on good terms with such officials, for "committees [have] sometimes allowed themselves to forget the demands of impartiality in order to reward friends and annoy enemies," at least in regard to minor issues.[51]

Beyond their participation in the CACs, NFU officials have at times been directly accorded devolved authority for the administration of extraordinary programs. For example, when blizzards of January 1978 caused extensive livestock losses in Scotland, the local NFU branch was called upon to play a role much like that which some FNSEA branches have played (see Chapter 5's discussion of fuel rationing in Aisne in 1973) during crises:

> The NFU (Scotland) was seen as the most suitable body to deal with compensation to Scottish farmers who had lost their livestock. . . . They established a fund to which the Government and the EEC contributed. Criteria for eligibility for compensation were negotiated between the NFU (Scotland) and the Government. This was an example of a scheme where it was held to be administratively easier for the union to manage the operation—and the Government was freed of some of the risk of criticisms of arbitrariness and lack of generosity.[52]

In unusual as well as routine situations, therefore, the British government has relied heavily on the NFU for the making of agricultural policy. Some observers have charged that the NFU-state relationship is "too close and unhealthy," but others have noted that the comanagement of policy within this sector is "much easier, and therefore less of a burden on the public purse" than any conceivable alternative. In fact, some analysts have contended that no realistic alternative exists: "It is no exaggeration to say that, without the willing cooperation of the NFU, the implementation, and, most probably, the formulation, of agricultural policy in Britain would simply not be possible."[53]

Needless to say, the NFU's "symbiotic" relationship with the state has been "an enormous advantage to the Union as an organization."[54] This has been evident in regard to both intragroup and intergroup relations. While many small farmers have resented the dominance of large farmers within the NFU and, especially on the poor Celtic fringe, have subjected the union to "constant attack for being insufficiently militant," they have generally lacked the means to organize effective splinter or rival unions. Only in Wales, where the Farmers' Union of Wales (FUW) was launched in 1955 as a result of Welsh nationalism and "feelings of neglect among small farmers," has the NFU ever faced a serious challenge. Through the mid-1970s, however, the NFU managed to recruit more Welsh members than the FUW, in large part because the government refused repeated FUW demands for official recognition.[55]

Two factors seemed to guarantee that the FUW's drive for recognition would continue to be frustrated. First, the highly centralized nature of the British government meant that a change in policy would have to be made in London. Given the slight weight of Wales in the national political balance (less than 5% of the total United Kingdom population), even pressure from sympathetic Welsh politicians would probably fail to bring about such a change in the face of NFU resistance. Second, an affront to the NFU seemed almost as unlikely to undertaken by a Labour government as a Conservative government, despite the fact that the political ties of the NFU's leaders and members were far stronger with the latter. The NFU had always worked to sustain an "apolitical" image and had played its official union role even with Labour governments, one of which had passed the celebrated Agricultural Act of 1947. Despite occasional "nippiness," fueled by rank-and-file discontent, the NFU had engaged only in "symbolic display[s] of militancy" so as to absorb the pressure from below "without compromising its general policy of . . . statesmanlike relations with government."[56] As for Labour leaders, they were faced with only limited pressure to recognize the FUW and traditionally viewed the maintenance of good relations with the NFU as the best way to maximize their hopes of winning farm votes in the few constituencies (in 1966 there were forty where more than 15% of the workforce was employed in farming) where such votes could be decisive.[57]

To the surprise of many observers, changes in governmental structure and political calculations combined in the late 1970s to bring about an alteration of the long-standing status quo. In the spring of 1978, as part of a general devolution effort, much of the responsibility for agricultural policy in Wales was formally transferred from the Ministry of Agriculture to the Welsh Office. In the face of local pressure, the secretary of state for Wales announced that this could entail recognition of the FUW if that union and the Wales branch of the NFU proved, as before, incapable of merging.[58] Meanwhile, relations between the NFU and the embattled Labour government were becoming badly strained. In March 1978, the NFU declared that Minister of Agriculture John Silkin's tenure in office had been "an unmitigated disaster for farming in Britain," and Silkin retorted in print that the NFU "want[ed] to take without giving in return" during an economic crisis affecting the entire nation.[59] The net result of these developments was that, in April 1978, the Labour government decided to grant official recognition to the FUW.[60] Given the small size of Wales, and the fact that the ministry deprived the NFU of few of its traditional privileges, this decision apparently amounted to only the mildest form of decorporatization. It did, however, underscore the fact that by the time the Labour government was ousted in 1979, the traditional "strong corporatism" system of British agriculture had become significantly destabilized.[61]

Italy

From the late 1940s onward, the system of interest intermediation in the Italian agricultural sector has stood as one of the most fully developed examples of "strong corporatism" within Western Europe. The key to the emergence of this system was the skillful exploitation by the leaders of the Coldiretti, especially Paolo Bonomi, of *parentela* ties with the ruling Christian Democratic Party. Bonomi and his associates used their influence within the party, the parliament, and especially the Ministry of Agriculture to establish a vast network of semipublic institutions consciously modelled after those created under the authoritarian corporatist system of the Fascist era. All of these institutions were designed in such a way as to limit the direct control of state agents by devolving authority for agricultural policy-making to representatives of "the profession," thus providing Italian farmers with a degree of *autogoverno* or *autogestione* unparalleled in other national sectors.[62] In practice, the most tangible effect of this system was to make the Coldiretti, whose membership grew from little more than 200,000 to nearly 8 million between 1944 and 1958, "the most powerful association operating on the Italian political scene."[63]

"In Italy we have two Ministers of Agriculture," wrote one observer in the early 1960s, "an actual one, Bonomi, and a complementary one, the minister temporarily in charge."[64] At the national level, the Coldiretti has traditionally exploited its power as the largest and most solid Christian Democratic bloc to influence heavily the composition and behavior of the agricultural committees in parliament as well as the various bureaucratic branches of the Ministry of Agriculture. Within the ministry, Coldiretti access and influence have been assured not only by the organization's political weight, but also by personal ties; through *operazione del trapasso*, many division heads have been selected from among elites of the dominant agricultural union and/or semipublic institutions which it controls.[65]

Representatives of the Coldiretti have not only influenced national policy through seats on advisory commissions and interactions with officials of the ministry, but have also played a direct, formal role in the policy-making process through their domination of many comanagement bodies similar to those found in France, for example, the Istituto Nazionale per la Istruzione Professionale Agricole (INIPA), the Ente di Patrocinio e Assistenza Coltivatori Agricoli, the Utenti Motori Agricoli, and the Ente Nazionale Risi. A brief examination of the INIPA's mode of operation will illustrate how these *ènti di riforma* (reform agencies) have served to enhance the status and power of the Coldiretti. Founded in 1953 as part of a general effort to encourage modernization in the countryside, the INIPA is controlled by a *paritaire*-style board whose president, by statute, is the president of the Coldiretti. In theory the INIPA was to be funded through a combination of contributions from private associations such as the Coldiretti and state subsidies; in practice, virtually all of the institution's activities have been financed by the state. The purpose of the INIPA is to promote technical education by covering the cost of special courses organized by committees in each of the provinces; in 1963–64, for example, the state expended over 516 million lire for a total of 1,341 courses during which farmers not only heard lectures but also received free notebooks, pens, books, scissors, knives, seeds, fertilizer, and other goods. What has made the INIPA appear to be a "freak from the museum of horrors" to its critics is the fact, in most provinces, Coldiretti leaders have managed to use these state-funded courses and goods primarily as recruiting devices; in many cases, it is charged, the state has simply been billed for "courses" which were never given, while the Coldiretti has distributed valuable goods to rank-and-file clients.[66]

At the subnational level, the Coldiretti's influence on policy making and its ability to attract members have been based primarily on its control of two other institutions, the Federconsorzi (Federazione dei Consorzi Agrari) and the

Federmutue (Casse Mutue Malattie per i Coltivatori Diretti). The provincial consorzi or syndicates are nominally private institutions but since the late 1940s have been "endowed with a number of quasi-public functions" and have served "as field agencies for certain of the national ministries at Rome, and particularly for the Ministry of Agriculture." Many of the syndicates' services are of vital importance for the farmers' welfare; among other things, they provide essential materials at cut-rate prices, arrange for the sale of farm machinery and the storage of crops, and facilitate the obtainment of credit. By the late 1950s, the Coldiretti had managed to gain control over 70% (sixty-five of ninety-two) of the *consorzi* and had thus obtained what one Communist critic termed "power of life and death over the small farmer."[67] In many regions the union and the syndicate have been so closely identified that they have been referred to as "two sides of the same coin: the commercial side and the political side." The intimate relationship between the two organizations has allowed the syndicate to engage in what critics term "predatory operations" for the benefit of the Coldiretti, extracting from farmers—including hostile members of the Leftist Alleanza Contadina—the sort of "forced dues" discussed in the French case.[68] As Joseph LaPalombara concluded some years ago, much of the Coldiretti's power must be attributed to "coerced membership," for "the individual farmer refuses to join the organization at his great peril."[69]

Since their establishment in 1955, the *casse mutue* have served as another source of "considerable power and prestige" for the Coldiretti. These public agencies are managed by elected boards of sectoral representatives and provide "a wide range of medical assistance" for the farmers.[70] They also serve as an important source of infrastructural support for the forces of "Bonomiana" in many parts of the country, for they have been used by the Coldiretti much as FDSEAs in France have used the local Chamber of Agriculture. In a good number of provinces the *mutue* and the local branch of the union have their offices in the same building, and the former pays all or most of the cost of the telephones, lights, publications, and employees utilized by the latter.[71] From the time of the first *mutue* elections onward, the Coldiretti has regularly received over 90% of the vote and has controlled virtually all of the boards. As one journal noted in the early 1960s, such an electoral result "is unparalleled in the political composition of the peasant electorate" and is largely attributable to "irregularities" committed by Coldiretti leaders. A more tart-tongued critic charged that the fraud of the "Bonomiana" and the complicity of officials had "transformed this democratic organization into a *grandiosa macchina per buggerare i contadini.*" Understandably, however, agents of the Ministry of Agriculture have generally pursued evidence of such "irregularities" with no more diligence than French officials have manifested in their investigation of questionable ties between the Chambers of Agriculture and the FNSEA.[72]

Through the early 1970s, the Coldiretti had thus succeeded more than any other "satellite" of the Christian Democratic Party in "occupying" its sector's institutional islands in what has been aptly termed the "archipelago state" of Italy.[73] The Coldiretti had not only acquired a major role in the administration of agricultural policy, but had also achieved a position of sectoral hegemony which rival organizations were unable to challenge effectively. Since the mid-1970s, however, the status of the Coldiretti has been impaired somewhat by several factors. First, the devolution of control over some aspects of agricultural policy to the regional governments has apparently enabled rival unions of the Left— Federterra, the Alleanza Contadina, and the more recently created Italian Confederation of Farmers—to exercise more influence than in the past within regions of Left orientation.[74] Second, not only is the Christian Democratic Party "no longer in a position to use the state apparatus as it wishes," but the influence of the Coldiretti within that party has declined as a result of the relentless rural exodus.[75] And third, elements within the Christian Democratic Party have felt compelled to make an effort to limit the abuses committed by the Coldiretti and to loosen the stranglehold of its leaders over the agricultural policy-making process.

When Italy was hit by high inflation and other signs of an economic crisis in the mid-1970s, the Christian Democratic government faced extreme pressure to curtail spending, improve efficiency, and eliminate corruption.[76] Since "the predicament of the agricultural sector [was] widely imputed to the poor performance of the relationship between Coldiretti and the Ministry of Agriculture," reformers within the Christian Democratic Party pushed for a special effort here which would amount to what we have termed decorporatization. Under a progressive minister of agriculture, Giovanni Marcora, the government took a variety of important steps intended to transfer control of some aspects of agricultural policy-making from "Bonomiana" to agents of the state, and to assure that "selection and efficiency" would replace clientelistic management and organizational gain as the guiding principles of state intervention.[77]

Predictably, the "Marcora Plan" met with stiff resistance on many fronts. The leaders of the Coldiretti were outraged at the implication that they were the cause of Italy's agricultural problems and argued that the minister's reform plan represented a threat to the country's poorest farmers. Tensions between Marcora and the Coldiretti reached such a point in 1977 that the minister refused to make a customary appearance at the union's annual congress, while the union countered by denouncing Marcora as the "Minister of Confagricoltura" (the organization of large farmers) and mobilizing its members for a wave of protest demonstrations. At the same time, Marcora faced a difficult battle within the Christian Democratic Party, which hotly debated the new reform policy at a special agricultural conference in April of 1977.[78] Despite their approval of attempts to curb the Coldiretti, the farmers' unions of the Left also rejected the Marcora Plan, viewing it as an unacceptable effort to accelerate capitalist development in the countryside.[79]

Although the ultimate effects of Marcora's proposed reforms have not yet been documented, it seems safe to assume that they have achieved only a modest

level of decorporatization. Given the problems inherent in attempts at decorporatization (see Chapter 8), the Italian government's record of failure in
regard to other reform ventures, and the broad-scale resistance the Marcora Plan
faced, the traditional "strong corporatism" system of the Italian agricultural
sector has most likely weathered the destabilization of the late 1970s and remained
essentially intact.[80]

United States

Two principal factors have combined to prevent the development of neocorporatist relationships between interest groups and the state in America. First, "peak
associations in the United States are either weak and incomplete or ineffectual.
None can claim quasi-monopolistic hegemony over a significant sector of socioeconomic interest." This incapacity of sectoral interest groups to mobilize and
discipline members nationwide has resulted not only from the social diversity and
vast size of the country, but also from the fact that American "political
institutions are designed to accommodate this spatially distributed diversity."
The federal system has hindered efforts to develop centralized interest groups of
national scope while "the continued existence of dispersed centers of authority"
has provided "opportunities for influence to interest groups which are similarly
organized in a fragmented, geographically dispersed manner." Second, this
incapacity of would-be organizational clients has been matched by (and to a great
extent caused by) the incapacity of the state to cultivate formal ties with interest
groups. As Robert Salisbury has cogently argued:

> If federalism makes it difficult, or unnecessary, for a sector to be mobilized on a
> nationwide basis, so all the devices for fragmenting governmental authority make it
> difficult, or impossible, to assemble the capacity to act in a focused and forceful
> fashion. The other side of the corporatism equation is "the state," an entity capable
> of recognizing, licensing or creating a peak association and then bargaining with it in
> a substantively meaningful way. But in the United States no such monistic state
> exists in any real behavioral sense.

While the inability of the state to seek and cultivate neocorporatist ties with
groups may be attributed primarily to the structural factors noted previously, one
additional social factor deserves mention as well: "monopolistic interest groups"
have been regarded "with deep suspicion in the American political culture." Even
in those few cases where governmental structure would permit or encourage it,
therefore, state officials have been hesitant to enlist the formal participation of
selected interest groups in the policy-making process.[81]

Does the American case thus stand as "deviant" in regard to the thesis that
there exists a corporatist imperative in the agricultural sector? As that
"imperative" has been defined here, it does not. Although the interest
intermediation system within the American agricultural sector has never been
highly corporatized by European standards, it has been highly corporatized
relative to other American sectors. When pressed to cite an exception to the rule of

"strong pluralism" in the United States, Salisbury and others have noted that "the best known" example is one from agriculture. Not only did an agency of the state help to form and strengthen the American Farm Bureau Federation, but it "took decades for this connection to be severed, and during at least part of the time from the Bureau's establishment . . . until the late 1940s there were many, inside of government and out, who asserted or acknowledged the Bureau's suzerainty."[82] At its peak of corporatization, it will be argued here, the interest intermediation system of American agriculture could properly be termed one of "weak corporatism" (with significant variance from state to state), while in recent decades it has remained at least at the "structured pluralism" level.

"The American Farm Bureau Federation . . . has had an extraordinarily curious history," David Truman notes, "in large part because of its close relation to government from its beginnings."[83] The AFBF, by far the largest of the American farm organizations and the "only one with a nationwide membership," originated for all practical purposes with the Smith-Lever Act of 1914. This legislation established through joint federal and state financing the Extension Service Program, administered by county agents who were intended to "furnish farmers information on improved methods of husbandry." Because many of the state governments made financial support of county agents contingent upon the presence of a county association of farmers evidencing an interest in the receipt of such information, agents were motivated to assist in the formation of what became known as "farm bureaus." County farm bureaus proliferated during World War I as government expenditures for "extension work" increased greatly. Along with this organizational growth came a "drive for federalization"; by 1919 many state bureaus had been formed, and a national organization (the AFBF) was begun. In the 1920s the leaders of the AFBF began to consider theirs a "voluntary" association; nevertheless, they maintained close ties to the Extension Service through the county agents, who were transformed into the "servants" of the local bureaus.[84]

For many years "Extension and Farm Bureau [were] almost synonymous terms in some areas" such as the Midwest and the South, and the link with Extension—the "long arm" of the Department of Agriculture—contributed greatly to the Farm Bureau's status as well as its ability to recruit members.[85] In some localities, the sign over the Extension Service office read simply "Farm Bureau," while in many cases the county agent was paid in part by and worked simultaneously for both the Extension Service and the Farm Bureau.[86] Some farmers were attracted by the Farm Bureau's "official" status, but more important was the fact that membership within the bureau assured (or seemed to assure) "first call on the county agent's services." Especially after the launching of the New Deal, when the county agent began to distribute not only information and technical assistance but also a variety of subsidy checks, "it was often expedient to join the county agent's organization: the Farm Bureau."[87]

The New Deal not only enhanced the role of the Extension Service, but more generally engendered a dramatic increase in the corporatization of the agricultural sector. It was during this period that a "weak corporatism" system was created with the AFBF as the central interest group actor. Under the Hoover administration, the AFBF had collaborated in the development of Republican farm policy and had achieved national "recognition . . . as a power in agricultural politics" when its president was appointed to the new Federal Farm Board.[88] However, the leaders of the AFBF soon became convinced that a more interventionist policy was necessary and, once Franklin D. Roosevelt had been elected, began eagerly to cultivate a close relationship with the new Democratic administration. Roosevelt sent representatives to the Farm Bureau conferences of 1932 and reportedly afforded the organization considerable influence over the selection of the new secretary of agriculture. In May 1933 the administration unveiled its initial response to the agricultural crisis, the Agricultural Adjustment Act, and established an agency (the AAA) intended to supervise its implementation. The AAA itself, however, was "confined principally to Washington," and government officials understood well that the new reform programs of the AAA could be launched and operated only through reliance on the Extension Service and the major agricultural organizations, especially the AFBF.[89] Organizational support was important to legitimate the government's farm policies in the face of resistance from radical groups such as the Farmers' Holiday Association, but it was even more crucial for logistical reasons: "the field operations necessary to the AAA, the allocation of quotas to individual farmers, and the checking of compliance with adjustment contracts were left largely to the farmers themselves. Thus, the AAA required that farmers not merely acquiesce in government intervention in their economic affairs, but that they actually participate in the federal program."[90]

The AFBF responded with alacrity to the Department of Agriculture's requests for assistance. The national leadership called upon the state federations to join in the organizational campaign, and in "many communities the local farm bureaus 'literally took over' the task of organizing the AAA committees. Thus, by exploiting the sudden opportunity given by government willingness to act, the Farm Bureau succeeded in making the AAA its own in administration as well as in policy."[91] At the same time, "with the assurance of a benevolent attitude in the department," the Farm Bureau utilized its link with the AAA to increase its membership, especially in the Southern states where its implantation had traditionally been weak. "Wherever practicable, AAA . . . production committees were . . . invited to serve as organization committees to organize a farm bureau in their local communities." Frequently "the chairman of the production control committees [became] the president of the county farm bureau and the members of the committee constitute[d] the board of directors."[92]

Although the AAA was struck down by the Supreme Court in 1936, it was soon replaced by a new structure which entailed simply the consolidation of local committees into "county agricultural conservation associations." Virtually all of the new bodies were directed by the local county agent, and the Farm Bureau succeeded to a remarkable extent in its effort to gain control of them. As of 1936,

Farm Bureau members held 69% (117 of 169) of the seats on the State Soil Conservation Committees in states where a Farm Bureau was organized, and in those same states "90 per cent or more of the county and township committeemen [were] Farm Bureau members."[93] By the late 1930s, therefore, the state's need for agricultural clients to facilitate intervention and achieve reform goals had provided representatives of American farm groups with an unprecedented, formal role in the policy-making process while reinforcing the Farm Bureau's "position of preeminence among farm organizations."[94] As Graham Wilson has argued, "Whether or not the Government had deliberately created a conservative farm group can be debated"; nevertheless, it is clear that the "soundness" of the AFBF's "views, particularly when contrasted with the radicalism of the NFU and other movements of the period," encouraged the state to pursue reform in the quasi-corporatist manner which it chose and "reduced the temptation to disrupt the cosy relationship between the AFBF and the Extension Service."[95]

In the 1930s, therefore, the AFBF enjoyed a good measure of the biased influence and competitive advantage characteristic of corporatist clients. Even at this time, however, the corporatization of the agricultural sector was limited by the political traditions and the fragmented federal structure of the United States. At the national level AFBF influence could be exercised only through informal channels, for the sort of formal consultative structures prevalent in Europe were unavailable after the liquidation of the Farm Board. Moreover, while the AFBF was accorded privileged access to governmental decision makers, it was not "officially recognized" as the sole representative of the sector. As Salisbury points out, "when there was a major consultation with the USDA or Congress about policy" the Grange and the National Farmers' Union also were included.[96] Even at the local level, the Farm Bureau was never treated as the sector's "official" union in every part of the country: "in those states in which another farm organization was strong and the Farm Bureau weak, the Extension Service was sometimes considered uncooperative by Farm Bureau officials."[97] Unlike the FNSEA in France, which has been able to count on special treatment from government officials even in regions where it is poorly organized and faces formidable rival unions, the AFBF was thus unable to entend its hegemony throughout the nation.

Although the National Farmers' Union and the Grange thus did not suffer a fate quite like that of MODEF and other rival unions in France during the 1960s and 1970s, they "were injured, deeply so in some states" by the "marriage" of the Extension Service and the Farm Bureau. "Their leaders," as Talbot and Hadwiger observe, "could only be criticized for not pursuing divorcement proceedings with more energy and acumen."[98] Pressure from the AFBF's rivals did lead to passage of the 1921 True-Howard agreement, which was intended to sever formal ties between the Farm Bureau and Extension, but this agreement was never enforced. During the 1930s, as has been shown, a Democratic administration actually moved not to eliminate, but rather to strengthen the Farm Bureau-Extension ties. A strong governmental push for abolition of the Farm Bureau's privileged status did not emerge until after World War II when, under the new leadership of staunch conservatives opposed to increased state intervention in agriculture, the AFBF developed a hostile relationship with Democrats in both the Department of Agriculture and Congress. Even then, a variety of political factors delayed resolution of the issue. Finally, in 1954, a Republican secretary of agriculture responded to pressure from Democrats on important agricultural committees in Congress and a wide variety of mobilized groups by issuing an order to end formal Farm Bureau-Extension ties. As William Block has documented, the AFBF failed to lobby against this move as it had done during earlier decorporatization campaigns. In part this was due to "the assumption that, where formal relationships had existed for more than two decades, the legal separation would have little practical effect." The acquiesence of the AFBF can also be attributed to the fact that, once the organization had developed the extensive "supermarket of services" discussed earlier, it had less need for formal Extension Service ties which had served their purpose and were now perceived as a political liability.[99]

In the context of America's unusual governmental structure and political culture, the corporatization of the 1930s thus failed to develop into a stronger version similar to that of many West European nations. Indeed, as the AFBF abandoned its practice of cooperating with whatever party happened to be in power, its privileges were significantly reduced if not eliminated. Since the late 1940s, the "dominant motif of American farm politics" has been "partisan division with each party joined in close working relationship with a general farm organization, Democrats with the Farmers' Union and Republicans with the AFBF."[100] Still, however, the decorporatized system of interest intermediation in the American agricultural sector has remained more similar to the model of "structured pluralism" than that of "strong pluralism." Given the continued importance of the role played by elected committees of farmers in the administration of many aspects of agricultural policy, it has been argued that American agriculture can best be characterized as "a system of self-government in which each leading farm interest controls a segment of agriculture through a delegation of national sovereignty." In Lowi's words, "Agriculture is that field of American government where the distinction between public and private has come closest to being completely eliminated."[101]

Predictions Versus Outcomes

What Lowi fails to acknowledge is that this characteristic of agriculture appears to be not a national exception, but rather a cross-national rule. As Figure C.5 summarizes schematically, the corporatist imperative hypothesis has been supported by all four of our crucial case studies. The level of corporatization within the agricultural sectors varies somewhat across nations and time, as predicted, but it is consistently higher than that achieved within the respective

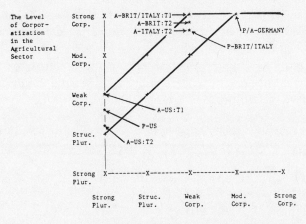

Figure C.5   Predicted/actual locations of the case studies on the curve(s) of Figure C.2. A = actual; P = predicted. For the United States, T1 = the New Deal era through the mid-1940s; T2 = the late 1940s onward. For Britain, T1 = the late 1940s through 1978; T2 = the period since 1978 (the T2 ranking is an estimate based on very little information). For Italy, T1 = the late 1940s to the mid-1970s; T2 = the mid-1970s to the present (as noted in the text, this T2 ranking is also an estimate based on relatively little information; the actual ranking may be somewhat lower, but it is difficult to believe that it could be lower than "moderate corporatism").

labor sectors. In this comparative context, one can stand Lowi's statement on its head: agriculture is that field of government where the distinction between public and private has come closest to being completely eliminated, but America is apparently the country in which that distinction has been most fully maintained.

SOME CONCLUDING REFLECTIONS

It is hoped that this elaboration and explanation of the "corporatist imperative" of the agricultural sector will serve to stimulate debate and encourage further research. Debate of a theoretical sort, focusing on issues ranging from the definition of "corporatism" to the conceptualization of the variables affecting the prospects for sectoral corporatization, is certainly to be expected. Ever since the appearance of Schmitter's seminal article on neocorporatism in 1974, analysts have worked—sometimes at cross purposes—to refine this concept and develop its implications. The scheme presented here settles nothing definitively, but it should provoke some to reconsider certain assumptions and convince others to embrace a more disaggregated, dynamic, and sectorally oriented approach.

Debate of an empirical sort is also to be expected. My ranking of national cases on the scale from "strong corporatism" to "strong pluralism" has of necessity been based on impressionistic grounds, and specialists on particular countries will no doubt raise questions concerning at least some categorizations. As Gerhard Lehmbruch noted some years ago, it is apparent that "interest organizations lend themselves much less to systematic cross-national comparison than political parties and party systems—or elections or parliaments—do," and "the lag in the comparative study of organized interests seems to be due primarily to methodological difficulties":

> Whereas standardized measurements for the cross-national comparison of party systems are relatively easy to establish, systems of interest intermediation constitute complex configurations subject to cross-cultural and cross-national variability. . . . To establish operational definitions with cross-cultural and cross-national validity and to arrive at reliable measurements is a much more complex and difficult task than in comparative party or electoral research.[102]

Needless to say, this study—like those of Lehmbruch and others—has proceeded from the assumption that cross-national (and longitudinal) comparative studies of interest intermediation systems are important and should be attempted even in the face of the obvious problems of measurement. Perhaps efforts to contest my relatively crude measurements will lead to some advances in this area.

Further research would also doubtless raise some empirical questions regarding my observations and conclusions, and such research is certainly to be encouraged. As Terry Moe acknowledged in his study of groups in the United States, not only is the area of interest groups "simply data-poor, to the point where even the most basic information about organizations and their members is lacking," but this problem is particularly severe in regard to the sector dealt with here: agriculture.[103] Useful national-level studies of agricultural groups and their relations with the state are available for the United States and Britain, but the standard source on the latter (Self and Storing) was published in 1963 and none on the former has yet been produced with the conscious intent of explaining the comparatively low level of corporatization in American agriculture. No book-length study of agricultural interest intermediation in postwar West Germany or Italy has yet appeared in English; the standard work on the former in German (Ackermann) is a slim volume dating from 1970, whereas the most informative book on the latter in Italian (Rossi) is a journalistic work published in 1965. Article-length studies on these cases have also been few and far between.

Finally, it is hoped that this book will encourage further research on agricultural interest intermediation beyond the cases discussed here and even beyond the sphere of the democratic, industrialized polities to which the corporatist imperative thesis elaborated in this chapter is intended to apply. One of the few available comparative studies of agricultural political economy provides some intriguing, if frustratingly inconclusive, evidence that the argument and explanatory model presented here may well be applicable, perhaps in a somewhat revised form, to a wide variety of countries. Hopkins, Puchala, and Talbot note that the state has enlisted farmers' associations as "vehicles of modernization and carriers of technological change—in effect as extensions of extension services" in nations such as Japan, Taiwan, and Pakistan. "With appropriately recruited and rewarded leadership," they conclude, organizations have served "as instruments of surveillance and even agents to enforce compliance with official policies. . . . More generally, farmers' organizations have been channels through which information about the impacts of policy has flowed back to governments. As such they have proven essential to monitoring the effects of policy and crucial to the governmental capacity for timely adjustment."[104] It thus seems probable, on the basis of inferences from the cases examined in depth here, that the agricultural interest intermediation systems in many non-Western and even nonindustrial polities feature a good number of the characteristics associated with neocorporatism. This would appear to be a potentially profitable topic for future research.

APPENDIX A

INTERVIEWS

This study is largely based on interviews I conducted during five separate visits to France: June–September 1974, September–December 1975, June–August 1976, July–August 1980, and August 1983. Interviews were undertaken at a great many different locations: Paris, Tulle, Brive, Mont-de-Marsan, Dax, Laon, Amiens, and a multitude of small towns and villages in the departments of Landes, Aisne, and Corrèze. The discussions with departmental union activists were structured loosely around the questionnaire given in Appendix B. In each case additional questions relevant to the particular individual were also posed, and discussions were generally lengthy and informal enough to allow interviewees to volunteer information on a wide variety of topics. The interviews were of varying duration, but in general they lasted from two to four hours. Some individuals were interviewed on several occasions; the names of individuals with whom I conversed for ten hours or more are underlined in the following list.

In the list of interviewees, each individual is identified by the position which he/she held at the time of his/her interview. Former offices or positions are mentioned only when particularly important or when the individual concerned no longer held an office; when possible, positions held after the time of the interview are also listed. An asterisk (*) appears next to the names of individuals who hold or have held national offices in the FNSEA, CNJA, APCA, MODEF, or MONATAR. Cross-references are given for individuals listed in more than one category.

I. ELECTED OFFICIALS AND ADMINISTRATIVE PERSONNEL OF THE FDSEA, CDJA, AND CHAMBER OF AGRICULTURE (CA)

A. Landes (Interviews conducted July–August 1976)

Elected Officials

* 1. Castaing, Jacques. President of the CA; vice-president and former president of the FDSEA. Also adjunct secretary-general of the APCA. Later elected vice-president of the APCA.

* 2. Damestoy, Laurent. Secretary-general of the FDSEA. Also former adjunct secretary-general of the CNJA.
  3. Daubin, André. Adjunct secretary-general of the FDSEA.
  4. Ducout, Jean. Cantonal delegate of the FDSEA; member of the CA.
  5. Lesparre, Paul. Former secretary-general of the FDSEA.
  6. Lubet, Henri. Vice-president of the FDSEA; member of the CA.
  7. Marcusse, Jean. Former secretary-general of FDSEA.
  8. Marcusse, Micheline. Vice-president of the FDSEA; president of the Women's Section.
  9. Marrocq, Maurice. Treasurer of the FDSEA; president of the Syndicat des Grandes Landes.
  10. Massetat, Raoul. Vice-president of the FDSEA; member of the CA.
* 11. Simon, Michel. President of the FDSEA. Also former president of the CNJA and member of the FNSEA bureau.

FDSEA Staff

12. Argouarch, Henri. Administrative secretary of the FDSEA.
13. Barets, Francis. Director of the FDSEA; member of the CA in the college of employees of agricultural organizations.
14. Capes, Didier. Administrative secretary of the FDSEA.
15. Ramon, Jacques. Editor of *Le Sillon* for Landes.

CA Staff

16. Bertrand, Yves. Secretary for the CA director.
17. Bourguignon, J. Administrative secretary for the CA.
18. Darrieulat, Jacques. Research director for the CA.
19. Sadoux, Philippe. Director of the CA.

B. Aisne (Interviews conducted November–December 1975, August 1976, and August 1980)

Elected Officials

20. Arnould, Dominique. Cantonal delegate of the FDSEA (USAA).
21. Arnould, Etienne. Former vice-president of the FDSEA.
22. de Benoist, Henri. Former president of the FDSEA.
23. Burlureaux, Annie. Member of the FDSEA bureau; president of the FDSEA Women's Section.
24. Burlureaux, Jean-Paul. Cantonal officer of the FDSEA.
* 25. Caffarelli, Gérard de. President of the CA; former president of the FDSEA. Also vice-president of the APCA and former president of the FNSEA.
26. Canon, Michel. President of the FDSEA; member of the CA.
27. Carlu, Maurice. Member of the FDSEA bureau; president of the FDSEA Small Farmer's Section; member of the CA.
28. Ferté, Claude. Former president of the FDSEA; member of the CA.
29. Guenard, Jacques. Cantonal delegate for the FDSEA.
30. Larangot, Jacques. Vice-president of the FDSEA; member of the CA.
31. Letrillart, Michel. Vice-president of the FDSEA.
32. Leurquin, Jean. Vice-president of the FDSEA.

33. Lhotte, Pierre. Vice-president of the FDSEA; member of the CA.
34. de La Maissoneuve, Ivan. Adjunct secretary-general of the FDSEA. Also president-of the FRSEA for the North and Parisian Basin.
35. Menu, Bernard. Cantonal delegate of the FDSEA; member of the CA.
36. Le Roux, Jean-Guy. Adjunct secretary-general of the FDSEA.
37. Vassant, Pierre. Member of the FDSEA bureau; president of the CDJA.
38. Venet, François. Secretary-general of the FDSEA; member of the CA.

FDSEA-CA Staff

39. Arnould, Dominique (Mme). FDSEA-CA librarian.
40. Braillon, François. Administrative secretary of the FDSEA's Animal Production Section; director of the CA's EDE (Departmental Agency for Livestock Production).
41. Carlu, Pierre. Cantonal secretary for the FDSEA-CA.
42. Depret, Michel. Editor of *Agriculteur de l'Aisne*; FDSEA administrative secretary.
43. Fache, Michel. Director of the CA's Cours Agricoles; director of the ADASEA.
44. Gentil, Jean-Marie. Counselor for the ADASEA.
45. Lefebvre, Philippe. Cantonal secretary for the FDSEA-CA.
46. Letissier, Alain. Cantonal secretary for the FDSEA-CA.
47. Petit-Four, Yves. Cantonal secretary for the FDSEA-CA.
*48. Prévot, Jean-Pierre. FDSEA-CA director (until 1 January 1976). Also former CNJA secretary-general (1949–54).
49. Quenardel, Bertrand. Administrator for the CDJA and the FDSEA's Women's Section.
50. Quizy, Jean-Pierre. Cantonal secretary for the FDSEA-CA.
51. Testu, Marie-Jo. Administrator for the CDJA and the FDSEA's Women's Section.
52. Tronche, Jean-Philippe. FDSEA-CA director (as of 1 January 1976).
53. Du Vivier, Marcellin. Administrative director of the FDSEA's Vegetable Production Section.

C. Corrèze (Interviews conducted September–October 1975 and August 1976)

Elected Officials

54. Bardolle, Xavier. Former cantonal delegate of the FDSEA; former CA member.
55. Baspeyre, Jean. Treasurer of the FDSEA.
56. Bousseyrol, Elie. Former FDSEA bureau member; former president of the FDSEA's Animal Production Section. See also under MADARAC/ MONATAR.
57. Chapelle, Georges. President of the FDSEA; member of the CA.
58. Chassaing, Jean Louis. Cantonal delegate of the FDSEA.
*59. Chezalviel, Michelle. Vice-president of the FDSEA. Also a member of the FNSEA bureau representing the national Women's Section. Later elected president of the FDSEA, president of the CA, and vice-president of the APCA.

60. Clement, Guy. Former CDJA vice-president.
61. Curbelie, Pierre. President of the CDJA.
*62. Deprun, Pierre. President of the CA; former president of the FDSEA. Also member of the FNSEA's administrative council and president of the FRSEA (Massif Central-Auvergne).
63. Estivie, Pierre. Cantonal delegate for the FDSEA.
64. Evrard, Johan. Former FDSEA bureau member; member of the CA.
65. Joly, Henri. Former adjunct secretary-general of the FDSEA; former CDJA president.
*66. Jos, Damien. Former FDSEA vice-president; former CGA president. Also former member of the FNSEA administrative council.
67. Labrousse, André. Secretary-general of the FDSEA.
68. Mante, Georges. Vice-president of the CA; member of the FDSEA bureau.
*69. Papin, Jean-Pierre. Adjunct secretary-general of the FDSEA; member of the CA. Also president of the CRJA (Massif Central-Auvergne) and adjunct secretary-general of the CNJA.

FDSEA-CA Staff

70. Crumeyrolle, Collette. Administrative secretary for the CA and FDSEA.
71. Demontjean, Pierre. Administrator for the FDSEA.
72. Faurie, Pierre. Technical advisor for the CA.
73. Leblanc, Gérard. Technical advisor for the CA.
74. Lemaire, Jeanne-Marie. Technical advisor for the CA.
75. Malmartel, René. Director of the FDSEA; director of the CA as of April 1976 (previously adjunct-director of the CA).
76. Mondet, Alain. Administrator for the CDJA.
77. Priolet, Aline. Administrator for the CDJA.
78. Sarraudie, Etienne. Librarian for the CA.
79. Terrieux, Yvonne. Director of the CA (until April 1976).
80. Vernat, Nicole. Secretary for the CA and director of SUAD.

D. FDSEA/CRJA Personnel from Other Departments (Interviews 81 and 82 conducted in Amiens, November 1975).

81. Hoel, Maurice. Director of the FDSEA in Somme.
—Lemaroc, Jean-Paul. Former FDSEA director in Lozère (see under MODEF-Landes, no. 94).
82. Malapert, Gervais. Member of the CDJA bureau in Nord.

II. FNSEA/APCA OFFICIALS AND STAFF (Interviews conducted June–September 1974, September 1975, August 1976, July–August 1980, and August 1983 in Paris)

83. Bonnetier, Christian. *Attaché de direction* for the FNSEA.
84. Bourgeois, Philippe. *Attaché parlementaire* for the FNSEA.

85. Genay, Monique. Chief librarian of the APCA.
86. Kerdraon, Paul. Assistant editor of the CNJA's *Jeunes Agriculteurs*.
*87. Lauga, Louis. President of the CNJA. Later adjunct secretary-general of the FNSEA. Elected a deputy (RPR) in 1986.
88. Trébous, Madeline. Editor of *Paysans*, a journal with close ties to the CNJA and FNSEA.

Note: See also numbers 1, 2, 11, 25, 48, 59, 62, 66, and 69.

III. ELECTED OFFICIALS AND STAFF OF MODEF, MONATAR, CNSTP and FNSP

A. MODEF

Landes (Interviews conducted July–August 1976).

89. Bourlon, Jean. Director of MODEF.
90. Cantiran, André. Vice-president of MODEF; president of MODEF's Section des Métayers et Fermiers. Also a *député-suppléant* for the Socialist Party.
91. Comet, Marcel. Vice-president of MODEF; member of the CA.
92. Juste, Albert. Adjunct secretary and administrator for MODEF.
93. Laborde, Bernard. Secretary-general of MODEF.
*94. LaCaule, Armel. Adjunct secretary-general of the CDJA-MODEF. Also national administrator for MODEF.
95. Lemaroc, Jean-Paul. Editor of *Les Informations agricoles*, the newspaper of MODEF in Landes.
96. Marcadé, Franck. President of MODEF. Also president of MODEF's regional federation for the Southwest.
*97. Sintas, Marcel. Vice-president of MODEF; former secretary-general of MODEF. Also national treasurer for MODEF.
98. Urrutiogoity, André. Adjunct secretary of MODEF.

Corrèze (Interviews conducted September–October 1975 and August 1976)

99. Boucheteil, Armand. President of MODEF.
100. Champseix, M. Former president of MODEF
101. Lacassagne, M. Secretary-general of MODEF.

B. MONATAR/MADARAC. (Interviews conducted September–October 1975 and August 1976 in Corrèze)

*—Bousseyrol, Elie. MADARAC president. Also member of the national bureau of MONATAR (see no. 56).
—Clement, Guy. Member of MADARAC bureau (see no. 60).
—Joly, Henri. Member of MADARAC bureau (see no. 65).
102. Terrieux, Yves. Vice-president of MADARAC; member of the CA.

C. CNSTP (Interview conducted August 1983 in Paris)

103. Jacopin, Jean-Charles. Member of national staff.

D. FNSP (Interview conducted August 1983 in Paris)

    104. Buffaria, Bruno. Member of national staff.

IV. MINISTRY OF AGRICULTURE (Interviews conducted August 1983 in Paris)

    105. Arbousse-Bastide, Joelle. Staff member, Public Relations.
    106. Descargues, Jacques. *Chef de cabinet, secretaire d'etat.*
    107. Petitdemange, Jean-Claude. *Chargé de mission, cabinet du ministre.*
    108. Well-Yulzari, Gentione. Staff member, *secretaire d'etat.*

V. MISCELLANEOUS

    109. Bechter, Jean-Pierre. *Chef de cabinet* for the prefect in Corrèze (October 1975).
    110. Domenges, Jean. Agricultural reporter for *Le Figaro* (August 1974).
    111. Olivier, Claude. Reporter for *La Terre*, Paris (August 1974).
    112. Tavernier, Yves. Professor at the Institut d'Etudes Politiques, Paris (August 1974). Elected a deputy (PS) in 1981.
    113. Tillinac, Denis. Reporter for *La Dépêche du Midi* (October 1975).

QUESTIONNAIRE

I. RENSEIGNEMENTS PERSONNELS

1. Nom: _____
2. Age: _____   Commune: _____
3. Présence de la famille: Exploitant seul _____
                               Avec conjoint (et enfants) _____
                               Avec famille (parents) _____
4. Depuis combien de temps travaillez-vous sur cette exploitation? Depuis quand avez-vous la direction effective de la ferme?
5. Quelles études avez-vous faites?
   Primaire _____   Secondaire _____   Supérieur _____

II. LA FERME

6. Quelle est la superficie de votre exploitation?
   Surface totale _____   Surface utile _____
7. Etes-vous actuellement: (indiquer les surfaces respectives)
   propriétaire-exploitant _____   métayer _____
   fermier _____   maître-valet _____
8. Employez-vous de salariés agricoles autres que les membres de votre famille? Régulièrement ou non?
9. Quelles sont vos principales productions? Dans l'ordre d'importance si possible:

   Culture (chiffrer en ha)   *Elevage* (nombre de têtes)

   _____ ____ ha   _____ ____ N
   _____ ____ ha   _____ ____ N
   _____ ____ ha   _____ ____ N
   _____ ____ ha   _____ ____ N

10. De l'élevage ou de la culture, qu'est-ce qui vous rapporte le plus?
    En partant des diverses productions (blé, maïs, vin, élevage pour le lait ou pour la viande, bovin ou ovin . . .) pouvez-vous indiquer, dans l'ordre si possible, ce qui vous rapporte le plus?
11. En dehors, de votre travail à la ferme, avez-vous un autre emploi?
    Lequel?
    Occasionnellement ou toute l'année?
12. Y a-t-il une SAFER dans la région? _____
    Marche-t-elle bien?_____

III. RÉFLEXION SUR LE MILIEU PAYSAN

13. Avez-vous le sentiment que les intérêts de tous les paysans sont les mêmes?
    Si *non*, quels sont les agriculteurs qui ont les mêmes intérêts que vous?
14. Quelles sont les catégories de travailleurs qui vous paraissent les plus proches des paysans?
    Et celles qui vous paraissent les plus eloignées?
15. Quand vous comparez votre situation actuelle à ce qu'elle était il y a dix ans, la trouvez-vous:
    meilleure _____   sensiblement égale _____   ou nettement plus mauvaise _____
16. Croyez-vous qu'en général cela ne va pas dans l'agriculture d'aujourd'hui?
    En quoi?
    Qu'est-ce qui, d'après vous, a provoqué cette situation difficile?
    Quelles solutions voyez-vous pour y remédier?
    Croyez-vous que les paysans peuvent faire quelque chose pour améliorer leur propre sort?

IV. SYNDICALISME

17. Depuis quand avez-vous milité au syndicalisme?
    Aux quelles positions étiez-vous élu ou delegué?

	FNSEA-CNJA	Autres Organisations Agricoles
au niveau local	_____	_____
au niveau cantonal	_____	_____
au niveau départemental	_____	_____
au niveau regional	_____	_____
au niveau national	_____	_____

18. Pourquoi militez-vous?
    Quelles sont les avantages à faire partie du syndicat?
19. En temps normal, en quoi consiste l'activité syndicale dans le village?

20. Combien de réunions local y a-t-il chaque année?
    Que fait-on à ces réunions?
    Y a-t-il parfois des discussions approfondies?
    Sur quel problème par exemple?
21. Est-ce qu'il est difficile ou facile à mobiliser les paysans du département?
    —pour les actions syndicales
    —pour les manifestations
22. Pour les syndicats agricoles, quel est, à votre avis, le type d'action le plus efficace?
    La concertation permanente avec les pouvoirs publics
    La négociation après une action de revendication politique
    Une action syndicale renforcée par une action politique
    Une opposition systématique
    Non précisé
23. Voici une liste de chose dont un syndicat agricole peut s'occuper. Quelles sont les trois
    qui vous semblent les plus importantes:
    La formation et l'information
    La développement des mesures sociales
    L'action en faveur des prix et des revenus
    L'action pour obtenir des prêts et des subventions
    La lutte pour la modernisation de l'agriculture
    L'organisation économique des producteurs
    L'action dans le domaine foncier
    La protection des agriculteurs dans les régions défavorisées
24. Et quelles sont les trois qui vous semblent les moins importantes?
25. Estimez-vous que la FNSEA/FDSEA se laisse influencer par le gouvernement, ou
    bien pensez-vous qu'elle est réellement indépendantes?
                Ils se laissent influencer par le gouvernement
                Ils sont réellement indépendants
                Sans opinion
26. Et pensez-vous que la FNSEA/FDSEA exerce sur le gouvernement une très grande
    influence, une grande influence, une influence assez faible ou une influence très
    faible?
27. Estimez-vous que la FNSEA/FDSEA défend les intérêts:
                uniquement des *gros* agriculteurs
                uniquement des *petits* et *moyens* agriculteurs
                de tous les agriculteurs
                sans opinion
28. A l'heure actuelle, les pouvoirs publics et le gouvernement n'acceptent comme
    interlocuteurs officels que deux syndicats d'agriculteurs, la FNSEA et le CNJA.
    A ce sujet, diriez-vous plutôt que la situation actuelle est satisfaisante ou que le
    gouvernement français devrait accepter comme interlocuteurs d'autres syndicats
    agricoles?
29. On parle souvent de l'unité syndicale. Selon vous, est-elle indispensable? utile?
    dangereuse?
    Pourquoi?
30. Y a-t-il de bonnes relations entre le syndicat départemental et la FNSEA?

31. Les élections aux Chambres d'Agriculture avait lieu il y a quelque mois. A votre avis, pour la défense des intérêts des agriculteurs, ces élections sont-elles:
    très importantes, assez importantes, assez peu importantes,
    très peu importantes, sans opinion
    Et pourquoi?

Note: Many of the questions in this questionnaire were derived from those of two previous surveys. By far the most important source was the questionnaire appended to Robert Bages, "Les Paysans et le syndicalisme agricole" (Thèse pour le Doctorat de Troisième Cycle, Groupe d'Ethnologie Rurale et de Sociologie, 1970, Université de Toulouse). The other major source was the survey of SOFRES included in Yves Tavernier, *Sociologie politique du monde rural et politique agricole* (fascicule III), pp. 319–26.

Notes

Introduction

1. *Le Monde*, 13–14 décembre 1981. All translations from French sources are my own unless otherwise indicated.

2. See *Le Monde*, décembre 1981 to février 1982; *Le Point*, 8 février 1982; *L'Express*, 12 février 1982; *Paris-Match*, 19 février 1982; *Le Nouvel Observateur*, 30 janvier 1982.

3. *Le Point*, 8 février 1982; *Le Monde*, 4 février 1982.

4. *Le Monde*, 24 mars 1982; New York *Times*, 24 March 1982.

5. *Le Monde*, 10 février 1982.

6. Michel Crozier, *La Société bloquée* (Paris: Editions du Seuil, 1970), p. 138.

7. *Le Monde*, 17 and 18–19 décembre 1977.

8. "Rapport Moral: Les Agriculteurs face à la corporation antipaysanne," delivered at the fourth national convention of the Fédération Française de l'Agriculture, 23–24 October 1974. For an excellent account of the creation and operation of the Corporation Paysanne, see Isabel Boussard, *Vichy et la corporation paysanne* (Paris: Fondation Nationale des Sciences Politiques, 1980).

9. *Le Monde*, 5 juin 1981 and 18 septembre 1981.

10. See *Paris-Match*, 19 février 1982; *Le Monde*, 19 décembre 1981 and 4 février 1982.

11. *L'Express*, 12 février 1982; a similar theme is developed in *Le Nouvel Observateur*, 30 janvier 1982.

12. Leo Panitch, "Recent Theorizations of Corporatism: Reflections on a Growth Industry," *British Journal of Sociology* 31:2 (June 1980), 159.

13. Ezra Suleiman, *Politics, Power and Bureaucracy in France* (Princeton: Princeton University Press, 1974), pp. 321–22, 351.

14. Philippe C. Schmitter, "Still the Century of Corporatism?" *Review of Politics* 36:1 (January 1974), 95.

15. Ibid., 96.

16. Ibid., 93–94.

17. Ruth Berins Collier and David Collier, "Inducements Versus Constraints: Disaggregating 'Corporatism,'" *American Political Science Review* 73:4 (December 1979), 967.

18. Charles W. Anderson speaks of "the state as architect of political order" in "Political Design and the Representation of Interests," *Comparative Political Studies* 10:1 (April 1977), 130.

19. Philippe C. Schmitter, "Reflections on Where the Theory of Neo-Corporatism Has Gone and Where the Praxis of Neo-Corporatism May Be Going," in Gerhard Lehmbruch and Philippe C. Schmitter, eds., *Patterns of Corporatist Policy-Making* (Beverly Hills, Calif.: Sage, 1982), 260.

20. Schmitter, "Still the Century," 99.

21. Birgitta Nedelmann and Kurt G. Meier, "Theories of Contemporary Corporatism: Static or Dynamic?" *Comparative Political Studies* 10:1 (April 1977), 49.

22. T. J. Pempel and Keiichi Tsunekawa, "Corporatism Without Labor?: The Japanese Anomaly," in Philippe C. Schmitter and Gerhard Lehmbruch, eds., *Trends Toward Corporatist Intermediation* (Beverly Hills, Calif.: Sage, 1979), 234. Gerhard Lehmbruch draws a distinction between "sectoral corporatism" and "corporatist concertation" in "Concertation and the Structure of Corporatist Networks," in John Goldthorpe, ed., *Order and Conflict in Contemporary Capitalism* (Oxford: Oxford University Press, 1984).

23. Philippe C. Schmitter, "Modes of Interest Intermediation and Models of Societal Change in Western Europe," *Comparative Political Studies* 10:1 (April 1977), 14.

24. Stanley Hoffmann mentions "what is sometimes called 'neo-corporatism,'" a group-state "symbiosis" which "has worked well only with the CNPF and the FNSEA" in "Conclusion: The Impact of the Fifth Republic on France," in William G. Andrews and Stanley Hoffmann, *The Fifth Republic at Twenty* (Albany: State University of New York Press, 1981), 455–56. Andrew Cox and Jack Hayward note that "the farm sector has come closest to a neo-corporatist relationship with government" and that industrial policies "have been the subject of a bipartite, not tripartite, corporatist relationship between government and large public or private firms" in "The Inapplicability of the Corporatist Model in Britain and France: The Case of Labor," *International Political Science Review* 4:2 (1983), 230 and 235. Jonathan Story acknowledges that in the business sector and (especially) the agricultural sector, there has been some development of "corporatism in economic policy" in "Capital in France: The Changing Patterns of Patrimony," *West European Politics* 6:2 (April 1983), 97–107. Hoffmann, Cox and Hayward, and Story all acknowledge that their analyses are based in part on my chapter in the Andrews and Hoffmann volume and/or my piece in Suzanne Berger, ed., *Organizing Interests in Western Europe* (Cambridge: Cambridge University Press, 1981). Gerhard Lehmbruch notes that "an institutional framework for neo-corporatist cooperation has been established" in France and that group-state relations there have developed at least to the point of "weak corporatism" in "Introduction: Neo-Corporatism in Comparative Perspective," in Lehmbruch and Schmitter, eds., *Patterns of Corporatist Policy-Making*, 22–23. See also Frank Wilson's works cited in note 27.

25. Some participants in the debate over corporatism have gone so far as to argue that "it is the involvement of organized labor that is distinctive about corporatism"

(Jessop) or, along similar lines, that what is "particularly distinctive" about corporatist state intervention is that it "involve[s] organized labour in institutionalized representation and administration of state policy, so that the functional interest groups of business and labour interact at the level of the state" (Panitch). For an elaboration of this "class-theoretical" approach to corporatism, see Panitch's article cited in note 12, above. My analytical perspective is obviously closer to what Panitch calls a "group-theoretical" approach as employed as Schmitter.

26. Martin Schain, "Corporatism and Industrial Relations in France," in Philip G. Cerny and Martin A. Schain, eds., *French Politics and Public Policy* (London: Frances Pinter, 1980), p. 193. See also Cox and Hayward, "The Inapplicability"; Pierre Birnbaum, "The State Versus Corporatism," *Politics and Society* 11:4 (1982).

27. Frank L. Wilson, "French Interest Group Politics: Pluralist or Neo-Corporatist?" *American Political Science Review* 77:4 (December 1983), 907–9; Wilson , "The Structures of French Interest Group Politics," paper presented at the 1983 annual meeting of the American Political Science Association, p. 39. For a critique of Wilson, see John T. S. Keeler, "Situating France on the Pluralism-Corporatism Continuum: A Critique of and Alternative to the Wilson Perspective," *Comparative Politics* 17:2 (January 1985).

28. For example, see Pempel and Tsunekawa, "Corporatism Without Labor?" 234.

29. Collier and Collier, "Inducements," 968–69.

30. Claus Offe, "The Attribution of Public Status to Interest Groups: Observations on the West German Case," in Berger, ed., *Organizing Interests*, 136–37.

31. Schmitter, "Reflections," 265.

32. Typologies of points on the continuum are suggested in Colin Crouch, "Pluralism and the New Corporatism: A Rejoinder, "*Political Studies* 31:3 (September 1983), 457; and Lehmbruch, "Concertation and the Structure of Corporatist Networks."

33. See Offe, "Attribution," 137.

34. For a brief discussion of the difference in emphasis between Offe and Schmitter, see Suzanne Berger's introduction to *Organizing Interests*. In large part because of the dichotmous distinction he makes between "societal corporatism" (the type said to be found in democracies) and "state corporatism" (the type said to be found in authoritarian polities), Schmitter sometimes seems to downplay excessively the role a "liberal" state may play in creating or sustaining corporatist relationships. In "Still the Century," for example, Schmitter asserts that recognition by the state is "a matter of political necessity imposed from below upon public officials" and that representational monopoly is "independently conquered" in the ideal-typical "societal corporatist" system (p. 104). A modification of this view is evident in one of his more recent articles. Here Schmitter argues that "the coercive intervention of the modern bureaucratic state" played a major role in giving rise to corporatism even in liberal democratic cases and stresses that "societal corporatist" arrangements "came into existence largely, *but not exclusively*, as the result of inter-associational demands and intraorganizational processes" (emphasis added). See "Interest Intermediation and Regime Governability in Contemporary Western Europe and North America," in Berger, ed., *Organizing Interests*, esp. 291–92.

35. See Eric A. Nordlinger, *On the Autonomy of the Democratic State* (Cambridge: Harvard University Press, 1981), p. 17.

36. Schmitter, "Interest Intermediation," 319.

37. Offe, "Attribution," 135. The phrase "the exchange of some gains for some losses" was taken from a draft of Offe's article and does not appear in the published version.

38. Leo Panitch, "The Development of Corporatism in Liberal Democracies," *Comparative Political Studies* 10:1 (April 1977), 67.

39. Offe, "Attribution," 137–38. The concept of "partial immunity" is discussed in somewhat different terms in the following articles: Panitch, "Recent Theorizations," 175; Schmitter, "Interest Intermediation," 292; Charles S. Sabel, "The Internal Politics of Trade Unions," in Berger, ed., *Organizing Interests*, 210.

40. Mancur Olson, *The Logic of Collective Action* (Cambridge: Harvard University Press, 1965), pp. 15–16, 133.

41. Terry M. Moe, *The Organization of Interests: Incentives and the Internal Dynamics of Political Interest Groups* (Chicago: University of Chicago Press, 1980), p. 9.

42. James Q. Wilson, *Political Organizations* (New York: Basic Books, 1973), pp. 26, 33–36.

43. For a discussion of the degree to which even American interest groups are dependent on exogenous sources ("funds from outside their membership which are needed to keep their groups in operation"), see Jack L. Walker, "The Origins and Maintenance of Interest Groups in America," *American Political Science Review* 77:2 (June 1983).

44. Schmitter, "Interest Intermediation," 323. On the dynamics of instability generated from below, see Sabel, "Internal Politics," 209–44; Leo Panitch, "The Development of Corporatism in Liberal Democracies," in Schmitter and Lehmbruch, eds., *Trends Toward Corporatist Intermediation*, 119–46; Schmitter, "Interest Intermediation," 319–22. Here it should be noted that I find rather confusing and contradictory Schmitter's insistence that ideal-typical "corporatism" specifies simply a mode of "interest intermediation" and does *not* necessarily entail "concertation," that is, the incorporation of groups "within the policy process as recognized, indispensable negotiators [which] are made co-responsible (and occasionally completely responsible) for the implementation of policy decisions." In his view, there *is* "an elective affinity, if not a strong element of historical causality, between the corporatization of interest intermediation and the emergence of 'concerted' forms of policymaking," but the two are "neither theoretically nor empirically synonymous." Schmitter argues that there has been "productive confusion" on this point in the literature, but does not acknowledge that the confusion—if it is that—stems from his own ideal-typical definition. Should not one logically assume that the granting by the state of "a deliberate representational monopoly" to a group entails the incorporation of that group into the policy-making process? Schmitter argues that the state could "deny [such groups] the access or capability to do more than 'pressure' for their preferred outcomes from without," but it is difficult to conceive of how such status could be termed "a deliberate representational monopoly." Moreover, it seems unlikely that groups granted only the right to engage in pressure activities "from without" would "in exchange" observe "controls on their selection of leaders and articulation of demands." To me it seems more theoretically consistent, in Schmitter's own terms, to assume that concertation is normally involved in "corporatism"

and is absent (or attenuated) only in what I have termed an "unstable" system. The passages from Schmitter are found in "Interest Intermediation," 296 and "Reflections," 262–63.

45. Schmitter, "Interest Intermediation," 291.

46. Samuel H. Beer, *Britain Against Itself* (London: Faber and Faber, 1982), p. 14.

47. Andrew Shonfield, *Modern Capitalism: The Changing Balance of Public and Private Power* (Oxford: Oxford University Press, 1976; orig. pub. 1965), p. 389.

48. Richard F. Kuisel, *Capitalism and the State in Modern France* (Cambridge: Cambridge University Press, 1981), pp. 248–49.

49. Georges E. Lavau, "Political Pressure by Interest Groups in France," in Henry W. Ehrmann, ed., *Interest Groups on Four Continents* (Pittsburgh: University of Pittsburgh Press, 1958), 82.

50. Hoffmann, "Conclusion," 450, 455–56.

51. Suzanne Berger, "D'Une Boutique à l'Autre: Changes in the Organization of the Traditional Middle Classes from the Fourth to Fifth Republics," *Comparative Politics* 10:1 (October 1977), 126.

52. Schmitter, "Interest Intermediation," 292.

53. Pempel and Tsunekawa, "Corporatism Without Labor?" 258, 266–67.

54. Kuisel, *Capitalism*, p. 259.

55. Stephen Cohen, *Modern Capitalist Planning: The French Model* (Cambridge: Harvard University Press, 1969), pp. 51, 197–98.

56. Panitch, "The Development of Corporatism," 73.

57. Gerhard Lehmbruch, "Liberal Corporatism and Party Government," *Comparative Political Studies* 10:1 (April 1977), 111.

58. Charles de Gaulle, *Memoirs of Hope: Renewal and Endeavor* (New York: Simon and Schuster, 1971), p. 162.

59. Cohen, *Modern Capitalist*, chs. 19–20.

60. Schain, "Corporatism," 203, 207.

61. A "CFTC" remained in existence after the CFDT was formed, but only as a very small organization now commonly referred to as CTFC-Maintenue.

62. Stephen Bornstein, "Unions and the Economy in France: The Changing Posture of the CFDT," *European Studies Newsletter* 7:5 (April-May 1978), 3–4. See also J. E. S. Hayward, *Private Interests and Public Policy: The Experience of the French Economic and Social Council* (London: Longmans, 1966), pp. 91–96, 106; Pierre Dubois, Claude Durand, and Sabine Erbes-Seguin, "The Contradictions of French Trade Unionism," in Colin Crouch and Alessandro Pizzorno, eds., *The Resurgence of Class Conflict in Western Europe Since 1968*, vol. 1 (London: MacMillan, 1978).

63. On the Grenelle talks, see George Ross, *Workers and Communists in France* (Berkeley: University of California Press; 1982), ch. 7.

64. On the "New Society" and the *politique contractuelle*, see Eric de Bodman and Bertrand Richard, *Changer les relations sociales: La politique de Jacques Delors* (Paris: Les Editions d'Organisation, 1976).

65. Bornstein, "Unions," 4.

66. Douglas Ashford, *Policy and Politics in France* (Philadelphia: Temple University Press, 1982), p. 201.

67. Ross, *Workers and Communists*, p. 219.

68. George Ross, "Party and Mass Organization: The Changing Relationship of PCF and CGT," in Donald Blackmer and Sidney Tarrow, eds., *Communism in Italy and France* (Princeton: Princeton University Press, 1975), 530–32; de Bodman and Richard, *Changer les relations sociales,* p. 145.

69. J. E. S. Hayward, "State Intervention in France: The Changing Style of Government-Industry Relations," *Political Studies* 20:3 (September 1972), 293–98; de Bodman and Richard, *Changer les relations sociales,* p. 164.

70. Schain, "Corporatism," 211.

71. Ibid., 211–12.

72. Ross, *Workers and Communists,* p. 159.

73. R. J. Harrison, *Pluralism and Corporatism* (London: Allen and Unwin, 1980), p. 81; Jean Bunel and Jean Saglio, *L'Action patronal du CNPF au petit patron* (Paris: Presses Universitaires de France, 1979), p. 173.

74. *Journal officiel,* 30 juin 1959, 1181.

75. Ibid.

76. Ibid., p. 1179.

77. Ibid., pp. 1184.

78. Ibid, 17 décembre 1959, 1863.

79. Ross, *Workers and Communists,* ch. 5.

80. Michel Bazex, *L'Administration et les syndicats* (Paris: Editions Berger-Levrault, 1973), pp. 146–49.

81. *L'Humanité,* 21 avril 1964.

82. *Le Monde,* 16 Juillet 1964.

83. Ross, *Workers and Communists,* p. 199; For a slightly different account, see Hervé Hamon and Patrick Rotman, *La Deuxième Gauche: Histoire intellectuelle et politique de la CFDT* (Paris: Editions Ramsay, 1982), ch. 7.

84. Ross, "Party and Mass Organization," 530–32.

85. Bazex, *L'Administration,* pp. 146–49; *Liaisons sociales,* supplement to no. 8237 ("Syndicats II, organisations syndicales"), avril 1980, p. 26; Gérard Adam, *Le Pouvoir syndical* (Paris: Dunod, 1983).

86. D. L. Hanley et al., *Contemporary France* (London: Routledge and Kegan Paul, 1979), p. 177.

87. See de Bodman and Richard, *Changer les relations sociales,* p. 148.

88. Janice McCormick, "Gaullism and Collective Bargaining: The Effect of the Fifth Republic on French Industrial Relations," in Andrews and Hoffmann, eds., *The Fifth Republic at Twenty,* 354.

89. On the ideology and strategy of Force Ouvrière, see Gabriel Ventejol, "Cogestion et participation," *Revue politique et parlementaire* (juin-juillet 1973), 33–41; René Mouriaux, *Les Syndicats dans la société française* (Paris: Fondation Nationale des Sciences Politiques, 1983), pp. 186–88.

90. George Ross, "Unions, State and Society in Mitterrand's France," paper presented at the 1983 annual meeting of the American Political Science Association. On the FO-FNSEA relationship, see *L'Information agricole* (hereafter *IA*), mars 1978, 26–28 and *Le Monde,* 26 février 1982. FO Secretary General André Bergeron was one of the official speakers at the FNSEA's annual conventions of 1978 and 1982.

91. For statistics on FO growth in membership and popularity, see Hamon and Rotman, *La Deuxième Gauche,* p. 419.

92. Henry W. Ehrmann, *Organized Business in France* (Princeton: Princeton University Press, 1957), p. 157.

93. Shonfield *Modern Capitalism,* p. 159.

94. Kuisel, *Capitalism,* p. 258.

95. Ehrmann, *Organized Business,* p. 149.

96. Bernard Brizay, *Le Patronat: Histoire, structure, strategie du CNPF* (Paris: Editions du Seuil, 1975), pp. 97–100.

97. John Zysman, *Governments, Markets and Growth: Financial Systems and the Politics of Industrial Change* (Ithaca: Cornell University Press, 1983), p. 107.

98. Ehrmann, *Organized Business,* p. 157.

99. Bunel and Saglio, *L'Action,* pp. 103–4; Brizay, *Le Patronat,* pp. 74–79.

100. Brizay, *Le Patronat,* pp. 82–96; Ehrmann, *Organized Business,* ch. 6.

101. Brizay, *Le Patronat,* p. 102; John Ardagh, *The New French Revolution* (New York: Harper & Row, 1968), p.33.

102. Brizay, *Le Patronat,* pp. 110–15.

103. Ezra Suleiman, *Elites in French Society* (Princeton: Princeton University Press, 1978), ch. 8. On the impact of the EEC, see Bunel and Saglio, *L'Action,* pp. 51–52.

104. Brizay, *Le Patronat,* pp. 107–10 and 117–21.

105. Ashford, *Policy,* p. 200; Brizay, *Le Patronat,* pp. 131–35.

106. Brizay, *Le Patronat,* pp. 129–38; André Harris and Alain de Sedouy, *Les Patrons* (Paris: Editions du Seuil, 1977), pp. 245–58; Philip M. Williams and Martin Harrison, *Politics and Society in de Gaulle's Republic* (New York: Anchor Books, 1971), p. 173.

107. Brizay, *Le Patronat,* pp. 138–46; Harris and Sedouy, *Les Patrons,* p. 7; Bunel and Saglio, *L'Action,* pp. 144–55; Jean-Maurice Martin, *Le CNPF* (Paris: Presses Universitaires de France, 1983), pp. 28–34.

108. Bunel and Saglio, *L'Action,* pp. 172–78.

109. Ibid., p. 180.

110. Jean-Gabriel Fredet and Denis Pingaud, *Les Patrons face à la gauche* (Paris: Editions Ramsay, 1982), p. 124; Story, "Capital," 97, 112; Ashford, *Policy,* p. 204.

111. Fredet and Pingaud, *Les Patrons,* chs. 6 and 12.

112. Ibid., pp. 104, 124, and 138; Brizay, *Le Patronat,* p. 248.

113. Fredet and Pingaud, *Les Patrons,* p. 102; Harris and Sedouy, *Les Patrons,* p. 240.

114. *Le Monde,* 29 octobre 1980.

115. Fredet and Pingaud, *Les Patrons,* pp. 184–85; Bunel and Saglio, *L'Action,* pp. 132–36.

116. F. L. Wilson, "French Interest Group Politics," p. 899.

117. Henri Mendras, "Les organisations agricoles," in Jacques Fauvet and Henri Mendras, eds., *Les Paysans et la politique dans la France contemporaine* (Paris: Armand Colin, 1958), 249–50; Paul Houée, *Les Etapes du développement rural,* vol. 2 (Paris: Editions Ouvrières, 1972), p. 71.

118. Crozier, *La Société bloquée,* p. 136.

119. Panitch, "Recent Theorizations," p. 161.

120. Harry Eckstein, "Case Study and Theory in Political Science," in Fred I. Greenstein and Nelson W. Polsby, eds., *Strategies of Inquiry* (Reading, Mass: Addison-Wesley, 1975), 108–13.

121. See Howard Machin, *The Prefect in French Public Administration* (London: Croom Helm, 1977); Pierre Grémion, *Le Pouvoir péripherique: Bureaucrats et notables dans le systeme politique français* (Paris: Editions du Seuil, 1976); Jean-Claude Thoenig, *L'Ere des technocrates* (Paris: Editions d'Organisation, 1973). For a brief summary of this literature, see Vincent Wright, *The Government and Politics of France* (London: Hutchinson, 1983), pp. 277–83.

Chapter 1

1. Gordon Wright, *Rural Revolution in France* (Stanford: Stanford University Press, 1964) p. 99.

2. Ibid., p. 86; see also François Guillaume, "Où va l'agriculture française?" *Le Débat*, janvier 1984, 50.

3. G. Wright, *Rural Revolution*, pp. 95–96; Michel Gervais, Marcel Jollivet, and Yves Tavernier, *La Fin de la France paysanne* (Paris: Editions du Seuil, 1976), pp. 410 and 449.

4. G. Wright, *Rural Revolution*, p. 99; Pierre Barral, *Les Agrariens français de Meline à Pisani* (Paris: Armand Colin, 1968), p. 285.

5. François Guillaume, *Le Pain de la liberté* (Paris: J.-C. Lattes, 1983), p. 119.

6. Gervais et al., *La Fin*, p. 454.

7. G. Wright, *Rural Revolution*, p. 102.

8. Gervais et al., *La Fin*, p. 454.

9. Ibid., p. 575.

10. Ibid., pp. 576–78; G. Wright, *Rural Revolution*, pp. 109–13; Barral, *Les Agrariens*, pp. 287–88.

11. Gervais et al., *La Fin*, p. 454; Wright, *Rural Revolution*, p. 95.

12. G. Wright, *Rural Revolution*, p. 98.

13. Ibid., pp. 100–101; Gervais et al., *La Fin*, p. 453.

14. G. Wright, *Rural Revolution*, p. 104; Barral, *Les Agrariens*, p. 289.

15. G. Wright, *Rural Revolution*, pp. 104–7 and 124–25.

16. Gervais et al., *La Fin*, p. 458.

17. Maurice Duverger, *La Cinquième République*, 3d ed. (Paris: Presses Universitaires de France, 1963), p. 237.

18. *Le Monde*, 25 février 1975.

19. David Butler and Donald Stokes, *Political Change in Britain*, coll. ed. (New York: St. Martin's, 1971), p. 177; see also the discussion of valence issues in William Schneider, "The Origins of Participation: Nation, Class, Issues and Party" (Ph.D. diss., Harvard University, 1971), esp. p. 318.

20. Suzanne Berger, *Peasants Against Politics* (Cambridge: Harvard University Press, 1972), p. 183.

21. G. Wright, *Rural Revolution*, p. 130.

22. The valence quality of the price issue was vividly demonstrated in a recent survey. When asked to name the three most important issues with which a farmers' union should be concerned, 86% of all respondents cited "action in favor of prices and income" while only 54% cited the next most popular issue ("the development of social measures").

See Yves Tavernier, *Sociologie politique du monde rural et politique agricole*, fascicule III (Paris: Fondation Nationale des Sciences Politiques, 1973), p. 320.

23. G. Wright, *Rural Revolution*, p. 131.

24. Laurence Wylie, "Social Change at the Grass Roots," in Stanley Hoffmann et al., *In Search of France* (New York; Harper & Row, 1965), 224. The emphasis is my own.

25. Berger, *Peasants Against Politics*, p. 183.

26. G. Wright, *Rural Revolution*, p. 131.

27. Cited in Berger, *Peasants Against Politics*, p. 183.

28. Houée, *Les Etapes*, p. 71. See also the interview with Michel Debatisse in *Le Point* 64 (10 décembre 1973); to the agricultural world in the 1950s, asserts Debatisse, "L'Etat, c'était l'ennemi."

29. Louis Prugnaud, *Les Etapes du syndicalisme agricole en France* (Paris: Editions de l'Epi, 1963), pp. 178–81; G. Wright, *Rural Revolution*, pp. 132–33.

30. G. Wright, *Rural Revolution*, p. 33.

31. Gervais et al., *La Fin*, pp. 460 and 579; G. Wright, *Rural Revolution*, p. 132.

32. Leon Dubois, "Partis politiques, syndicats et pouvoir," *Paysans* 33 (décembre 1961–janvier 1962), 19.

33. As Isabel Boussard has noted, every FNSEA president (Eugène Forget, René Blondelle, Jacques Lepicard, and Joseph Courau) and secretary-general (Blondelle, Jean Laborde, and Albert Génin) until 1961 was a former official of Vichy's Corporation Paysanne. See p. 443 of Boussard's "La Corporation paysanne: Une Etape dans l'histoire du syndicalism agricole français (1940–1944)" (Thèse pour le doctorat de recherches, Fondation Nationale des Sciences Politiques, Paris, 1971).

34. G. Wright, *Rural Revolution* p. 109; Tavernier, *Sociologie politique*, pp. 353, 392.

35. Houée, *Les Etapes*, p. 70.

36. G. Wright, *Rural Revolution*, p. 118.

37. For details on this questionnaire, see Tavernier, *Sociologie politique*, pp. 307–8.

38. G. Wright, *Rural Revolution*, pp. 117–18; Philip M. Williams, *Crisis and Compromise: Politics in the Fourth Republic* (Garden City: Doubleday, 1966), p. 388.

39. G. Wright, *Rural Revolution*, p. 118 ff.; Tavernier, *Sociologie politique*, p. 310. For a list of the ministers of agriculture (and their political affiliations) from 1881 to 1956, see pp. 262–63 of Fauvet and Mendras, eds., *Les Paysans*.

40. G. Wright, *Rural Revolution*, p. 137.

41. Ibid., pp. 140–41 and 122–23; Houée, *Les Etapes*, p. 71; Philippe Gratton, *Les Paysans français contre l'agrarisme* (Paris: François Maspero, 1972), pp. 213–18.

42. G. Wright, *Rural Revolution*, pp. 140–41.

43. Ibid., p. 116.

44. Gervais et al., *La Fin*, p. 463.

45. G. Wright, *Rural Revolution*, p. 127.

46. Ibid., pp. 122–23.

47. Yves Tavernier, "Le XVIIIᵉ congres de la FNSEA," *Revue française de science politique* 14:5 (octobre 1964), 974.

48. While the Communist program for agriculture was in accord with the essentials of the FNSEA program it did differ in nuance. For example, the Communists

supported the "prices first" policy, but they demanded relatively higher prices for the products (such as meat and milk) in which many small farmers specialized as well as differential price schemes favoring small farmers for products produced by large and small farmers alike.

49. G. Wright, *Rural Revolution*, p. 128.

50. Yves Tavernier, "Le Mouvement de coordination et de défense des exploitations agricoles familiales (M.O.D.E.F.)," *Revue française de science politique* 18:3 (juin 1968), 470–72.

51. Moe, *Organization of Interests*, pp. 206–10.

52. Mendras, "Les Organisations agricoles."

53. Tavernier, *Le Syndicalisme paysan*, p. 33.

54. Ibid., p. 65; Tavernier, *Sociologie politique*, p. 278. Also interview 70.

55. Berger describes the merger of union and cooperative activities in Finistère—see p. 194 of *Peasants Against Politics*.

56. Cited in *Compte-rendu d'activité au cours de l'année 1955*, FDSEA, Tulle (Corrèze), p. 1.

57. A much more extensive discussion of departmental services will be given in Part II; Moe, *Organization of Interests*, p. 246.

58. Barral, *Les Agrariens*, pp. 290 and 340. Also see the concluding chapter of this book.

59. See Chapters 5 and 6. Budget statistics for the period before January 1960 (when France converted to a "new franc" worth 100 "old francs") have been translated into new francs.

60. See Chapter 6.

61. Tavernier, *Le Syndicalisme paysan*, pp. 104–5.

62. *Compte de gestion de l'exercice*, Union des Syndicats Agricoles de l'Aisne, 1957; *Rapport financier*, FDSEA de la Corrèze, 1957.

63. See Tavernier, *Le Syndicalisme paysan*, pp. 94–97; see also the case studies of Part II.

64. G. Wright, *Rural Revolution*, p. 126.

65. Gervais et al., *La Fin*, pp. 459–60.

Chapter 2

1. For discussions of the significance of the JAC, see Berger, *Peasants Against Politics*, pp. 195–200; G. Wright, *Rural Revolution*, ch. 8; Ardagh, *New French Revolution*, pp. 70–72; Barral, *Les Agrariens*, pp. 312–14.

2. G. Wright, *Rural Revolution*, p. 123.

3. Tavernier, *Le Syndicalisme paysan*, p. 142.

4. Ibid., pp. 42, 142, 155.

5. G. Wright, *Rural Revolution*, p. 154.

6. Roy Pierce, *French Politics and Political Institutions* (New York: Harper & Row, 1968), p. 199; G. Wright and Tavernier (in virtually all of his works cited) discuss the "conflict of generations" in considerable detail.

7. Louis Lauga discusses the end of this "systematic opposition" in a book written while he was president of the CNJA in 1971; see his *CNJA* (Paris: EPI, 1971), p. 101. As

Pierre Grémion has noted, systematic opposition ended as the popularity of the new generation leaders placed them in a "posture of succession." As they were "very quickly integrated" into what Grémion terms the *treillis des caciques*, the CNJA itself became less important. The traditional, hierarchical system of agricultural organizations was thus not renovated but remained intact. See Grémion, *Le Pouvoir périphérique* pp. 225–27.

8. G. Wright, *Rural Revolution*, pp. 154–55.

9. P. Coulomb and H. Nallet, "Les Organisations syndicales agricoles à l'épreuve de l'unité," in Yves Tavernier et al., *L'Univers politique des paysans dans la France contemporaine* (Paris: Armand Colin, 1972), 393.

10. Michel Debatisse, *La Révolution silencieuse* (Paris: Calmann-Lévy, 1963), p. 197.

11. François-H. de Virieu, *La Fin d'une agriculture* (Paris: Calmann-Lévy, 1967), p. 197.

12. Lucien Douroux, "Réflexions sur la politique agricole," *Paysans* 68 (octobre–novembre 1967), p. 29.

13. Debatisse, *Révolution*, p. 94.

14. Ibid., p. 235.

15. Ibid., p. 162; Coulomb and Nallet, "Les Organisations," 393.

16. André Lefebvre, "Subir l'exode ou l'organiser," *Paysans* 51 (decembre 1964–janvier 1965), 50–51; see also Douroux, "Réflexions," 25; Coulomb and Nallet, "Les Organisations," 394; and Michel Debatisse, "Préparer, aménager, organiser," *Jeunes agriculteurs*, juin 1959, 112.

17. Coulomb and Nallet, "Les Organisations," 394.

18. See p. 205 of Claude Servolin and Yves Tavernier, "La France: Reform de structures on politique des prix?" in Henri Mendras and Yves Tavernier, eds., *Terre, paysans et politique*, Vol. 1 (Paris: SEDEIS, 1969).

19. See Debatisse, *Révolution*, pp. 242–44; Marcel Faure, "Où en est l'agriculture de groupe?" *Paysans* 65 (avril–mai 1967), 19; Thomas Lafon, "Questions aux agriculteurs associés dans les formules de groupe," *Paysans* 65 (avril–mai 1967), 30.

20. G. Boudy, "Non, M. Debatisse," *Jeunes agriculteurs*, septembre 1959, 2.

21. See Jacques Pelletier, "Liberté, liberté chérie," *Jeunes agriculteurs*, novembre 1959.

22. G. Wright, *Rural Revolution*, p. 160; Tavernier, "Le XVIIIᵉ congrès," 975.

23. Tavernier, "Le. XVIIIᵉ congrès," 975.

24. It should be noted that, ironically enough, the young reformers were originally apprehensive about the Fifth Republic: "their profound attachment to democracy made them fear the worst with the arrival of the new regime." See p. 126 of Marcel Faure, *Les Paysans dans la société française* (Paris: Armand Colin, 1966).

25. G. Wright, *Rural Revolution*, p. 162.

26. See de Virieu, *La Fin*, p. 200 ff.; G. Wright, *Rural Revolution*, pp. 162–63.

27. See de Virieu, *La Fin*, p. 202.

28. Yves Tavernier, "Le Syndicalisme paysan et la politique agricole du gouvernement," *Revue française de science politique* 12:3 (septembre 1962), 621. This reference will henceforth be referred to as "Le Syndicalisme et la politique." From 1949 through the 1960s, the APCA was known as the APPCA (Assemblée Permanente des Présidents de Chambres d'Agriculture).

29. Ibid.

30. Bazex, *L'Administration*, p. 112.

31. The CNJA is quite proud of this fact, as its president (Louis Lauga) stressed in an interview with the author in September 1974 (interview 87). For a discussion of the CNJA's unique status, see Jean Meynaud and Dusan Sidjanski, *Les Groupes de pression dans la communauté européene 1958–1968* (Brussels: Editions de l'Institut de Sociologie, 1971), p. 173.

32. See Bazex, *L'Administration*, pp. 111–14.

33. Cited in Tavernier, "Le Syndicalisme et la politique," 621–22.

34. François Guillaume, "Où va l'agriculture Française?" *Le Débat*, janvier 1984, 56.

35. See Pierre Muller, *Grandeur et décadence du professeur d'agriculture: Les transformations du systeme d'intervention de l'état en agriculture 1955–1965* (Grenoble: Institut d'Etudes Politiques de Grenoble/CERAT, 1978), pp. 171–72.

36. Cited in de Virieu, *La Fin*, p. 201.

37. Michel Debatisse, "Inventer l'avenir," *Paysans* 56 (octobre–novembre 1965), p. 19.

38. Marcel Faure, "Le Combat syndical et l'avenir des agricultures," *Paysans* 68 (octobre–novembre 1967), 9.

39. Pelletier, "Liberté," 10.

40. See Michel Debatisse, "Les Groupes économiques face à la participation au pouvoir," *Paysans* 33 (décembre 1961–janvier 1962); G. Wright, *Rural Revolution*, pp. 133–34; John Hackett and Anne-Marie Hackett, *Economic Planning in France* (Cambridge: Harvard University Press, 1965), ch. 15.

41. Tavernier, "Le Syndicalisme et la politique," 622.

42. Gaston Rimareix and Yves Tavernier, "L'Elaboration et le vote de la loi complémentaire à la loi d'orientation agricole," *Revue française de science politique* 13:2 (juin 1963), 390.

43. Servolin and Tavernier, "La France," 196.

44. G. Wright, *Rural Revolution*, pp. 166–67.

45. Ibid., p. 167; Serge Mallet, *Les Paysans contre le passé* (Paris: Editions du Seuil, 1962), esp. ch. 8 and the conclusion; Henri Mendras and Yves Tavernier, "Les Manifestations de juin 1961," *Revue française de science politique* 12:3 (septembre 1962), 647–71.

46. See de Virieu, *La Fin*, p. 202.

47. Faure, *Les Paysans*, p. 132.

48. G. Wright, *Rural Revolution*, p. 170.

49. Ibid., p. 165.

50. Ibid., p. 170.

51. Hackett and Hackett, *Economic Planning*, pp. 284–85.

52. G. Wright, *Rural Revolution*, p. 171; Berger, *Peasants Against Politics*, pp. 214–15.

53. "Agriculture de groupe," *Paysans* 73–74 (août–novembre 1968), 82; Marc Hanrot, "Les Groupements agricoles en commun ont enfin une cadre juridique," *Paysans* 53 (avril–mai 1965), 59; see also, G. Wright, *Rural Revolution*, p. 171.

54. A phrase from the orientation law cited in de Virieu, *La Fin*, p. 73.

55. Pierre Muller, *Le Technocrate et le paysan* (Paris: Editions Ouvrières, 1984), pp. 50 and 122.

56. *Le Monde*, 4 octobre 1967.

57. The CNJA's "absorption through success" was so complete that by 1970 many farmers began to question the necessity for the CNJA's continued existence as a quasi-independent union. The CNJA president, in an official report at the organization's twelfth congress in 1970, noted that observers outside of agriculture and even "some within the organizations of agriculture . . . draw the conclusion that the mission of the CNJA is terminated at present. Having served as a trampoline for a generation which forced a change in the orientations of the FNSEA, [they contend], the latter should assume the task of defending all farmers, the young along with the others." Not surprisingly, the CNJA president disagreed that the organization had lost its raison d'être. See Louis Lauga, "L'Agriculteur et la société industrielle: Le role du CNJA," Rapport d'Orientation, XIIᵉ Congrès du CNJA, 5–6 juillet 1970, Blois.

58. Tavernier, "Le Syndicalisme et la politique," 615–16; G. Wright, *Rural Revolution*, pp. 160–61; *Le Monde*, 28 février 1962.

59. Cited in G. Wright, *Rural Revolution*, p. 244.

60. Tavernier, "Le XVIIIᵉ congrès," esp. 976–81; *Le Monde*, 4 mars 1964 and 6 mars 1964.

61. *Jeunes agriculteurs*, novembre 1971, 8. See also Debatisse's initial editorial as FNSEA president: "Changement et continuité," *IA*, octobre 1971, 5.

62. Tavernier, *Le Syndicalisme paysan*, pp. 190 and 203.

Chapter 3

1. Michel Crozier, *On ne change pas la société par décret* (Paris: Bernard Grasset, 1979), pp. 284–85.

2. See Michel Debatisse, "Rapport moral," XXIVᵉ Congrès Fédéral, FNSEA, 3–4 mars 1970, Lyon. See also *30 ans de combat*, pp. 28–29.

3. Debatisse has argued that the "originality" of the FNSEA has been its desire to "prepare the future"; see *IA*, octobre 1971, 5.

4. Coulomb et Nallet, "Les organisations," 404.

5. Raoul Serieys, "Rapport moral," CNJA, 25–26 décembre 1967; for commentary on the report, see Coulomb and Nallet "Les Organisations," 402–3.

6. Coulomb and Nallet, "Les Organisations," 404.

7. Ibid., 399.

8. Andre Vial, "Editorial," *Paysans* 81 (juin-juillet 1970), 7–8.

9. Bernard Lambert, *Les Paysans dans les luttes des classes* (Paris: Editions de Seuil, 1970), p. 103.

10. Interviews 22, 26, and 27. More details are given in Chapter 5.

11. The journal was *Paysans*; see G. Wright, *Rural Revolution*, p. 246.

12. *Graph-agri 80: Annuaires de graphiques agricoles* (Paris: Ministere de l'Agriculture, 1980), pp. 14 and 53.

13. See Joseph Klatzmann, *Les Politiques agricoles* (Paris: Presses Universitaires de France, 1972), p. 88; Servolin and Tavernier, "La France," 200–201.

14. *30 ans de combat*, p. 92.

15. Ibid., p. 95. See also "Devenir-être-rester agriculteur, agricultrice," Programme d'Action Syndicale 1975/1976, CNJA (pages unmarked).

16. Michel Monteil, "Les 'Oubliés' de la dotation," *Jeunes agriculteurs*, décembre 1976, 12–13.

17. Interviews 13 and 15. See also Chapter 4.

18. Extracts from the "Rapport moral" presented by Secretary-General M. P. Cormoreche at the twenty-sixth FNSEA congress (1972), pp. 9–17 of *IA*, février 1972; for a similar analysis of the necessity of *concertation*, see Marcel Bruel, "Le Syndicalisme agricole et le pouvoir politique," *L'Union paysanne* (Corrèze), 30 octobre 1965.

19. Cited in *Le Point* 133 (7 avril 1975), 67.

20. *IA*, février 1972, 16–17.

21. *30 ans de combat*, p. 30.

22. Ibid., p. 81; see also *Annuaire statistique de la France 1978: Résultats de 1976/1977* (Paris: Ministère de l'Economie, 1978), p. 167.

23. *IA*, février 1972, 16.

24. Tavernier, *Sociologie politique*, pp. 322–23, 358. The figures cited here are percentages of the farmers who responded.

25. *30 ans combat*, p. 30.

26. See *IA*, mai 1979, 5.

27. This quotation is taken from p. 10 of a report delivered by the dissident *paysans-travailleurs* faction at the CNJA congress of 1970: Antoine Richard, "Pour un syndicalisme de travailleurs" (Rapport d'Orientation), XIIᵉ Congrès du CNJA, 5–6 juillet 1970, Blois.

28. Yves Tavernier, "Le Syndicalisme paysan et la Cinquième République: 1962–1965," *Revue francaise de science politique* 16:5 (octobre 1966), 878–84.

29. Tavernier, "Cinquième République," 886–909.

30. See *Le Monde*, 3 octobre 1967.

31. Coulomb and Nallet, "La France," 402.

32. See *Le Monde*, 4 octobre 1967; *Le Monde*, 3 octobre 1967; Coulomb and Nallet, "La France," 402.

33. *Le Monde*, 17–18 décembre 1969; *IA*, novembre 1969, 7; and *IA*, janvier 1970, 6.

34. *Jeunes agriculteurs*, mars 1962, 4.

35. *IA*, novembre 1969, 9–11.

36. Ibid., 11.

37. *Le Monde*, 17 décembre 1969; see also *Le Monde*, 25 novembre 1969.

38. This citation is extracted from a letter sent by the president of the FDSEA of Indre-et-Loire to Caffarelli on 5 November 1969, explaining the FDSEA's decision to secede from the Federation. A copy of the letter was forwarded by the dissident federation to every other FDSEA; I read the copy sent to the FDSEA of Landes in Mont-de-Marsan.

39. *Le Monde*, 18 décembre 1969.

40. Ibid., 18 décembre 1969; the article on the *congrès extraordinaire* in *IA*, janvier 1970.

41. *IA*, juillet-août 1974, 6.

42. Pierre Cormorèche, "Rapport Moral," XXIXᵉ Congrès de la FNSEA, 18–20 mars 1975, 5.

43. *Le Monde*, 25 juillet 1974.

44. See *Le Monde* for virtually every day of July and August, especially 3 août; see also *Le Figaro*, 27–28 juillet, for specific comments on the violence of the demonstrations.

45. Cormorèche, "Rapport moral" (1975), p. 10.

46. Ibid, pp. 40–41.

47. Tavernier, *Sociologie politique*, 394–95.

48. Ibid., p. 391.

49. Ibid., p. 413.

50. "Le MODEF: Ses origines, son activité, ses buts," mimeographed pamphlet prepared by the Landes branch of MODEF in 1975; see also Tavernier, *Sociologie politique*, p. 410.

51. Tavernier, *Sociologie politique*, p. 412.

52. "Programme national du MODEF," IVe Congrès National du MODEF, 1–2 mars 1975, Paris.

53. Ibid.; see also *Le Monde*, 4 mars 1975.

54. Tavernier, *Sociologie politique*, pp. 400–´406.

55. *Le Monde*, 11 juin 1981.

56. See, for example, *Les Informations agricoles* (Landes), 9 mai 1975.

57. While MODEF received approximately 20% of the vote in Chamber of Agriculture elections during the 1970s, the Communist party reportedly received 8% of the farm vote in 1973, 9% in 1978, and 6% in the assembly election of 1981. See Roy C. Macridis, *French Politics in Transition* (Cambridge: Winthrop, 1975), p. 84; Howard Penniman, ed., *The French National Assembly Elections of 1978* (Washington D. C.: American Enterprise Institute, 1980); *Le Nouvel Observateur*, 4–10 juillet 1981, 42.

58. *IA*, juillet-août 1977, p. III of the "Connaissance de l'agriculture" insert.

59. See Chapter 7 for discussion of the MODEF in Landes.

60. Interviews 56, 65, and 102.

61. Tavernier, *Sociologie politique*, pp. 366–73.

62. Ibid., p. 356.

63. *Vent d'ouest* 1 (novembre 1969).

64. Lambert, *Les Paysans*, p. 111.

65. Richard, "Pour un syndicalisme de travailleurs," Rapport d'orientation, XIIe Congrès du CNJA, 5–6 juillet 1970, Blois, p. 11. This was a "counterreport" presented by the CNJA's *paysans-travailleurs* faction.

66. Tavernier, *Sociologie politique*, p. 369.

67. Richard, "Pour un syndicalisme de travailleurs," 17.

68. Ibid., 15.

69. Ibid., 8 and 17.

70. *Le Monde*, 6 juin 1981 and 12 mars 1982.

71. *Vent d'ouest* 69 (janvier 1976), p. 4.

72. See nearly every issue of *Vent d'ouest* published during the 1970s; also see Tavernier, *Sociologie politique*, p. 379.

73. Tavernier, *Sociologie politique*, pp. 378–80.

74. *Vent d'ouest* 74 (juillet 1976), 4.

75. Ibid., 68 (décembre 1975), 16.

76. *PSU-Germinal*, mai 1975.

77. See *Monatar*, mai 1975 and janvier 1976; interviews 65 and 102.

78. Interviews 56, 65, and 102; see Chapter 6.

79. *Le Monde*, 30–31 octobre 1977.

80. Ibid., 6 juin 1981 and 23 mars 1982.

81. "Rapport moral: Les agriculteurs face à la corporation anti-paysanne," IVe Congrès national, Fédération Française de l'Agriculture, Saint-Lô, 23–24 octobre 1974.

82. Ibid.

83. *Le Monde*, 10 juin 1981.

84. Diana Green with Philip Cerny, "Economic Policy and the Governing Coalition," in Philip G. Cerny and Martin A. Schain, *French Politics and Public Policy* (London: Frances Pinter, 1980), 159–60.

85. *Le Monde*, 17 and 18–19 décembre 1977.

86. *The Economist*, 15 December 1979.

87. "International Economic Survey," New York *Times*, 3 February 1980.

88. *IA*, juin 1979, 19.

89. *Graph-agri 80*, p. 38.

90. *Journal officiel de la République française: Débats parlementaires, assemblée nationale*, 12 décembre 1979, 11588; see also *The Economist*, 11 December 1979.

91. *Graph-agri 80*, pp. 81–83.

92. *Journal officiel*, 12 décembre 1979, 11592.

93. *IA*, septembre 1977, p. II of the "Connaissance de l'agriculture" insert.

94. *Agricultural Policy of the European Community* (Brussels: European Communities—Information, 1979), p. 7.

95. *IA*, septembre 1977, p. IV of the "Connaissance de l'agriculture" insert; *Graph–agri 80*, p. 25.

96. *Le Monde*, 17 and 18–19 décembre 1977.

97. Pierre Boulnois, "Europe: Le défi des jeunes agriculteurs," report presented at the Journées d'Etudes du CNJA, 3–4 juin 1975, Caen, pp. 34, 51 and 55.

98. *Graph-agri 80*, p. 39.

99. Ibid., pp. 39–41.

100. *IA*, juillet-août 1977, p. III of the "Connaissance de l'agriculture" insert.

101. Ibid., mai 1980, 51.

102. *Graph-agri 80*, pp. 46 and 48.

103. "Rapport moral: Les responsabilités des agriculteurs," XXXIVe Congrès Fédéral, FNSEA, 11–13 mars 1980, Bordeaux, p. 17.

104. Green and Cerny, "Economic Policy," 161.

105. *IA*, mai 1980, 36–39.

106. Ibid., mars 1978, 8.

107. Ibid., 5 and 27; *Le Monde*, 24 février 1978.

108. *IA*, mars 1978, 27; *Le Monde*, 23 février 1980.

109. Interviews 52 and 20 (July 1980).

110. *IA*, juillet-août 1977, p. IV. of the "Connaissance de l'agriculture" insert.

111. *Le Monde*, 7 avril 1977; *L'Agriculteur de l'Aisne*, 9 mars 1979.

112. *Le Monde*, 23 février 1978 and 2 mars 1979.

113. Ibid., 23 février 1978.

114. Ibid., 16 septembre 1977.

115. Ibid, 16 and 18–19 septembre 1977, 30–31 octobre 1977.

116. Ibid, 18–19 septembre 1977, 30–31 octobre 1977, 23 février 1978; for a description and discussion of Interpaysanne, see ibid., 20 juin 1981 and 25 février 1982.

117. Ibid., 23 and 24 février 1978.

118. *IA*, mars 1978, 8.

119. *Le Monde*, 24 and 25 février 1978.

120. Ibid., 20 avril 1979.

121. Ibid., 23 octobre 1979; see also *IA*, novembre 1979, 13.

122. Interviews 52 (July 1980) and 83 (August 1983).

123. *IA*, mars 1978, 8, and juin 1980, 13.

124. "Rapport Moral," FNSEA, 1980, p. 7.

125. *Le Monde*, 13 octobre 1979.

126. Ibid., 11 and 13 décembre 1979; *Journal officiel*, 12 décembre 1979, 11583.

127. "Rapport Moral," FNSEA, 1980, p. 7.

128. *Journal officiel*, 12 décembre 1979, 11587; *Le Monde*, 18 décembre 1979.

129. *Le Monde*, 18 décembre 1979; for a description of the role of the *groupements fonciers agricoles*, see *IA*, mai 1978, 31–33; for the complete text of the 1980 orientation law, see *IA*, juin 1980.

130. *Le Monde*, 18–19 décembre 1977.

131. *IA*, juin 1980, 4, 19, and 30.

132. Ibid., 13.

133. "Rapport Moral," FNSEA, 1980, p. 8.

134. See *Le Monde*, 24 novembre 1979, 15 mars 1980, and 28 février 1981.

135. *L'Exploitant familial*, février 1980.

136. *Le Monde*, 2–3 décembre 1979.

137. See the speech of Maurice Cornette (RPR) in *Le Monde*, 13 décembre 1979.

138. Interviews 83 and 87.

139. Interview 97.

140. François Clerc, "Le Syndicalisme agricole: De l'unité agricole à l'unite syndicale," *IA*, janvier 1974, 25.

141. See for example, "Les Candidats face aux problèmes agricoles," *IA*, juillet-août 1974, 9–17. This article does contain some mild criticism of Giscard d'Estaing, for example, "Hasn't he been led, in his concern for a society of liberty, to weaken somewhat certain *dirigistes* aspects of the structural reform policy…?" However, it contains much more extensive and harsh criticism of Mitterrand. "From a formal point of view, it is clearly evident that the least good (*la moins bonne*) campaign on agricultural issues was that of M. Mitterrand who, along the way, was led to change his themes, his theses and his vocabulary, while the other two candidates pursued the same line from the beginning to the end." Mitterrand was also criticized for employing "the classic distinction of the left between the large farmers of the Parisian Basin and the others" and for making "a personal attack against the President of the FNSEA, a rare personal attack, the only one of the entire campaign." See also "Les Programmes agricoles des partis politiques," *IA*, octobre 1973.

142. Clerc, "Le Syndicalisme agricole," 142.

143. See Henry W. Ehrmann, *Politics in France*, 4th ed. (Boston: Little, Brown, 1982), pp. 253 and 255.

144. See *IA*, mai 1975, 20–22.

145. Tavernier, *Sociologie politique*, p. 407.

146. See *IA*, mars 1978, 27.

147. Tavernier, *Sociologie politique*, pp. 291, 295, and 407. See also Tavernier's "Les

Paysans français et la politique," in Tavernier et al., eds., *L'Univers politique des paysans*, esp. 113 and 123; and Pierre Rémy's "Le Gaullisme et les paysans," 255–72 of the same collection.

148. See Jean Domenge's article in *Le Figaro*, 18 mars 1975.

149. *Le Monde*, 28 février 1981.

Chapter 4

1. Suleiman, *Politics, Power and Bureaucracy in France*, p. 331.

2. The "Cotisations 1975" document cited as a source for Figure 3.5 indicates that the FNSEA had 537,000 dues-paying members in 1975, a figure that would give the Federation a national membership density of approximately 44% if one assumes—with Prugnaud—that the number of eligible farmers equals the number of farms larger than 2 hectares. In recent years the FNSEA has publicly claimed a membership of 750,000 (*Le Point*, 7 avril 1975), 700,000 (in *30 ans de combat syndical*), and even 850,000 (see the interview with François Guillaume in *Paris-Match*, 19 février 1982). Such inflated figures are, of course, given to impress the public and the government. Even if these membership figures can be dismissed, however, the FNSEA may be said to have a legitimate claim to membership density higher than 44%; it is true, as FNSEA leaders argue, that farms smaller than 5 or even 10 hectares are usually farmed on a part-time basis by individuals who cannot be expected to pay union dues and should perhaps not be counted when estimating the number of farmers "eligible" for membership. It has been estimated that all French industrial trade unions combined have managed to organize "probably not more than 20 to 25 percent of eligible wage earners." See p. 185 of Henry W. Ehrmann's *Politics in France*, 3rd ed., and Gérard Adam, ed., *L'Ouvrier français en 1970* (Paris: Armand Colin, 1970), pp. 15 ff. For a discussion of elections to the Chambers of Agriculture, see André Vial, "Elections aux Chambers d'Agriculture: La signification d'un vote," *Paysans* 117 (février–mars 1976), 11–15.

3. Gilles Allaire, "L'Etat des forces à la vielle des élections aux Chambres d'Agriculture," *Nouvelles Campagnes*, novembre 1982, 16.

4. Exclusive of other farmers' unions, though not of other professional organizations; representatives of the Chambers of Agriculture and the cooperative associations are accorded seats along with the FNSEA-CNJA.

5. Lavau, "Political Pressures by Interest Groups in France," 83.

6. In denying a request for recognition of FFA in 1973, Jacques Chirac (then minister of agriculture) argued that governmental negotiation with a plurality of unions would simply lead to a process of *surenchère* which would serve neither the interests of the agricultural profession nor the "general interest." "The existence of a single union representative of all *tendances d'esprit*," he asserted, "was a source of strength for agriculture and permitted *concertation* to be "fully effective." Thus the government considered "inopportune the creation of new union organizations distinct from the FNSEA" and would refuse to deal with them. Not without some reason, the FFA interpreted such grounds for the refusal of recognition as an infringement of syndical freedom. See the "Rapport moral" ("Les Agriculteurs face à la corporation anti-paysanne"), IVᵉ Congrès National, Fédération Française de l'Agriculture, 23–24 octobre 1974, Saint-Lô.

7. Prugnaud, *Les Etapes*, p. 238.

8. See ibid., pp. 219–20; G. Wright, *Rural Revolution*, p. 165; Houée, *Les Etapes*, pp. 179–80.

9. On the 1975 and 1980 legislation related to the *interprofessions*, see *I.A.*, juin 1980, novembre 1981, and juin 1982.

10. Jacques Cloarec, "Un éxemple d' intervention de l'état: Le financement public de l'agriculture," *Etudes rurales* 69 (janvier–mars 1978), 19 and 24.

11. For a discussion of the Annual Review in Britain, see Graham K. Wilson, *Special Interests and Policymaking: Agricultural Policies and Politics in Britain and the United States of America, 1956–70* (New York: Wiley, 1977), ch. 4.

12. See *IA*, novembre 1974, 10–11.

13. See page "d" of the FFA "Rapport moral" cited in note 6; also, interviews 15, 94, 95, 96, 97, 99, and 56.

14. Andre Vial, "L'Exploitation agricole: Realités 1973," *Paysans* 100 (juin–juillet 1973), 25.

15. See "La SAFER Marche-Limousin au service de l'agriculture régionale," *Corrèze-Magazine*, 163 (juillet-août 1975); *IA*, decembre 1974, vi.

16. *SAFER: Organisation, fonctionnement* (Paris: FNSAFER, 1972), pp. 5–15.

17. Raoul Massetat, "Rapport moral," XXVIᵉ Congrès, FDSEA (Landes), p. 29.

18. Interviews 13, 52, 72, 89, 92, 94, 97, 99, 101, 56, and 65.

19. Interviews 89, 97, 99. As discussed in Chapter 6, such discrimination is virtually impossible in a department in which a rival union is well established, extremely powerful, and capable of applying external pressure on SAFER decisions.

20. Interview 72.

21. *L'ADASEA au service des agriculteurs* (Laon: ADASEA de l'Aisne, mars 1972), p. 8.

22. Ibid., p. 23.

23. ADASEA personnel have performed FDSEA functions for a variety of reasons; some have done so out of a commitment to the FDSEA's values and goals (many are former FDSEA members), some have done so because they are friends (or even relatives) of FDSEA staff or members, others have done so simply because they—or their bosses— consider it to be part of their job. This assessment is based on my personal observations and many interviews, for example, 14, 15, 52, 56, 61, 65, 72, 73, 74.

24. The "development"program was prepared under Pisani but was not enacted until after his departure, in October 1966.

25. *Le Monde;* 7 octobre 1966.

26. Ibid.; Pierre Muller's *Grandeur et décadence du professeur d'agriculture* provides the most comprehensive available account of the controversial transfer of authority for the implementation of development programs from the administration to "the profession"; see also ch. 6 of Houée, *Les Etapes*.

27. R. Thierry de Ville d'Avray, "Les Grandes étapes de la diffusion du progrès technique en France," *Paysans* 111 (avril–mai 1975), 25; see also, in the same issue of *Paysans*, Gérard de Caffarelli, "Les Nouvelles orientations de L'ANDA pour un meilleur service des agriculteurs," 38–43.

28. R. Thierry de Ville d'Avray, "Les Grandes étapes," 25.

29. Even the non-FDSEA members appointed to the SUAD council are generally

FDSEA sympathizers. Rival union members have obtained seats on the SUAD council only on the rare occasions in which a rival union controlled a majority of seats in the Chamber of Agriculture. The reaction of the state to this anomalous situation will be discussed in Chapter 7.

30. Houée, *Les Etapes*, pp. 61, 124; "Le Développement agricole dans les Landes," Assemblée Générale, 18 mars 1972 (Saint-Vincent-de-Tyrosse), esp. p. 3; "Dotation aux organismes maîtres d'oeuvre: 1976," SUAD, Chambre d'Agriculture de la Corrèze; "Programme pluriannuel de développement agricole," SUAD, Chambre d'Agriculture des Landes, septembre 1974; "Programme pluriennal de développement agricole: 1974–1976," SUAD, Chambre d'Agriculture de l'Aisne. For a discussion of the importance of the SUAD subsidy to the CNJA, see Tavernier, *Sociologie politique*, p. 281.

31. F. Maurel, "Quel est le rôle des chambres d' agriculture?" *Paysans* 44 (octobre–novembre 1963), 11–19; F. Maurel, "Syndicalisme et chambres d'agriculture," *Paysans* 42 (juin-juillet 1963), 5–14; *Le Monde*, 1 février 1964, p. 18; Christiane Mora, "Les Chambres d' agriculture et l'unité paysanne," in Tavernier et al., eds., *L'Univers politique des paysans*, 507–31; "Le Budget des chambers d'agriculture: 1973," APCA (Paris).

32. The DSA (now DDA) is the chief departmental state bureaucrat for agriculture.

33. See the two articles by Maurel in note 31, above. The president of the Chamber of Agriculture in Aisne was referred to as the "préfet vert" in interview 52; the director of the chamber in Corrèze was referred to as the "préfet agricole" in interview 99.

34. The most noteworthy exceptions to the rule of FNSEA dominance before 1981 were Indre-et-Loire (where FFA controlled the chamber) and Puy-de-Dôme (where anti-Debatisse forces controlled the chamber); MODEF controlled the Landes chamber from 1964 to 1970.

35. In Corrèze, for example, the FDSEA director performed the functions of the chamber director for almost two decades while maintaining the title of chamber subdirector; the activity of the de jure chamber director was limited to relatively mundane chores such as bookkeeping, bill paying, and supervision of personnel (Interviews 75, 78, and 79). Informed sources indicate that this is a rather common arrangement (Interviews 13, 52, 79, 81).

36. Interview 56. This particular individual eventually did leave the FDSEA to organize MONATAR in Corrèze—and admitted doubts as to whether he had made the proper decision, a decision that entailed abandoning his positions of influence within the powerful decision-making structures of the department. Had the FDSEA not been an "official union" with a monopoly on departmental power, he noted, he would have resigned from it long before he actually did.

37. Interviews 56, 78.

38. Interview 72.

39. Sharing a newspaper with the chamber has been a great advantage for the FDSEA even in cases in which the FDSEA has paid its fair portion of the publication costs. For many farmers, the technical chamber news—concerning prices, newly available equipment, and so on—is much more interesting than the union news; such farmers will buy the FDSEA-chamber newspaper primarily for its technical content, and in the process expose themselves to the FDSEA's interpretation of local events. No such farmers would buy a purely union newspaper—either that of the FDSEA or a rival union. Local businessmen have recognized this fact as well; they have thus been likely to advertise in an

FDSEA-chamber newspaper with a fairly wide circulation and unlikely to advertise in a purely union paper. This relative facility in obtaining advertising revenue has made the publication cost of an FDSEA-chamber newspaper much lower than that of a rival union newspaper. Interviews 13, 15, 42, 52, 56, 95, 113.

40. *Le Monde*, 19 août 1971.

41. See, for example, *L'Exploitant familial: Organe national du MODEF* 140 (septembre 1971); *Le Monde*, 19 août, 1971.

42. See Yves Tavernier, "Le Mouvement de coordination et de défense des exploitations agricoles familiales (M.O.D.E.F.)," *Revue française de science politique*, 18:3 (juin 1968), 479; see also the discussion of the Landes case in Chapter 7.

43. See *Les Informations agricoles* (MODEF-Mont-de-Marsan), no. 789, 6 juin 1975.

44. The "hierarchical-vertical" and "political-horizontal" terms are borrowed from Jean-Claude Thoenig, "State Bureaucracies and Local Government in France" (paper presented at the Harvard Center for European Studies, March 1975), p. 10.

45. "Quelques données chiffrées sur le développement agricole," *Paysans* 111 (avril–mai 1975), 108–9; *IA*, mai 1968; Tavernier, *Sociologie politique*, p. 281; "La Situation de l'agriculture et l'activite syndicale en 1974," XXIXe Congrès Fédéral-FNSEA, 18–20 mars, 1975 (Versailles), p. 72. "Le financement public du CNJA et de la FNSEA et le nombre réel de leurs adherents," *Nouvelles campagnes*, novembre 1982, p. 26.

46. See the series of articles by Joanne Roy on "L'Aide gouvernementale à la formation des syndicalistes," *Le Monde*, 16, 17, 18 juillet 1964.

47. *IA*, décembre 1972, 43; mai 1971, 48.

48. See Bazex, *L'Administration*, pp. 146–49.

49. *Le Monde*, 18 juillet 1964; "Le financement public," p. 26.

50. *IA*, avril 1972 and juin 1974.

51. Ibid., mai 1971, 49; p. 66 of the FNSEA report ("la Situation") cited in note 45, above.

52. "Rapport moral: Les Agriculteurs face à la corporation anti-paysanne," IVe Congrès National, Fédération Française de l'Agriculture, 23–24 octobre 1974, Saint-Lô.

Chapter 5

1. Maxime de Sars, "Soixante ans de syndicalisme agricole dans le département de l'Aisne" (unpublished official history of the USAA written by one of its former administrators), 1952, p. 132.

2. Ibid., p. 133.

3. Ibid., p. 125.

4. See *30 ans de combat syndical*, p. 27.

5. Michel Canon, "Compte rendu d'activité," USAA Assemblée Générale, 1973; reprinted in *L'Agriculteur de l'Aisne* (henceforth cited as *AA*), 24 février 1973.

6. USAA, "Réflexion sur l'étude faite par les FDSEA du Finistère, de Loire-Atlantique, de Mayenne et du Morbihan, intitulée: Le droit au travail et le revenu minimum garanti," 18 mars 1975, p. 1.

7. Interview 26.

8. Chambre d'Agriculture de l'Aisne, "Visage méconnu de l'agriculture de l'Aisne," mai 1975, p. 1.

9. USAA, "Réflexion," p. 2.

10. Henri de Benoist, *AA*, 2 décembre 1972.

11. *AA*, 22 décembre 1973; the validity of this claim was confirmed by the director of the FDSEA of Somme (interview 81).

12. *AA*, 2 juin 1973.

13. Interviews 22, 25, 28.

14. Michael Canon, "Compte rendu d'activité," USAA Assemblée Général 1971; reprinted in *AA*, 20 février 1971.

15. See *Paysans* 73–74 (août–novembre 1968), 117–19.

16. "Visage," p. 5.

17. In 1951 almost 30% of Aisne voters cast their ballots for the PCF; in the first ballot of the 1969 presidential election, Aisne ranked eleventh among non-Parisian departments in support for PCF candidate Jacques Duclos; in the 1978 legislative elections, 28.7% of Aisne voters supported the PCF and two of the five deputies elected by the department were Communists.

18. Juan Linz, "Patterns of Land Tenure, Division of Labor and Voting Behavior in Europe," *Comparative Politics* 8:3 (April 1976), 388. For the population statistics, see pp. 29–30 of *Paysans* 73–74 (août–novembre 1968).

19. Linz, "Patterns of Land Tenure," 390.

20. Calculated from statistics in Jean Duplex, ed., *Atlas de la France rurale* (Paris: Armand Colin, 1968); see the pages listing election results by canton in Aisne.

21. Interview 27.

22. Interview 52.

23. Interview 41.

24. These statistics are derived from information collected in the interviews of elected USAA officials.

25. Interviews 20, 22, 27, 34, 41, 52.

26. Interviews 41, 49, 52.

27. See de Sars, "Soixante ans," pp. 79–95.

28. Ibid., pp. 91–94; see also pp. 53–59 on pre–World War II services.

29. Ibid., pp. 88–90.

30. Ibid., pp. 90–93.

31. Ibid., pp. 90–91.

32. Interview 48.

33. See de Sars, ch. 4, for an interesting if tendentious discussion of the Vichy period.

34. Ibid., pp. 103–19. Judging from the statistics cited by Gordon Wright in *Rural Revolution*, the Aisne case was not unusual. Vichy corporation officials were elected to postwar union positions in many regions. See also pp. 440–45 of Isabel Boussard's "La Corporation paysanne: Une étape dans l'histoire du syndicalisme agricole français (1940–1944)" (Thèse, Fondation Nationale des Sciences Politiques, Paris, 1971).

35. See de Sars, pp. 105 and 109.

36. Ibid., pp. 116–17.

37. Ibid., p. 107; interview 48.

38. See de Sars, p. 127.

39. "Statuts de l'union des syndicats agricoles de l'Aisne," pp. 2–3.

40. See de Sars, "Soixante ans," ch. 5, esp. pp. 128–64.

41. Ibid., p. 115; *AA*, 24 février 1973.

42. See Chapter 3; interviews 28 and 48 confirmed that Paris was a major distraction for Blondelle and other USAA leaders during this period.

43. See de Sars, "Soixante ans," pp. 151–52.

44. A statistic provided by interview 48.

45. See de Sars, "Soixante ans," p. 164.

46. Statistics obtained in interview 48. The figures for membership density were computed according to the following formula: union members divided by the number of departmental farms larger than 2 hectares.

47. See Berger, *Peasants Against Politics*, ch. 6.

48. Interviews 22, 25, 26, 27, 28, 30, 34, 38, 48, 52, and notes taken at a meeting of the USAA bureau on 5 December 1975.

49. Interviews 22, 25, 34, 48, 52, 53.

50. Interview 48; the monetary figures for 1948 have been converted to new francs.

51. "Compte de gestion de l'exercice—USAA," 1955; "Budget—USAA," 1974; inflation rates taken from *Annuaire statistique de la France 1966; résumé retrospectif 1948—1965* (Paris: Ministère de l'Economie et de Finances, 1966), pp. 377–78.

52. "Au Service des agriculteurs de l'Aisne" (Laon, USAA, 1975), pages not numbered.

53. Interview 48 (Prévot) provided me with the nature and number of USAA employees for most years between 1955 and 1974.

54. Interview 75.

55. Interview 48.

56. "Au Service des agriculteurs de l'Aisne," and interviews 41, 45, 47, 50, 52.

57. "Au Service des agriculteurs de l'Aisne."

58. Interview 50.

59. Interviews 22, 26, 32, 34, 41, 45, 46, 47, 50.

60. Interviews 45, 47, 50.

61. Interviews 33, 41, 45, 46, 50, 52.

62. Interviews 45, 47.

63. "Au Service des agriculteurs de l'Aisne."

64. Interview 81.

65. Interviews 41, 47, 50.

66. Interview 41.

67. Interview 47.

68. Interview 81.

69. Interviews 34, 52.

70. Interviews 41 and 52.

71. Interviews 31 and 41, discussion with several farmers in the canton and observation at the farm of M. Letrillart.

72. Interview 52.

73. Overheard in the office of the adjunct-director of both the USAA and the Chamber of Agriculture (Tronche).

74. "Membres des commissions et comités—1975," and interview 48.
75. "Membres des commissions et comités—1975," and interviews 27, 34, 48, 52.
76. Interviews 48, 52, and observation in the office of the USAA director.
77. Jean-Philippe Tronche, "Organigramme administratif de l'union des syndicats agricoles et de la chambre d'agriculture de l'Aisne," 1974.
78. Ibid.
79. Ibid.
80. "Au Service des agriculteurs de l'Aisne."
81. Tronche, "Organigramme."
82. Interview 53.
83. "Au Service des agriculteurs de l'Aisne," and interview 52.
84. Interviews 48, 52.
85. "Budget de la chambre d'agriculture," 1958 and 1975; the 1975 figure is composed of the "general budget" and the SUAD budget.
86. "Budget de la chambre," 1975.
87. Interviews 41, 45, 46, 47, 50.
88. "Budget de la chambre," 1975.
89. *AA*, 24 février 1973.
90. "Budget de la chambre," 1975.
91. Interviews 40, 43, 44.
92. The Fonds National d'Assurance Formation des Exploitants Agricoles administers the national programs for *promotion collective* and the *perfectionnement des cadres*; at the department level its subsidies are distributed by a twelve-member committee composed of representatives of the "recognized" organizations. In Aisne, of course, this committee has been dominated by leaders of the USAA.
93. Chambre d'Agriculture, "Programme pluriennal de développement agricole 1974–1976: Compte rendu d'activité 1975"; "Au Service des agriculteurs de l'Aisne."
94. *Le Monde*, 15 décembre 1973; interview 53.
95. Interviews 41, 52.
96. Interview 41.
97. Interview 52.
98. "Cotisations 1971," a document prepared by Prévot.
99. Interviews 27, 48, 52.
100. Interviews 22, 25, 26, 27, 52.
101. Interview 52; see *Le Monde*, 6 avril 1977.
102. *AA*, 2 mars 1979; letter from Jean-Philippe Tronche, USAA director, to the author—7 mars 1979.
103. Interview 94.

Chapter 6

1. *Paysans* 73–74 (août–novembre 1968), 141.
2. See Table 5.1; the quotation is from Gratton, *Les Paysans*, p. 18.
3. "Compte rendu de la réunion de travail," Chambre d'Agriculture de la Corrèze, 9 juin 1972, Meymac, p. 6.
4. "Aperçu sur la Corrèze," Chambre d'Agriculture de la Corrèze, avril 1974, p. 6.
5. See Jean-Marie Denquin, *Le Renversement de la majorité dans le département de la*

Corrèze 1958–1973 (Paris: Presses Universitaires de France, 1976), esp. pp. 9–11; Juan Linz, "Patterns of Land Tenure," 390–92; G. Wright, *Rural Revolution*, pp. 190–201; Alain Bastardie, "Le Syndicalisme paysan en Corrèze depuis 1945," Memoires de Fin d'Etudes, Institute d'Etudes Politiques de Paris, 1970–71, 58; Jean Charlot, ed. *Quand la gauche peut gagner* (Paris: Editions Alain Moreau, 1973), appended electoral results (no page numbers given).

6. The 1952 results are taken from Bastardie, "Le Syndicalisme paysan," 49. The results from the 1970 election were given to me in handwritten form by the director of the Chamber of Agriculture. For the remaining elections, the results were taken from the following issues of the FDSEA's newspaper, *L'Union paysanne* (henceforth cited as *UP*): mai 1959, 15 février 1964, 15 février 1967, 28 février 1974, 15 février 1976.

7. Bastardie, "Le Syndicalisme paysan," 33–37.

8. Ibid., 33–37.

9. "Rapport presenté à l'assemblée général du 15 mars par Monsieur Champseix, president de la fédération des exploitants" (1947), p. 3.

10. Bastardie, "Le Syndicalisme paysan," 40.

11. Ibid., 41–45.

12. Ibid., 45, 52.

13. Guy Lord, "Le P.C.F.: Structure et organisation d'une fédération dé-partementale," paper presented at the Workshop sur le Communisme en Europe Occidentale (European Consortium for Political Research), Paris, juin 1973, p. 25.

14. None of the union elites denied that this was the case, although MODEF leaders stressed that not all of their members or supporters were Communists.

15. These correlation coefficients and those that follow are based only on the rural cantons in Corrèze. The definition of "rural canton" used here essentially follows that employed by the editors of the *Atlas de la France rurale*: all cantons except those with a commune whose population exceeded 20,000 in 1962. By this definition all but one (Brive) of the twenty-nine cantons of Corrèze were rural in 1962; to control further for the influence of urban votes, however, I also excluded the two cantons of Tulle from the computations. In short, the correlation coefficients are based on statistics for twenty-six of the twenty-nine cantons of the department. Electoral returns for the Chamber of Agriculture elections were taken from the sources listed above in note 6. Returns for the legislative elections were taken from the *Atlas de la France rurale* for 1962 and *Les Elections legislatives de 1973—4 et 11 mars* (Paris: Ministère de l'Interieur, 1972), pp. 266–71. "Left votes" for 1962 were those defined as such by the *Atlas*. For 1973 the "left" was defined as the Communist Party, the Socialist Party, the PSU, and the Mouvement Lutte Ouvrière. For both 1962 and 1973, the results used were those of the first ballot.

16. Bastardie, "Le Syndicalisme paysan," 40, 86–87; also interviews 65, 72, 99.

17. The FDSEA membership statistics were taken from union notebooks entitled "Cotisations."

18. Interviews 62, 75.

19. Denquin, *Le Renversement*, p. 74.

20. *UP*, 30 janvier 1976.

21. Bastardie, "Le Syndicalisme paysan," 48.

22. See, for example, the remarks of M. Biset in the "Procès verbal de l'assemblée générale de la FDSEA du 19 février 1953," p. 5.

23. Bastardie, "Le Syndicalisme paysan," 51.

24. "Procès verbal de la réunion du conseil d'administration de la FDSEA du 12 décembre 1953," esp. pp. 3–4. See also the "Procès verbal de la réunion du conseil fédéral du 2 octobre 1953."

25. Bastardie, "Le Syndicalisme paysan," 79–80; interview 66.

26. Interviews 62, 75. While Deprun has held no major position in the Jaciste movement, Malmartel served as *secrétaire fédérale* between 1940 and 1944. From "Renseignements concernant M. Malmartel," a photocopied document at the FDSEA in Tulle.

27. "Procès verbal de la réunion de conseil fédéral du lundi 15 juin 1974," p. 3.

28. Interview 62 and "Compte rendu de la réunion des membres du conseil d'administration du 23 octobre 1969." At this meeting Deprun explained that the goal of the Comité de Gueret had originally been "the defense of the interests of the farmers of the Centre region. But gradually the *personnes politiques de MODEF* infiltrated it" and changed the course of its activities.

29. Bastardie, "Le Syndicalisme paysan," 79–80; interview 62.

30. Ibid., 80; interview 62.

31. See *IA*, mai 1975, 20; interviews 59 (with Michelle Chezalviel, president of the Women's Commission) and 69 (with Jean-Pierre Papin, adjunct secretary-general of the FDSEA and CRJA president).

32. Interviews 56, 57 (with the current FDSEA president Georges Chapelle), and 62.

33. See "Procès verbal de l'assemblée générale de la FDSEA du 12 mars 1957."

34. Bastardie, "Le Syndicalisme paysan," 40.

35. The statistics for 1950 and 1957 are taken from Bastardie, p. 66; the statistics for 1963 and 1973 are taken from the FDSEA's membership notebooks ("Cotisations") for those two years. The membership density figure for "all farmers" was calculated by dividing membership by the number of farms larger than 2 hectares. Here it must be noted that the FDSEA of Corrèze has failed to give an accurate public accounting of its membership since the dawn of the 1960s—when its membership began to decline at a rate faster than the rural exodus. In its reports to the FNSEA, for example, the FDSEA provided an inflated figure of 5,300 members in 1966 and an even more blatantly inflated figure of 6,400 in 1975. As Yves Tavernier has noted, such manipulation of membership statistics is not at all uncommon in the FNSEA—see p. 64 of *Le Syndicalisme paysan: FNSEA, CNJA* (Paris: Armand Colin, 1969). When confronted with the discrepancy between the official and actual figures, Pierre Deprun admitted that the 6,400 figure was "perhaps a bit exaggerated—like all departments, we want to have the best representation possible at national and regional assemblies." A former FDSEA bureau member, now a MONATAR activist, provided a more detailed and precise explanation for the exaggeration: "The principal reason for the inflated figures is to guarantee control of the FRSEA for Limousin-Auvergne, of which Deprun has long been president and Debatisse secretary-general. To be elected they need the extra votes which this exaggeration provides, since three of the eight member federations are controlled by anti-Debatisse forces: Haute-Vienne, Creuse and Allier. The votes of Cantal, Haute-Loire, Lozère and the inflated votes for Corrèze and Puy-de-Dôme assure their retention of power" (Interview 56).

36. These percentages were calculated from the voting statistics cited above in note 6 and the membership statistics in the "Cotisations" notebooks.

37. "Procès verbal de l'assemblée générale de la FDSEA du 17 février 1954."

38. "Compte-rendu d'activités—FDSEA de la Corrèze, 1955," pp. 1–2.

39. "Rapport financier de la FDSEA," 1957 and 1973; for the sources of the USAA statistics, see Chapter 5; the figure given for 1957 here has been converted into new francs.

40. Interviews 70, 72, 75.

41. Interview 75, observation of Malmartel's work and *UP*, 30 mai 1965.

42. Interviews 59, 67.

43. Interviews 57, 59, 67, 68; "Cotisations" notebooks for 1973 and 1974.

44. "Cotisations" notebooks for 1973 and 1974; estimates of the number of departmental farms larger than 2 hectares in these two years were provided by interview 78.

45. The membership figure for 1950 is taken from Bastardie, "Le Syndicalisme paysan," 66. FCSEA-MODEF leaders would not allow me to examine their membership statistics, but did give estimates of 3,000 for the 1950s and 2,000 for the 1970s (interviews 99, 100, 101). Judging from direct observation of FCSEA meetings and interviews with fairly objective sources, it seems clear that these figures are as inflated as those made public by the FDSEA. Several sources agreed that if the present FDSEA membership was near 3,400, the FCSEA membership could be no more than 1,000 (interviews 56, 65, 72, 113).

46. Interview 56.

47. Interviews 59, 61, 64, respectively.

48. Interview 99.

49. Bastardie, "Le Syndicalisme paysan," 50.

50. "Procès verbal de la réunion du bureau de la FDSEA du 10 decembre 1956."

51. "My job," stated the formal director in 1975, "has been to take care of the *boulot*: I pay the bills, fill out forms and hire and supervise the employees of the buildings. M. Malmartel takes care of policy and external relations, for example, dealing with the prefecture" (interview 79).

52. "Procès verbal de la réunion du bureau de la FDSEA du 10 decembre 1956."

53. Interviews 56, 72, 75.

54. Bastardie, "Le Syndicalisme paysan," 52.

55. Interviews 75.

56. Interviews 75, 109, and observation of the monthly conference of 30 October 1975.

57. This portrayal of Malmartel is based on interviews with him, conversations with some of his "clients," and weeks of observation in and outside of his office.

58. Interviews 55, 56, 60, 65, 68, 72, 99.

59. Interview 109.

60. Interview 99.

61. Interview 109.

62. Interview 72.

63. Interview 56.

64. "Procès-verbaux des délibérations," Conseil Général, Département de la Corrèze, 2e Session Ordinaire de 1975.

65. Interview 56.

66. "Dotation aux organismes maîtres d'oeuvre: 1976," Chambre d'Agriculture de la Corrèze—SUAD.

67. Interview 102.

68. *UP*, janvier 1976.

69. Interviews 56, 101, 102.

70. "Compte rendu d'activités—FDSEA de la Corrèze," 1971; "Compte rendu de la réunion des membres du conseil fédéral du 12 mars 1975"; interview 75.

71. "Procès verbal: Session de la chambre d'agriculture de la Corrèze, 6 mai 1975 (Tulle)."

72. "Liste du personnel en place au 1 octobre 1975," Chambre d'Agriculture de la Corrèze; interview 79.

73. Interviews 56, 72, 75, 99; see also the exposé in the "Supplément au *Monatar*," no. 6, janvier 1976.

74. "Supplément au *Monatar*," no. 6, janvier 1976.

75. "Compte rendu de la réunion des membres du bureau de la FDSEA du 19 novembre 1973," p. 5.

76. "Compte rendu de la réunion des membres du bureau de la FDSEA du 16 avril 1974," p. 2.

77. Interview 72. Also, see "Paille: Une opération sans précédent," *Jeunes agriculteurs*, septembre 1976, 13.

78. Interviews 70, 80.

79. Interview 78: I observed the librarian as he worked every day to compile this file.

80. "Procès verbal: Session de la chambre d'agriculture de la Corrèze, 6 mai 1975 (Tulle)," p. 16.

81. "Procès-verbaux des délibérations," Conseil Général, Département de la Corrèze, 2e Session Ordinaire de 1975, pp. 225–27.

82. "Procès verbal de la réunion des membres du bureau de la FDSEA du lundi 9 octobre 1967."

83. "Compte rendu de la réunion des membres du conseil d'administration du 23 octobre 1969." See also the criticism of Debatisse in "Procès verbal de la réunion du conseil fédéral du 12 mai 1969."

84. "Cotisations" notebooks for 1968–74.

85. "Compte rendu de la réunion des membres du conseil fédéral du 8 avril 1974"; "Compte rendu de la réunion des membres du bureau du 19 mars 1974"; "Compte rendu de la réunion du conseil fédéral du 22 janvier 1974."

86. "Supplément au *Monatar*," no. 6, janvier 1976; also interview 56. Bousseyrol stated that he was "very close" to but not a "card holder" of the Socialist Party.

87. "Supplément" and *L'Avenir agricole de la Corrèze: Organe du MADARAC*, no. 2, octobre 1974.

88. See *UP* for the preelection period, esp. 15 février 1974.

89. See note 6 above for the sources of these electoral statistics.

90. "Compte rendu de la réunion du conseil fédéral du 22 janvier 1974."

91. "Assemblée général du vendredi 22 mars 1974: Intervention de M. Roland Meyjonade."

92. "Compte rendu de la réunion des membres du conseil fédéral du 15 juillet 1974."

93. *L'Exploitant familial*, mars 1979.

Chapter 7

1. See Table 5.1 and *Paysans* 73–74 (août–novembre 1968), 140–41.

2. "Le Département des Landes: Agriculture et forêt," Chambre d'Agriculture des Landes, 1975, pp. 1, 4, 7, 10; *Recensement générale de l'agriculture: 1970—fascicule 1* (Mont-de-Marsan: Direction Départementale de l'Agriculture—Service de Statistique Agricole, 1971), pp. 15, 23, 75; *Paysans* 73–74 (août–novembre 1968), 23.

3. *Statistique agricole de la France: Résultats généraux de l'enquête de 1929* (Paris: Ministère de l'Agriculture, 1936).

4. *Recensement général de l'agriculture de 1955: Premiers résultats par région agricole* (Paris: Ministère de l'Agriculture, 1959), pp. 55, 61.

5. *Recensement général de l'agriculture: 1970*, p. 26.

6. See Philippe Gratton, *Les Luttes de classes dans les campagnes* (Paris: Editions Anthropos, 1971), pp. 115–132 and 441–43.

7. See ibid., pp. 345–57; "Schéma sur le syndicalisme," MODEF des Landes, janvier 1973.

8. Linz, "Patterns of Land Tenure," 401–3.

9. Ibid., 404; Charlot, ed., *Quand la gauche peut gagner*, appended electoral statistics for 1967–73 (pages not numbered).

10. *Recensement générale de l'agriculture: 1970*, p. 30. The electoral statistics are from *Les Elections législatives de 1967—5 et 12 mars* (Paris: Ministère de l'Intérieur, 1967), pp. 492–97); *Les Elections legislatives de 1968—23 et 30 juin* (Paris: Ministère de l'Intérieur, 1968), pp. 453–57; *Les Elections législatives de 1973—4 et 11 mars* (Paris: Ministère de l'Intérieur, 1973), pp. 456–63.

11. "Schéma sur le syndicalisme," pp. 4–6; interviews 5, 92, 97.

12. "Schéma sur le syndicalisme," p. 5; Paul Fabra, "La S.F.I.O.," in Fauvet and Mendras, eds., *Les Paysans et la politique dans le France contemporaine*, 90–91.

13. "Schéma sur le syndicalisme," p. 7; *Les Informations agricoles* (henceforth cited as *LIA*) 96 (1 juin 1950); interviews 7, 92, 97.

14. *LIA* 115 (15 mars 1951) "Les Fermiers et métayers landais face à la decision du congrès de la FNSEA"; see also *LIA* 122 (1 juillet 1951) and 152 (1 octobre 1952).

15. "Le Réveil landais" in *Le Courrier français*, 26 août 1950. The new FDSEA was commonly termed the FLSEA (*Fédération Landaise*) during the 1950s to avoid confusion with its predecessor.

16. *Le Réveil landais* (henceforth cited as *RL*) 3 (juillet 1950); *RL* 20 (janvier 1952); *RL* 85 (2ᵉ quinzaine novembre 1955); *LIA* 96 (1 juin 1950).

17. Interview 13.

18. Interviews 89, 90, 91, 92, and 98.

19. "Objet: A/s des responsables de la fédération des syndicats agricoles (MODEF) et des mouvements annexes"; interviews 90, 96, 97.

20. Interviews 89, 90, 91, 92, and 98.

21. The results of the Chamber of Agriculture elections are taken from *LIA* 425 (2ᵉ quinzaine de février 1964); *Le Sillon* 442 (1 mars 1974); *LIA* 825 (20 février 1976). For the results of the 1967 and 1970 chamber elections, see *LIA* 497 (2ᵉ quinzaine de février 1967) and 574 (1ᵉʳ quinzaine de mai 1970). The results of the legislative elections were taken from the *Atlas de la France rurale* for 1962 and from *Les Elections legislatives de 1973—4 et*

11 mars. "Left" votes for 1962 were those defined as such by the *Atlas*. For 1973, the "Left" included the votes for the Communist, Socialist, Radical-Socialist, and Lutte Ouvrière candidates. For both 1962 and 1973, the results used were those of the first ballot. These correlation coefficients and those that follow are based only the rural cantons in Landes. The definition of "rural canton" used here essentially follows that employed by the editors of the *Atlas de la France rurale*: all cantons except those with a commune whose population exceeded 20,000 in 1962. By this definition all of the twenty-eight cantons of Landes were rural in 1962; to control further for the influence of urban votes, however, I excluded the cantons containing the department's three largest cities (Mont-de-Marsan, Dax, and Saint Sever) from the computations. The coefficients for 1973/1974–76 are thus based on statistics for twenty-five of the cantons in Landes. Because the Chamber elections of 1964 were uncontested in the northwestern *circonscription* (the cantons of Parentis-en-Born, Mimizan, Pissos, Sabres, Morcenx, Sore, and Labrit), the coefficients for 1964/1962 are based on electoral results in eighteen cantons. For the eighteen cantons which yielded the coefficients cited for 1964/1962, the 1973/1974–76 coefficients were +.377 (MODEF-Communist votes) and +.592 (MODEF-Left votes).

22. "Schéma sur le syndicalisme," pp. 12–13; interviews 90, 91, 95, 96, 98. See also *LIA* 668 (19 janvier 1973); 669 (26 janvier 1973); 735 (3 mai 1974); 737 (17 mai 1974).

23. Interviews 5, 7; the "cigarette paper" quote is from Paul Lesparre.

24. Interviews 5, 13, 92.

25. *LIA* 497 (février 1967); for Ducourneau's self-described occupation on the ballot, see p. 492 of *Les Elections legislatives de 1967—5 et 12 mars*; interviews 1, 13, 91, 92, 97.

26. For the source of the FDSEA-Right vote correlations, see above, note 21. "Right" votes for 1962 were those defined as such by the *Atlas de la France rurale*. For 1973 the "Right " was defined as those parties not included among the "Left" in note 21.

27. Interview 5.

28. Interviews 1, 5, 6, 7, 9, 92, 97.

29. Interviews 5, 7, 89, 92, 97.

30. The statistics for the number of *salariés* and farms larger than 100 hectares in Landes are taken from *Recensement général de l'agriculture: 1970*, pp. 15, 86. The socioeconomic profile of the FDSEA bureau is based on data obtained from interviews 1, 2, 3, 6, 8, 9, 10, 11, 13.

31. The socioeconomic profile of the MODEF elite is based on data obtained in interviews 89, 90, 91, 92, 93, 96, 97, 98.

32. *LIA* 712 (23 novembre 1973); *Le Sillon* 419 (15 février 1974). See also Raoul Massetat, "Rapport moral," XXVIIIᵉ Congrès de la FDSEA, 23 mars 1974 (Mont-de-Marsan), p. 15.

33. The membership statistics are taken from the FDSEA's "Cotisations" notebook for 1963 and a MODEF document entitled "Nombre d'adhérents" listing the total departmental membership for each year from 1946 to 1975.

34. The "syndicalisme de sentiment" quote is from interview 2. The FDSEA budget statistic is an estimate given in interview 9; the MODEF budget statistic (93, 529.55 francs to be exact) is taken from MODEF's "Rapport financier de l'Année 1963."

The staff personnel statistics were given in interviews 13 (for the FDSEA) and 89 (for MODEF). The traditional policy of presenting "united lists" at chamber elections was discussed in interviews 1, 5, 13, 89, 97; Joseph Courau was the "independent" chamber president during the "united list" period.

35. Interviews 89, 97.

36. "Elections à la chambre d'agriculture," an undated memo marked "confidential" and included in the FDSEA's dossier on the 1964 elections.

37. *RL* 270 (janvier 1964).

38. Detailed 1964 election results may be found in *LIA* 425 (2e quinzaine de février 1964). The FDSEA obtained a majority of the votes in only four cantons (Geaune, 78%; Hagetmau, 59%; Aire-sur-l'Adour, 67%; Gabarret, 64%), three located in the Tùrsan region and the other the home of a major FDSEA leader; MODEF received more than 70% of the vote in nine cantons—90% in Soustons. The results of the election (by the members of the chamber) for chamber president are taken from "Procès verbal: 1er session de la chambre d'agriculture des Landes, 1964."

39. *RL* 271 (février 1974).

40. The 1974 membership figure is taken from the FDSEA's "Cotisations" notebook for 1974; the formula used to calculate membership density here and elsewhere is members/departmental farms larger than 2 hectares.

41. Untitled memo sent by Lafourcade to the members of the administrative council, 13 mars 1964.

42. Interview 2.

43. Interview 1.

44. Interview 13.

45. Delorme's visit is discussed in a letter of 13 mars 1964 sent by Lafourcade to the members of the union council; also see interviews 1 and 13.

46. Memo of 3 avril 1964 from Lafourcade and Castaing to the local union presidents.

47. A letter of 7 octobre 1965 from Ducourneau to the FNSEA.

48. Letter of 9 novembre 1965 from B. Delorme (speaking in the name of Gérard de Caffarelli) to J. Castaing; letter of 16 november 1965 from Castaing to Delorme; letter of 7 février 1966 from J. P. Haberkorn to J. Castaing.

49. See, for example, the form letter sent by the FNSEA to the FDSEA in 1966 entitled "Formation et promotion."

50. Memo from Lafourcade to the members of the union council, 13 mai 1964.

51. Interviews 1, 13.

52. "Circulaire no. 652" sent by Ducourneau to the local union presidents, 18 novembre 1965; see the responses from such presidents as Cagnotte and Onard.

53. A handwritten letter from the president of the Toulouzette union to Ducourneau, undated.

54. Letter of 24 juillet 1965 from the mayor of Saint Vincent-de-Tyrosse to Francis Barets.

55. Interview 14.

56. See any issue of *LIA* for 1965.

57. Interview 5.

58. See "Circular 64604," 1964, Ducourneau to the local union presidents.

59. Interviews 1, 13, 92, 97; *Le Sillon* (26 janvier 1967); letter of 6 avril 1964 from the president of the SNFM to J. Castaing.

60. "Circular 66–127," Ducourneau to the local union presidents; *RL*, no. 274, mars 1964; letter of 5 février 1965 from René Lafitte to Ducourneau; interview 13.

61. Interview 13; see any 1965 issue of *RL*.

62. Interview 13.

63. Interview 8.

64. "Le Développement agricole dans les Landes," CDJA des Landes, Assemblée Générale du 18 mars 1972.

65. See *Jeunes agriculteurs*, septembre 1970, 24.

66. Interview 25.

67. "A Propos des élections à la chambre d'agriculture," a "bilan de l'activité de la FDSEA," 1967; Michel Simon, "Lignes force et d'action," XXVIe Congrès de la FDSEA (Mont-de-Marsan) 1er mars 1972, pp. 3–6; "Rapport moral présenté par le secrétaire général de la FDSEA, M. Raoul Massetat," XXIVe Congres de la FDSEA des Landes (Hagetmau), 16 janvier 1970, pp. 4–5.

68. *RL*, 271 (février 1964); "Le Département des Landes: Agriculture et forêt," pp. 10–11.

69. The budget statistics are taken from "Budget de la FDSEA—1968" and "Rapport financier de l'année 1968—CGA des Landes, MODEF."

70. Interview 9.

71. "Assemblée général du 13 février 1976," Syndicat des Exploitations de la Grande Lande, Solferino; interview 9.

72. Interview 9.

73. Ibid.

74. Ibid.

75. "Nombre d'adherents," MODEF; "Rapport financier de l'année 1974—CGA des Landes, MODEF"; interviews 1, 13.

76. "Comité special pour la chambre d'agriculture," a confidential 1967 memo sent by M. Simon to all local union presidents; "Quelles constatations tirer de l'élection à la chambre d'agriculture," a confidential analysis of the elections written by F. Barets and distributed to FDSEA bureau members in 1970; "Notes d'observation sur le déroulement des élections à la chambre d'agriculture (24 février 1974)," another confidential election analysis by Barets.

77. See note 21 above for the sources of chamber election returns through 1976; the 1979 statistics are taken from *L'Exploitant familial*, mars 1979.

78. See note 40, Chapter 3; the changes in the electoral laws are described in detail in *Le Sillon* 217 (17 avril 1970), and "Informations syndicales agricoles—service d'action syndicale, FNSEA," no. 2, 23 janvier 1970.

79. *LIA*, 576 (juin 1970).

80. See note 21, above, for the sources of chamber election results.

81. "Notes d'observation sur le déroulement des élections á la chambre d'agriculture (24 février 1974)," p. 3.

82. "Chambre d'agriculture des Landes: Composition 1974"; "Composition de la chambre d'agriculture des Landes 1976"; interview 97. For an interesting discussion of the manner in which *"pseudo-syndicats sans statuts* have contributed to the victory of

Debatisse's U.D.S.E.A. in the Chamber's college for "agricultural groups," see *LIA* 791 (20 juin 1975).

83. For the results of the election for the chamber bureau, see "Procès verbal: Session de la chambre d'agriculture du 21 mai 1974," Mont-de-Marsan, p. 13.

84. *LIA* 543 (2ᵉ quinzaine de janvier 1969).

85. Ibid., 652 (29 septembre 1972); interview 97.

86. *LIA* 755 (4 octobre 1974); 772 (7 février 1975).

87. Machin, *The Prefect in French Public Administration*, p. 201.

88. *LIA* 792 (27 juin 1975); 819 (16 janvier 1976); 827 (12 mars 1976); 844 (9 juillet 1976).

89. Interview 96.

90. *LIA* 757 (18 octobre 1974).

91. Interviews 1, 2, 13, 89, 97; observation of personnel interactions at the *Maison*.

92. *Le Sillon* 219 (30 avril 1970); "Rapport moral," XXVIᵉ Congrès de la FDSEA, 1972; interviews 12, 13, 14, 89, 97.

93. The statistics are taken from "Programme pluriannuel de développement agricole," Chambre d'Agriculture des Landes—SUAD, septembre 1974, pp. 69, 85, 86; the description of the groupements fonciers agricoles (GVA) is taken from "Le développement agricole dans les Landes," CDJA des Landes, Assemblée Générale du 18 mars 1972, p. 3. It has been noted in the Conseil Général that the GVA subsidies "passait par le canal" of the FDSEA—see "Procès-verbaux des délibérations du conseil général: Département des Landes," 2ᵉ Session Ordinaire de 1967, p. 256.

94. *LIA* 773 (14 février 1975); 779 (27 mars 1975).

95. "Procès-verbaux des délibérations du conseil général: Département des Landes," 2ᵉ Session Ordinaire de 1968, pp. 79, 80, 82.

96. Ibid., p. 80.

97. Ibid.

98. See *LIA* 725 (22 février 1974); interviews 96, 97.

99. "Procès-verbaux des délibérations du conseil général: Département des Landes," 2ᵉ Session Ordinaire de 1967, p. 255.

100. "Procès-verbaux des délibérations du conseil général: Département des Landes," 2ᵉ Session Ordinaire de 1972, pp. 141–49. The statistics in Table 7.2 are taken from these 1972 deliberations, from those listed in note 99 above (for 1967) and from those that follow: 2ᵉ Session Ordinaire, pp. 436–38; 1ᵉʳ Session Ordinaire, 1974, pp. 177–82; 2ᵉ Session Ordinaire de 1975, pp. 317–337.

101. See the deliberations for 1975 listed in note 100, above, esp. pages 322, 325, 326, 330.

Chapter 8

1. Eugene Bardach, *The Implementation Game: What Happens After a Bill Becomes a Law* (Cambridge: MIT Press, 1977), p. 93.

2. *La Lettre des Syndicats Paysans* (FNSP), 1 janvier 1983, p. 1.

3. See F. L. Wilson, "French Interest Group Politics," 909; Suzanne Berger, "Protest Under the French Socialists," *Stato e Mercato* (December 1984), p. 6.

4. Schmitter, "Reflections on Where the Theory of Neo-Corporatism Has Gone and Where the Praxis of Neo-Corporatism May Be Going," 266–67.

5. Brian W. Hogwood and B. Guy Peters, *Policy Dynamics* (Brighton: Wheatsheaf, 1983), pp. 157–60.

6. *Le Monde*, 3 mars 1981.

7. Ibid.

8. *Programme commun de gouvernement* (Paris: Flammarion, 1973), pp. 55–57; *Projet socialiste: Pour la France des années 80* (Paris: Club Socialiste du Livre, 1980), pp. 204–8; "110 propositions pour la France presentées par François Mitterrand, candidat à la Présidence de la République," in Jean-Louis Quermonne, *Le Gouvernement de la France sous la Ve République* (Paris: Dalloz, 1983), p. 681.

9. *Le Monde*, 3 mars 1981.

10. For a discussion of the *office du blé*, see G. Wright, *Rural Revolution*, pp. 60–65.

11. *Le Monde*, 3 mars 1981.

12. Ibid.

13. Ibid.; for a discussion of tensions between the United States and the EEC over agricultural policy, see *IA*, octobre 1982.

14. See *IA*, juillet–août 1974, 17.

15. For a Socialist critique of the FNSEA's attitude regarding the *offices par produits*, see *Vent d'ouest*, mars 1981, 4.

16. *Le Monde*, 3 mars 1981.

17. For statistics concerning the voting behavior of the various occupational groups during the 1981 elections, see Ehrmann, *Politics in France*, 4th ed., pp. 253, 255.

18. *Le Point*, 12 avril 1982.

19. *Paris-Match*, 28 janvier 1983.

20. *Le Point*, 12 avril 1982.

21. "Biographical Sketches: Second Cabinet of Pierre Mauroy, June 23, 1981" (Documents from France—Press and Information Service of the French Embassy); *Le Point*, 12 avril 1982. Cresson was the mayor of Thuré (population 2,500) from 1977 through 1983; in the 1983 municipal elections, she was elected mayor of Chatellerault (over 40,000). For an account of her victory in the 1983 election, see *Le Nouvel Observateur*, 11 mars 1983.

22. *Paris-Match*, 19 février 1982; "Biographical Sketches."

23. *Le Point*, 12 avril 1982.

24. Edith Cresson, *Avec le soleil* (Paris: J. -C. Lattès, 1976), p. 219.

25. *Le Nouvel Observateur*, 30 janvier 1982.

26. Monique Dagnaud and Dominique Mehl, *L'Elite rose: Qui gouverne?* (Paris: Editions Ramsay, 1982), pp. 306–7; interview 104; *Le Nouvel Observateur*, 30 janvier 1982.

27. For a defense of Cresson by Tavernier, see *Le Monde*, 24 février 1982.

28. Ibid., 5 juin 1981.

29. For an account of the founding of the CNSTP, see *Le Monde*, 6 juin 1981; see also "Pour une alternative syndicale en agriculture," a sixteen-page mimeo produced by the CNSTP Collectif National in August 1982.

30. *Le Point*, 12 avril 1982.

31. *Paris-Match*, 19 février 1982.

32. See Article L.133–32 of the Code du Travail, reprinted on p. 22 of *IA*, novembre 1982.

33. *Le Monde*, 20 juin 1981; interview 104.

34. *Le Monde*, 20 juin 1981.

35. Ibid., 2 février 1982.

36. See the critique of the *concertation* system in the official report prepared for Mitterrand and Mauroy by the special *commission du bilan* in 1981: *La France en mai 1981: Forces et faiblesses* (Paris: La Documentation Française, 1982), pp. 123–25.

37. Interviews 83, 84, 104; see also Gilles Allaire, "L'Etat des forces à la veille des élections aux Chambres d'Agriculture," *Nouvelles campagnes*, novembre 1982, 16.

38. *Le Monde*, 5 juin and 18 septembre 1981.

39. Ibid., 18 septembre and 8 décembre 1981.

40. Ibid., 8 décembre 1981.

41. Ibid., 5 juin and 18 septembre 1981.

42. Ibid., 6 août 1981.

43. Ibid., 1–2 novembre and 9 décembre 1981; *IA*, novembre 1981.

44. *Le Monde*, 1–2 novembre 1981; *IA*, novembre 1981.

45. *Le Monde*, 10 décembre 1981.

46. *IA*, décembre 1981.

47. *Le Monde*, 10 décembre 1981.

48. *IA*, décembre 1981; *Le Monde*, 10 décembre 1981.

49. *Le Monde*, 10 décembre 1981.

50. *Vent d'ouest*, décembre 1981, 2.

51. See *Le Monde*, most issues from December 1981 through February 1982; *Le Point*, 8 février 1982; *L'Express*, 12 février 1982; *Paris-Match*, 19 février 1982; *Le Nouvel Observateur*, 30 janvier 1982; *Le Figaro Magazine*, 13–19 février 1982.

52. *Le Monde*, 17 décembre 1981.

53. Ibid., 10 février 1982.

54. Ibid., 20–21 décembre 1981.

55. *Le Nouvel Observateur*, 30 janvier 1982; *Le Monde*, 22 janvier 1982; Dagnaud and Mehl, *L'Elite rose*, p. 307.

56. *Le Monde*, 22 janvier 1982.

57. Ibid., 2 février 1982.

58. *Le Point*, 8 février 1982; *Le Monde*, 4 février 1982. Many newspapers unsympathetic to the government printed political cartoons mocking Cresson after the helicopter incident. One depicted her leaving the Ministry of Agriculture in a suit of armor with an official in the background saying, "Have a nice trip in the countryside, Madame"; another blended sexism with sarcasm, showing a beaten and apparently raped Cresson explaining that "In fact it's my body which drives them crazy." See the cartoons from *Minute* reprinted in *Le Crapouillot* 67 (1982), 36.

59. *Paris-Match*, 19 février 1982.

60. *Le Monde*, 10 février 1982.

61. Ibid., 4 février 1982.

62. *Le Point*, 8 février 1982.

63. *Le Monde*, 9 février 1982; see also *Le Travailleur paysan* (CNSTP), mars 1982 and novembere 1982.

64. *Le Travailleur paysan*, novembre 1982, p. 4.

65. *Le Monde*, 27 février 1982.

66. Ibid., 20 mars 1982.

67. Ibid., 27 février 1982.

68. Ibid., 24 mars 1982; *IA*, avril 1982; New York *Times*, 24 March 1982.

69. Interview 104.

70. *La Lettre des syndicats paysans*, janvier 1983, p. 1.

71. *IA*, juin 1982.

72. *Le Travailleur paysan*, juin 1982, 6; see also Allaire, "L'Etat des Forces," 15.

73. Fredet and Pingaud, *Les Patrons*, pp. 61–66; *The Economist*, 8 May 1982.

74. Quermonne, *Le Gouvernement*, p. 681.

75. *Projet socialiste*, p. 208; see also "Une autre politique foncière applicable à toutes les exploitations agricoles," a thirty-seven-page mimeo produced by the CNSTP in December 1982. Socialist minister of agriculture Pierre Tanguy-Prigent considered instituting an *office national foncier* during the Liberation era, but was forced to abandon the idea after encountering "violent opposition"—see G. Wright, *Rural Revolution*, pp. 111–12.

76. *Projet socialiste*, p. 208; for statistics concerning the SAFERs' performance since 1970, see *Graph-Agri 80* (Paris: Ministère de l'Agriculture, 1980), p. 14.

77. *IA*, mars 1982; *Le Monde*, 22–23 novembre 1982; Guillaume, *Le Pain de la liberté*, pp. 82–84.

78. *Le Monde*, 24 mars 1983; *Le Travailleur paysan*, mars 1983, 4.

79. *Le Monde*, 10 février 1982.

80. *Le Travailleur paysan*, mars 1982, 4.

81. Ibid., juin 1982, 5.

82. *Le Monde*, 20 mai 1982.

83. Ibid., 5 juin 1982; *La Travailleur paysan*, septembre 1982, 8.

84. *Le Monde*, 9 novembre 1982.

85. Ibid., 11 décembre 1982.

86. Ibid., 24 mars 1983; *Le Travailleur paysan*, mars 1983, 3.

87. *Le Monde*, 29 juin 1982.

88. Ibid., 3 juin 1982.

89. Ibid., 29 juin 1982.

90. According to *The Economist* of 6 March 1982, France registered a gain of 259 million pounds from the CAP budget system in 1981 and was thus—as it had long been—the policy's principal benficiary in absolute terms. See also Werner Feld, "Implementation of the European Community's Common Agricultural policy: Expectations, Fears, Failures," *International Organization* 33:4 (Summer 1979).

91. *Le Travailleur paysan*, juin 1982, 6.

92. An extensive critique of the bill from the perspective of the FNSEA can be found in *IA*, juillet–août 1982; for the views of the disappointed Socialists, see *Le Monde*, 29 juin and 7 août 1982.

93. *IA*, juin 1982.

94. *Le Monde*, 29 juin 1982; *IA*, juillet-août 1982.

95. See the comments of M. Sourcy (PCF) in *Le Monde*, 1 juillet 1982.

96. Ibid., 1 juillet 1982.

97. Ibid., 3 juillet 1982. The legislative process that produced the *office par produits* law demonstrated the weakness of the Senate in the Fifth Republic. On its first reading of the bill, the Senate approved by a vote of 192–91 (with the PS and PCF senators in

opposition) a version so different that the "offices" were not even mentioned. The *commission mixte* was unable to produce a compromise bill, so on the second reading the government invoked Article 45 of the Constitution and reintroduced, in slightly altered form, the original version prepared by the National Assembly. The Senate rejected this version by a vote of 192–107 (with the PS, PCF, and MRG in opposition), so the government simply bypassed the Senate by asking the National Assembly to rule definitively. See *Le Monde*, 24 and 25 septembre and 1, 2, and 3–4 octobre 1982.

98. *IA*, octobre and novembre 1982; *Le Monde*, 27 février 1982; Guillaume, *Le Pain de la liberté*, pp. 179–180.

99. George C. Edwards, *Implementing Public Policy* (Washington, D.C.: Congressional Quarterly, 1980), p. 1.

100. *Le Travailleur paysan*, janvier 1983, 8.

101. Interviews 83, 84, 103, and 106.

102. *Le Monde*, 11 février 1983.

103. *Le Travailleur paysan*, décembre 1982, 7 and mars 1982, 3.

104. Interviews 103 and 104.

105. *Le Travailleur paysan*, janvier 1983, 5.

106. *Les Informations agricoles* (MODEF in Landes), 15 octobre 1982; see also the 24 juillet 1981 and 2 octobre 1981 issues.

107. *Le Monde*, 11 décembre 1982.

108. *Le Travailleur paysan*, juin 1982, 6; interview 103.

109. *La Lettre des syndicats paysans*, 16 décembre 1982, p. 8.

110. Interview 83.

111. *Pays et paysans!* novembre 1984, 9. For the ANDA figures, see also *Journal officiel*, 14 mars 1983, 1209.

112. *Le Travailleur paysan*, juin 1982, 6.

113. *Les Informations agricoles* (MODEF in Landes), 21 mai 1982.

114. "Les Elections aux Chambres d'Agriculture," décret no. 82–688 du 3 août 1982 (pamphlet published by the Ministry of Agriculture).

115. *IA*, janvier 1983, 4–5, and février 1983, 4–5.

116. *Le Travailleur paysan*, septembre 1982, 4–6; interview 104.

117. *Le Travailleur paysan*, juin 1982, 5–6; septembre 1982, 3; octobre 1982, 3; novembre 1982, 4.

118. The problems of the CNSTP can be traced in *Le Monde* of 11 and 12 septembre 1981, 12 mars 1982, 17 août 1982 and 30–31 janvier 1983. On the FNSP, see *Le Monde*, 15 septembre 1982 and 30–31 janvier 1983; "Pour construire le syndicalisme d'une paysannerie solidaire," undated FNSP pamphlet; "Un Revenu minimum garanti pour tous les paysans," report of the first FNSP congress, Paris, 16–17 novembre 1982.

119. See G. Wright, *Rural Revolution*, ch.6.

120. Guillaume, *Le Pain de la liberté*, pp. 203–9; *Libération*, 28 janvier 1983.

121. Guillaume, *Le Pain de la liberté*, pp. 203–9; Isabel Boussard, "Elections aux chambres d'agriculture et municipales: Le Vote des agriculteurs," *Revue politique et parlementaire* 85 (avril 1984), 79–94.

122. *Le Monde*, 30–31 janvier and 8 février 1983; *Agra-France*, 29 janvier 1983.

123. *Le Monde*, 9 mars 1983.

124. *L'Agriculteur de l'Aisne*, 3 février 1983.

125. *L'Union paysanne* (Corrèze), 11 février 1983.

126. *Le Sillon des Landes et des Pyrénées* (FDSEA), 11 février 1983.

127. *Le Monde*, 9 mars 1983; *Les Informations agricoles* (Landes), 4 mars 1983.

128. *Le Monde*, 26 novembre 1982; *IA*, décembre 1982.

129. *Le Monde*, 5 mai 1984.

130. Ibid., 16 novembre 1982.

131. *Le Travailleur paysan*, décembre 1982, 4; *Le Monde*, 15 septembre 1982.

132. *Le Monde*, 26 novembre 1982; *IA*, décembre 1982.

133. *Le Monde*, 26 novembre 1982.

134. *The Economist*, 22 May 1982.

135. Interview 83.

136. *Le Monde*, 16 avril 1983.

137. *La Travailleur paysan*, avril 1983, 3, and mai 1983, 4.

138. *Ibid.*, juin 1983, 7.

139. Interview 107.

140. Interviews 83 and 84; *L'Humanité*, 15 avril 1983.

141. *Le Monde*, 16 avril 1983.

142. *IA*, avril 1983, 4; *Le Monde*, 19–20 février 1984.

143. *Le Monde*, 28 juillet 1983; *L'Humanité*, 28 juillet 1983; *IA*, septembre 1983, 14–15.

144. *Le Monde*, 5 and 6 avril 1984, 8 juin 1984; *IA*, juillet–août 1984, 38.

145. *La Lettre des syndicats paysans*, mai 1983, pp. 3–4.

146. Ibid., juin 1983, p. 2.

147. Interviews 83, 84, 103, 104, and 106.

148. *Le Monde*, 28 octobre 1983; *La Lettre des syndicats paysans*, juin 1983, p. 2.

149. *Le Monde*, 18, 28, and 29 octobre 1983; *Pays et paysan!* janvier 1984, p. 7.

150. *Le Monde*, 19–20 février 1984; *Pays et paysan!* février 1984, p. 6; *IA*, février 1984, 28.

151. *Le Monde*, 17 novembre 1983; interview 107.

152. *Le Travailleur paysan*, juillet-août 1983, 4; *Pays et paysan!* mai 1984, 7. From the accounts available to me, it appears that only one special conference has been held since the arrival of Rocard: the "milk conference" of 9–10 mai 1984.

153. Interviews 104 and 106; *IA*, avril 1984, 48–49; *Libération*, 29 mai 1984.

154. See *Pays et paysan!* janvier–mars 1984; *Le Travailleur paysan*, juillet-août 1983, 7.

155. *IA*, juin 1984, 46–47.

156. *Le Monde*, 19–20 février 1984; *Le Travailleur paysan*, juin 1983.

157. *Pays et paysan!* février 1984, 7, and juin–juillet 1984, 2.

158. *Le Monde*, 17 mai 1983.

159. Ibid., 18 and 19 mai 1983; 9 septembre 1983.

160. Ibid., 30 septembre 1983 and 29 octobre 1983.

161. Ibid., 24 novembre 1983.

162. Ibid., 18 novembre 1983; *IA*, novembre 1983.

163. *Le Monde*, 3 décembre 1983.

164. Ibid., 19–20 février 1984.

165. Ibid., 14 mars and 1–2 avril 1984; *The Economist*, 7 April 1984.

166. *Le Monde*, 18 mai 1984.

167. Ibid., 15 mars 1984.

168. Ibid., 24 mars 1984.

169. Ibid., 21 avril 1984.

170. Ibid., 28 mars 1984; see also 29 mai 1984.

171. Ibid., 26 avril 1984.

172. Ibid., 30 and 31 mai 1984; *Pays et paysan!* juin–juillet 1984, 4–6; *Libération*, 29 mai 1984.

173. *Le Monde*, 31 mai 1984.

174. Ibid., 23 juin 1984 and 12 juillet 1984; *L'Express*, 3 août 1984.

175. *Le Monde*, 23 juin 1984.

176. The publication timetable for this book precludes a detailed treatment of events since mid-1984, but two developments of the 1984–86 period should be noted. First, relations between the FNSEA and the Ministry of Agriculture worsened considerably from May 1984 until Rocard left the rue de Varenne, in April 1985. They remained rather tense, with Henri Nallet as minister of agriculture, until the Socialist majority in the National Assembly was ousted in the March 1986 elections. The FNSEA was not subjected to systematic attacks à la Cresson during this era, but it was deeply troubled by the government's insistence on retention of milk quotas and its support for enlargement of the European Economic Community. As a result, although the FNSEA continued to play a privileged role in the administration of policy throughout the countryside, *concertation* at times deteriorated into a sort of "dialogue of the deaf" at the national level (see *Le Figaro*, 29 mars 1985; *Le Monde*, 20 mars 1986). Second, the FNSEA emerged as one of the principal victors in the 1986 elections, for on 20 March the new prime minister, Jacques Chirac, stunned observers by naming François Guillaume his minister of agriculture. Raymond Lacombe, formerly FNSEA secretary-general, was named to replace Guillaume as president of the Federation. Soon after assuming his government post, Guillaume announced his intention to revivify *cogestion* and to prepare a new orientation law designed to dismantle the central structural reforms of the Socialist era. As a number of commentators have noted, the unprecedented elevation of an FNSEA president to the minister's office could eventually prove politically compromising and embarrassing for the farmers' union. Nevertheless, it seems certain to produce, at least in the short run, a reversion to the pre-1981 pattern of group-state relations (see *Le Monde*, 29 mars 1986).

177. The Mitterrand quotation is from his *The Wheat and the Chaff* (New York: Seaver, 1982), p. 173.

Conclusion

1. Eckstein, "Case Study and Theory in Political Science," 104–5.

2. Gerhard Lehmbruch, "Liberal Corporatism and Party Government," *Comparative Political Studies* 10:1 (April 1977), 96.

3. Beer, *Britain Against Itself*, p. 14.

4. *IA*, février 1972, 16–17, emphasis added.

5. V. O. Key, *Politics, Parties and Pressure Groups*, 5th ed. (New York: Thomas Y. Crowell, 1964), p. 30.

6. Peter Self and Herbert J. Storing, *The State and the Farmer: British Agricultural Policies and Politics* (Berkeley: University of California Press, 1963), pp. 24–25.

7. Ibid., p. 25; see also Key, *Politics*, p. 30, and G. K. Wilson, *Special Interests and Policymaking*, pp. 1–4.

8. See for example, Barral, *Les Agrariens*, p. 256.

9. D. Gale Johnson, *World Agriculture in Disarray* (London: Fontana, 1973), ch. 2; G. K. Wilson, *Special Interests and Policymaking*, p.1.

10. Key, *Politics*, p. 30; G. K. Wilson, p. 1.

11. Samuel H. Beer, *British Politics in the Collectivist Age* (New York: Vintage, 1969), p. 322.

12. Paul Ackermann, *Der Deutsche Bauernverband im Politischen Kräftespiel der Bundesrepublik* (Tubingen: Mohr, 1970), p. 50; Rolf G. Heinze, *Zur Politisch-Sozialen Funktion des Deutschen Bauernverbandes (DBV)* (thesis, Faculty of Sociology, Universität Bielefeld, 1976), pp. 67–68 and 96. (The translations from German are my own.)

13. Self and Storing, *The State and the Farmer*, pp. 55 and 60–61; G. K. Wilson, *Special Interests and Policymaking*, p. 35.

14. Giuseppe Ciranna, "Un Gruppo di pressione: La Confederazione Nazionale Coltivatori Diretti," *Nord e Sud* 5 (1958), 33–34.

15. G. K. Wilson, *Special Interests and Policymaking*, p. 33.

16. Ackermann, *Deutsche Bauernverband*, p. 28.

17. Olson, *Logic of Collective Action*, pp. 72–73; Derek C. Bok and John T. Dunlop, *Labor and the American Community* (New York: Simon and Schuster, 1970), p. 82.

18. Olson, *Logic of Collective Action*, p. 75.

19. Johnson, *World Agriculture in Disarray*, ch. 2; *Agricultural Policy of the European Community*, p. 23; Michael Lewis-Beck, "The Electoral Politics of the French Peasantry: 1946–1978," *Political Studies* 29:4 (December 1981).

20. Erich Andrlik, "The Farmers and the State: Agricultural Interests in West German Politics," *West European Politics* 4:1 (January 1981), 106; Ackermann, *Deutsche Bauernverband*, p. 49; Heinze, *Zur Politisch*, p. 93.

21. A number of French interviewees agreed that such practices were probably common in West Germany.

22. G. K. Wilson, *Special Interests and Policymaking*, p. 31.

23. Self and Storing, *The State and the Farmer*, pp. 48–49.

24. Ibid., p. 49; G. K. Wilson, *Special Interests and Policymaking*, p. 41.

25. Joseph LaPalombara, *Interest Groups in Italian Politics* (Princeton: Princeton University Press, 1964), p. 238.

26. Ibid., pp. 243–44; Ernesto Rossi, *Viaggio nel feudo di Bonomi* (Rome: Riuniti, 1965), pp. 198–212.

27. LaPalombara, *Interest Groups*, p. 236.

28. Moe, *Organization of Interests*, p. 185; Olson, *Logic of Collective Action*, p. 157.

29. Samuel R. Berger, *Dollar Harvest: The Story of the Farm Bureau* (Lexington, mass.: Heath, 1971), p. 33, and pp. 30–32 for a discussion of the difficulty involved in trying to ascertain the precise membership of the Farm Bureau.

30. Olson, *Logic of Collective Action*, pp. 153–57.

31. S. R. Berger, *Dollar Harvest*, pp. 33, 53, and 69.

32. Moe, *Organization of Interests*, p. 183.

33. Ibid., p. 184.

34. Eckstein, "Case study and Theory in Political Science," 116–18 and 127.

35. Lehmbruch, "Concertation and the Structure of Corporatist Networks." Lehmbruch provides rankings of the OECD countries "according to the degree of corporatism that they display," using as his indicator "the nature of trade-union participation in public policy formation" (pp. 65–66). His categories have been translated into my own as follows: L's "strong corporatism" = K's "strong corporatism"; L's "medium corporatism" = K's "moderate corporatism"; L's "weak corporatism" = K's "weak corporatism"; L's "pluralism" = K's "strong pluralism." Some of Lehmbruch's "pluralism" cases (e. g., Canada, Australia, New Zealand) might qualify for my "structured pluralism" category, but it seems safe to categorize the United States as an example of what I term "strong pluralism." Curiously, Lehmbruch does not discuss the possibility that particular national cases may change from one category to another over time. Implicitly, his rankings are based on the contemporary period, that is, the mid-1970s to early 1980s.

36. William F. Averyt, *Agropolitics in the European Community: Interest Groups and the Common Agricultural Policy* (New York: Praeger, 1977), p. 9.

37. Ibid., pp. 10 and 19.

38. Rolf G. Heinze, "Neokorporatistische Strategien in Politikaren und die Herausforderung durch neue Konfliktpotentiale," in Ulrich von Alemann, ed., *Neokorporatismus* (Frankfurt/Main: Campus-Verlag, 1979), 144.

39. Heinze, *Zur Politisch*, pp. 105–7; Heinze, "Neokorporatistische Strategien," 144.

40. Averyt, *Agropolitics*, pp. 15–19.

41. Ackermann, *Deutsche Bauernverband*, pp. 30–35; see also Hans-Jurgen Puhle, *Politische Agrarbewegungen in kapitalistischen Industriegesellschaften* (Göttingen: Vandenhoeck & Ruprecht, 1975), pp. 106–7.

42. Heinze, *Zur Politisch*, pp. 111–12.

43. Averyt, *Agropolitics*, pp. 13–14.

44. Ackermann, *Deutsche Bauernverband*, p. 99; Averyt, *Agropolitics*, p. 12; see also Andrlik, "Farmers and the State."

45. Self and Storing, *The State and the Farmer*, pp. 230–31; Robert J. Lieber, *British Politics and European Unity: Parties, Elites and Pressure Groups* (Berkeley: University of California Press, 1970), p. 118; Geoffrey Alderman, *Pressure Groups and Government in Great Britain* (London: Longman, 1984), p. 93; W. Grant, "The National Farmers Union: The Classic Case of Incorporation?" in David E. Marsh, ed., *Pressure Politics: Interest Groups in Britain* (London: Junction, 1983), 129.

46. Self and Storing, *The State and the Farmer*, p. 37.

47. Ibid., pp. 39–47.

48. Alderman, *Pressure Groups*, p. 114.

49. Self and Storing, *The State and the Farmer*, pp. 139–45; J. J. Richardson and A. G. Jordan, *Governing Under Pressure: The Policy Process in Post-Parliamentary Democracy* (London: Martin Robertson, 1979), p. 113.

50. Self and Storing, *The State and the Farmer*, pp. 142–43, 145, and 117.

51. Ibid., pp. 139–47 and 111–17.

52. Richardson and Jordan, *Governing Under Pressure*, p. 150.

53. Alderman, *Pressure Groups*, pp. 81 and 90.

54. Grant, "National Farmers Union," 141; G. K. Wilson, *Special Interests and Policymaking*, pp. 34–35.

55. G. K. Wilson, *Special Interests and Policymaking*, pp. 34–35.

56. Ibid., pp. 34–36.

57. Ibid., pp. 22–26 and 38–39.

58. *Hansard—Parliamentary Debates* (London: HMSO, 1978), 26 January 1978, pp. 757–59 and 6 February 1978, pp. 452–54.

59. *The Times*, 6 March 1978.

60. Ibid., 4 April 1978.

61. See *The Economist*, 16 March 1985 for a brief mention of the NFU's problems in Wales as of 1985.

62. Rossi, *Viaggio*, p. 295 ("autogovérno"); Ciranna, esp. p. 25 (on "autogestione"); see also Sidney Tarrow, *Peasant Communism in Southern Italy* (New Haven: Yale University Press, 1967), p. 334; Giorgio Galli, *Storia della D.C.* (Rome: Laterza, 1978), pp. 37 and 57.

63. LaPalombara, *Interest Groups*, pp. 236–37.

64. Rossi, *Viaggio*, p. 290.

65. Ibid., pp. 3 and 115–17; Gianfranco Pasquino, "Italian Christian Democracy: A Party for All Seasons?" in Peter Lange and Sidney Tarrow, eds., *Italy in Transition* (London: Frank Cass, 1980), 101; Carlo Donolo, "Social Change and Transformation of the State in Italy," in Richard Scase, ed., *The State in Western Europe* (London: Croom Helm, 1980), 175.

66. Rossi, *Viaggio*, pp. 91–105, 143, 187, and 265.

67. LaPalombara, *Interest Groups*, pp. 236–44; P. A. Allum, *Italy: Republic Without Government* (New York: Norton, 1973), p. 98.

68. Rossi, *Viaggio*, pp. 301 and 102.

69. LaPalombara, *Interest Groups*, p. 149.

70. Ibid., pp. 241–42.

71. Rossi, *Viaggio*, p. 265.

72. LaPalombara, *Interest Groups*, pp. 241–42; Rossi, *Viaggio*, pp. 265–73.

73. Donolo, "Social Change," esp. 168–69.

74. Arturo Parisi and Gianfranco Pasquino, "Changes in Italian Electoral Behavior: The Relationships Between Party and Voters," in Lange and Tarrow, eds., *Italy in Transition*, 12; Geoffrey Pridham, *The Nature of the Italian Party System* (London: Croom Helm, 1981), p. 233.

75. Parisi and Pasquino, "Changes," 12; Pasquino, "Italian Christian Democracy," 96; Giuseppe Di Palma, "The Available State: Problems of Reform," in Lange and Tarrow, eds., *Italy in Transition*, 160; Giorgio Galli and Alfonso Prandi, *Patterns of Political Participation in Italy* (New Haven: Yale University Press, 1970), pp. 186–87.

76. Pasquino, "Italian Christian Democracy," 95–103.

77. Parisi and Pasquino, "Changes," 12; Giovanni Mottura, "Continuita e svòlta nella politica agrària italiana: Le linee programmatiche del ministro Marcora," in Claudio M. Cesaretti et al., eds., *L'Imbroglio agricolo alimentare* (Torino: Rosenberg and Sellier,

1977); Claudio M. Cesaretti and Antonio Russi, "Governo delle astensioni e politica agrària: Storia del piano agricolo-alimentare," in Cessaerti et al., eds., esp. 61.

78. Cesaretti and Russi, "Governo," esp. 61–82.

79. Ibid., esp. 36–44, 60–61, and 69–74.

80. See Pasquino, "Italian Christian Democracy," 101; Di Palma, "Available State," 163–64. Rossi discusses the futility of earlier efforts to mount a decorporatization campaign against the Coldiretti, for example, during the "Opening to the Left" in the early 1960s when the Socialists argued that Bonomi's organization was the "major obstacle to a reform of Italian agriculture"; see *Viaggio*, pp. 95–121.

81. Robert H. Salisbury, "Why No Corporatism in America?" in Philippe C. Schmitter and Gerhard Lehmbruch, eds., *Trends Toward Corporatist Intermediation*, 217–21.

82. Ibid., 216.

83. David Truman, *The Governmental Process: Political Interests and Public Opinion*, 2d ed. (New York: Knopf, 1971), p. 90.

84. Grant McConnell, *The Decline of Agrarian Democracy* (New York: Atheneum, 1969), pp. 44–52; Olson, *Logic of Collective Action*, pp. 149–50.

85. Ross B. Talbot and Don F. Hadwiger, *The Policy Process in American Agriculture* (San Francisco: Chandler, 1968), p. 105; McConnell, *Decline*, p. 85.

86. William Block, *The Separation of the Farm Bureau and the Extension Service* (Urbana: University of Illinois Press, 1960), p. 108.

87. Olson, *Logic of Collective Action*, pp. 150–52.

88. McConnell, *Decline*, p. 67.

89. Ibid., pp. 70–75.

90. Kenneth Finegold, "From Agrarianism to Adjustment: The Political Origins of New Deal Agricultural Policy," *Politics and Society* 11:1 (1981), 25.

91. McConnell, *Decline*, p. 75.

92. Ibid., p. 75; Christiana M. Campbell, *The Farm Bureau and the New Deal* (Urbana: University of Illinois Press, 1962), p. 89.

93. McConnell, *Decline*, pp. 77–78.

94. Ibid., p. 79.

95. G. K. Wilson, *Special Interests and Policymaking*, p. 78.

96. Salisbury, "Why No Corporatism?" 216.

97. Campbell, *Farm Bureau*, p. 91.

98. Talbot and Hadwiger, *Policy Process*, p. 135.

99. See Block, *Separation*, esp. chs. 9–10 and p. 276.

100. Salisbury, "Why No Corporatism?" 216; Key, *Politics*, p. 34.

101. Theodore Lowi, *The End of Liberalism* (New York: Norton, 1969), ch. 4 and esp. pp. 68–69.

102. Gerhard Lehmbruch, "Interest Intermediation in Capitalist and Socialist Systems: Some Structural and Functional Perspectives in Comparative Research," *International Political Science Review* 4:2 (1983), 154.

103. Moe, *Organization of Interests*, pp. 228 and 181.

104. Raymond Hopkins, Donald Puchala, and Ross Talbot, eds., *Food, Politics and Agricultural Development: Case Studies in the Public Policy of Rural Modernization.* (Boulder, Colo.: Westview, 1979), p. 12.

Bibliography

The sources utilized in the preparation of this study were obtained for the most part from the following libraries, archives, and offices. United States: Widener Library, Littauer Library, and the Center for European Studies Library at Harvard University; Suzzallo Library, University of Washington. Paris: the library and archives of the Assemblée Permanente des Chambres d'Agriculture; the library of the Ministère de l'Agriculture; the archives of the FNSEA; the archives of the CNJA; the library of the Fondation Nationale des Sciences Politiques; the offices of *Paysans*, *La Terre*, and *Economie Agricole*. Laon (Aisne): the library and archives of the USAA-Chambre d'Agriculture; the Archives Départementales. Tulle (Corrèze): the archives of the FDSEA; the library and archives of the Chambre d'Agriculture; the archives of MODEF; the "office" (home of the president) of MADARAC-MONATAR; the Archives Départementales. Mont-de-Marsan (Landes): the archives of the FDSEA; the archives and library of the Chambre d'Agriculture; the archives of MODEF; the Archives Départementales.

The books, articles, and documents listed in this bibliography are divided into six topical categories: (1) organizational theory, interest group politics, and public policy (general/France); (2) farm organizations and agricultural politics outside of France; (3) national farm organizations and agricultural politics in France; (4) farm organizations and agricultural politics in Aisne; (5) farm organizations and agricultural politics in Corrèze; (6) farm organizations and agricultural politics in Landes. The bibliography includes virtually all sources cited in the notes as well as a few additional books and articles that contributed to the development of my study.

I. ORGANIZATIONAL THEORY, INTEREST GROUP POLITICS, AND PUBLIC POLICY

General

Almond, Gabriel A., and G. Bingham Powell. *Comparative Politics: A Developmental Approach*. Boston: Little, Brown, 1966.
Almond, Gabriel A., and Sidney Verba. *Civic Culture*. Boston: Little, Brown, 1965.

Bardach, Eugene. *The Implementation Game: What Happens After a Bill Becomes a Law.* Cambridge: MIT Press, 1977.

Beer, Samuel H. *British Politics in the Collectivist Age.* New York: Vintage, 1969.

_____. *Britain Against Itself.* London: Faber and Faber, 1982.

Berger, Suzanne, ed. *Organizing Interests in Western Europe.* Cambridge: Cambridge University Press, 1981.

Bok, Derek C., and John T. Dunlop. *Labor and the American Community.* New York: Simon and Schuster, 1970.

Brenner, Michael J. "Functional Representation and Interest Group Theory." *Comparative Politics* 2:1 (October 1969).

Butler, David, and Donald Stokes. *Political Change in Britain.* College ed. New York: St. Martin's, 1971.

Clark, Peter B., and James Q. Wilson. "Incentive Systems: A Theory of Organizations." *Administrative Science Quarterly* 6 (September 1961).

Collier, Ruth Berins, and David Collier. "Inducements Versus Constraints: Disaggregating 'Corporatism.'" *American Political Science Review* 73:4 (December 1979).

Cox, Andrew, and Jack Hayward. "The Inapplicability of the Corporatist Model in Britain and France: The Case of Labor." *International Political Science Review* 4:2 (1983).

Crouch, Colin. "Pluralism and the New Corporatism: A Rejoinder." *Political Studies* 31:3 (September 1983).

Crouch, Colin, and Alessandro Pizzorno, eds. *The Resurgence of Class Conflict in Western Europe Since 1968.* Vol. 1. London: MacMillan, 1978.

Eckstein, Harry. "Case Study and Theory in Political Science." In Fred I. Greenstein and Nelson W. Polsby, eds., *Strategies of Inquiry.* Vol. 7 of the *Handbook of Political Science.* Reading, Mass.: Addison-Wesley, 1975.

Edwards, George. *Implementing Public Policy.* Washington, D.C.: Congressional Quarterly, Inc., 1980.

Ehrmann, Henry W. "Interest Groups and the Bureaucracy in Western Democracies." In Reinhard Bendix, ed., *State and Society.* Berkeley: University of California Press, 1968.

Finer, S. E. *Anonymous Empire: A Study of the Lobby in Great Britain.* London: Pall Mall Press, 1966.

Goldthorpe, John, ed. *Order and Conflict in Contemporary Capitalism.* Oxford: Oxford University Press, 1984.

Harrison, R. J. *Pluralism and Corporatism.* London: Allen and Unwin, 1980.

Hogwood, Brian W., and B. Guy Peters. *Policy Dynamics.* Brighton: Wheatsheaf, 1983.

Key, V. O. *Politics, Parties and Pressure Groups.* 5th ed. New York: Thomas Y. Crowell Co., 1964.

Kvavik, Robert B. "Interest Groups in a 'Cooptive' Political System: The Case of Norway." In Martin Heisler, ed., *Politics in Europe.* New York: David McKay, 1974.

Lange, Peter. "Change and Choice in the Italian Communist Party: Strategy and Organization in the Post-War Period." Ph.D. diss., Massachusetts Institute of Technology, 1974.

LaPalombara, Joseph. *Interest Groups in Italian Politics.* Princeton: Princeton University Press, 1964.

Lehmbruch, Gerhard, and Philippe C. Schmitter, eds. *Patterns of Corporatist Policy-Making*. Beverly Hills, Calif.: Sage, 1982.

Lowi, Theodore J. *The End of Liberalism*. New York: Norton, 1969.

Marsh, David. "On Joining Interest Groups: An Empirical Consideration of the Work of Mancur Olson, Jr." *British Journal of Political Science* 6:3 (July 1976).

Moe, Terry M. *The Organization of Interests: Incentives and the Internal Dynamics of Political Interest Groups*. Chicago: University of Chicago Press, 1980.

Nordlinger, Eric A. *On the Autonomy of the Democratic State*. Cambridge: Harvard University Press, 1981.

Olson, Mancur. *The Logic of Collective Action*. Cambridge: Harvard University Press, 1965.

Panitch, Leo. "Recent Theorizations of Corporatism: Reflections on a Growth Industry." *British Journal of Sociology* 31:2 (June 1980).

Salisbury, Robert H. "Interest Groups." In Fred I. Greenstein and Nelson W. Polsby, eds., *Nongovernmental Politics*. Vol. 4 of the *Handbook of Political Science*. Reading, Mass.: Addison-Wesley, 1975.

Sapolsky, Harvey M. "Organizational Competition and Monopoly." *Public Policy* 17 (1968).

Schattsschneider, E. E. *The Semi-Sovereign People*. Hinsdale, Ill.: Dryden Press, 1960.

Schmitter, Phillippe C. "Still the Century of Corporatism?" *Review of Politics* 36:1 (January 1974).

Schmitter, Phillippe C., ed. "Corporatism and Policy-Making in Contemporary Western Europe." Special issue of *Comparative Political Studies* 10:1 (April 1977).

Schmitter, Philippe C., and Gerhard Lehmbruch, eds. *Trends Toward Corporatist Intermediation*. Beverly Hills, Calif.: Sage, 1979.

Schneider, William. "The Origins of Participation: Nation, Class, Issues and Party." Ph.D. diss., Harvard University, 1971.

Shonfield, Andrew. *Modern Capitalism: The Changing Balance of Public and Private Power*. New York: Oxford University Press, 1976, orig. pub. 1965.

Truman, David. *The Governmental Process: Political Interests and Public Opinion*. 2d ed. New York: Knopf, 1971.

von Beyme, Klaus. "Neo-Corporatism: A New Nut in an Old Shell?" *International Political Science Review* 4:2 (1983).

Walker, Jack L. "The Origins and Maintenance of Interest Groups in America." *American Political Science Review* 77:2 (June 1983).

Wilson, James Q. *Political Organizations*. New York: Basic Books, 1973.

France

Adam, Gérard. *Le Pouvoir syndical*. Paris: Dunod, 1983.

————, ed. *L'Ouvrier français en 1970*. Paris: Armand Colin, 1970.

Andrews, William, and Stanley Hoffmann, eds. *The Fifth Republic at Twenty*. Albany: State University of New York Press, 1981.

Ardagh, John. *The New French Revolution*. New York: Harper & Row, 1968.

Bazex, Michel. *L'Administration et les syndicats*. Paris: Editions Berger-Levrault, 1973.

Berger, Suzanne. "D'Une Boutique à l'Autre: Changes in the Organization of the Traditional Middle Classes from the Fourth to Fifth Republics." *Comparative Politics* 10:1 (October 1977).

Birnbaum, Pierre. "The State Versus Corporatism." *Politics and Society* 11:4 (1982).

Bornstein, Stephen. "Unions and the Economy in France: The Changing Posture of the CFDT." *European Studies Newsletter* 7:5 (April–May 1978).

Brizay, Bernard. *Le Patronat: Histoire, structure, stratégie du CNPF.* Paris: Editions du Seuil, 1975.

Bunel, Jean, and Jean Saglio. *L'Action patronal du CNPF au petit patron.* Paris: Presses Universitaires de France, 1979.

Cerny, Philp G., and Martin A. Schain. *French Politics and Public Policy.* London: Frances Pinter, 1980.

Clark, James M. *Teachers and Politics in France: A Pressure Group Study of the Fédération de l'Education Nationale.* Syracuse: Syracuse University Press, 1967.

Commission du Bilan. *La France en mai 1981: Forces et faiblesses.* Paris: La Documentation Française, 1982.

Cresson, Edith. *Avec le soleil.* Paris: J.-C. Lattes, 1976.

Crozier, Michel. *La Société bloquée.* Paris: Editions du Seuil, 1970.

Dagnaud, Monique, and Dominique Mehl. *L'Elite rose: Qui gouverne?* Paris: Editions Ramsay, 1982.

de Bodman, Eric, and Bertrand Richard. *Changer les relations sociales: La politique de Jacques Delors.* Paris: Les Editions d'Organisation, 1976.

de Gaulle, Charles. *Memoirs of Hope: Renewal and Endeavor.* New York: Simon and Schuster, 1971.

Duverger, Maurice. *La Cinquième République.* 3d ed. Paris: Presses Universitaries de France, 1963.

Ehrmann, Henry W. *Organized Business in France.* Princeton: Princeton University Press, 1957.

———. *Politics in France.* 3d ed. Boston: Little, Brown, 1976.

———. *Politics in France.* 4th ed. Boston: Little, Brown, 1982.

———. "Pressure Groups in France." *Annals of the American Academy of Political and Social Science* 319 (September 1958).

France. *Journal officiel de la République française,* 30 juin 1959, 17 décembre 1959, 12 décembre 1979, 14 mars 1983.

Frears, J. R., and Jean-Luc Parodi. *War Will Not Take Place: The French Parliamentary Elections, March 1978.* New York: Holmes and Meier, 1979.

Fredet, Jean-Gabriel, and Denis Pingaud. *Les Patrons face à la gauche.* Paris: Editions Ramsay, 1982.

Grémion, Pierre. *Le Pouvoir périphérique: Bureaucrats et notables dans le système politique français.* Paris: Editions du Seuil, 1976.

Hackett, John, and Anne-Marie Hackett. *Economic Planning in France.* Cambridge: Harvard University Press, 1965.

Hanley, D. L. et al. *Contemporary France.* London: Routledge and Kegan Paul, 1979.

Harris, André, and Alain de Sedouy. *Les Patrons.* Paris: Editions du Seuil, 1977.

Hayward, Jack. *Private Interests and Public Policy: The Experience of the French Economic and Social Council.* London: Longman, 1966.

_____. "State Intervention in France: The Changing Style of Government-Industry Relations." *Political Studies* 20:3 (September 1972).

Hoffmann, Stanley. *Decline or Renewal? France Since the 1930s*. New York: Viking Press, 1974.

_____ et al. *In Search of France*. New York: Harper & Row, 1965.

Keeler, John T. S. "Situating France on the Pluralism-Corporatism Continuum: A Critique of and Alternative to the Wilson Perspective." *Comparative Politics* 17:2 (January 1985).

Kuisel, Richard F. *Capitalism and the State in Modern France*. Cambridge: Cambridge University Press, 1981.

Lavau, Georges. "Political Pressures by Interest Groups in France." In Henry W. Ehrmann, ed., *Interest Groups on Four Continents*. Pittsburgh: University of Pittsburgh Press, 1958.

Machin, Howard. *The Prefect in French Public Administration*. London: Croom Helm, 1977.

Macridis, Roy. *French Politics in Transition*. Cambridge: Winthrop, 1975.

Maus, Didier, ed. *Textes et documents relatifs à l'élection présidentielle des 26 avril et 10 mai 1981*. Paris: La Documentation Française, 1981.

Meynaud, Jean. *Nouvelles études sur les groupes de pression en France*. Paris: Armand Colin, 1962.

Mitterrand, François. *The Wheat and the Chaff*. New York: Seaver, 1982.

Mouriaux, René. *Les Syndicats dans la société française*. Paris: Fondation Nationale des Sciences Politiques, 1983.

Penniman, Howard, ed. *France at the Polls: The Presidential Election of 1974*. Washington, D.C.: American Enterprise Institute, 1975.

Pierce, Roy. *French Politics and Political Institutions*. New York: Harper & Row, 1968.

Programme commun de gouvernement. Paris: Flammarion, 1973.

Projet socialiste. Paris: Club Socialiste du Livre, 1980.

Quermonne, Jean-Louis. *Le Gouvernement de la France sous la Ve Republique*. Paris: Dalloz, 1983.

Ross, George. "Party and Mass Organization: The Changing Relationship of the PCF and CGT." In Donald Blackmer and Sidney Tarrow, eds., *Communism in Italy and France*. Princeton: Princeton University Press, 1975.

_____. *Workers and Communists in France*. Berkeley: University of California Press, 1982.

Schain, Martin A. "Corporatism and Industrial Relations in France." In Philip G. Cerny and Martin A. Schain, eds., *French Politics and Public Policy*. London: Frances Pinter, 1980.

Story, Jonathan. "Capital in France: The Changing Patterns of Patrimony." *West European Politics* 6:2 (April 1983).

Suleiman, Ezra. *Politics, Power and Bureaucracy in France*. Princeton: Princeton University Press, 1974.

_____. *Elites in French Society*. Princeton: Princeton University Press, 1978.

Tarrow, Sidney. *Between Center and Periphery: Grassroots Politicians in Italy and France*. New Haven: Yale University Press, 1977.

Thoenig, Jean-Claude. *L'Ere des technocrates*. Paris: Editions d'Organisation, 1973.

_____. "State Bureaucracies and Local Government in France." Manuscript at Harvard University Center for European Studies, March 1975.

Ventejol, Gabriel. "Cogestion et participation." *Revue politique et parlementaire* (juin-juillet 1973).

Williams, Philip M. *Crisis and Compromise: Politics in the Fourth Republic*. Garden City: Doubleday, 1966.

_____, and Martin Harrison. *Politics and Society in de Gaulle's Republic*. Garden City: Doubleday, 1971.

Wilson, Frank. "French Interest Group Politics: Pluralist or Neo-Corporatist?" *American Political Science Review* 77:4 (December 1983).

Zysman, John. *Governments, Markets and Growth: Financial Systems and the Politics of Industrial Change*. Ithaca: Cornell University Press, 1983.

II. FARM ORGANIZATIONS AND AGRICULTURAL POLITICS OUTSIDE OF FRANCE

Ackermann, Paul. *Der Deutsche Bauernverband im Politischen Kraftespiel der Bundesrepublik*. Tubingen: Mohr, 1970.

Agricultural Policy of the European Community. Brussels: European Communities-Information, 1979.

Alderman, Geoffrey. *Pressure Groups and Government in Great Britain*. London: Longman, 1984.

Allum, Percy. *Italy: Republic Without Government?*. New York: Norton, 1973.

_____. "Les Groupes de pression en Italie." *Revue française de science politique* 30:5 (octobre 1980).

Andrlik, Erich. "The Farmers and the State: Agricultural Interests in West German Politics." *West European Politics* 4:1 (January 1981).

Averyt, William. *Agropolitics in the European Community: Interest Groups and the Common Agricultural Policy*. New York: Praeger, 1977.

Berger, Samuel R. *Dollar Harvest: The Story of the Farm Bureau*. Lexington, Mass: D. C. Heath, 1971.

Block, William. *The Separation of the Farm Bureau and the Extension Service*. Urbana: University of Illinois Press, 1960.

Campbell, Christiana M. *The Farm Bureau and the New Deal*. Urbana: University of Illinois Press, 1962.

Cesaretti, Claudio M. et al., eds. *L'Imbroglio agricoltoro alimentare*. Turin: Rosenberg and Sellier, 1977.

Ciranna, Giuseppe. "Un Gruppo di pressione: La Confederazione Nationale Coltivatori Diretti." *Nord e Sud* 5 (1958).

Feld, Werner. "Implementation of the European Community's Common Agricultural Policy: Expectations, Fears, Failures." *International Organization* 33:4 (Summer 1979).

Finegold, Kenneth. "From Agrarianism to Adjustment: The Political Origins of New Deal Agricultural Policy." *Politics and Society* 11:1 (1981).

Galli, Giorgio, and Alfonso Prandi. *Patterns of Political Participation in Italy*. New Haven: Yale University Press, 1970.

Heinze, Rolf G. *Zur Politisch-Sozialen Funktion des Deutschen Bauernverbandes (DBV)*. Thesis, Faculty of Sociology, Universitat Bielefeld, 1976.

————. "Neokorporatistische Strategien in Politikarenen und die Herausforderung durch neue Konfliktpotentiale." In Ulrich von Alemann, ed., *Neokorporatismus*. Frankfurt/Main: Campus-Verlag, 1979.

Hopkins, Raymond, Donald Puchala, and Ross Talbot, eds. *Food, Politics and Agricultural Development: Case Studies in the Public Policy of Rural Modernization*. Boulder, Colo.: Westview, 1979.

Howarth, Richard W. "The Political Structure of British Agriculture." *Political Studies* 17:4 (1969).

Johnson, D. Gale. *World Agriculture in Disarray*. London: Fontana, 1973.

Lange, Peter, and Sidney Tarrow, eds. *Italy in Transition*. London: Frank Cass, 1980.

LaPalombara, Joseph. *Interest Groups in Italian Politics*. Princeton: Princeton University Press, 1964.

Lieber, Robert J. *British Politics and European Unity: Parties, Elites and Pressure Groups*. Berkeley: University of California Press, 1970.

Linz, Juan. "Patterns of Land Tenure, Division of Labor, and Voting Behavior in Europe." *Comparative Politics* 8:3 (1976).

McConnell, Grant. *The Decline of Agrarian Democracy*. New York: Atheneum, 1969.

Marselli, Gilberto. "Le Cas italien." In Henri Mendras and Yves Tavernier, eds., *Terre, paysans et politique*, vol. 2. Paris: SEDEIS, 1970.

Marsh, David, ed. *Pressure Politics: Interest Groups in Britain*. London: Junction Books, 1983.

Meynaud, Jean, and Susan Sidjanski. *Les Groupes de pression dans la communauté européene: 1958–1968*. Brussels: Editions de l'Institute de Sociologie, 1971.

Pridham, Geoffrey. *The Nature of the Italian Party System*. London: Croom Helm, 1981.

Puhle, Hans-Jurgen. *Politische Agrarbewegungen in Kapitalistischen Industriegesellschaften*. Gottingen: Vandenhoeck and Ruprecht, 1975.

Richardson, J. J., and A. G. Jordan. *Governing Under Pressure: The Policy Process in a Post-Parliamentary Democracy*. London: Martin Robertson, 1979.

Rossi, Ernesto. *Viaggio nel feudo di Bonomi*. Roma: Riuniti, 1965.

Scase, Richard, ed. *The State in Western Europe*. London: Croom Helm, 1980.

Self, Peter, and Herbert J. Storing. *The State and the Farmer: British Agricultural Policies and Politics*. Berkeley: University of California Press, 1963.

Talbot, Ross B., and Don F. Hadwiger. *The Policy Process in American Agriculture*. San Francisco: Chandler, 1968.

Tarrow, Sidney. *Peasant Communism in Southern Italy*. New Haven: Yale University Press, 1967.

Wilson, Graham K. *Special Interests and Policymaking: Agricultural Policies and Politics in Britain and the United States of America, 1956–70*. London: Wiley, 1977.

III. NATIONAL FARM ORGANIZATIONS AND AGRICULTURAL POLITICS IN FRANCE

Secondary Sources

Allaire, Gilles. "L'Etat des forces à la veille des élections aux chambres d'agriculture." *Nouvelles campagnes*, novembre 1982.

Bages, Robert. "Les Paysans et le syndicalisme agricole." Thèse pour le doctorat de troisième cycle. Groupe d'Ethnologie Rurale et de Sociologie, Université de Toulouse, 1970.

Barral, Pierre. *Les Agrariens français de Meline à Pisani*. Paris: Armand Colin, 1968.

Berger, Suzanne. *Peasants Against Politics*. Cambridge: Harvard University Press, 1972.

_____. "Corporative Organization: The Case of a French Rural Association." In J. Roland Pennock and John W. Chapman, eds., *Voluntary Associations*. New York: Atherton Press, 1969.

_____. "Postface to *Peasants Against Politics*." Unpublished paper, Massachusetts Institute of Technology, February 1974.

Boussard, Isabel. *Vichy et la corporation paysanne*. Paris: Fondation Nationale des Sciences Politiques, 1980.

_____. "La Corporation paysanne: Une étape dans l'histoire du syndicalisme agricole français (1940–1944)." Thèse pour le doctorat de recherches, Fondation Nationale des Sciences Politiques, Paris, 1971.

_____. "Elections aux chambres d'agriculture et municipales: Le vote des agriculteurs." *Revue politique et parlementaire* 85 (avril 1983).

Cloarec, Jacques. Un exemple d'intervention de l'état: Le financement public de l'agriculture." *Etudes rurales* 69 (janvier–mars 1978).

de Virieu, François-H. *La Fin d'une agriculture*. Paris: Calmann-Lévy, 1967.

Delorme, Hélène, and Yves Tavernier. *Les Paysans français et l'Europe*. Paris: Armand Colin, 1969.

Duplex, Jean, ed. *Atlas de la France rurale*. Paris: Armand Colin, 1968.

Faure, Marcel. *Les Paysans dans la société française*. Paris: Armand Colin, 1966.

Fauvet, Jacques, and Henri Mendras, eds. *Les Paysans et la politique dans la France contemporaine*. Paris: Armand Colin, 1958.

"Le Financement public du CNJA et de la FNSEA et le nombre réel de leurs adhérents." *Nouvelles campagnes*, novembre 1982.

France. *Annuaire statistique de la France 1966: Résumé retrospectif 1948–1965*. Paris: Ministère de l'Economie et de Finances, 1966.

_____. *Statistique agricole: Enquête communautaire sur la structure des exploitations agricoles en 1967*. Paris: Ministère de l'Agriculture, mars, 1969.

_____. *Graph-Agri 80*. Paris: Ministère de l'Agriculture, 1980.

Gervais, Michel, Marcel Jollivet, and Yves Tavernier. *La fin de la France paysanne de 1914 à nos jours*. Vol. 4 of *Histoire de la France rurale*, under the direction of Georges Duby and Armand Wallon. Paris: Editions du Seuil, 1976.

Gervais, Michel, Claude Servolin, and Jean Weil. *Une France sans paysans*. Paris: Editions du Seuil, 1965.

Gratton, Philippe. *Les Luttes de classes dans les campagnes*. Paris: Editions Anthropos, 1971.

———. *Les Paysans français contre l'agrarisme*. Paris: François Maspero, 1972.

Guillaume, François. "Où va l'agriculture française? François Guillaume, entretien avec Emmanuel Le Roy Ladurie." *Le Débat*, janvier 1984.

Houée, Paul. *Les Etapes du développement rural*. Vol. 2 of *La Révolution contemporaine (1950–1970)*. Paris: Editions Ouvrières, 1972.

Jollivet, M., and Henri Mendras, eds. *Les Collectivités rurales françaises: Etudes comparative de changement social*. 2 vol. Paris: Armand Colin, 1971.

Klatzmann, Joseph. *Géographie agricole de la France*. Paris: Presses Universitaires de France, 1972.

———. *Les Politiques agricoles*. Paris: Presses Universitaires de France, 1972.

Lalignant, Marcel. *L'Intervention de l'état dans le secteur agricole*. Paris: Librairie Générale de Droit et de Jurisprudence, 1968.

Lewis-Beck, Michael S. "The Electoral Politics of the French Peasantry: 1946–1978." *Political Studies* 29: 4 (December 1981).

Mallet, Serge. *Les Paysans contre le passé*. Paris: Editions du Seuil, 1962.

Mendras, Henri, and Yves Tavernier. "Les Manifestations de juin 1961." *Revue française de science politique* 12:3 (septembre 1962).

———. and Yves Tavernier, eds. *Terre, paysans et politique*. 2 vols. Paris: SEDEIS, 1969.

Michelet, Claude. *J'ai choisi la terre*. Paris: Editions Robert Laffont, 1975.

Muller, Pierre. *Grandeur et décadence du professeur d'agriculture*. Grenoble: Institut d'Etudes Politiques de Grenoble, 1978.

———. *Le Technocrate et le paysan*. Paris: Editions Ouvrières, 1984.

Prugnaud, Louis. *Les Etapes du syndicalisme agricole en France*. Paris: Editions de l'Epi, 1963.

Quiers-Valette, Suzanne. "Les Causes économiques du mécontentement des agriculteurs français en 1961." *Revue française de science politique* 12:3 (septembre 1962).

Rimareix, Gaston, and Yves Tavernier. "L'Elaboration et le vote de la loi complémentaire à la loi d'orientation agricole." *Revue française de science politique* 13:2 (juin 1963).

Tarrow, Sidney. "The Urban-Rural Cleavage in Political Involvement: The Case of France." *American Political Science Review* 65 (June 1971).

Tavernier, Yves. *Le Syndicalisme paysan: FNSEA, CNJA*. Paris: Armand Colin, 1969.

———. *Sociologie politique du monde rural et politique agricole* (fascicule III). Paris: Fondation Nationale des Sciences Politiques, 1973.

———. "Le Syndicalisme paysan et la politique agricole du gouvernement." *Revue française de science politique* 12:3 (septembre 1962).

———. "Le XVIIIe Congrès de la FNSEA." *Revue française de science politique* 14:5 (octobre 1964).

———. "Le Mouvement de coordination et de défense des exploitations agricoles familiales (M.O.D.E.F.)." *Revue française de science politique* 18:3 (juin 1968).

———, Michel Gervais, and Claude Servolin, eds. *L'Univers politique des paysans dans la France contemporaine*. Paris: Armand Colin, 1972.

Wright, Gordon. *Rural Revolution in France*. Stanford: Stanford University Press, 1964.

Wylie, Laurence. *Village in the Vaucluse*. Cambridge: Harvard University Press, 1957.

Primary Sources

1. *General newspapers and magazines.* Selected articles from 1959 to 1984.
   Le Crapouillot
   The Economist
   Le Figaro
   Le Figaro Magazine
   France-Soir
   L'Humanité
   Libération
   Le Monde
   New York *Times*
   Le Nouvel Observateur
   Paris-Match
   Le Point
   The Times (of London)

2. *Newspapers and magazines of French farm organizations*
   Agra-France, 1983–84.
   L'Action agricole de Touraine (FFA), 1971–75
   L'Exploitant familial: Organe national du MODEF, 1971–84
   L'Information agricole (FNSEA), 1962–84
   Jeunes agriculteurs (CNJA), 1959–76
   La Lettre des syndicats paysans (FNSP), 1983
   Monatar, 1975–76
   Nouvelles campagnes, 1982–84
   Pays et paysans! (FNSP), 1983–85.
   Paysans, 1957–76
   Le Travailleur paysan, 1982–83
   Vent d'ouest: Journal des paysans-travailleurs, 1969–81

3. *FNSEA and CNJA congress reports.* The following are selected reports cited in the text (listed in chronological order).

   "Le Syndicalisme, moyen d'expression et d'action des agriculteurs." XIXe Congrès Fédéral-FNSEA, 3–4 mars 1965.
   Serieys, Raoul. "Rapport moral." Journées d'Etude—CNJA, 25–26 octobre 1967.
   _____. "Rapport moral." CNJA, 25–26 décembre 1967.
   Debatisse, Michel. "Rapport moral." XXIVe Congrès Fédéral-FNSEA, 3–4 mars 1970, Lyon.
   Lauga, Louis, "L'Agriculteur et la société industrielle: Le role du CNJA" (Rapport d'orientation). XXIIe Congrès du CNJA, 5–6 juillet 1970.
   Richard, Antoine. "Pour un syndicalisme de travailleurs." XIIe Congrès du CNJA, 5–6 juillet 1970, Blois.
   "Rapport financier." XXVe Congrès Fédéral-FNSEA, 24–26 février 1971, Nimes.

"La Situation de l'agriculture et l'activité syndicale en 1972." XXVIIe Congrès Fédéral-FNSEA, 11–12 avril 1973, Saint Malo.

Cormorèche, Pierre. "Rapport moral (1 partie)." XXVIIe Congrès Fédéral 11–12 avril 1973.

"La Situation de l'agriculture et l'activité syndicale en 1974." XXIXe Congrès Fédéral-FNSEA, 18–20 mars, 1975, Versailles.

Cormorèche, Pierre. "Rapport moral." XXIXe Congrès de la FNSEA, 18–20 mars, 1975.

Boulnois, Pierre. "Europe: Le défi des jeunes agriculteurs." Journées d'Etudes du CNJA, 3–4 juin 1975, Caen.

"Devenir-être-rester agriculteur, agricultrice." Programme d'Action Syndicale 1975/76, CNJA.

Grit, Auguste, and Raoul Serieys. "Rapport moral: Les responsabilités des agriculteurs." XXXIVe Congrès Fédéral-FNSEA, 11–13 mars 1980, Bordeaux.

4. *Reports and pamphlets of the rival unions*

"Agriculteurs et société." Eleven-page mimeographed statement of the MONATAR program, 1975.

"Les Agriculteurs face à la corporation anti-paysanne" (Rapport moral), IVe Congrès Nationale, Fédération Française de l'Agriculture, 23–24 octobre 1974, Saint-Lô.

"Le MODEF: Ses origines, son activité, ses buts." Four-page mimeographed document prepared by MODEF, 1975.

"Programme national du MODEF: Pour une politiqué agricole nouvelle assurant le bienêtre des expoitants familiaux dans une agriculture prospère." IVe Congrès National du MODEF, 1–2 mars 1975, Paris.

5. *Books by participants in union politics*

Debatisse, Michel. *Le Révolution silencieuse*. Paris: Calmann-Lévy, 1963.

Guillaume, François. *Le Pain de la liberté*. Paris: J. C. Lattes, 1983.

Lambert, Bernard. *Les Paysans dans les luttes des classes*. Paris: Editions de Seuil, 1970.

Lauga, Louis. *CNJA*. Paris: EPI, 1971.

6. *Miscellaneous pamphlets and documents*

"Le Budget des chambres d'agriculture: 1973." Paris: APCA, 1973.

"Cotisations 1966." FNSEA-ISA, no. 18, 27 mai 1966. Mimeographed list of the membership and dues payments of each FDSEA.

"Cotisations 1975." 7 juillet 1975, Action Syndicale-FNSEA. Mimeographed list of the membership and dues payments of each FDSEA.

"Les Chambres d'agriculture: 1975." Paris: APCA. Pamphlet listing the address, members, and staff of each chamber of agriculture.

"Elections aux chambres d'agriculture: Collèges des chefs d'exploitation— circonscriptions renouvelables en février 1974." Paris: Ministère de l'Agriculture. A twenty-page list of the returns in each department.

SAFER: Organisation, fonctionnement. Paris: FNSAFER, 1972.

30 ans de combat syndical. Supplement to *L'Information agricole*, no. 467, mars 1976. Official history of the FNSEA published on its thirtieth anniversary.

IV. FARM ORGANIZATIONS AND AGRICULTURAL POLITICS IN AISNE

Secondary Sources

de Sars, Maxime. "Soixante ans de syndicalisme agricole dans le départment de l'Aisne." 1952. Unpublished, official history of the USAA written by one of its former administrators; the 164-page typescript is available only at the USAA in Laon.

Primary Sources

1. *USAA newspaper*
   L'Agriculteur de l'Aisne. 1946–83.

2. *Typed or handwritten documents of the USAA and Chambre d'Agriculture*
   "Adhérents—USAA." 1947, 1950, 1953, 1962, 1967, 1971, 1974. File cards listing membership by canton.
   "Budget—chambre d'agriculture." 1958, 1967, 1975.
   "Budget—USAA." Mimeographed document for each year from 1964 to 1975.
   "Compte de gestion de l'exercice." Mimeographed documents for each year from 1952 to 1963.
   "Cotisations 1971." Document prepared by the USAA director notes the membership density of the USAA in each canton and for each category of farm (e.g., 1–5 hectares).
   "Membres des commissions et comités—1975." Prepared for the author by a USAA secretary.
   "Organigramme administratif de l'union des syndicats agricoles et de la chambre d'agriculture de l'Aisne." 1974.
   "Réflexion sur l'étude faite par les FDSEA du Finistère, de Loire-Atlantique, de Mayenne et du Morbihan, intitulée: 'Le Droit au·travail et le revenu minimum garanti.'" USAA, 18 mars 1975.
   "Les Responsables de l'USAA: 1953–1976." List of USAA bureau members prepared for the author by the USAA director.
   "Les Résultats des élections aux chambres d'agriculture: 1955, 1959, 1964, 1967, 1970, 1974, 1976." Document prepared for the author by the archivist of the Chamber of Agriculture.
   "Statuts de l'union des syndicats agricoles de l'Aisne."

3. *Mimeographed or printed pamphlets*
   "L'ADASEA au service des agriculteurs." ADASEA de l'Aisne, mars 1972. Fifty-six page pamphlet.
   "L'Aisne agricole." Ten-page pamphlet of the Chamber of Agriculture, 1975.
   "Programme pluriannuel de développement agricole 1974–1976, compte rendu d'activité." Chambre d'Agriculture—SUAD (Aisne), Laon, 1975.
   "Au Service des agriculteurs de l'Aisne—présentation des services de: l'union des syndicats agricoles; la chambre d'agriculture; des autres organismes agricoles de

la Place Edouard Herriot à Laon." USAA-Laon, 1975. Thirty-four-page
pamphlet.

"Visage méconnu de l'agriculture de l'Aisne." Chambre d'Agriculture de l'Aisne, mai
1975. Eleven-page pamphlet.

V. FARM ORGANIZATIONS AND AGRICULTURAL POLITICS IN CORRÈZE

Secondary Sources

Bastardie, Alain. "Le Syndicalisme paysan en Corrèze depuis 1945." Mémoire de Fin
d'Etudes sous la Direction de Monsieur Tavernier, 1970–71. Institut d'Etudes
Politiques de Paris.

Denquin, Jean-Marie. *Le Renversement de la majorité électorale dans le département de la
Corrèze 1958–1973.* Paris: Presses Universitaires de France, 1976.

Gràtton, Philippe. "Le Communisme rural en Corrèze," Chap. 1 of *Les Paysans français
contre l'agrarisme.* Paris: François Maspero, 1972.

Lord, Guy. "Le P. C. F.: Structure et organisation d'une fédération départementale."
Paper prepared for the Workshop sur le communisme en Europe occidentale
(European Consortium for Political Research). Juin 1973, Paris.

Lord, J. H. G., A. J. Petrie, and L. A. Whitehead. "Political Change in Rural France: The
1967 Election in a Communist Stronghold." *Political Studies* 16 (June 1968).

Primary Sources

1. *Newspapers and magazines*
   L'Avenir agricole de la Corrèze: Organe du Madarac, no. 2 (octobre 1974) to no. 5
   (juillet 1975).
   Corrèze-Magazine, no. 163, juillet–aout, 1975.
   L'Union paysanne. 1946–83. The official newspaper of the FDSEA and—since the
   mid-50s—of the Chamber of Agriculture.

2. *FDSEA documents*
   "Compte rendu d'activités—FDSEA de la Corrèze." 1955–74. Printed pamphlets.
   "Compte rendu" or "Procès-verbal" for each meeting of the FDSEA Bureau, Conseil
   d'Administration and Conseil Fédéral between 1952 and 1975. Typescripts and
   mimeographs.
   "Cotisations." 1962–74. Notebooks listing FDSEA membership by commune. Those
   for the years before 1962 are not available and have apparently been discarded.
   "Procès-verbal: Assemblée générale, FDSEA de la Corrèze." 1948–75. Typescripts
   and mimeographs.
   "Rapport financier" for 1949 and for each year from 1957 to 1974.
   "Rapport moral" and "Interventions" for each FDSEA assemblée général from 1965
   to 1975. Mimeographs and typescripts.
   "Statuts—FDSEA de la Corrèze." Undated. FDSEA archives in Tulle.

3. *Chambre d'Agriculture: Typed and mimeographed documents*
   "Compte rendu de la réunion de travail." 9 juin 1972, Meymac, Chambre
      d'Agriculture de la Corrèze.
   "Dotation aux organismes maîtres d'oeuvre: 1976, chambre d'agriculture de la
      Corrèze-SUAD."
   "Liste complète des membres titulaires de la chambre d'agriculture (après les élections
      des 17 février et 15 mars 1974)." Chambre d'Agriculture, mars, 1975.
   "Liste du personnel en place au 1 octobre 1975, chambre d'agriculture de la Corrèze—
      services généraux et SUAD."
   "Organigramme au 25 octobre 1975, chambre d'agriculture de la Corrèze."
   "Procès-verbal: session de la chambre d'agriculture de la Corrèze, 6 mai 1975 (Tulle)."
   "Programme d'action 1974—1978, chambre d'agriculture de la Corrèze."

4. *Chambre d'Agriculture: Printed documents*
   "Aperçu sur la Corrèze agricole." Chambre d'Agriculture de la Corrèze, avril 1974.
   "Les Chambres d'agriculture du Limousin au service des agriculteurs, 1924–1974."
      Chambre d'Agriculture de la Corrèze, de la Creuse, de la Haute-Vienne, et la
      Chambre Régionale du Limousin.
   Mémoires de Joseph Faure, 1875–1944. Paris: APCA, 1974.

5. *Miscellaneous*
   "L'Agriculture en Corrèze: 1974" Direction Départementale de l'Agriculture—
      Service Statistique, Tulle, 1974.
   "Chiffres clés du départment de la Corrèze." Comité Permanent des Chambres
      Economiques de la Corrèze, Préfecture de la Corrèze, Tulle, 1969.
   "Procès-verbaux des délibérations." Conseil Général, Département de la Corrèze.
      The following are of special interest.
   2ᵉ Session Ordinaire de 1967, p. 363
   2ᵉ Session Ordinaire de 1968, pp. 68–72
   1ᵉʳ Session Extraordinaire de 1970, pp. 237–41
   2ᵉ Session Ordinaire de 1973, pp. 107–8
   2ᵉ Session Ordinaire de 1975, pp. 225–27

VI. FARM ORGANIZATIONS AND AGRICULTURAL POLITICS IN LANDES

Secondary Sources

Gratton, Philippe. *Les Luttes de classes dans les campagnes.* Paris: Editions Anthropos,
   1971. Pages 115–32 and 345–57 deal with the organization of farm workers in Landes
   from the turn of the century to 1920.
Répression des luttes: Les paysans parlent. Paris: François Maspero, 1972. Pages 109–15
   deal with a strike of farm workers in Landes from 1969 to 1971.

Primary Sources

1. *Newspapers*

  Les Informations agricoles. 1945–83. The newspaper of what is now the "CGA des Landes—MODEF."

  Le Réveil landais. 1945–66. The SLIR and later FDSEA newspaper, which ceased publication in 1966.

  Le Sillon des Landes et des Pyrénées. 1966–83. FDSEA newspaper published jointly by the FDSEA of Landes and Basses-Pyrénées.

2. *FDSEA-CDJA documents*

  "Assemblée générale du 13 février 1976." Syndicat des Exploitations de la Grande Lande—Solferino.

  "Bilan de l'action syndicale de la FDSEA" for each year from 1967 to 1975.

  "Budget." 1967–75.

  "Cotisations." 1959–75. Notebooks listing FDSEA membership by commune and by canton. No records of the pre-1959 period are available.

  "Le Développement agricole dans les Landes." CDJA des Landes, Assemblée Générale, 18 mars, 1972.

  "Notes d'observation sur le déroulement des élections." FDSEA bureau memo, 1974.

  "Quelles constations tirer de l'élection à la chambre d'agriculture." FDSEA bureau memo, 1970.

  "Rapport moral" for each FDSEA assemblée générale from 1963 to 1975.

3. *Chambre d'Agriculture documents*

  "Chambre d'agriculture des Landes: Composition 1974."

  "Composition de la chambre d'agriculture: 1976."

  "Le Département des Landes: Agriculture et forêt." Chambre d'Agriculture des Landes, Mont-de-Marsan, 1975.

  "Procès-verbal: Session de la chambre d'agriculture des Landes." 1950–76.

  "Programme pluriannuel de développement agricole." Chambre d'Agriculture des Landes-SUAD, septembre 1974.

  "Règlement intérieur de la chambre d'agriculture des Landes."

4. *MODEF documents*

  "Nombre d'adhérents." Departmental membership totals from 1946 to 1975.

  "Object: A/s des responsables de la fédération des syndicats agricoles (MODEF) et des mouvements annexes." An undated FDSEA memo listing the professional and political positions held by the principal MODEF officials.

  "Rapport financier" for each year from 1958 to 1974.

  "Rapport moral." 34 Congrès de la Fédération des Syndicats Agricoles—C.G.A. des Landes MODEF, Mugron, 2 juillet 1976.

  "Schéma sur le syndicalisme." Janvier 1973. A short history of Landes-MODEF and statement of purpose for use by local elites in organizational meetings.

  "Statuts de syndicat agricole MODEF."

5. *Miscellaneous*
   Etude sur les structures des exploitations agricoles. Pau: Service Régional de Statistique
      Agricole (Région Aquitaine), 1969.
   "Procès-verbaux des déliberations." Conseil Général, Département des Landes. The
   following are of special interest:
      2ᵉ Session Extraordinaire de 1967, pp. 254–59
      2ᵉ Session Ordinaire, 1968, pp. 78–86
      2ᵉ Session Ordinaire, 1970, pp. 436–38
      2ᵉ Session Ordinaire, 1971, pp. 234–37
      2ᵉ Session Ordinaire, 1972, pp. 141–49
      1ᵉʳ Session Ordinaire, 1974, pp. 177–82
      2ᵉ Session Ordinaire, 1975, pp. 317–37
Recensement général de l'agriculture 1970. Fascicule 1. Direction Départementale de
   l'Agriculture—Service de Statistique Agricole, Mont-de-Marsan, 1971.

Index